Luca della Robbia

Luca della Robbia

JOHN POPE-HENNESSY

Cornell University Press
Ithaca · New York

© 1980 by Phaidon Press Limited, Oxford

All rights reserved. Except for brief quotations in a
review, this book, or parts thereof, must not be reproduced
in any form without permission in writing from the
publisher. For information address Cornell University
Press, 124 Roberts Place, Ithaca, New York 14850.

First published 1980 by Cornell University Press.

Library of Congress Cataloging in Publication Data

Pope-Hennessy, John Wyndham, Sir, 1913–

   Luca della Robbia.
   Bibliography: p.
   Includes index.
   1. Robbia, Luca della, 1400?–1482.
NB623.R72P66   730'.92'4   79-13566
ISBN 0-8014-1256-0

Printed in Great Britain

Text printed by Clark and Constable Limited, Edinburgh
Color plates printed by Burgess & Son Limited, Abingdon
Monochrome plates printed by W. & J. Mackay Limited,
Chatham

To Andrew Porter

CONTENTS

PREFACE

I remember clearly the moment at which this book was conceived. It was in August 1950 at Vallombrosa, where Orlando, a former Prime Minister of Italy, had come to tea with Berenson. As he was leaving—in his country clothes he looked a little like Lloyd-George at Churt—Orlando started talking about La Verna and the Della Robbia altarpieces there. They were made, he said, of sky and snow. Political rhetoric? Perhaps it was. But it stirred up memories of Pater's apostrophe of Luca della Robbia's sculptures 'like fragments of the milky sky itself, falling into the cool street, and breaking into the darkened churches,' and that afternoon I decided to write this book. In the publication queue, however, other works had precedence, first my general volumes on Italian sculpture, then the catalogue of the Italian sculpture at South Kensington, then the Mellon lectures on the Renaissance portrait and the Wrightsman lectures on Raphael; and after that, for ten long years, I was constrained to dedicate most of my time and thought to museum administration. In effect, therefore, work on the book was not begun until the summer of 1973.

That it has been concluded is due to the help I have received from many quarters. My first debt is to Professor Ulrich Middeldorf and to the Kunsthistorisches Institut in Florence. Without the incomparable facilities of the Institute and the unfailing helpfulness of its staff the task would have consumed ten years not six. Ulrich Middeldorf supported the project, as he has supported so many others, with unstinting generosity. Some of the great pleasures in the years I have been working on it have been the free, discursive conversations with him in which problems arising from the work of Luca della Robbia were thrashed out. My second debt is to Dr. Gino Corti. To someone like myself who is not by temperament or training an archivist, documentary research is fraught with hazards, and I have therefore left the documentation of this book in Dr. Corti's hands. Despite his efforts, the contract for the Cantoria is still untraced and absolutely nothing has been added to our knowledge of the Impruneta altars or the roundels in the Pazzi Chapel, but known documents (documents known to Poggi, Mather and Marquand that is) have been re-transcribed and sometimes supplemented, and the ver-

sions printed here are, to the best of my belief, correct. I have deliberately omitted documents which were irrelevant or uninformative. I am under a special obligation to Dr. Margaret Haynes, who has generously made available the partly unpublished documentation of Luca della Robbia's bronze door in the Cathedral, and has also supplied me with the transcript from the *Memorie* of Benedetto Dei referred to on p. 59. To Dr. Marco Spallanzani I owe some interesting references to Andrea della Robbia. Other debts I must acknowledge are to Ruth Rubinstein for help in connection with the classical sources of the Cantoria, to Robert Carson of the British Museum in respect of the medallic sources of the Peretola tabernacle, and to Michael Tyte of the British Museum Research Laboratory for assistance with spectroscopic glaze analysis. Roberto Longhi once referred, in a suggestive phrase, to the 'Atticismo' of Luca della Robbia, but only in 1973 was the classical background of his style seriously explored in a remarkable article by Carlo Del Bravo (from whom I have received innumerable kindnesses while engaged upon this book). The completion of the book would hardly have been possible but for the tenacious help of Laurence B. Kanter, who has spent two summers tirelessly checking the text and notes against the works in the original and has compiled the bibliography. The colour photographs of works in Tuscany used throughout the book are due to the Istituto Fotografico Scala, and have been made available through the good offices of my friends John and Thekla Clark. New black-and-white photography of the Cantoria, the Pazzi Chapel and many other works has been undertaken by the firm of Alinari; the quality of the results is due to the sensibility and patience of Francesco Lazzeri.

As so often in the past, I am indebted to the critical acumen which Dr. I. Grafe has brought to bear on the editing of the manuscript.

Luca della Robbia is the only one of the great Florentine Early Renaissance sculptors on whom there is no modern monograph. One reason for this is the excellence of the volume on his work published by Marquand sixty-four years ago. My own conclusions differ from Marquand's in a number of respects, but I feel, as all students of Luca della Robbia's work must do, unbounded respect for his powers of observation, his sobriety and his self-effacing thoroughness. The omission none the less is serious. Luca della Robbia is the most popular sculptor of the fifteenth century. He coined a language more universal than that of Donatello and his sculptures are accepted, for the human consolation or the acute aesthetic pleasure that they offer, by a vast public to which Renaissance art is all but a closed book. It is this that makes it necessary and timely to take a new look at his work.

Florence, 1978   JOHN POPE-HENNESSY

I THE LIFE OF LUCA DELLA ROBBIA

Luca della Robbia was born in 1399 or 1400.[1] His father, Simone di Marco della Robbia, was aged fifty-seven at the time. The Della Robbia family were involved in the wool trade and had long-standing associations with the Arte della Lana. Two of Simone's brothers matriculated in the Arte della Lana in July 1389,[2] and on 21 March 1427 Luca della Robbia and his two elder brothers, Marco (b. 1386) and Giovanni (b. 1394), likewise matriculated in the guild.[3] Of the three, only Marco continued in the family profession, becoming a partner in a firm of wool merchants. To judge from a tax return of 1427, their father Simone was engaged in the sale or manufacturing of textiles; the list of debtors from whom money was due includes two dyers, a *conciatore* (tanner), and a wool carder, and among the creditors to whom obligations were outstanding are a linen merchant and three firms of *ritagliatori* (cutters).[4] In all likelihood the Della Robbia received their name from the colour of a crimson dye,[5] like the Ruccellai who derived their patronymic from the wool dye *oricello* (orchil).[6]

The Della Robbia family seem to have been relatively well-to-do. In 1413 Simone della Robbia shared a house near the hospital of Santa Maria Nuova with two brothers, Filippo and Jacopo,[7] and this house, in the district of San Pier Maggiore, on the corner of Via Albertinelli and Via Sant'Egidio, is mentioned once more in his Catasto (tax) return of 1427, when it was divided into two, one half inhabited by a widow who paid no rent and the other by a certain Ugolino di messer Giovanni, who had signed no formal lease but usually paid three florins a year. At this time Simone della Robbia himself leased a second, larger house in Via Sant' Egidio for nineteen florins a year, and there he, his sixty-five year old wife Monna Margherita, his three sons, a daughter-in-law, wife of the notary ser Giovanni, and a single grandchild, Pulisena, lived. The tax return also describes 'uno podere con chasa da signore e da llavoratore ... posto ... nel popolo di San Tommè a Baroncelli.' Dwelling houses were exempt from tax, and no valuation is therefore given for this property. The two pieces of land in the *podere* were surrounded by Peruzzi holdings, and included a small vineyard, producing 'barili quaranta di vino', and in addition yielded modest quantities of wheat, flax and fruit. The term 'casa da

1. Luca della Robbia's age is given as twenty-seven in his father's Catasto return of 1427 (Appendix 1 A) and thirty in his father's Catasto return of 1430 (Appendix 1 B). The first of these returns dates from 10 July 1427, and Luca must therefore have been born between July 1399 and July 1400.
2. Florence, Archivio di Stato: Arte della Lana 20 (Matricole 1352–1405, f. 46v.).
3. Florence, Archivio di Stato: Arte della Lana 21 (Matricole 1401–1456, f. 45r.).
   Ser Iohannes
   Marcus   fratres et filii Simonis quondam Marci
   et Lucas Vannis,* populi S. Petri Maioris de Florentia, positi et descripti fuerunt in presenti matricula per me Puccium notarium antedictum dictis anno indictione et die, vigore deliberationis facte per consules dicte Artis sub die XXVIII mensis Ianuarii MCCCCXXVI, ex benefitio eis collato ex persona dicti Simonis in matricula descripti. Et quia etiam iuraverunt, promiserunt et alia fecerunt secundum ordinamenta dicte Artis.

*(in margin)** Additum fuit post nomina dictorum ser Ioannis, Marci et Luce, fratrum et filiorum Simonis quondam Marci Vannis, cognomen casale videlicet della Robbia vigore deliberationis Magnificorum consiliorum Reipublice Florentine sub die 27 mensis Octobris 1429, hac die XVIII Martii 1429 [= 1430 m.st.].

4. Appendix 1 A. The thesis of Marquand (1914, p. xxv) that '... Simone had been a farmer and once lived upon his *podere* in the village of S. Maria in Tartigliese' is based on a misinterpretation of this Catasto return.
5. *Dizionario etimologico italiano*, ed. C. Battisti, Florence, 1957, v. 3272, s. voce Robbia. The name was current by 1380, see n. 7 below.
6. Kent, 1977, p. 254.
7. Florence, Archivio di Stato: Prestanze 2900 (S. Giovanni, Chiavi, 1413, c.17r.). Earlier references to the house, in Prestanze of 1380 and 1390, show that at that time it was already occupied by 'Filippo di Marcho della Robbia et frategli.' One of the 'frategli' was presumably Simone della Robbia.

signore' suggests a background of some prosperity, and the site of the house owned by Simone della Robbia at Baroncelli outside Florence can still be identified.[8] In addition, Simone was the owner of a small farm in the Arno valley, seemingly held for productive or investment purposes. It was situated in the village of Santa Maria di Tartigliese near Figline and comprised a 'chasa da llavoratore' with a 'chasecta' nearby used for stabling farm animals (two oxen, an ass, five full-grown pigs, a sow and seven piglets). Adjacent to the cottage were nineteen pieces of arable or agricultural land worked by a farmer, Marco di Berto dal Tartigliese. Their annual yield was just over eighty-seven lire, and their capital value was declared at three hundred and fourteen florins. From a later tax return put in by Luca della Robbia himself in 1457,[9] we learn that part of the land lay between the highway and the river Arno, and was vulnerable to flooding ('oggi detto podere è buona parte in Arno'). Simone's property also included a smallholding at Castel San Giovanni, where a 'chasetta' was rented to a tenant named Francesco di Luca; another tenant, Antonio di Conte da Castel San Giovanni, leased three pieces of land in the vicinity. It has been calculated that on the institution of the new tax system in 1427, eighty-two per cent of the population of Florence paid less than one florin in tax, and that between this indigent majority and a small body of two hundred and eighty-eight citizens of substantial wealth came a group of about fifteen hundred middle-class householders, who were taxed at between one and ten florins.[10] The tax imposed on Simone della Robbia of four florins fourteen soldi places him in the centre of this third group.

Catasto returns prepared by Simone della Robbia in 1430 and 1433[11] reveal the same material picture as before, save that a further *podere* had been purchased, at Sant'Andrea a Liviano. The main changes are in the composition of the Della Robbia family. Simone's daughter-in-law Mona Papera and her child Pulisena were dead, ser Giovanni della Robbia had remarried, and at the age of forty-three Marco della Robbia had married a girl of twenty, who had borne him three children: a baby, Filippo, who died at six months, a girl Cecca, and a son Jacopo. Marco's fourth child, Andrea della Robbia, the sculptor, was born only in 1435. At some time between 1433 and 1442, when Luca della Robbia made

his first independent Catasto return,[12] Simone della Robbia died. His property was shared by his three sons, who became joint owners of the land at Santa Maria di Tartigliese and of the house in Via Albertinelli. There is no reference to the Baroncelli property in this return or in a Catasto return of 1456-8,[13] but in later Catasto returns of 1469 and 1480[14] the house and land appear once more, as the joint property of Luca and of two of his nephews, Andrea (b. 1435) and Simone (b. 1438), the sons of Marco della Robbia. It seems, therefore, that the 'casa da signore' at Baroncelli and the adjacent land remained in Luca's hands throughout his life.

There are no further references in Luca's tax returns to the notary ser Giovanni, who enjoyed a successful official career and died between 1446 and 1451, but in 1442 he was sharing a house with his brother Marco (presumably that in Via Sant'Egidio) and in August 1446 he acquired, jointly with his brother, for two hundred and twenty florins, a house in Via Guelfa in which he lived for the remainder of his life. After Marco's death in 1448 it was vested first in Luca and the beneficiaries of his brother's estate, five nephews and nieces, and then jointly in Luca and two nephews, Andrea and Simone di Marco della Robbia. The house stood almost at the end of Via Guelfa, and was therefore on the periphery of the town. What we know about the property derives in the main from litigation after Luca's death, from which it transpires that it consisted of one house with outbuildings or two houses ('dictam domum sive dictas domos'), with a courtyard, a large garden and a well. Its purchase may have been dictated by the change of emphasis in Luca's work in the fourteen-forties from marble sculpture to enamelled terracotta. In the fifteenth century the use of kilns and furnaces in built-up areas of cities was commonly discouraged, and though there is no conclusive evidence from documents that the Della Robbia kiln was situated in the Via Guelfa house or in the garden adjacent to it, this is very probable.[15] In August 1451, the house in Via Albertinelli owned by Luca's father was sold for forty florins; half the sum raised was paid to Luca and the balance was distributed among his brother's children, Andrea (aged fifteen), Simone (aged thirteen), Paolo (twelve), Francesco (eight) and Margherita (seven). Later Catasto returns put in by Luca in 1457-8, 1469 and 1480 show

---

8. The site of the house is identified by Carocci, ii, pp. 86-7, as that of the present Villa Candrion at Poggio Baronti. After Luca della Robbia's death his half-interest in it passed by sale to Marco di Domenico Mellini, who in 1486 secured the remaining half-interest from Andrea della Robbia.

9. Appendix 1 G.

10. G. Brucker, 1977, pp. 403-4.

11. Appendix 1 B, C.

12. Appendix 1 D.

13. Appendix 1 G.

14. Appendix 1 H, I.

15. Marquand, 1920, p. xi, who infers that the kiln was in the *anticucina*.

no significant changes in the property held by him and by his family.

Luca matriculated in the Arte dei Maestri di Pietra e di Legname in September 1432.[16] His application for admission must have been precipitated by the contract for his first great commission, that for the Cantoria in the Cathedral, which was awarded him early in 1432 or in the preceding year. Membership in the Guild of Sculptors was not a prerequisite of independent sculptural activity, and Luca's admission at the age of thirty-two follows the same pattern as that of Ghiberti, who matriculated at thirty-one, and of the marble sculptor Piero di Giovanni Tedesco, who matriculated in 1388 when he had been in practice for some three years. We know, however, from his father's tax returns, that Luca must already have been practising as a sculptor. In Simone della Robbia's Catasto return of 1430, 'Lucha mio figliuolo' is credited with one hundred and fifty florins invested in the Monte di Prestanzioni, while in the return for 1433 he is credited with three hundred florins in the Monte di Prestanzioni, plus two hundred florins in the Monte Comune. The payments made to Luca in 1432 and 1433 in connection with the Cantoria account for no more than a part of this sum.

Until the last decade of his life the graph of the capital invested in Luca's name in the Monte Comune follows an upward curve. In 1442, it was four hundred and twenty-three florins, in 1446 it was nine hundred and ten (plus a further sum held in his father's name), in 1457–8 it was one thousand two hundred and three, and in 1469 it was one thousand four hundred and sixty-three. In 1480, however, his capital assets showed a sharp decline, and his tax assessment was less than half the previous total (one florin three soldi as against two florins nine soldi eleven years before). He was aged eighty when his last Catasto return was prepared, and the figures suggest that his professional activity must have been much reduced in his last years.

It has been stated that in addition to his affiliation to the Arte dei Maestri di Pietra e di Legname, Luca also matriculated in the Guild of Painters, the Arte dei Medici e degli Speziali, 'where he served several times as one of its Consuls, thirty times as a member of its council, three times as a Syndic, and twice as Treasurer.'[17] Search of the Guild records has failed to substantiate this claim. He was, however, an active member of the Guild of Sculptors, serving repeatedly as Consul and *Sindaco*.[18] On 2 September 1471, he signed a declaration of inability to assume the position of Consul of the Guild on the ground that his age and infirmity were such that he could not discharge the duties of the office without risk ('quod sine periculo sue persone dictum officium commode exercere non posset'),[19] but he recovered from this decline, and was again appointed Consul on 1 May 1475. His name also appears in 1472 in the records of the Compagnia di San Luca, to which he made regular annual contributions.[20] Confirmation that Luca suffered a serious illness in 1470 or 1471 is provided by the fact that on 19 February 1471 he made his will (almost invariably in the fifteenth century a sign of failing health).[21]

16. Florence, Archivio di Stato: Maestri di Pietra e di Legname 2 (Matricole, 1388–1518, c. 37r.): 'Lucas Simonis della Robbia scultor receptus fuit ad matriculam civitatis die primo setembris MCCCCXXX secundo, et solvit pro matricula libras vigintaquatuor camerario dicte artis, ut patet in libro campionis a foleis 262.'

17. According to Marquand (1914, p. xxviii), Luca 'was enrolled in the Guild of the Doctors and Apothecaries and in that of the Stone Masons and Woodcarvers.' For his alleged matriculation in the Arte dei Medici e Speziali see also *ibid.*, pp. xxvii, 130. This confusion seems to have arisen from a misreading by Marquand of a passage in Staley (1906, p. 270) which relates to the Compagnia di San Luca, not to the Arte dei Medici e Speziali. See n. 20 below.

18. According to the Guild records (Florence, Archivio di Stato: Maestri di Pietra e di Legname 2: Matricole, 1388–1518, c. 38v., 98r., 104r., 107v., 109v., 113v., 122v., 128r. and 144r.; and Debitori e creditori per matricole, 1465–1522, c. 28), Luca served as Consul in 1434, 1445, 1453, 1456, 1457, 1460, 1464, 1466, and 1475, and as *Sindaco* in 1467, 1471 and 1476. He was still a member of the Council of the Guild in April 1480.

19. Florence, Archivio di Stato: Notarile ante-cosimiano, C.5 25 (ser Agnolo di Cinozczo Cini, 1463–1474, c. 304v.).

20. Florence, Archivio di Stato: Accademia del Disegno, 2 (Debitori e creditori, segnato A, della Compagnia di San Luca di Firenze, 1472–1522, f. 86):

MCCCCLXXII

Lucha di Simone della Robia, intagliatore a San Bernaba, de' dare per tutto giugnio 1472 soldi sei per lla grazia fatta d'ogni debito aveva choll'arte per insino adì primo di luglio 1472; in questo a carte 2 . . . . L…s.6..

E de'dare per lla oferta del dì di Santo Lucha adì 18 d'ottobre 1472, e per ogni anno, soldi cinque. L…s.5..

E de'dare per lla sovenzione e aiuto e sosidio dell'arte, e per ogni anno, soldi sedici, paghando ogni mese s.1 d.4, inchominciando adì primo di luglio 1472 . . . . L… s. 16 ..

E de'dare per tuto novembre 1472 soldi cinque, per lla imposta fatta adì 18 d'ottobre 1472, per gli penoni de'trombetti . . . . L…s.5..

21. Appendix 2 A.

His death occurred on 20 February 1482, and three days later he was buried in the same church as other members of his family, San Pier Maggiore.[22]

At the time of his death he was still living in the house shared with his nephews Andrea and Simone and their families in Via Guelfa. Luca in his will says that Simone 'exercuit aliam artem,' and so indeed he did; he was a hosier with a shop near Or San Michele.[23] Andrea, on the other hand, was a mature artist of forty-six or forty-seven. His name appears in a document for the first time in August 1451, when he visited Maso di Bartolomeo's house on his uncle's behalf, taking with him a florin towards the expenses of retrieving some tackle used in installing the lunette made by Luca for the doorway of San Domenico at Urbino.[24] In 1455 he was already in receipt of independent commissions, receiving a down-payment of two florins on 25 September for a *Madonna* to be delivered in the following May.[25] Before this time, no doubt, he served an apprenticeship in Luca's shop, and for a few years after 1455 uncle and nephew may have maintained some loose form of collaboration. But we must assume that at least from 1458, when he matriculated in the Arte dei Maestri di Pietra e di Legname, Andrea della Robbia was an independent artist. Since he and Luca practised the same technique, they are likely to have used the same kiln and the same technical assistants, but after about 1460 the distinction between their work is very marked. There may indeed have been some tension between them. In a tax return of 1469, Andrea, who was then thirty-four, complains that his uncle Luca is demanding from him a 'buona somma di danari.'[26] If, he explains, he were really in debt to his uncle to the extent that Luca claimed, he would have very little money left. The sums demanded by Luca from his nephew cannot have represented rent, since Andrea was joint owner of the house, and may have arisen from Andrea's use of the kiln and technical facilities or from some form of technical copyright. In Luca's will of 1471 his relationship to his two nephews is carefully spelled out.[27] He had, he records, instructed Andrea in his own sculptural techniques, and while still alive had relinquished to him 'omne creditum dicti Luce' (this phrase seems to refer to the goodwill of the Della Robbia shop). In consequence, at the time the will was written, Andrea, by virtue of Luca's industry 'et eius documentis' (it is open to us to interpret this term as a reference either to instruction or to written formulae), practised a remunerative profession, as a result of which he was already 'superlucratus'. In the future, by continuing use of the technique, he was liable to become richer still and would be able without difficulty to ensure an honourable living for himself and for his family. The total resources of his estate, Luca asserts, were less than the earning potential of Andrea, and since he was anxious that he should not be charged, either by Simone or by other informed people, with ingratitude, he names Simone as beneficiary of his whole estate ('universalem haeredem'). The will was signed in the Dominican refectory at San Marco, in the presence of seven members of the community. No sooner was Luca dead than litigation ensued. The arbitrators came down decisively on the side of Andrea della Robbia.[28] Not only was he permitted to remain in Via Guelfa, but Simone della Robbia was constrained to sell him his share of the property for two hundred and fifty florins payable over a two-year term, was forbidden access to the garden (where the kiln probably was), and was ordered to have a window overlooking Andrea's premises blocked up. The decision may have been influenced by the sheer size of Andrea's family—when Luca died Andrea had eight children, of whom the eldest was sixteen and the youngest two—but a prime consideration must have been his reputation as an artist and the economic significance of the by then highly productive Della Robbia shop.

22. Florence, Archivio di Stato: Libri dei morti in Firenze (Serie della Grascia), 5 (Morti dal 1457 al 1506) c. 160r.: 'Lucha della Robbia, riposto in San Piero Maggiore adì 23 detto.'

23. In a document of 9 December 1473 (Florence, Archivio di Stato: Notarile ante-cosimiano, S 501, ser Bastiano Serforesi, 1466–1476, f. 52v.), he is described as 'Simon Marci della Robbia, calzaiuolus, conductor apotece posite in sul canto Orti S. Micaelis a Capitaneis Partis Guelfe.'

24. Florence, Biblioteca Nazionale, MSS Baldovinetti. 70 (Libro di conti di Maso di Bartolomeo da Firenze, 1449–1456, c. 51r.): 'E de' avere adì 21 d'agosto un fiorino largho, el quale mi presto per pagare el vetturale che m'arechò cierte cose da Urbino; mandomelo insino a chasa per Andrea suo nipote.'

25. Corti/Hartt, 1962, p. 164: 'E adì 25 detto f. dua, per lui a Andrea di Marcho dela Robia, portò contanti: sono per capara di una Nostra Donna gli debe fare per tutto magio prosimo.'

26. Florence, Archivio di Stato: Catasto 927 (S. Giovanni, Chiavi, 1469, c. 52r., v.): 'Lucha di Simone della Robbia mio zio mi domanda buona somma di danari, della quale s'io ne fussi debitore chome lui dicie, mi rimarebbe picchola chose: e pero mi vi rachomando.'

27. Appendix 2 A.

28. Appendix 2 B.

Not long after Luca's death, a paragraph about him was included in the *De' Viri illustri di Firenze* of Antonio Manetti.[29] He was, says Manetti, a master sculptor in bronze, marble and clay, and was the first artist to discover the technique of making enamelled terracottas. He goes on to enumerate Luca's works in the Cathedral —the bronze door of the North Sacristy, the enamelled terracotta lunette of the *Resurrection* above it, the lunette of the *Ascension* opposite, and the Cantoria—and closes with a sentence describing Luca's human not his artistic personality: 'Uomo buono e di costumata vita e di grande intelletto.' For Manetti, therefore, Luca was an artist distinguished for moral and intellectual qualities, not simply for productiveness or technical facility. The only book we know that he possessed is a copy of the poems of Jacopone da Todi which is now in Paris,[30] but his works compel us to suppose that he was, as Manetti indicates, both a pious and a literate sculptor.

Earlier references to Luca della Robbia lend colour to this view. As is well known, Alberti in 1436, in the preface to the Italian translation of his *De Pictura*, records the names of the five artists who set the course of Florentine Renaissance style.[31] One of them was Brunelleschi, whose importance was attested at the time by a number of great buildings and by the cupola of the Cathedral. The second, Masaccio, on his death in 1428 had left behind him frescoes in Santa Maria Novella and in the Carmine which testified to his stature and significance. The third, Ghiberti, had completed the first of his bronze doors for the Bapistry and was engaged, at the time Alberti wrote, on the Porta del Paradiso, while the fourth, Donatello, had to his credit a host of great statues on Or San Michele, the Duomo and the Campanile and a quantity of other public works. Luca della Robbia was a relatively unproved artist, and in 1436 his first major commission, the Cantoria for the Cathedral, was still incomplete. But those parts of it which could be seen in the Opera del Duomo must have impressed Alberti so forcibly that he included Luca in his list.

The same grouping is preserved by Vespasiano da Bisticci in his life of the humanist Niccolò Niccoli. The passage alludes to Niccoli's influence on the fine arts and reads as follows: 'Non solo Nicolaio prestò favori a uomini litterati, ma intendendosi di pitura, scoltura, architettura, con tutti ebbe grandissima notitia, et prestò loro grandissimo favore nel loro exercicio, Pipo di ser Brunellesco, Donatello, Luca della Robbia, Lorenzo di Bartoluccio, et di tutti fu amicissimo.'[32] The phrase 'prestò loro grandissimo favore nel loro exercicio' is ambiguous, but is likely to mean that Niccoli, who was a philologist and a collector of great distinction, participated in the planning of works by all four artists either with advice or with the loan of coins and other objects from his own collection. 'Amicissimo' suggests true intimacy. 'A vederlo a tavola,' writes Vespasiano of Niccoli, 'così antico come egli era, era una gentileza,' and it may well be that Luca from time to time was privileged to eat at Niccoli's table, loaded with classical vases as we know it to have been, and to watch him drinking from his hardstone and crystal cups. As a collector Niccoli had got in on the ground floor, before the price of antiques reached the level they attained later in the century, and those who visited his house were shown 'infinite degne cose'. There were classical statues and vases, inscriptions, 'molte cose di musaico in tavolette', paintings by artists of distinction, a seemingly limitless number of classical coins, in bronze, copper and silver, and classical bronze statues and statuettes.[33] All

29. G. Milanesi, 1887 (i), p. 168: 'Luca, che si disse della Robbia, maestro scultore di getti e di marmi e di terra, e fu el primo che trovò lo invetriare le figure. Fece molte cose: ma in Santa Maria del Fiore di Firenze si vede di lui insieme tre opere mirabili; la porta di bronzo della sagrestia, che si dice col tramontano lato, el pergamo di sopra, dove sono gli organi, et sopra le porte della sagrestia, cioè d'amendue gli archetti, cioè le figure di vetro, ovvero di terra invetriata, dov'è una Resurrezione di Cristo, e l'Ascensione. E fece molte altre cose per la città a per altrove. Uomo buono e di costumata vita e di grande intelletto.'

30. Paris, Bibliothèque Nationale. I am indebted for this reference to Professor Federico Zeri.

31. Alberti, iii, p. 7: '. . . qui fui in questa nostra sopra l'altre ornatissima patria ridutto, compresi in molti, ma prima in te Filippo, e in quel amicissimo Donato scultore e in quegli altri Nencio e Luca e Masaccio, essere a ogni

lodata cosa ingegno da non posporli e qual si sia stato antiquo e famoso in queste arti.'

32. Vespasiano da Bisticci, ii, p. 237.

33. *Ibid.*, pp. 239–40: 'Quando era a tavola mangiava in vasi antichi bellissimi, e così tutta la sua tavola era piena di vasi di porcellana, o d'altri ornatissimi vasi. Quello con che egli beveva erano coppe di cristallo o d'altri pietre fine. A vederlo a tavola, così antico come egli era, era una gentileza. . . . Saranno alcuni che si maraviglieranno di tanti vasi quanti egli aveva, a che si risponde che in questo tempo non erano queste cose in tanta riputatione, nè tanto istimate, quanto sono istate di poi; et avendo Nicolaio notitia per tutto il mondo, chi gli voleva gratificare gli mandava o statue di marmo, o vasi fatti dagli antichi o piture o isculture di marmo, d'epitafi di marmo, di piture di mano di singulari maestri, di molte cose di musaico in tavolette. Aveva numero infinito di medaglie di bronzo et d'otone e alcuna d'ariento. Aveva molte figure antiche di

these Luca della Robbia must have seen, and their influence is reflected in the only major work he undertook before Niccoli's death in 1437, the Cantoria.

These passages leave little doubt as to the circle in which Luca della Robbia moved as a young man. What we know of his professional training is based on stylistic inference. Vasari (whose life of Luca is of no more than secondary value)[34] states that he was educated as a goldsmith, as Brunelleschi had been before him. This was a not unusual practice in the early fifteenth century, but there is no confirmation that it was followed in Luca's case. If he started to learn his trade as sculptor at fourteen or fifteen, he would have embarked on his career at a time when progressive activity in Florence was focused on three buildings: the Baptistry, for which the first of Ghiberti's bronze doors was completed in 1423, Or San Michele, and the Cathedral. A letter, written by Pietro Cennini in 1475 while Luca was still alive, implies that he was for a time a member of Ghiberti's shop.[35] It refers to the second of Ghiberti's bronze doors, the Porta del Paradiso, 'in quo tamen et Michelotius et Luca Robia sculptores egregii, his melior Donatellus, et Bernardus aurifex pater meus, florentini omnes, non minimam partem fecere.' We know that Donatello, in the second half of 1407, and

Michelozzo, about 1420, worked on Ghiberti's first bronze door, but there is no record of Luca della Robbia's presence in the workshop. None the less, as the commission for the door of the North Sacristy of the Cathedral demonstrates, he was regarded as a capable bronze sculptor, and Ghiberti's was the only shop in which his experience could have been gained. Possibly he was employed there in 1423, when work began on the floreated jambs of the first bronze door, and in 1424, when the door and the jambs were installed, or between 1427 and 1429 during the first phase of work on the narrative reliefs of the Porta del Paradiso. The first hypothesis would explain why the floreated borders of Luca's later works depend from the jambs of Ghiberti's first bronze door rather than those of the second, while the second would account for resemblances between the formulation of individual figures on the Porta del Paradiso and on the Cantoria.

In the Cathedral, however, Luca was employed initially as a marble not as a bronze sculptor. To an aspirant marble sculptor in the middle of the second decade of the fifteenth century, one workshop, that of Nanni di Banco, would have been more attractive than any other. It had a dual appeal. In the first place it offered, unlike the capriciously constituted studio of

bronzo et d'otone, et grandi et picole. Aveva uno bellissimo universale, dove erano tutti i siti della terra, aveva Italie, Ispagne tutti di pittura. Non era casa in Firenze che fusse più ornata che la sua, et dove fussino più gentili cose che erano in quella, in modo che ognuno che v'andava in ogni facultà n'aveva infinite degne cose.'

34. Relevant passages from the 1550 and 1568 editions of Vasari's *Lives* are transcribed in the notes on individual sculptures throughout this book. In the jejune and rather contemptuous biography of 1550 (Vasari-Ricci, i, pp. 248–51) Vasari describes Luca as a rival of Donatello, and refers to the Campanile reliefs, the Cantoria, the lunettes in the Duomo ('La onde essendo cosa nuova piacque a' popoli sommamente per la vaghezza di quella'), the San Pier Buonconsiglio and Via dell'Agnolo lunettes, the Pazzi Chapel roundels, the Chapel of the Cardinal of Portugal, and a royal tomb for Naples. The text includes three passages which are omitted from the later life:
(i) 'Dicono, che Luca fu molto costumata et savia persona, et alla religione Christiana mirabilmente devoto.'
(ii) 'Et per tornare a Luca vecchio, essendo egli d'anni LXXV. et fieramente di mal di renella aggravato, non potendo resistere al dolore, che tale malattia gli dava, passò di questa a miglior vita.'
(iii) 'Et co'l tempo fu onorato con questi versi:
    Terra vivi per me cara et gradita
    Che alle acque e a'ghiacci come il marmo induri.

    Perche quanto men cedi, o ti matturi
    Tanto più la mia fama in terra ha vita.'
In the biography of 1568 Vasari states that Luca was trained as a goldsmith in the shop of Leonardo di ser Giovanni, and at the age of fifteen, with other young sculptors, started work at Rimini on a chapel for Sigismondo Pandolfo Malatesta and on the tomb of Isotta degli Atti. Returning to Florence, he undertook the reliefs on the Campanile, and on the insistence of Vieri de' Medici, was awarded the commission for the Cantoria. The list of works included in the earlier life is extended by references to the bronze door in the Cathedral (where the relief of St. John the Baptist at the top of the right wing is wrongly described as 'Gesù Cristo che esce dal sepolcro'), the *scrittoio* in the Palazzo Medici, the Chapel of the Crucifix at San Miniato al Monte, the *stemmi* on Or San Michele, and the Federighi monument. The belief that Luca worked at Rimini led Vasari, in the revised *Life*, to claim that he was the brother of Agostino and Ottaviano di Duccio (Vasari-Milanesi, II, p. 174: 'E perchè egli solo non poteva al tutto supplire, levò dallo scarpello Ottaviano e Agostino suoi fratelli'). It is implied in the second *Life* that Luca died at a younger age than Vasari had previously supposed (*ibid.*, p. 177: '. . . se la morte, che quasi sempre rapisce i migliori quando sono per fare qualche giovamento al mondo, non l'avesse levato, prima che bisogno non era, di vita').

35. G. Mancini, 1909, p. 221.

I. *Tabernacle* (Cat. No. 5). Marble and enamelled terracotta. Santa Maria, Peretola

II. *The Resurrection* (Cat. No. 6). Enamelled terracotta. Duomo, Florence

III. *The Ascension* (Cat. No. 7). Enamelled terracotta. Duomo, Florence

IV. *Angel with Candlestick* (Cat. No. 8). Enamelled terracotta. Duomo, Florence

V. *The Visitation* (Cat. No. 10). Enamelled terracotta. San Giovanni Fuorcivitas, Pistoia

VI. *Saint Matthew* (Cat. No. 9). Enamelled terracotta. Pazzi Chapel, Santa Croce, Florence

VII. *Saint John the Evangelist* (Cat. No. 9). Enamelled terracotta. Pazzi Chapel, Santa Croce, Florence

VIII. *Saint James the Great* (Cat. No. 9). Enamelled terracotta. Pazzi Chapel, Santa Croce, Florence

Donatello, the prospect of continuing employment. It was engaged on the filling of niches on Or San Michele, and had also received, in the summer of 1414, a contract from the Opera del Duomo for a relief over the Porta della Mandorla of the Cathedral which could not, on the most optimistic estimate, be completed in less than four or five years. In the second place it was the bulwark of classicising style in Florence. Its preconceptions are summed up in the great seated figure of St. Luke on the façade of the Cathedral and in the statues on Or San Michele and the reliefs beneath them, works whose relationship to the antique is unambiguous. There are a number of reasons for thinking that this was the course Luca chose. When he began work in 1437 on five marble reliefs for the Campanile, and in 1439 on two reliefs for an altar in the Cathedral, the relief style he employed was adapted from that of the marble predellas by Nanni di Banco on Or San Michele, and when in the fourteen-forties he started modelling the *Apostles* for the Pazzi Chapel, the ideal in his mind was that established by the *St. Luke*. There were other studios in Florence whose orientation was classical, like that of Ciuffagni, whose waterspout of 1422, in the form of a naked youth pressing a wine-skin, made for a position outside the South Sacristy of the Cathedral,[36] he must have known. But in the absence of evidence from documents, the view that he was trained as a marble sculptor by Nanni di Banco is very plausible.

The *Assumption* relief over the Porta della Mandorla of the Cathedral was commissioned from Nanni di Banco in June 1414, and payments for it continued till 1421, when the sculptor died. An analysis of them seems to show that the relief was between one-half and two-thirds completed before the sculptor's death, and that the bulk of this work was undertaken in a two-year period between 1418 and 1420, when he was free of other commitments and could concentrate on the relief.[37] It is possible that Luca, if he were a member of the studio, not only worked on the relief in Nanni di Banco's lifetime but continued to work on it after his death. The Virgin on the Porta della Mandorla is carved in one with

its surrounding frames from a single piece of marble, and the figures round it are carved from separate marble slabs. We cannot tell whether Nanni di Banco's practice was to bring the sections of his reliefs individually to a state of near completion or whether the sections were blocked out and put aside to be worked up together in a last stage. The issue of Luca's conjectural intervention can be posed only in terms of interrogatives. The Virgin was evidently carved by Nanni di Banco, but how do we account for two small cherub heads (Fig. 12) which appear to her right and left? Are they by Nanni di Banco or are they by a younger sculptor who completed the relief? Above and to the left of the Virgin is a flying angel playing a pipe (Fig. 13), whose swollen, flattened head is strangely similar to the central head in low relief in the *Choral Dancers* on Luca's Cantoria. Is the angel on the Porta della Mandorla by Luca, or does the head on the Cantoria derive from Nanni di Banco? At the apex, above the figure of the Virgin, is another music-making angel. Was this brought to its present state by Nanni di Banco, or was it begun by Nanni di Banco and finished by Luca della Robbia? All these possibilities must be borne in mind, though they are not supported by documentary evidence.

Whether Luca della Robbia worked on the Porta della Mandorla or no, it was a work that he knew well and that exercised a profound influence on his style. The appearance it presented in the second quarter of the fifteenth century was very different from the drab, monochrome effect it makes today. The marble was white and was touched up in gold, there was an abundance of blue paint presumably on the flat ground (it was bought for use on the relief by the painter Bicci di Lorenzo), the Virgin held a lily which was either painted or gilt, and in 1422 the girdle she dropped to St. Thomas was silk with a gold edge, later replaced by a metal girdle made by a coppersmith from Siena, Andrea di Ciecho.[38] The work belonged indeed to the same class of pictorial marble sculptures as the painted reliefs of *Virtues* on the Loggia dei Lanzi, and the Sacrament reliefs on the Campanile, where white marble figures were set off

36. Poggi, 1909, Doc. 428. The payment relates to 'unam buccam seu docciam marmoris albi, super qua sculta sit et facta figura unius pueri cum utre quem stringat.' Other payments refer to *doccioni* (Doc. 422) by Niccolò di Pietro Lamberti ('pro manifatura unius teste unius mastini, de marmore, da gittare acqua') and (Doc. 429) by Nanni di Bartolo. The *doccione* by Ciuffagni was purchased early in this century by Bernard Berenson, and until 1959 stood in the garden at the Villa I Tatti,

Florence. The discrepancy between the well preserved head and left shoulder and the remainder of the body suggests that in its original position the upper part of the figure was protected by a projecting ledge. For its intended position over the South Sacristy see Paatz, iii, p. 398.
37. Janson, 1963.
38. For the documentation of the relief see Poggi, 1909, Nos. 375–98.

against a blue glass ground. After 1440 it gave rise to the polychrome enamelled terracotta reliefs made by Luca della Robbia for the interior of the Cathedral.[39]

Luca was twenty-two when the relief over the Porta della Mandorla was installed, and thirty-one when he received the commission for the Organ Loft of the Cathedral. The Cantoria cannot have been entrusted to an inexperienced sculptor, yet we know no documented works by Luca from the half decade before it was begun. Between 1425 and 1432 Donatello was in partnership with Michelozzo, and both sculptors were engaged on the Coscia monument for the Baptistry in Florence, the Brancacci monument for Naples, and the Aragazzi monument for Montepulciano. Michelozzo was some four years older than Luca, and hypothetically Luca might have gravitated to his shop when it was engaged on the small figures over the niche containing Ghiberti's statue of St. Matthew on Or San Michele and on the reliefs of Virtues and the Virgin and Child on the Coscia monument. None of these works is, however, directly ascribable to Luca. More probably he was already associated in the fourteen-twenties with the artist with whom he was aligned a decade later, the architect and sculptor Brunelleschi. We can infer, moreover, from the panels of the Cantoria, that before starting work on them Luca went to Rome, and it is likely that his training in the late fourteen-twenties was designed to fit him for his historic task, the execution of the first great humanist commission in the Cathedral.

39. Seymour, 1963, carefully and thoroughly elaborates the case for Luca's presence in Nanni di Banco's shop. While his arguments are compelling, his conclusions are compromised by misinterpretation of Luca's development in the following decade.

II THE CANTORIA

Since the eighteenth century Luca della Robbia's first documented work, the Organ Loft in the Cathedral (Cat. No. 1, Plates 1–28), has been called the Cantoria, or Singing Gallery. There is no proof that it was designed to house a choir, but it will be referred to as the Cantoria throughout this book. Its recorded history opens on 9 April 1432, when Luca received a payment of six florins for the 'lavorio del perghamo degli orghani', though a small sum paid to him 'de quodam marmore albo' in October of the preceding year may also have been connected with the commission. It was substantially completed by March 1438, when authority was given to insert the consoles on which it rested in the wall over the entrance to the North Sacristy, and it was fully installed by the end of August of that year. Between 1432 and 1438 the progress of work on it is very fully documented, but the initial contract is not preserved. It is likely, however, to have been under discussion for some years before it was formally commissioned, and a long period of gestation must be presumed if its cogitated, highly self-conscious structure and imagery are to be explained.

The decision-making process in the Duomo in the fourteen-twenties was cautious and tentative, and the timespan of the thinking of the Operaii was very long and very slow. By character they were tenacious, and they did not feel the least impatience if a relief in marble over one of the north entrances took eight years to complete, or if in the Baptistry one third of a normal lifetime was consumed in the production of one door. On the outside of the Cathedral and on the Campanile, thanks to the superhuman zest of Donatello and of a new generation of sculptors trained, as a second nature, to carve life-size, free-standing statues, satisfactory progress was being made. Inside the church, on the other hand, things were more difficult. The choir with its three tribunes had been completed, and when in 1421 the third tribune was roofed over it became apparent how embarrassingly large the new space was. The cupola, after a protracted dialogue, had been entrusted to Brunelleschi, and, with Ghiberti looking across his shoulder, its building was under way, but the space beneath it was fraught with problems. The fact was that the Operaii had on their hands one of the largest churches in the whole of Italy, and that their duty was to bring it to a state in which it could be put to use. The choir stalls and high altar were in the nave, the culminating point of the preceding structure, and logically they should now be moved to a central place beneath the cupola. Moreover, fifteen subsidiary chapels, five in each tribune, had to be fitted out and decorated. Money was short—while the cupola was building that was bound to be the case—and the objective was not the erection of temporary altars, but an interior that was solid, stable and dignified. When the time came to consecrate the church, its state should in all essentials be definitive.

For the board it was a matter of determining priorities. One project, it was agreed, could be deferred. It would be sufficient for the present to leave the choir stalls and the high altar where they were, investing just a little money in painting or repainting the outside of the stalls and hoping that in ten years time a new high altar could be built. As for the tribune chapels, it seemed prudent initially to concentrate on one, that in the centre at the east end of the church, which was to be dedicated to the patron saint of Florence, St. Zenobius. Once this decision had been reached, expert advice had obviously to be elicited, so with some delay in 1428 a committee was formed; it included painters, sculptors and theologians, and it recommended that the Opera commission an altar for the chapel, a shrine for the Saint's relics (which were kept in a box in the crypt), a statue of the Saint, and a stained-glass window of the Saint and his two disciples. Even so, three and a half years elapsed before the committee's recommendations were translated into action, and only in 1432 was it finally agreed that the building of the altar should be entrusted to Brunelleschi, that a stained-glass window should be ordered, and that the shrine of St. Zenobius should be formally commissioned from Ghiberti, who was engaged on it, spasmodically, for upwards of nine years.

This was a liturgical decision, and the second project to which priority was given was liturgical as well. The organ of the Cathedral dated from 1388 and had been commissioned from Fra Domenico da Siena when complaints were made that the preceding organ 'was now so sad no one could get pleasure from the sound that it produced.' A wooden casing was provided for it in 1411, and in 1413 it was supplied with a blue curtain decorated with lilies, but by the fourteen-twenties it too was regarded as inadequate. In 1422-3 the most celebrated organ-maker in Tuscany, Matteo di Paolo da Prato, was called in to repair or recondition it. He did what he could, but the organ was still unsatisfactory, having regard to the fact that when the high altar and choir stalls were moved, the organ would necessarily be moved as well, to the vast space beneath the cupola. By the winter of 1426 the Operaii were reconciled to the fact that a new organ had to be built so that it, and the old renovated organ, could be installed in the choir. They were fortified in this decision by the fact that a superior organ existed in the Baptistry, and that an organ, by Matteo da Prato, had been ordered for Or San Michele, where it was fitted in 1429 with painted shutters by Francesco d'Antonio of music-making angels singing from scrolls of music. But once more there was a delay, this time of six years, and not till March 1432 was the order for the new organ confirmed. A year later, in 1433, a model of the organ was despatched from Prato.

New organs (more strictly one new organ and one re-pristinated organ) involved new organ lofts, and since the positions designated for the organs over the doors of the two sacristies, to right and left of the central tribune (Fig. 1), were determined by the prospective position of the new altar, the lofts were of great consequence. Facing west, towards the high altar, and fully visible from two thirds of the way up the nave of the church, they were the first significant addition to the interior architecture beneath the cupola. In the Cathedral, as we have seen, the date at which a contract was placed is not in itself an indication of the date when the work to which it relates was conceived. The contract for Luca della Robbia's Cantoria almost certainly dates from 1431, and that for the second Cantoria (Fig. 2) was placed in the second half of 1433, when Donatello, who had been in Rome, returned to Florence. In books on Luca della Robbia and Donatello the two organ lofts are often treated as though they were planned independently of one another, but that cannot have been the case. Though the end products were, in the event, strikingly diverse, there were from the start two organs, and two organs required two organ lofts. If the time schedule for the commissions in the Chapel of St. Zenobius is any guide, the commissions would have been preceded by three or more years of discussion, and the plan for the two Cantorias, conceived as conterparts, not as a true pair, must have been in gestation at least from 1428, when decisions of principle would have been reached about their form and style and iconography.

As we see it today in the Museo dell'Opera de Duomo, the first Cantoria, Luca della Robbia's, comprises ten figure reliefs enclosed in an architectural frame. But in its original position, sixteen metres from the ground over the door of the North Sacristy, it would have registered quite differently, as an architectural unit decorated with reliefs that were (if the sources are to be believed) less than fully legible. Looking up at it from the floor of the Cathedral, we would have seen a gallery supported on five massive consoles (Plate 1). The front face of the parapet was articulated with paired pilasters corresponding with the consoles beneath, and across it ran emphatic horizontal strips of incised lettering, which was coloured black and could (unlike the reliefs) be read from some distance away. The upper part, the gallery proper, was removed from its original position in 1688, and though the six figure reliefs were carefully preserved, its architectural framing was destroyed or put to other use. The present reconstruction is based on a single set of paired pilasters which happens to have survived and on a small piece of the inscription at the top. The cornice above was carved separately, and its reconstruction is conjectural. The consoles, on the other hand, with the central inscription and the inscription across the base, remained in position till the nineteenth century, and are preserved intact.

At the time the Cantoria was conceived, the dominant voice in the Cathedral was that of Brunelleschi, and we might expect that Brunelleschi either would have designed it or would have overseen its plan. The architecture of the Organ Loft is not ascribed to Brunelleschi by any early source, but this is not in itself evidence that Brunelleschi was not responsible for its design. In the fifteenth century works of art were commonly credited to the executant, not to the ideator, and for that matter Antonio di Tuccio Manetti, when he wrote the life of Brunelleschi, omitted, from forgetfulness or for some other reason, all reference to the Pazzi Chapel.

The evidence for Brunelleschi's association with the Cantoria is stylistic, and is not therefore of a perfectly conclusive kind. Its architectural ornament is of the very highest quality. The paired pilasters with composite Corinthian capitals which punctuate the balustrade are consistent with Brunelleschi's architectural vocabulary, and so are the consoles (Plates 26, 27), their leading edges carved with bold acanthus decoration, visually segregated from the volutes at the back, and their lateral faces carved with floreated motifs reminiscent of the Ara Pacis. Especially bold is the carving of the flowers in the centre of each side. Similar decorative carving appears, in the middle of the fourteen-twenties, on the consoles of Donatello's Coscia monument, which are, however, more constricted and more meagre than the consoles of the Cantoria. The soffit reliefs above the consoles (Plate

28A) are carved with moulded rectangles containing a fluted design, framed in the two outer spaces by olive wreaths and in the inner spaces by perspective discs. Similar motifs are employed, again to less effect, in the upper part of Donatello's Brancacci monument in Naples, as well as in the spandrels of the Brunelleschi-designed architecture of Masaccio's *Trinity*. The effect of the structure is vigorous and confident. There is no later evidence that Luca della Robbia functioned as an architect, and confronted as we are with the options of regarding the Cantoria as a work designed by Luca on the basis of those works by Brunelleschi available for study in 1431, or as an original work by Brunelleschi, we must conclude that the second alternative is the less implausible.

On more than one occasion between 1432 and his death in 1446, Brunelleschi concerned himself with projects involving a component of figure sculpture. In 1432 a lavabo designed by him for the North Sacristy of the Cathedral was carried out by his adopted son, Buggiano. The grotesque putti who preside over the flow of water are Buggiano's, but it was Brunelleschi, not Buggiano, who was responsible for the concept of classicising style they represent. In a second lavabo, ordered in 1442 for the South Sacristy, the same relationship obtains. When an altar was designed by Brunelleschi for the Sagrestia Vecchia of San Lorenzo, provision was again made for figure sculpture, and once more it was executed by Buggiano. In 1439 this pattern was repeated in two altars designed by Brunelleschi for the Cathedral; in this case, however, the execution was entrusted to two major sculptors, Luca della Robbia and Donatello. Finally in 1443 a model for a pulpit in Santa Maria Novella was prepared by Brunelleschi on the commission of the Ruccellai. Four scenes were incorporated in the balustrade, and they too were entrusted to Buggiano. We might well suppose that this same procedure was followed with the Cantoria, that its design was due to Brunelleschi and that Luca della Robbia performed a role analogous to that played by Buggiano in the altar, pulpit and lavabos; that Brunelleschi's was the controlling mind and that Luca was the inspired executant.

The Cantoria is a hard work to analyse, and epigraphy may be the best point at which to start. Across the front in three incised bands run the words of Psalm 150. The top band contains the first two verses of the Psalm: LAVDATE D⟨OMI⟩N⟨V⟩M IN S⟨AN⟩C⟨T⟩IS EIVS · LA⟨VDATE⟩EV⟨M⟩ IN F⟨IR⟩MAMENTO V⟨IR⟩TVTIS EI⟨VS⟩ · LA⟨VDATE⟩ EV⟨M⟩ IN V⟨IR⟩- TVTIB⟨VS⟩ EI⟨VS⟩ · LA⟨VDATE⟩ EV⟨M⟩ S⟨ECVUN⟩- D⟨V⟩M MVLTITVDINEM MAGNITVD⟨IN⟩IS EI⟨VS⟩. The only original section is that with the words IN V⟨IR⟩TVTIB⟨VS⟩EI⟨VS⟩ · LA⟨VDATE⟩EV⟨M⟩- S⟨ECVNDV⟩ (Plate 28B). On the central band are the third verse and the first half of the fourth: LAVDATE EVM IN SONO TVBAE · LAVDATE EVM IN PSALTERIO ET CYTHARA · LAVDATE EVM IN TIMPANO; and on the lowest band, beneath the consoles, is the remainder of the Psalm, from the second half of the fourth verse to the sixth verse: ET CHORO · LA⟨VDATE⟩ EV⟨M⟩ IN CORDIS ET ORGANO LA⟨VDATE⟩EV⟨M⟩ IN CIM- BALIS BENE SONA⟨N⟩TIBVS LA⟨VDATE⟩ EV⟨M⟩ INCIMBALIS IVBILATIONIS O⟨MN⟩IS SP⟨IRITV⟩S LAVDET D⟨OMI⟩N⟨V⟩M. The size of the letters and the elisions were dictated by the length of the lines, and these in turn seem to have been determined by the figure content of the Organ Loft. If, for example, the words ET CHORO had been inserted at the end of the second line, the length of the three lines would have been equalised, but the relation between the inscription and the image would have been disturbed. The contraction of LAVDATE in the first and last lines is unusual, and is indicated by a spray of foliage running through the two initial letters. Classical formata lettering appears in a number of codices written by Poggio Bracciolini between 1408 and 1422, and was adopted by Ghiberti on the *Arca of the Three Martyrs* between 1424 and 1428. Variants of classical majuscule lettering appear in the second half of the fourteen-twenties on the Dati tomb slab of Ghiberti (1425–7?), the Pecci tomb slab of Donatello (1426), and, in an illusionistic form, on the Coscia monument (after 1425). The inscription on the Cantoria is, however, the earliest large-scale affirmation of humanist epigraphy in a public monument, and given its prominence we may guess that a humanist epigrapher, perhaps Niccolò Niccoli, advised on its design.

The four reliefs on the front of the parapet (Plates 2, 5, 7, 10) illustrate the words inscribed beneath them, IN SONO TVBAE (the relief known as the *Trumpeters*), IN PSALTERIO (the *Players on the Psaltery*) ET CYTHARA (the *Players on the Cithara*), and IN TIMPANO (*Players on the Drum*). Similarly the reliefs between the consoles (Plates 14, 16, 17, 20) relate to the bottom line of the inscription, and illustrate the words ET CHORO (the *Choral Dancers*), IN CORDIS ET ORGANO (the *Players on the Organ, Lute and Harp*), IN CIMBALIS BENE SONANTIBVS (the *Players on the Tambourine*), and IN CIMBALIS IVBILATIONIS (the *Cymbal Players*). It would be well at this point to look at Luca's ten reliefs individually, in the order in which they appear on the Cantoria, first at the four on the front of the parapet, then at the four between the consoles, and finally at the two side reliefs at the ends of the gallery.

The first relief, the *Trumpeters* (Plates 2–4), shows six youths in two symmetrical lines that recede diagonally towards the centre of the scene. The three on the right are shown in repose. Two rest the stems of trumpets on their shoulders, and the third holds a pipe, or the mouth-piece of a trumpet, in his right hand. The group on the left is active. Two of the boys are blowing straight trumpets, and the third, behind, is sounding a folded trumpet. Villani describes men and women going through Florence 'con trombi e diversi strumenti,' and a similar combination of straight and folded trumpets is depicted on the Adimari marriage cassone. The only earlier representation of a folded trumpet occurs in a manuscript in the British Library (Harley Roll Ms. 7353), but there can be little doubt that when the relief was carved the two types of trumpet were commonly played together on festive occasions. To judge from its effect on the four dancing girls who occupy the centre foreground, the sound was an exciting one. One of them, in the middle, reaches up to touch the foremost trumpet, bending her head back so that her long, heavily drilled hair flows out behind her. This motif derives, and would in the fourteen-thirties have been recognised as deriving, from a maenad figure on some Roman or Hellenistic relief. One of the closest parallels is with a figure on the left of a Dionysiac scene now in the Uffizi (Fig. 11), which was formerly in the Palazzo Riccardi. More important than the exact source of the motif is the success with which Luca reproduces the orgiastic movement in classical Dionysiac reliefs. The verticals of the two musicians at the sides and the horizontal of the trumpets, which extend across the greater part of the relief, supply the dancing figures with an emphatic rectangular frame.

The second scene (Plates 5, 6) shows three standing girls playing on psalteries and singing. In the background to right and left are two boy auditors, one of whom sings while the other places his hand on the shoulder of a player. At the back are the heads of three other listeners in very low relief, while in the foreground are two seated children plucking smaller psalteries. The three female figures in the centre wear diaphanous dresses, which fall loosely over their high girdles. They evidently derive from a Muse sarcophagus, and almost certainly—if their poses, the smooth movement of their legs, and the pattern of raised forearms running across the scene constitute valid proof—from the famous Muse sarcophagus in Vienna (Fig. 4), which in the sixteenth century stood outside Santa Maria Maggiore in Rome, and which was also known in the Quattrocento. It has been suggested, persuasively, that the two heads in low relief to right and left of centre derive from Greek coins of the class of those from Metapontum and Clazomenae. One of the children in the foreground, that on the left, is adapted from a Roman statuette, the *Boy with a Goose* in the Uffizi (Fig. 9), which was also copied, from another angle, in the middle of the fourteen-twenties, for the Christ in Masaccio's *Virgin and Child with St. Anne* in the Uffizi. No doubt the second child, to the right,

also depends from a classical original. Here it is the outer auditors, ranged stiffly against the frame, who establish the controlling verticals of the composition. The figures in the Vienna Muse sarcophagus stand in a single plane against a curtain. In Luca's relief, however, heads in low relief inserted beside the central Psaltery player establish the space content of the scene.

In the third relief (Plates 7–9) are two singing girls, in long dresses and full cloaks, who accompany themselves on citharas. Whereas the psalteries in the preceding scene are uniform and are played with the fingers, not a plectrum, the two citharas are of different sizes, one with five frets extending from the neck and the other with three. They are of regular fifteenth-century types, and occur again in a relief by Agostino di Duccio in the Tempio Malatestiano. At the sides, pressed against the frame, are two girls in profile enraptured by the music, and at the back appear the heads of three more female figures. In the foreground are two seated children, one, on the left, pointing diagonally to the right-hand cithara player, and the other, on the right, pointing with raised right arm and an extended finger to the same figure and endeavouring with the open palm of his left hand to attract the attention of unseen spectators beneath. The source of the main figures is once more a Muse sarcophagus, at Woburn Abbey (Fig. 5), from the Villa Giustiniani, which is reproduced in the Codex Coburgensis and must have been available for study at an earlier time. In the Woburn relief the treatment of space is less rigid than in the Vienna Muse sarcophagus, and a head is inserted at the back between the central figures of Apollo and Athena. The dialogue which appears to be in progress between the second and third figures from the left of the sarcophagus and the second and third figures from the right and between Athena and the muse behind her, seems to have inspired the colloquy between the background figures which is one of the great beauties of Luca della Robbia's relief. The child in front on the left, with right leg extended and the left knee flat on the ground, depends from a child playing with a goat on a Bacchic sarcophagus, also at Woburn (Fig. 6), which is recorded in the Villa Aldobrandini in 1603 and was also known in the sixteenth century. The arm and left knee of the child in the Roman relief were repaired in the eighteenth or nineteenth century, and the figure may already have been broken when Luca copied it.

The fourth relief (Plates 10–13), on the extreme right of the balustrade, shows in the centre and on the left two boys playing on hand drums. A third boy, on the right, has a drum hooked to his chest, and moistens his drum stick in his mouth. The instruments are once more of different sizes and, though they do not exactly correspond with the drums shown in the Tempio Malatestiano, are of regular fifteenth-century types. At the back are the faces of two smiling onlookers, and in the centre, in front, in very deep relief, is a confronting pair of dancing boys, watched from the sides by two naked children. The drummer on the left wears a rose in his hair and one of the two dancing boys carries a rose in his left hand. Probably the drummer on the left, with cloak billowing out over his shoulders and right thigh, derives from a cymbal player on a Dionysus sarcophagus of the class of that at Hever Castle.

Moving down to the lower register, between the consoles on the left we encounter a group of seven dancing figures with hands linked (Plates 14, 15). This is not the formal dance that is depicted in Ambrogio Lorenzetti's fresco of *Good Government*, but a spontaneous round. It has been suggested very plausibly that the linked hands and extended arms of the forward figures were inspired by the great Neo-Attic vase in the Camposanto at Pisa (Fig. 8). The two central figures are carved in deep relief, middle relief is used for the two profile figures at the sides, and very low relief for the focal figure with head slightly foreshortened at the back. The antithesis between the outer figures, a boy on the left looking up and a girl on the right with her demure head turned down, is once more classical.

In the adjacent relief to the right (Plates 16, 18) a boy playing a portable organ is seated in the centre on a classical stool—clearly of Roman origin, though the closest parallel, in reverse, is with the seat on a sarcophagus relief excavated in 1858, now in the Lateran. On the right are two boys with a lute and harp. The portatif is of an orthodox type, which is carried by an angel in a marble statuette by Piero di Giovanni Tedesco from the façade of the Cathedral and appears once more in Lorenzo di Bicci's fresco of the *Marriage of St. Cecilia and Valerianus* in the sacristy of the Carmine. In the Tempio Malatestiano at Rimini it is shown played in conjunction with a harp, just as it is here. There are six child onlookers, and one of them, an almost naked boy standing with legs crossed on the left, has a parallel on an Endymion sarcophagus in the Palazzo Rospigliosi.

The centralised form of this relief is retained in the next and penultimate relief (Plates 17, 19), which shows a boy in full face, naked save for a garland, singing and striking a tambourine. At the sides are four other children, two boys and two girls, sounding tambourines, and at the back are two listening children with heads upturned. An analogy has been found for the central figure in a Daedalus sarcophagus in the Louvre (Fig. 10), where the genitals of the naked child are masked by a garland in somewhat the same way. The head, and probably also the body, of a wreathed boy on the extreme right seem also to have been adapted from the antique. The two outer figures have wings.

In the last scene, the *Cymbal Players* (Plates 20, 21), a child on the left appears likewise to be derived from a Bacchic relief, and the head of the wreathed boy on the right is also of classical origin. The strong forward propulsion of the whole group is established by a striding girl in the centre, with weight thrown forward on the right leg, a formula that is employed again by Ghiberti for a frightened warrior in the *Moses* relief on the Gate of Paradise and by Donatello for a putto on the extreme left of the pulpit at Prato. All these figures are likely to have a common source in sarcophagus reliefs, perhaps in that from Santa Maria Maggiore in the British Museum. A somewhat similar figure, with head turned frontally, also occurs on a Marsyas sarcophagus in the Palazzo Barberini.

The two narrow reliefs of *Singing Boys* (Plates 22–25) at the sides of the parapet stand a little apart from these eight scenes. On the left five boys are shown singing under the direction of a youth on the right, who gives them their entries with his raised left hand. From the left another youth looks on attentively. The two foremost singers, evidently younger children since their dresses reach only to the thigh, hold a volume of music which the other three read over their heads. The older figures wear ankle-length boots and robes fastened on the shoulder with full cloaks. The relief reads well at eye level, but in its original position one and possibly both the heads of the small boys would have been hidden by the protruding choir book. In the corresponding relief on the right, three youths in half-relief are seen singing from a scroll which extends horizontally across the scene. At the back are the heads of a fourth singing boy and of a youth listening with one hand pressed against his cheek. The intention in these scenes manifestly is more literal than in the other reliefs. They portray the members of two choirs engaged in their professional task. Given the care with which the musical detail in the other eight reliefs is planned, the antithesis between the choir book on the left and the scroll on the right can only be deliberate; perhaps the contrast is between plainchant and polyphonic singing. According to Villani polyphonic music was sung in the Cathedral in the fourteenth century, and it seems to have been this that gave rise, in the fifteenth century, to the practice of including two *cantores* in the plainchant choir of the church. Interest in polyphonic music increased after 1430, and reached a climax in 1436, when a well-known motet, *Nuper rosarum flores*, was commissioned for the consecration ceremony from Dufay. A chapel of polyphony was established in 1438, staffed by four Ferrarese singers. Very possibly the imagery of the lateral reliefs of the Cantoria relates to these developments.

When the content of the ten reliefs is examined in this way, one conclusion is mandatory: that they were planned with the advice of a musician in a relief style based, by intention not by accident, on Roman sarcophagus reliefs. Their style becomes intelligible only if we assume that the decision to commission the Organ Loft was taken in the late fourteen-twenties, that it originated in the mind of Brunelleschi, and that Luca della Robbia before 1431 visited Rome in order to familiarise himself not simply with a wider range of sarcophagus reliefs than was available in Tuscany but more broadly with the syntax of Roman sculpture. When the eight panels on the front face of the Cantoria were installed in their intended place, however, they would not have been looked at, as we have been looking at them here, sequentially. They would have been regarded as a group, and only when they are so seen does an essential aspect of their style become apparent. It has been said that 'the periodic sentence is the basic art form of the early humanists,' and on the Cantoria that concept is worked out on a visual plane. In the centre of the balustrade are two reliefs, each of which contains a vertical figure in the centre of a static composition. Outside, to left and right, are two reliefs of dancing figures closed at the end by a music-making youth turned inwards, in the left-hand panel in profile to the right, in the right-hand panel in profile to the left. Between the consoles the same pattern is repeated. In the centre are two scenes with figures in repose, with the same vertical emphasis as those above, provided on this occasion by the seated boy playing a harp and the child holding a tambourine, and outside these are two more groups in movement, on one side a circle of dancing figures rotating clockwise and on the other, moving to the left, a troop of cymbal players.

One of the paramount impressions left by early humanist literature is of the ubiquity of the notion of style. 'What is there,' asks Poggio Bracciolini in a letter to Guarino in 1416, 'that could be more delightful, more pleasant and more agreeable to the youth and the rest of the learned world than the knowledge of those things whose acquisition makes us more learned and, what seems even more important, stylistically more polished?' This is the thinking from which the Cantoria springs. In the first half of the fifteenth century there was a premium on assimilation, and the successful style was the style whose sources were imperceptible. The classical sources of Ghiberti have been studied in great depth, but no one looking at his reliefs can doubt that the classical culture from which they proceed was wider than the aggregation of known borrowings might suggest. The case of the Cantoria is very similar. It proceeds not only from thorough knowledge of sarcophagus reliefs (a few of which can be tentatively identified), but also from sources of a less obvious kind. Some of the heads in low reliefs have, for example, been convincingly related to Greek coins. This is not surprising since we know that

a later work of Luca, carved after the Cantoria was complete, is based on two coins of Constantine or Constans. In this area his intimacy with Niccoli must have been of special consequence. It cannot indeed be wholly ruled out that the planning of the Cantoria as a succession of carefully equilibrated, isocephalous, rectangular panels was not bound up with early knowledge of Greek fifth and fourth century metope reliefs. Ciriaco of Ancona was in Florence in 1432–3, when work on the Cantoria was begun, and though at that time he had not visited either Athens or Olympia, he may have been the channel through which reports on the character of classical Greek sculpture were transmitted to the Florentine humanists of the day. Certainly we should misjudge Luca della Robbia's Cantoria if we did not accept it as the closely cogitated product of a group of learned men.

One of the puzzling things about the great monuments of the Early Renaissance is that they changed as work on them progressed. This happened (to take one exceptionally well-documented case) with the Prato pulpit of Donatello. At the time it was commissioned, in 1428, its balustrade was to be decorated with six reliefs of paired putti holding shields. But by the time the balustrade was executed, about 1433, the six reliefs had become seven, and the putti with shields had been scrapped and replaced by reliefs of playing children based on the antique. Something of this sort also occurred with the Cantoria of Donatello in the Cathedral (Fig. 2). It has been argued conclusively by Janson that the balustrade was originally to be decorated with a sequence of separately framed panels, and that only in a second stage were these supplanted by the continuous frieze that we see now. So it is not surprising that the Cantoria of Luca della Robbia changed as well. Here luckily we have a good deal of evidence as to precisely what occurred.

From 1432 till its completion in 1438 the progress of Luca's Cantoria is very fully documented. We are cognisant in detail of the sums due to him and we are cognisant of the sums that he received, and the correspondence between them is extremely close. We know that the most important architectural elements, the consoles, the paired pilasters, and the strips of incised lettering belong to a late stage in the history of the Organ Loft, and we know that the figure reliefs were executed between 1432 and the spring of 1437. Two records are of special consequence. The first dates from August 1434, and explains that the Operaii had examined and assessed four figurated reliefs ('quatuor petia seu quatuor petiis storiarum'). Two of them were large reliefs, valued at sixty florins apiece, and two of them were small and were valued at thirty-five florins. The second record dates from April 1435, when payment for the large reliefs was increased to seventy florins, with a pro rata increase for those reliefs which were less large. The reason for the increase is spelled out in the document, that their execution had consumed more time than that of the earlier reliefs ('in quibus maiorem laborem et longius tempus misit') and that the reliefs themselves were better and more beautiful ('dicte storie quas fecit ad presens sunt pulcriores ac meliores').

Since two reliefs on the Cantoria are smaller than the rest, and since two small reliefs were completed by August 1434, it can be inferred that the small reliefs, the *Boys singing from a Book* and the *Boys singing from a Scroll*, are among the earliest of the carvings. That has been contested but is not open to serious dispute. It follows that the two large reliefs carved by 1434 must be the two most closely related to the small reliefs. These are the central reliefs on the balustrade, the *Players on the Psaltery* and the *Players on the Cithara*. The ovoid form of the head of the second boy from the right in the *Boys singing from a Scroll* recurs in the second figure from the left in the *Players on the Psaltery*, and there are affinities as well between the head of the further boy holding an antiphonal in the *Boys singing from a Book* and the upturned head to right of centre in the *Players on the Cithara*.

There are other conclusive reasons for supposing that the *Cithara* and *Psaltery Players* precede the other large reliefs. When we look at the front face of the Cantoria, we find that six of the large reliefs are filled with children (the four bottom reliefs and the outer reliefs on the balustrade) while the two in the centre of the gallery are occupied by figures of an older age group. There must, therefore, have been a change of plan after the completion of the two exceptional reliefs. Alone of the eight large carvings, the *Players on the Cithara and Psaltery* have an origin in Muse sarcophagus reliefs. The document of 1435 could, therefore, imply not simply that the subsequent reliefs were more exacting and more deeply cut, but that the decision to employ a relief style based on Muse sarcophagi was revised. Instead the six remaining rectangles would be filled with big boisterous children, inspired by Hadrianic reliefs like the *Sacrifice of a Bull* in the Uffizi (Fig. 7), by Roman child sarcophagus reliefs, and by reliefs of children like those in the Palazzo Medici, which Donatello adopted as his models for the figure carvings of the second Cantoria.

The sequence of the six reliefs occupied by children can also be established with some confidence. They fall into three pairs. The first pair comprises the two central reliefs between the consoles, the *Tambourine Players* and the *Players on the Organ and Harp* (where a concave group of children forms a niche behind the central figure). The second pair comprises the more highly activated *Drummers* and *Cymbal Players*, where the emphasis on movement reflects the innovations of

Donatello on the Prato pulpit and the second Cantoria. The third pair comprises the *Trumpeters* (the only relief which is unfinished, five feet on the right and in the centre and the head and hair of one of the dancing children being left in the rough) and the *Choral Dancers*, for which Luca must have made a model which was executed by another hand. The reason for regarding this as the last of the reliefs is that it implies a deeper space than the notional depth of the carving, and in this respect has a parallel only in the *Trumpeters*. Its execution, however, is more flaccid and perfunctory; the back of the forward figure lacks anatomical definition, the forward limbs and legs are flattened, and the pupils of the eyes are void. Another work possibly by the same sculptor is a *Madonna and Child* in the Museo dell'Opera del Duomo (Cat. No. 61, Fig. 40) sometimes given to Pagno di Lapo Portigiani. The late date of the *Choral Dancers* can be corroborated in another way, for Luca, after 1438, added two bronze candle-bearing angels to the balustrade (Cat. No. 46, Plates 108–111). They are described by Vasari and Baldinucci, and they remained on the Cantoria until it was dismantled in 1688. They are now in Paris in the Musée Jacquemart-André, and are discussed in this book in the context of Luca della Robbia's bronze sculptures. Their heads agree closely in one case with the central head in the background of the *Choral Dancers* panel and in the other with a figure to the right of centre in the same scene.

Today in the Museo dell'Opera del Duomo, as we turn from the Organ Loft of Luca to that of Donatello (Plate 1, Fig. 2), what we are conscious of is contrast. Externally Donatello's Cantoria differs from Luca's in almost every respect—in its use of coloured inlay, in the summariness of its execution, in its aggressive imagery. None the less it springs from the same seed. It fulfilled the same function as Luca's; its size, to within a very few centimetres, is the same; its consoles are also carved with classicising ornament (related in this case to the decoration of the Temple of Concord); and what may well be the earliest of its carvings, the figure reliefs at the bottom between the consoles, follow known classical originals—in one case a relief from the Throne of Ceres at Ravenna, in the other a section of the Throne of Neptune in Milan—much more punctiliously than any carvings in the companion Cantoria. Probably the two Cantorias had a common programme as well. It has been suggested that since Luca's Cantoria illustrates Psalm 150, the frieze of dancing angels devised by Donatello must illustrate Psalm 148 or 149. But if this is so it is surprising that there was at no time an inscription on the second Cantoria. The readiest explanation is one so simple that it has never been seriously advanced— that the two Cantorias illustrate one and the same Psalm, and that the subjects allotted to Donatello were the opening verses which were not illustrated on Luca's Cantoria: Laudate Dominum in sanctis eius: laudate eum in firmamento virtutis eius. Laudate eum in virtutibus eius: laudate eum secundum multitudinem magnitudinis eius. Hence the distinction between the winged angels of Donatello, praising the Lord in a heavenly sphere, and the almost invariably wingless boys and girls sounding their instruments on an ambiguous platform of cloud on the first Cantoria. This unity of purpose must have been laid down from the first, and when, in July 1433, Neri di Gino Capponi was entrusted by the Operaii with determining the 'storiis' as well as the terms of the contract for Donatello's Organ Loft, his concern must have been not with its thematic content, but with the way in which its thematic content was to be illustrated.

The process went through two distinct phases which can be inferred from the surviving documents. In the first the panels were to be rectangular with separate framing, and we can imagine that at this time they would have more than a little in common with the panels decided upon for the Prato pulpit in 1433, that they would, in other words, have shown groups of four or five angels dancing and playing instruments, each distinct from that adjacent to it and each perhaps framed, as the Prato pulpit reliefs are framed, with double pilasters at the sides. But in a second stage this was revised, first in favour of a continuous frieze (and here Donatello's model, as Janson has shown, was almost certainly a Byzantine ivory carving of the type of the Veroli Casket in London), and second in favour of extremely deep relief with colonnettes marking the front plane. The new scheme placed a premium on movement and tactility, which in turn exercised a reflex action on the later reliefs, the *Drummers* and the *Cymbal Players*, of Luca della Robbia.

Granted that all this is so, why then is the figure style of the two organ lofts so very different? Because the creative psychology and aesthetic intentions of the two artists were different, and because these were reflected in their method and technique. In the fourteen-thirties there were two ways in which figure reliefs could be produced. The first is described by Filelfo in 1429. 'For the masters,' he writes, 'when they have resolved to fashion some rare masterpieces out of raw wood or stone, have been used to entrust the first tasks, of beginning and rough-hewing the work, to some apprentices (not quite unskilled, but still not deeply versed in it), they themselves either just adding the finishing touch or improving such parts as are more conspicuous or more difficult.' The Prato pulpit of Donatello was carved in that fashion. Models, that is, were made by Donatello and the marble reliefs based on them were executed, with varying degrees of intervention by the master, in Donatello's

shop. The Cantoria was turned out in that way as well. That is why attempts to ascribe the individual panels of the Prato pulpit and individual sections of the Cantoria to Michelozzo and Buggiano and other artists are fallacious; there is none of them which did not proceed from Donatello's mind and in which he did not, in some way, albeit in some small way, intervene. The reliefs of Luca della Robbia's Cantoria, on the other hand, are stylistically consistent and are likely to be almost wholly autograph. Clay models for them must naturally have been prepared, but they were translated into marble slowly, and the hand that carved them was in the main that of one sculptor. In expressive terms the result was a different kind of sculpture. No one can guess whether the God-intoxicated putti who bump into one another on Donatello's Cantoria are enjoying the experience or no. The children on Luca della Robbia's Cantoria, on the other hand, are humanly persuasive images which offer a mimetic record of the world the sculptor saw. The notion of mimetic sculpture was by no means new. In the thirteen-eighties a group of marble sculptors, headed by Giovanni d'Ambrogio, had carved for the front of the Cathedral a number of statuettes of music-making angels, and these self-absorbed, contented figures seem to have provided a taking-off point for the Cantoria project. They were followed by a work of great significance, Nanni di Banco's relief over the Porta della Mandorla, where instrumental playing is depicted with remarkable resource. It was from the first fundamental to the programme of the Cantoria that current choral practice and contemporary instruments should be portrayed. Important as were classical models for its style, there was therefore a second term to the equation, that the figures in the ten carvings must appear to listen, appear to dance, appear to sing, and that the sculptor, by his own terms of reference, must study singing, dancing, playing figures and record precisely how they looked. The two objectives were not easy to reconcile. On the right of the *Tambourine Players* (Plate 17) we see a figure whose features are contorted in a bogus classical smile—it reads as though the sculptor were no more than a superior Buggiano—while a boy opposite with furrowed forehead, trying to keep time, is a masterpiece of naturalism. Much the same contrast is found in the *Trumpeters* (Plate 2), where, amid the resolute classicism of the main figures, we encounter on the right a little girl with a head that reads like a Pigalle.

This is the quality that differentiates the Cantoria carvings from the closely contemporary reliefs made by Michelozzo for the Aragazzi monument. Michelozzo was a great and an experienced sculptor, but his strength lay in the dynamic of free-standing statuary, not in relief. His two carvings would indeed be almost wholly inexpressive if we were not intellectually aware of the emotions they are intended to depict. In the scene of *Aragazzi taking leave of his Family* reason tells us that the faces of the main figures must be meant to register regret, and that the children in the foreground are intended to appear disconsolate, while in the scene of *Aragazzi before the Virgin and Child* we realise that the welcome extended to the dead man must convey a message of tranquillity and peace, though the message is communicated neither by the grimacing children nor by the impassive features of the protagonists. How vivid and how comprehensible by contrast are Luca della Robbia's reliefs.

The only way in which the ten figure reliefs could have been arrived at is by the making of life studies, presumably in clay, which were then synthesised in models for the individual scenes. For at least a decade before his emergence as a master of enamelled terracotta, therefore, Luca must have practised as a modeller, and from the start he was confronted with the task of preserving the quality and lifelikeness of the clay model in a carved relief. The representational gain throughout the sequence of reliefs is very marked. To take two examples only, the third head to the right of centre in the *Players on the Cithara* (Plate 7) is flat and unaccomplished, whereas the comparable head in the later *Players on the Organ* (Plate 16) takes on an almost sensual expressiveness. Similarly if we compare the parted lips of the *Boys singing from a Book* (Plate 22) with those of the *Choral Dancers* (Plate 14), we shall find a marked advance in the later of the two reliefs. These experiments were central to Luca della Robbia's artistic personality, and long after the Cantoria was complete, when Brunelleschi was dead, and Luca had himself escaped from the rigid discipline of the Cathedral, they triumphed in a series of modelled reliefs in enamelled terracotta of incomparable subtlety and truthfulness.

On the Cantoria, however, the individual heads were not thought of in isolation, since it was central to its conception that each scene should depict a moment of action in which the figures were emotionally linked. As the modelled sculptures of Ghiberti constantly remind us, there were lessons to be learned here from the antique. Thus the Woburn Abbey and Vienna Muse sarcophagi (Figs. 4, 5) must have been the source not only of poses and motifs, but of the gentle, unemphatic converse that is put, in the *Players on the Cithara* and *Players on the Psaltery* (Plates 5, 7), to such poetic use. In the last relief, the *Choral Dancers* (Plate 14), which was carved from Luca's model, the linking of the figures is so free and so accomplished as demonstrably to surpass its antique source. In the fourteen-thirties one painter and one only, Fra Filippo Lippi, concerned himself with this mimetic problem, and if we look first at the lunette in Milan, in which, in the very early fourteen-thirties, he

broached the task—how awkward as representation the six angels are—and then at the Sant'Ambrogio *Coronation* of 1441, where the seductive heads of the angelic choir are posed with greater variety and artifice, we cannot but suspect that Lippi's sights were set on Luca della Robbia's reliefs.

There are later works in marble which provide at least a general indication of the working procedure in Luca's studio. In 1439 he was commissioned to execute two marble reliefs with *Scenes from the Life of St. Peter* (Cat. No. 3, Plates 34–36) for an altar in the Cathedral. The reliefs survive, in the Bargello, and are both unfinished, though in one of them the degree of finish is rather greater than in the other. At about the same time he undertook five reliefs for the Campanile (Cat. No. 2, Plates 29–33), and there is some reason to suppose that these were carved concurrently and were finished off together before delivery. In these circumstances it would be unrealistic to suppose that the later Cantoria carvings were completed one by one, and some features of them suggest that this cannot have been the case. In the *Players on the Organ, Lute and Harp* (Plate 16) we find on the extreme left a boy with strongly modelled torso and accurately rendered legs. On the right of the *Tambourine Players* (Plate 17) is a related figure holding a tambourine whose body and legs are far from perfectly articulated. Faced with differences like these, it is tempting to ascribe the figures to two different hands, but the truth may be that both were carved by Luca, the first having been brought to its intended state and the second being left unfinished and then smoothed down before the Cantoria was installed. It may be to this process that a document of April 1437 refers; it enjoins that the Capomaestro of the Cathedral 'poliri faciat omnes figuras que sunt miste cum marmore opere in laborerio decte opere in terra per Lucam Simonis della Robbia'.

Of the respect with which Luca della Robbia was regarded while working on the Cantoria there can be no doubt. In 1434, when no more than the first four figure reliefs were complete, we find him competing with Donatello for a model for a colossal head for the summit of the cupola of the Cathedral, and in 1436, in the preface to the Italian edition of the *Della Pittura*, he is mentioned along with Donatello and with two other older artists. Alberti's reference would be intelligible only if he were personally cognisant of Luca della Robbia's aspirations and capacity. Whether or not Luca and Alberti met in Rome when the Cantoria was in gestation, they must certainly have known each other after 1434, when Alberti arrived in Florence. Just as Alberti, in Florence, left his stamp on the perspective structure and on the figure compositions of the Gate of Paradise, so too he seems to have exercised an influence on the Cantoria. The passages in the *Della Pittura* that are relevant to the

Cantoria occur, as we might expect, in the second book. 'The painter,' says Alberti (and for 'painter' we may here read 'artist') 'must know all about the movements of the body, which I believe he must take from Nature with great skill. It is extremely difficult to vary the movements of the body in accordance with the almost infinite movements of the heart. Who, unless he had tried, would believe it was such a difficult thing, when you want to represent laughing faces, to avoid their appearing tearful rather than happy, and who without the greatest labour, study and care, could represent faces in which the mouth and chin and eyes and cheeks and forehead and eyebrows all accord together in grief or hilarity? All these things, then, must be sought with the greatest diligence from Nature.' Alberti goes on: 'I have observed how in every attitude a man positions his whole body beneath his head, which is the heaviest member of all. And if he rests his entire weight on one foot, this foot is always perpendicularly beneath his head like the base of a column, and the face of a person standing is usually turned in the direction in which his foot is pointing . . . I have also seen that if we stretch our hand upwards as far as possible, all the other parts of that side follow that movement right down to the foot, so that with the movement of that arm even the heel of the foot is lifted from the ground.' If we look at any of the later Cantoria panels (for example the *Cymbal Players*, Plate 20), we shall find there precisely the peculiarities of stance Alberti describes. In the penultimate paragraph of the *Della Pittura*, Alberti presses the case for consultation while artists are at work. 'Friends,' he says, 'should be consulted, and while work is in progress, any chance spectators should be welcomed and their opinion heard.' While the carving of the Cantoria panels was in progress in the Opera del Duomo, this particular friend must indeed have been consulted, and must have given Luca sound, indeed infallible, advice.

When Alberti, more than a decade later, was called upon to plan the interior decoration of the Tempio Malatestiano at Rimini, the model he recalled was Luca's Cantoria. At Rimini the piers are decorated with isolated carvings in middle and low relief integrated in the architecture. They derive their unity, however, not from the unflagging concentration of a single sculptor, but from the Neo-Attic relief style within whose framework the sculptors employed there were constrained to operate. The connection with the Cantoria was indeed apparent to Vasari, though the deduction he drew from it was false, that the earliest of the chapels at Rimini was carved by Luca when he was fifteen, before he began work on the Cantoria.

Writing in 1436, Leonardo Bruni describes two types of poet, represented by St. Francis and by Dante. 'To explain my meaning better to the reader,' he writes, 'I shall say that one becomes a poet in two different ways. One way is through sheer genius, whipped up by some hidden internal power which is called fury and mental obsessiveness . . . The other way is through science, and study, and discipline, and skill, and judgement.' Though it originates in literature, this passage is applicable also to the visual arts, and specifically to the two Organ Lofts. A condescending echo of it appears in Vasari's life of Luca della Robbia. 'It often happens,' says Vasari, 'that rough sketches which are born in an instant in the heat of inspiration, express the idea of their author in a few strokes, while on the other hand too much effort and diligence sometimes sap the vitality and powers of those who never know when to leave off. Anyone who realises that all the arts of design, and not painting alone, are allied to poetry, also knows that as poems composed in a poetic fervour are the true and genuine, and far better than those produced with effort, so the works of men who excel in the arts of design are better when they are the result of a single impulse of the force of that fervour than if they are produced little by little with toil and labour.' 'The vulgar,' he goes on, 'prefer a certain external and apparent delicacy, where the lack of what is essential is concealed by the care bestowed, to a good work produced with reason and judgement but not so smooth or so highly finished.' This post-Michelangelesque view of Luca's Cantoria is, by and large, the view that still persists today.

But it was not the view taken in the fifteenth century. The style of the Prato pulpit and the Cantoria was personal to Donatello; it sprang from an interior vision that other artists did not share and was propagated by a technique they did not understand. When, five years after the Cantoria was complete, Donatello moved his studio to Padua, the brief chapter in the history of sculpture in relief represented by his two commissions was at an end. Not so the style evolved by Luca della Robbia on the other Organ Loft. He himself, with the encouragement it seems of Brunelleschi, abandoned marble sculpture, and concentrated, at first largely and then exclusively, on sculpture in enamelled terracotta. But the aspirations established on the Cantoria were shared by sculptors for more than half a century, and when one stands before the tender, classicising putti on Antonio Rossellino's Monument of the Cardinal of Portugal, or looks at the closely observed yet highly artificial Child in the *Altman Madonna* by Antonio Rossellino in New York, or at the putti on Desiderio da Settignano's Marsuppini Monument, it must be remembered that the seed-bed in which their aesthetic grew was the Cantoria of Luca della Robbia. Precisely how its influence was transmitted we can only guess. Antonio Rossellino was eleven when it was set in place, and Desiderio was eight or nine. Bernardo Rossellino was active as an independent artist from 1433 but can have had no part in it. The only major sculptor of the middle of the century who might hypothetically have worked at some time in the fourteen-thirties in Luca's shop is Agostino di Duccio, but his having done so is highly questionable. The right side of the *Players on the Tambourine* is the single section in whose carving he could conceivably have had a share. What was involved may have been precept and not training, for when Donatello left Florence in 1443, the most experienced marble sculptor remaining in the city was Luca della Robbia. How natural that he, together with Ghiberti, whose attitude to the antique he shared, should dominate the thinking of the younger sculptors who, by the middle of the century, were filling the churches of the city with their work. When Alberti prepared his *De Statua* in Rome in the fourteen-forties, the battle had been won.

His concern is not with the objective at which sculptors ought to aim, but with the means by which the objective is best reached, for all sculptors, says Alberti, modellers and carvers and silversmiths alike, aspire to the same goal, 'namely that as nearly as possible the works that they have undertaken shall appear to the observer to be extremely like real natural bodies.' This sentence brings us up against the central mystery of Luca della Robbia's Cantoria and of the sculptures which depend from it, the imaginative alchemy whereby the *disjecta membra* of what we now look on as archaeology, the casual residue of an art that had dealt in the main in generalities, became a receptacle for private emotions and individual sensibility, and were transformed into particularised images which for five hundred years have continued to exercise their spell and with which even today uninhibited communication is still possible.

III OTHER MARBLE SCULPTURES FOR THE CATHEDRAL AND THE CAMPANILE

Payments for Luca della Robbia's Cantoria continue through the summer of 1438, but in the spring of the preceding year his creative thought was redirected to a commission of a very different kind, the carving of reliefs (Cat. No. 2, Plates 29–33) for the Campanile outside the Cathedral. The lowest register of the Campanile (Fig. 17) was decorated with twenty-one hexagonal reliefs, which had been carved in the first half of the fourteenth century by and in the workshop of Andrea Pisano, and in the fifteenth century were commonly ascribed to Giotto, the father of Florentine painting. The reliefs were disposed in groups of seven on the west, south and east faces of the building. When, in the third quarter of the fourteenth century, the doorway which gave access to the Campanile from the street on the east side was reconstructed, two of the seven reliefs on the east face were displaced and were reinstalled on the north face of the building. The upper register on the north side was already decorated with reliefs, and in the fourteen-thirties it was deemed desirable, in the interests of order and intellectual symmetry, that the lower register of the north face be brought into conformity with that of the three other faces by the addition of five further reliefs. On 30 May 1437 the carving of the supplementary reliefs was entrusted to Luca della Robbia.

The twenty-one existing reliefs illustrated the Creation of Man and the mechanical and some liberal arts, and their programme was drawn in the main from Genesis, Isidore of Seville and Brunetto Latini. If new reliefs were to be added, the first prerequisite was that they should appear to be a logical continuation of this sequence. The two fourteenth-century reliefs on the north face portrayed *Phidias*, or *Sculpture*, and *Apelles*, or *Painting*, and the subjects selected for the new reliefs were Astrology, Arithmetic, Poetry or Rhetoric, Philosophy, and Grammar. They represent an interest in systematised thought that was peculiar to the fifteenth century, and it may be inferred from the range of sources and ideas reflected in their iconography that they were carved to a humanist programme influenced, perhaps devised, by Leonardo Bruni.

The marble for the carvings was supplied by the Opera del Duomo, and for each of them Luca della Robbia received a fee of twenty florins. Payment was made in two instalments, on 2 December 1438, when he was paid a sum of thirty florins, and on 10 March 1439, when he received the balance of seventy florins. Probably all five reliefs were executed in the rough in the second half of 1437 and the first half of 1438, and were finished in part in the winter of 1438 and in part in the early spring of the following year. It was essential that not only the programme but the style of the new reliefs should harmonise with the earlier scenes. The five new hexagons were, however, carved from deeper slabs of marble than those used in the fourteenth century. In Andrea Pisano's carvings the frame establishes the front plane of the relief, whereas in Luca's the figures project beyond the moulding. In only one relief does the design extend, as it does in so many of the earlier scenes, to the base of the hexagonal field. In the four cases in which the sculptor has recourse to the expedient of a platform running across the scene, the exergue beneath is not excavated, as it was by Andrea Pisano, but is filled with shallow decorative carvings, in one case a fluted disc, in two more foliated designs, and in another a suspended garland.

Grammar, the first of the reliefs (Plate 29), shows a male figure, wearing a cloak and cap, seated at a reading desk and gesticulating with raised left hand to an open window in the centre of the rear wall. Opposite him, in profile to the left, are two youths seated on a bench, one writing and the other holding an open book. The figure on the left is identified by Vasari as the mid-fourth-century grammarian Aelius Donatus. If this interpretation is correct, the boy writing may illustrate the teaching of the *Ars minor* or *prima* designed for 'infantes, pueri et tirones,' and the older youth behind, who wears a robe or surplice, the teaching of the *Ars major* or *secunda*, 'de voce, de littera, de syllabe.' The writings of Donatus had been the subject of frequent comment since antiquity, and interest in the field they covered was heightened in the fourteen-twenties by Bruni's *De studiis et litteris* and by his translation of Plutarch's *De liberis educandis*. The motif of an open door occurs in Roman sarcophagus reliefs, and the window is here used symbolically to indicate that Grammar is a casement opening on enlightenment. The relief thus adds a poetic dimension to Bruni's writings, and is an allegory of the usefulness of knowledge and the means by which it can be inculcated. Owing to long exposure much of the naturalistic detail has been effaced, but traces of it can still be seen in the puzzled profile of the older youth and in the wrinkled stocking on the raised leg of the boy in front.

The second relief, *Philosophy* (Plate 30), shows a shallow platform with two confronting figures in classical dress, identified by Vasari as Plato and Aristotle. One expostulates with raised arms, and the other points with his index finger to the pages of a book. The formula whereby two confronting figures are shown in debate is employed by Donatello throughout the bronze doors in the Sagrestia Vecchia of San Lorenzo. From 1437 on, Donatello was under contract to provide bronze doors for the two sacristies of the Cathedral, and we must suppose either that the doors in the Old Sacristy were adapted from a rejected model for the Cathedral doors, or that Luca had access to a model for one of the two pairs of doors in the Old Sacristy, or that Luca's relief was designed by Donatello. Once more, Luca's relief has an oblique connection with the known interests of Bruni, who translated the *Nicomachean Ethics* of Aristotle and the *Gorgias* and other dialogues of Plato.

The third relief, *Poetry* or *Rhetoric* (Plate 31), like certain of the earlier carvings, is set in the open air and for that reason dispenses with an exergue, so that the composition extends to the bottom of the hexagonal field. Orpheus (whose head must derive from the antique) is shown in the centre, seated on the ground. Vasari, confronted with the figure of Orpheus playing the lute, described the subject of the scene as Music. Music is, however, personified by Jubal in the earlier reliefs. The meaning of the imagery here has been explained by a passage in Dante's *Convivio*, which describes how Orpheus with his cithara tamed beasts and trees and stones, 'which is to say that the wise man, with the instrument of his voice, can tame even cruel hearts, and move at his will those who are incapable of learning the disciplines of science and art; for those who are devoid of the rational life of science resemble stones.'

The fourth relief, *Arithmetic* (Plate 32), is occupied by two confronting bearded figures. One, on the left, is dressed in a long robe, which extends almost to his feet. Over his left shoulder he wears a scarf or cloak, and in his hands he holds a tablet or board. The other, on the right, has a shorter, more heavily embroidered dress and a full cloak, which falls over his left shoulder and down his back. Both wear turbans and are therefore orientals. The scene has been explained by reference to a passage in Calandri's *De Arithmetica Opusculum*, which describes two methods of computation in use in the late

fifteenth century. One was to record figures 'with their own characters, which are popularly called abacus figures,' while the other was to indicate them with the fingers of the hand. The latter is the task in which the figure on the right of the relief is apparently engaged. According to Calandri, the practice of numeracy was brought to Italy from India about the year 1200, while digital computation was of Latin origin. The figures in Luca's carving, however, both wear oriental dress, and the scene seems to represent not two antithetical methods of computation, but digital computation and the means by which a record of it was made.

The last relief (Plate 33) shows a bearded man in full face seated on a bench, wearing a hat and a long robe and cloak. He strikes an anvil, to his left, with hammers held in both hands. The subject is identified by Vasari as *Astrology*, and the figure as Ptolemy. The first part of Vasari's explanation is correct, but the figure is Pythagoras, who listens to the harmony of the sounds he has produced. The imagery is inspired by Boethius, and illustrates the belief that the intervals of the musical scale correspond with the distances between the planets and fixed stars. This grave and beautiful relief must have been inspired by Andrea Pisano's *Jubal* and *Tubalcain*.

Though Luca's reliefs bear a close resemblance to the earlier reliefs on the Campanile, they are constructed on different principles. In the relief of *Grammar* the left edge of the closed section of the window falls on a vertical line between the upper and lower corners of the hexagonal frame, while the lower of the two glazing bars lies on a horizontal line drawn from a median point on the two sides of the hexagon. The left hand of the lector, pointing to the open window, rests on a horizontal established by the upper glazing bar. Similarly in *Philosophy* the narrative focus of the scene is established by a book held by the figure on the left, whose pointing finger rests on a central vertical. The *Poetry* or *Rhetoric* also, to a greater extent than is apparent at first sight, observes the geometrical conventions of the two previous reliefs; a central vertical is established by the tree trunk at the back and a central horizontal by the lute of Orpheus, which extends across the composition. In the fifth relief the top edge of the anvil lies on a median line between the edges of the hexagon, and is reinforced by the forearm of the seated figure and by the upper surface of the bench. That these geometrical expedients were central to Luca's thinking in the late fourteen-thirties is evident from their recurrence in two reliefs for an altar in the Cathedral, on which he started work in April 1439.

In the spring of 1439 *provveditori* were appointed to oversee the construction of three altars in the central tribune. The first was in the chapel of St. Zenobius and the second and third were in the adjacent chapels of St.

Peter and St. Paul. From the documents it has been inferred that four altars were commissioned for the lateral chapels, two on 6 April from Donatello and two from Luca della Robbia. What was at issue, however, was not four altars but two, in each of which two artists were involved. Both commissions are qualified by phrases ('in certo modo e disegno' in the case of Donatello, 'secondo cierto disegnio' in that of Luca) which suggest that the form of the altars was predetermined, almost certainly by Brunelleschi. In the altar of St. Paul, Luca della Robbia was required to follow a wax model by Donatello, which rested on four columns and had in or on it ('parte intus') an oval field to be filled with a scene or scenes from the life of the Saint. The altar of St. Peter was to conform to a full-scale wooden model, measuring three and seven-eighths braccia in length, and was to contain on its front face two or more scenes from the life of the Saint. In both cases, if the documents are read at their face value, the reliefs were to be built into, not superimposed on, the altars. Probably the intended form was that established by Brunelleschi in the altar of the Sagrestia Vecchia of San Lorenzo (Fig. 16), where the front face incorporates two reliefs of Prophets flanking a central space, which was originally occupied by Brunelleschi's trial relief of the *Sacrifice of Isaac*. For reasons which can no longer be established, the project for the altars was abandoned, and all that survives of them today is two reliefs of the *Deliverance of St. Peter* and the *Crucifixion of St. Peter* by Luca della Robbia.

The *Deliverance of St. Peter* (Cat. No. 3, Plates 34, 36) is the more accomplished of the two reliefs. The principal unfinished areas are the upper surface of the rear wall, where the receding surface of the ceiling is no more than summarily indicated, and a strip left in the rough above, across the whole width of the scene, where the artist's intentions are unclear. The *Crucifixion of St. Peter* (Plate 35) was abandoned in a more rudimentary state, when the Saint's body and loin cloth, the lower part of the cross, and details such as the spear or banner carried by a bearded man in the background on the right, were still undefined.

The *Deliverance* is framed in half-columns, which recall those framing the reliefs made by Buggiano for the altar in the Sagrestia Vecchia. At the back through a window grille we see the profiles of St. Peter and the Angel, and to the left on a bench are two sleeping soldiers with a third soldier on the ground beside them. To the right St. Peter is led from prison by an Angel derived from a Victory figure on a late Roman coin. Both here and in the *Crucifixion of St. Peter* the imagery is strongly

classical, and the figures in the *Crucifixion* scene have much in common with those in the predella of Masaccio's Pisa polyptych. But the iconography of the two scenes belies the evidence of style, for they depend from two of the most celebrated Gothic cycles of scenes from the life of St. Peter available in Florence, a predella by Jacopo di Cione on the high altar of San Pier Maggiore (Fig. 14) and a predella by Giovanni dal Ponte in San Pier Scheraggio (Fig. 15). Whether it was stipulated that Luca should refer back to these predellas we do not know, but refer to them he did, in terms so explicit that his sources are in no doubt. From Giovanni dal Ponte's *Deliverance of St. Peter* he adopted the window, reversing the two figures, eliminating the wall surface on the left, concentrating the group of soldiers, and investing the robes and poses of St. Peter and the Angel in the foreground with a strongly classical stamp. In the *Crucifixion of St. Peter* the cross is set, as it is by Jacopo di Cione, flat across the foreground, but the two executioners hammering nails into the Saint's hands derive from the *Crucifixion* panel of Giovanni dal Ponte. Both reliefs are marked by the same insistence on geometry as in the Campanile carvings. In the *Deliverance of St. Peter* the vertical bar of the window falls in the exact centre of the relief, and the right foreleg of St. Peter rests on a diagonal drawn between the centre of the base and the upper right corner of the marble slab. The *Crucifixion* is dominated by the assertive vertical and horizontal of the cross, and would, had it been finished, have been elaborated with diagonal spears held by the soldiers on the right. The sloping foregrounds of the scenes are more pronounced than in the Campanile carvings, and are planned (as we should expect if the reliefs were to be incorporated in an altar) for inspection from above.

The commission for the altars in the Cathedral was followed in March 1440 by negotiations for a second abortive project (Cat. No. 4). Its scene was the Badia, not the Duomo, and what we know of it derives from a single payment to Luca della Robbia for a drawing and a terracotta model 'per fare la sepoltura d'Ughone.' Ughone was Count Hugo of Tuscany, the founder of the Badia, whose remains were preserved till 1439 in a porphyry sarcophagus in the Cappella Maggiore of the church, and were transferred, in 1440, to a newly constructed wooden sarcophagus, painted by a certain Piero di Lorenzo, in the Sacristy. The marble tomb designed by Luca seems to have formed part of a scheme for the replanning of the church by Brunelleschi, which was promoted by Cosimo de' Medici, but which attracted opposition from the monks and was abandoned on that account.

IX. *Interior of the Cupola of the Portico* (Cat. No. 9). Enamelled terracotta. Pazzi Chapel, Santa Croce, Florence

X. *January* (Cat. No. 12). Enamelled terracotta. Victoria & Albert Museum, London

XI. *May* (Cat. No. 12). Enamelled terracotta. Victoria & Albert Museum, London

XII. *November* (Cat. No. 12). Enamelled terracotta. Victoria & Albert Museum, London

XIII. *Detail from the Border of the Monument of Benozzo Federighi* (Cat. No. 13).
Enamelled terracotta. Santa Trinita, Florence

XIV. *Detail from the Border of the Monument of Benozzo Federighi* (Cat. No. 13).
Enamelled terracotta. Santa Trinita, Florence

XV. *Prudence*. Detail from the Ceiling of the Chapel of the Cardinal of Portugal (Cat. No. 14).
Enamelled terracotta. San Miniato al Monte, Florence

XVI. *Fortitude*. Detail from the Ceiling of the Chapel of the Cardinal of Portugal (Cat. No. 14). Enamelled terracotta. San Miniato al Monte, Florence

IV THE TRANSITION TO ENAMELLED TERRACOTTA

Until 1441, so far as major commissions were concerned, Luca della Robbia practised solely as a marble sculptor. In 1442, however, he contracted to undertake the first of two lunettes in enamelled terracotta above the doorway of the North Sacristy of the Cathedral, and thereafter, with the single exception of the Federighi Monument in 1454, he worked exclusively in the new medium. What were the reasons for the change? The first attempt to answer this question was made in 1550 by Vasari. Luca della Robbia, he explains, after completing the bronze door of the North Sacristy of the Cathedral, 'made an estimate of what he had gained upon it, and of the time he had expended in making it, and came to realise how slight had been his advantage and how great his labour. Accordingly he determined to abandon marble and bronze, and to see if he could derive greater advantage from other methods. It then occurred to him that clay can be manipulated with ease and little trouble, and that the only thing required was to discover a means whereby work produced in this material could be preserved for a long time. . . . By this method he won loud praise, and all succeeding ages are under an obligation to him.' From the time these words were written down to our own the legend has held currency that Luca's works in enamelled terracotta were an inexpensive substitute for sculpture in other media, and were glazed in order to protect them from decay. It is understandable that in the middle of the sixteenth century the technique should be explained along these lines, for by that time the entrances to countless churches throughout Tuscany were surmounted by lunettes in enamelled terracotta, the full freshness of whose colouring was perfectly preserved. This was, however, an *ex post facto* argument, and the little evidence we have for the introduction of enamelled terracotta shows quite conclusively that it is wrong.

The likely reasons for the change of medium can be established readily enough from the earliest documented works in which enamelled terracotta is employed. The first of them, a marble tabernacle at Peretola (Cat. No. 5, Col. Plate I, Plates 37–41), was commissioned for the church of Sant' Egidio in Florence in 1441. Payments for it run from 4 August 1441 till 1443, and we know from

the concluding payment that the sum received by Luca was one hundred and seven florins. This included the cost of marble made available by the Opera del Duomo, which amounted to just over forty lire, and a sum of thirty florins paid to an assistant, Agnolo di Cristofano, who may have worked on the architectural surround. There is no reference in documents to the use of enamelled terracotta in the tabernacle, and it may be best initially to study it as though its surface were monochrome. Its architecture has two precedents, the Parte Guelfa niche of 1422 on Or San Michele and the painted surround of Masaccio's *Trinity* in Santa Maria Novella of the mid-fourteen-twenties. The former provides analogies for the pediment, the frieze with garlands under it, and the central lunette, while the second offers parallels for the circular motif in the spandrels (treated in the fresco as a decorative architectural feature and in the tabernacle as a background for the crutch which formed the emblem of the Hospital of Santa Maria Nuova) and the platform at the base. The lateral pilasters are Brunelleschan; they recall the pilasters designed by Brunelleschi about 1440 for the interior of the Pazzi Chapel. The carved detail in the pediment and in the moulding beneath the frieze is developed from the decorative detail on the Cantoria.

In the second quarter of the fifteenth century close attention was given to the form and programme of Sacrament tabernacles. In November 1426 Fra Giuliano Benini determined to present a 'tabernacholo del Corpo di Christo' to the church of San Jacopo in Campo Corbellini. On the advice of Brunelleschi he bought a slab of marble from the Opera del Duomo and transported it to San Lorenzo, where, under Brunelleschi's direction and from his design, a tabernacle was carved from it by a stonemason whose services were made available by the Cathedral, Giusto di Francesco da Settignano. This lost work may have had some influence on Luca della Robbia's tabernacle. In 1436 a second important tabernacle was commissioned, from Bernardo Rossellino, for the Badia. Two small pieces of it survive, and from one of them, a console with an eagle, we can deduce that its imagery was bound up with a sentence in the Gospel of St. John: 'Et verbum caro factum est.' The most inventive of these tabernacles was carved by Donatello in Rome shortly before 1430 and is now in the Sagrestia dei Beneficiati of St. Peter's. It has a relief of the Entombment at the top, and though it exercised no influence in Florence, its programme, the mystery of the Redemption, anticipates that of the Sant' Egidio tabernacle of Luca della Robbia.

In the pediment of Luca's tabernacle is a half-length figure of God the Father in benediction, and in the lunette is the Dead Christ supported by an angel and accompanied by the Virgin and St. John. Christ's left hand rests on a moulding, which serves as the edge of the tomb, and his open right hand is directed to the ciborium beneath. Below, on a much larger scale, are two winged figures holding an olive wreath, which contains a gilt bronze roundel of the Holy Ghost plunging down towards the tabernacle door (Plate 37). The present door is of later date—it shows Christ as Man of Sorrows with a chalice at his side—and may have been substituted for an earlier grille. Behind the angels is a patterned curtain, designed in such a way as to transform the flat surface of the marble into a shallow niche. The imagery of the upper part depends from works by Masaccio and Masolino. One of these is the fresco of the *Trinity*, which seems to have influenced the type of the God the Father in the pediment, and which was certainly responsible for two figures in the lunette, the Virgin with head turned towards the spectator pointing to the Dead Christ and the profile figure of St. John with clasped hands on the right (Plates 40, 41). The other is Masolino's fresco of the *Pietà* at Empoli, from which the type of Luca's Christ derives. The two large Victory angels supporting a central wreath (Plates 38, 39), depend either from a gold medallion of Constantine the Great, in which the wreath is held in place by the raised arms of the two figures and is not supported from beneath, or from a solidus of Constans, where it is also supported with the forward arms. In both cases the two figures are represented in profile, but other coins of the first half of the fourth century show Roma and Constantinopolis holding up a wreath with heads turned in full face. These strongly classical figures and the relief of the *Pieta* in the lunette are some of the most moving and accomplished marble sculptures of the first half of the fifteenth century.

The effect made by the tabernacle is not, however, due to its figure carvings alone. The brocaded curtain behind the angels seems to have been pigmented, the haloes above were gilt, and the surface, save for the pediment and the pilasters, is enriched with enamelled terracotta. Enamelled terracotta is used throughout the tabernacle in three different ways. The first occurs in the lunette, where the marble slab from which the relief is carved has been cut back to permit the superimposition of irregular slabs of blue-glazed terracotta. The function these fulfil is closely analogous to that performed by the blue glass backgrounds of Orcagna on the Or San Michele tabernacle or of Arnoldi on the Campanile. The second is in the frieze, where three cherub heads and garlands with blue ribbons protrude from the surface of the marble. The garlands are composed of a variety of foliage, with flowers of morning glory and convolvulus, the cherub in the centre is coloured purple and the two outer heads are blue with strongly marked white eyes. In the spandrels the marble surface is relieved with glazed terracotta inlay of green fern leaves on a violet-purple ground, and similar glazed decoration appears on the base in the interstices of nine large circles framed with a white guilloche strip. Eight of the nine circles are filled with twelve-petalled blue flowers on a bisected blue ground, painted as though lit from above, and that in the centre shows a white quadrilobe with the emblem of the Hospital. The eight small circles which intervene contain blue discs.

By 1443 the use of enamelling (that is the application of a lead glaze made white and opaque by the addition of oxide of tin, or blue, turquoise and brown by the addition of other metallic oxides) was an established practice among ceramicists. A glaze with a tin component is already mentioned in the *Margherita Preciosa* of Piero dal Dono in 1330. Majolica vessels were made at Montelupo, and a number of makers of majolica were at work in Florence, in the district of Santo Spirito, in Santa Croce (where the principal potter was Piero di Mazeo), and at Ricorboli (where a majolica kiln was operated by three brothers, Maso, Miniato and Piero di Domenico). In 1431-2 a set of drug jars was commissioned for the Hospital of Santa Maria Nuova from Giunta di Tagio. At the end of the first quarter of the fifteenth century, moreover, there were produced in Florence what we now know as Oak-leaf Jars, in which the colour was stronger and more resonant than any that had been achieved before, and the glaze was no longer a simple colouristic agency, but took on a tactile character. But the design of those parts of the Santa Maria Nuova tabernacle which are flat, and might be expected to relate most closely to majolica, has no direct connection with surviving majolica jars or dishes or tiles, least of all with the highly conventional drug jars made by Giunta di Tagio for the hospital. The oak-leaves in the spandrels and the floreated roundels and green foliage in the base are on a level of delicacy and sophistication that far transcends the work of Florentine ceramicists. Hispano-Mauresque pottery was known in Italy, and Islamic pottery was known there too. In Emilia and Romagna, at Pomposa and Sant'Apollinare Nuovo at Ravenna, there were towers inlaid with Islamic bowls. Analogies for the leaf decoration on the tabernacle (which should be cited, though they are insufficiently exact to be insisted on) occur in tiles of the first quarter of the fifteenth century at Bursa, while the flowers in the frieze recall motifs on Iznik pottery. Once the decision had been taken to include enamelled terracotta panels in the tabernacle, the range of models to which reference could be made was very wide.

The reason why colour was invoked in the planning of the tabernacle was bound up with the function it fulfilled. It is described in the records of interim payments as 'il tabernacholo dove sta el Chorpo di Christo nella chappella di Santo Lucha.' The chapel of St. Luke was the Cappella Maggiore of the hospital church of Sant' Egidio, and was so called because the Compagnia di San Luca had its headquarters in the hospital. The tabernacle was one element in a scheme for the redecoration of the choir of Sant'Egidio, which opened with a commission to Domenico Veneziano for a famous cycle of *Scenes from the Life of the Virgin*. These frescoes, on which Domenico Veneziano worked from 1439 till 1455, assisted in September 1439 by Piero della Francesca, were whitewashed in the course of renovation of the Cappella Maggiore in 1594. The scanty fragments of them which have been recovered show framing in the form of ribs of foliage with a pierced circular design, and it is this supporting decoration with which the tabernacle in the choir was from the first associated. Whether the tabernacle was installed on the right or the left wall, it would from the first have been seen in conjunction with Domenico Veneziano's frescoes, and it is the frescoes that account for its vivid polychromy.

The fact that the tabernacle is the first documented work by Luca in which use is made of enamelled terracotta does not imply that it was the first work he executed in this medium. The skill evinced in the enamelling is indeed a strong argument to the contrary, and we have therefore to ask ourselves when and why he started to produce enamelled terracotta sculptures. The first part of this question can be answered with some confidence. While working on the Cantoria, about 1434, he made two terracotta reliefs of a half-length *Virgin and Child*, one of which bears traces of defective enamelling covered by normal pigmentation, while the other is enamelled more proficiently in white and blue (Cat. Nos. 26, 27. Plates 91b, 93). A little later, between 1435 and 1440, he produced two more reliefs in enamelled terracotta. These are versions of a single composition, the so-called *Friedrichstein Madonna*, formerly in Berlin and in the Albright-Knox Art Gallery at Buffalo (Cat. No. 28, Col. Plate XXV). In both of them the glazing is defective and was subject to scaling and firing cracks. We must, then, suppose that in the fourteen-thirties Luca conducted a number of experiments in works on a small scale which resulted, about 1440, in a

technique that was of proved dependability. A recent writer has protested that 'Vasari was wrong in giving (Luca della Robbia) credit for the invention of the technique of glazed terracotta.' The fact is, however, that Vasari, in presenting enamelled terracotta sculpture as an invention, spoke the simple truth. From time immemorial glaze had been applied to flat or to unincidented surfaces, but there was no post-classical precedent for the glazing of terracotta sculpture, and when it was perfected to the state in which we find it in the cherub heads and garlands at Peretola, the technique was an invention of the first consequence. It was accepted in the fifteenth century as a major technical advance, and for three quarters of a century the formulae that made it possible remained the exclusive property of the Della Robbia shop.

It may be well at this point briefly to describe what the technique involved. A very large number of terracotta sculptures were produced in Florence in the third and fourth decades of the fifteenth century, and their surface was commonly covered with priming and colour. This was the practice in the itinerant shop of Michele da Firenze, and it was adopted in 1420-4 for an important group of sculptures commissioned for Sant'Egidio. They comprised twelve statues of Apostles made for the interior of the church, which have disappeared, and a relief of the *Coronation of the Virgin* over the entrance, which is still preserved. Like the lost Apostles, it was modelled by a sculptor, possibly Dello Delli, and was coloured by a painter, Bicci di Lorenzo, who first covered its surface with priming (which was at one time mistaken for white slip) and then added colour and gilding. The substitution of enamelling for pigmentation was not a simple change; it meant that an elementary technique open to any journeyman sculptor or painter was replaced by a procedure that was immeasurably more complex and more specialised. The first stage was the modelling of the clay relief, which received its first firing *a bistugio*. If it were of substantial size, it was, before firing, cut into sections, but wherever possible the figure, to preserve its continuity of modelling, was fired as a whole. The hazard of irregular shrinkage was considerable, and measures were taken to ensure that the firing was uniform. The relief was then reassembled and covered with *marzacotto* (a transparent fusible glass frit) which, when absorbed, left on the terracotta a powdery surface of unfired glaze. The composition of the *marzacotto* used by Luca della Robbia differed materially from that employed in the making of majolica. At a much later date lead was added to standard *marzacotto* by ceramicists to make the resulting surface whiter, and this may from the first have been the practice in the Della Robbia shop. Colour was then superimposed on the *marzacotto* and the sections were fired again, probably at a lower temperature than before. In this second firing the pigment and glaze amalgamated. With majolica the pigment was sometimes covered with a transparent overglaze or *coperta* before the second firing, and this procedure seems also to have been followed in Luca's reliefs. The result was an enamelled surface which was not only of great brilliance but was hard and durable.

The earliest account of the technique employed in the Della Robbia shop is supplied by Vasari. In the first edition of his life of Luca della Robbia he was content to observe that 'ancora che gli invetriati delle figure di terra cotta non siano in grandissima stima, sono molto utili et perpetui et necessarii.' In his second edition of 1568, however, he describes in some detail how Luca 'dopo avere molte cose esperimentato, trovò che il dar loro una coperta d'invetriato addosso, fatto con stagno, terraghetta, antimonio ed altri minerali, e misture cotte al fuoco d'una fornace apposta, faceva benissimo quest' affetto, e faceva le opere di terra quasi eterne.' This simple and generally accurate account has given rise to a number of misconceptions. Thus we read, in a standard ceramic dictionary by a scholar of some authority, 'the claim formerly made (originally by Vasari) that Luca invented, or was the first to practice in Italy, the process of making an opaque tin glaze is now known to be untenable.' Vasari makes no such claim; he asserts not that Luca della Robbia was the inventor of tin-glazing, but that he was the first artist to develop a technique whereby tin-glazing could be applied successfully to sculpture. In at least one other Florentine workshop (as we know from a Ghibertesque cassone front in the Victoria & Albert Museum and from a handful of other works) experiments were conducted in the fourteen-thirties with the application of a transparent tin glaze to terracotta reliefs, with a view to gilding, not to polychromy.

For obvious reasons it is impossible to subject to technical examination those works by Luca della Robbia which are still *in situ*. One large figure relief, however, at Urbino, is now shown in conditions in which its structure can be studied. It depicts the Virgin and Child flanked by four Saints (Cat. No. 30, Plate 95, Figs. 23, 24). In it the central group was glazed and fired in three sections, and the two pairs of lateral Saints were each glazed and fired in four parts. The blue background is composed of irregular sections of enamelled terracotta with a depth of 3.3 cm. From the standpoint of pigmentation one of the most elaborate of Luca's works is the *Stemma of King René of Anjou* in London (Cat. No. 21, Col. Plate XXIII, Plate 87). In specimens of coloured glaze from this work submitted to the Research Laboratory of the British Museum, the glaze layer was generally 0.1–0.2 mm. thick. Examined by means of X-ray diffraction and qualitative emission spectrography, the blue glaze proved to be cobalt in solution with a tin oxide

opacifier. The colour and opacity of the white surface were induced by particles of tin oxide. The yellow derived its colour and opacity from the presence of lead antimonate. In a dark-green specimen lead antimonate was also present, and the colour resulted from the simultaneous presence of copper in solution in a lead glaze, while a light-green specimen resulted from a mixture of this and of the yellow glaze. With a purple specimen the colour was due to manganese in solution in the glaze, which again derived its opacity from tin oxide. Since no red glaze could be produced, manganese purple was commonly substituted. It has sometimes been suggested that the colour range of Della Robbia glazes was much extended in Luca's later works. In practice, however, Luca's first documented work in enamelled terracotta, the Peretola tabernacle, makes use of a greater range of colouring agencies than any of his later works, and the subsequent contraction of his palette must therefore have been due not to limitations of technique, but to aesthetic choice.

When we ask ourselves why Luca della Robbia developed the technique of enamelling, one explanation can be ruled out at once. This is the reason given by Vasari, that enamelled terracotta was designed for sculpture in the open air, and that the prime function of enamelling was preservative. The view is inadmissible since Luca's earliest documented sculptures in enamelled terracotta were, without exception, commissioned for interiors. The first document relating to a work wholly executed in enamelled terracotta dates from 21 July 1442. Signed by Brunelleschi, it is the commission for a lunette of the *Resurrection* (Cat. No. 6, Col. Plate II, Plates 42, 43) to be set over the door of the North Sacristy of the Cathedral. Much trouble was taken to ensure that the appearance presented by the entrances to the two sacristies was uniform (each was surmounted with an Organ Loft, and in 1442 it was still intended that each should be provided with bronze doors by Donatello), and we must therefore assume that what was envisaged at this time was not one lunette but two, though the second relief, of the *Ascension* (Cat. No. 7, Col. Plate III, Plates 44, 45) over the door of the South Sacristy, was not in fact contracted for till 1446. The view that these lunettes were inexpensive substitutes for reliefs in marble cannot be entertained for the cogent reason that in these positions marble reliefs would have been imperfectly visible and would therefore have been inapposite. When the lunettes were commissioned, the decisive factor must have been qualities that made them superior for their purpose to works in other media, namely their colour and their legibility. The space beneath the cupola was cold and featureless, and thought was given at this time to supplying it with points of colouristic emphasis. The outcome was the commission to Donatello in 1437 for the stained-glass window of the *Coronation of the Virgin* on the east face of the drum under the cupola, and to Ghiberti, Castagno and Uccello in the mid-fourteen-forties for other stained-glass windows. That this was indeed the motivation behind enamelled terracotta sculpture is confirmed by the fact that in 1442, when work began in earnest on Brunelleschi's Pazzi Chapel in the cloister of Santa Croce, the articulation of the wall spaces provided for twelve circular stone frames which can only have been intended to receive the works that were actually installed in them, roundels of the *Apostles* in enamelled terracotta. We are bound therefore to infer that the use of enamelled terracotta was promoted by Brunelleschi as a means of enriching the buildings of which he was in charge.

By temperament Brunelleschi was an empiricist. In Rome as a young man he engaged in archaeological study of classical building techniques. Manetti describes how 'he made clocks and alarm bells with sundry types of springs geared by many diverse contrivances.' He received *ex gratia* payments for machinery which he invented in connection with work on the cupola. He devised the highly ingenious technical basis of the annual Annunciation play at San Felice. He was a well-known military engineer, and in 1421 he patented a cargo boat. In all these circumstances we may presume that it was he who first envisaged a type of terracotta sculpture in which the colour was more resonant and more emphatic than in conventional pigmented terracottas and which was more durable in that the surface was not subject to fading or organic change and adhered firmly to its ground.

The terms of the contract for the *Resurrection* lunette (Cat. No. 6) were agreed at a meeting attended by Brunelleschi, Ridolfo Lotti, Buggiano, Simone di Lorenzo and others, and bound Luca to complete, within a year, a relief 'in terra cotta invetriata prout videntur alia laboreria fieri et secundum designum factum et melius si melius fieri potest.' The fee was to be determined by nominees of the Consuls and Operaii when the relief was complete. As with the Cantoria, so here it is likely that the scheme had been discussed in detail over a long period. The phrase 'prout videntur alia laboreria fieri' seems to refer to an antecedent work in enamelled terracotta which had been submitted to the Operaii, along with a cartoon of the lunette. By the standard of fifteenth-century relief sculpture in Florence the *Resurrection* is exceptionally large; it measures two metres in height and is 2.65 metres wide. The only directly comparable relief was in marble, the *Assumption of the Virgin* by Nanni di Banco over the Porta della Mandorla, and in 1443 the minds of the Operaii would have been filled with memories of the travail through which it had been produced; it was commissioned in

1414 and only in 1422 was it set in place. By contrast the commission for the *Resurrection* bound Luca della Robbia to complete it within one year, and though in practice this schedule was not adhered to, it was completely finished in a period of two years and seven months. For the administrators of the Cathedral the speed with which results could be anticipated must have been one of the prime attractions of the new technique. An interim payment of 18 January 1445 shows that by that time part of the relief had been installed in its intended place over the Sacristy door. The final sum credited to Luca on 26 February 1445 was 440 lire, of which 140 was paid 'pro sua industria et inventione ad inveniendum dictum laborerium' and the balance of 300 lire was due 'pro suo magisterio dicti laborerii.' A further sum of 100 lire had already been paid in respect of the lunette.

The technical mastery evinced by the relief is indeed remarkable (Col. Plate II, Plates 42, 43). The sections of the composition are so planned as to preserve the continuity and where possible the integrity of the individual figures. The figure of the Risen Christ is modelled and glazed in two pieces with a join across the waist, and the sleeping soldier in the right foreground is modelled and glazed in one save for the left foot. The soldier on the left is treated in the same way save that the extended leg is modelled in one with the body of the soldier in the centre, whose legs are in turn modelled in one with the front face of the tomb. The figures, the tomb, trees and ground are glazed in white, and the background is blue. A single deviation is the cloud beneath Christ's feet and the small clouds accompanying the angels, which are a paler blue than the flat ground. The colouristic effect was originally enhanced by surface gilding, of which traces can be seen in the cruciform halo of Christ, in the wound on His right hand, in the rays which emanate from His body (better preserved on the left than on the right), in the hair and wings of the angels, and locally in the armour of the soldiers.

The drawing of the lunette which was prepared before the signing of the contract must have been the subject of close thought. The design is rigorously classical. The scene is constructed round the vertical axis of Christ, in the exact centre of the lunette, and the horizontal of the tomb, whose ends are hidden and which appears therefore to extend across the whole width of the scene. The winding cloth of Christ is represented as a form of *toga*, and the armour of the soldiers is reconstructed with great care. The features of the soldier on the right seem to derive from a classical bronze head like that which Donatello incorporated in the second Cantoria. A sleeping soldier, silhouetted against the tomb, with left arm and leg raised so that they form two triangles, derives from an Endymion sarcophagus from St. John Lateran now in the Palazzo Rospigliosi, while the tree on the left and the plant beside the right foot of Christ recall the detail of the Hadrianic roundels on the arch of Constantine. To this extent the thinking in the *Resurrection* is an extension of the thinking that produced the Cantoria.

What is involved, however, in the *Resurrection* is not simply the assimilation of classical motifs; it is rather the rethinking of one of the key scenes of Christian iconography in terms derived from the antique. The relief is the first and in some respects the most profound Early Renaissance interpretation of the theme. Seen today across the choir over the Sacristy door of the Cathedral, the impression that it makes is overpowering, and it must have been still stronger in the fifteenth century. Its influence was very great. Castagno returned from Venice to Florence in the year in which it was installed, and when, at some point in the following half decade, he painted his fresco of the *Resurrection* at Sant'Apollonia, Luca's relief was evidently in the forefront of his mind. Piero della Francesca, in the *Resurrection* at Borgo San Sepolcro of about 1460, likewise acknowledges a debt to the relief, and so does Verrocchio in his painted terracotta *Resurrection* for Careggi. The importance of the relief as a paradigm of style, moreover, transcends analogies like these. What Luca formulated in it were principles of classicism which were of cardinal significance for later artists.

The lunette of the *Resurrection* has been compared with the panel of the *Resurrection* on Ghiberti's first bronze door, but the two schemes are totally distinct. In the companion lunette, the *Ascension* (Cat. No. 7, Col. Plate III, Plates 44, 45) over the door of the South Sacristy, on the other hand, the influence of the late style of Ghiberti is manifest. It is apparent in the looser organisation of the design and in the rhythmical figure of the ascending Christ. The decision to commission two lunettes, not one, must have been taken before the initial contract was drawn up, but the commission for the second lunette did not follow immediately on the first. It was contracted for after an interval in October 1446, and was completed in June 1451. In April 1446 Brunelleschi died, and this may be reflected in the decision, recorded in the contract, to substitute limited polychromy for the bichromatic palette of the earlier scene. The contract on this occasion refers to a small model, not to a preliminary cartoon, and stipulates that local colour should be employed. The hill was to be 'sui coloris' (that is a purplish brown) and the trees were to be 'sui coloris' (that is green with greenish brown stems). The naturalistic ground protrudes irregularly over the lintel of the door. The method of manufacture corresponds with that of the earlier lunette, but the glaze is drier and less resonant and the surface reveals a quantity of shallow firing cracks, which may result either from the use of a more varied palette or from a reduction in the thickness of the relief. The figure of Christ seems to have been modelled and fired in a single piece. In the *Resurrection* the eyes of Christ are dark, and the eyebrows and eyelashes are not indicated, whereas in the *Ascension* the eyebrows and eyelashes of Christ are stippled blue, and the upper and sometimes the lower eyelashes of the Apostles are reinforced. The gilt rays surrounding Christ are better preserved than in the earlier scene. The relief makes a less strongly classical effect by virtue both of its polychromy and its pictorial design. It is planned in greater notional depth, as a kind of stage backed by a diorama of pale-blue sky, and the figures of the Virgin and Apostles are grouped in semi-circles at the sides. The Christ, a little to the left of centre, again establishes a controlling vertical, and in the absence of the tomb the corresponding horizontal is achieved by aligning the left legs of the kneeling figures along the base of the relief. The pose of Christ and the treatment of the body beneath the linear drapery may derive from a headless female figure of the type of the Hellenistic *Aphrodite* in Mantua, but the features are softer and less classical. Impressive as it is, the scene is a less imposing image than the *Resurrection* and its influence was less great. Perhaps the use of colour was introduced at the insistence of the Opera of the Cathedral, or that of Ghiberti, who was working on the stained-glass windows of the church throughout these years. Luca della Robbia seems to have concluded that the innovation was unjustified, and he had no further recourse to descriptive local colouring till late in his career, when his nephew Andrea was an active partner in his shop.

One of the contributory factors in the five-year delay before the execution of the *Ascension* may have been a further commission Luca received from the Opera of the Cathedral, which appears to have enjoyed priority over the lunette. When St. Antoninus took over the Archbishopric of Florence in 1446, one of his prime concerns was with the housing of the Host. No doubt on his initiative it was decided that the Chapel of the Sacrament, which hitherto had been established in the Chapel of St. Anthony the Abbot in the south tribune, should be moved to the central chapel in the north tribune, that of St. Stephen. This was a comparatively simple operation; it involved no more than the transfer of a marble tabernacle executed by Buggiano in 1443 from the south to the north side of the church. But matters did not rest there, for in December 1446 a new altar was ordered for the chapel, probably from Michelozzo, and in February 1447 Michelozzo was commissioned to equip the altar with a bronze grille. The new altar was dedicated by St. Antoninus on 2 July 1447. At this point, however, it seems to have been recognised that Buggiano's tabernacle was an inadequate central feature of the altar, and it was decided that it should be reinforced with two kneeling *Angels* in enamelled terracotta by Luca della Robbia (Cat. No. 8, Col. Plate IV, Plate 46). A part payment for Luca's *Angels* is recorded in June 1448, and early in 1449 they were equipped with wings executed by a woodcarver, Giovanni di Domenico da Gaiole. Traces of surface gilding or painting can be seen on the two *Angels* in old photographs. For reasons which cannot be reconstructed the value of the *Angels* was assessed only in August 1451, by the sculptors Bernardo Rossellino and Pagno di Lapo Portigiani, who recommended that Luca should receive ninety lire. The *Angels* were thus modelled concurrently with the lunette of the *Ascension*, and their affinities are with this work rather than with the earlier *Resurrection*. They show firing cracks and other local damage, and in the *Angel* facing to the left the glaze on both sides of the face is damaged and restored. This was a small but in no sense a casual commission. The *Angels* are the first documented free-standing works executed by Luca in enamelled terracotta. With heads turned in full-face they gaze confidently at the onlooker, as though inviting his participation in the act of adoration in which they are engaged. The modelling of the necks and of the still classical heads is confident and strong, and their cloaks are disposed over their shoulders and their beautifully modelled legs with exemplary lucidity.

It is hardly conceivable that the lunette of the *Resurrection* would have been commissioned for the Cathedral if the efficacy of its technique had not been fully demonstrated. One group of reliefs exactly corresponds with it in style and may in part be somewhat earlier in date, the *Apostle* roundels in the Pazzi Chapel (Cat. No. 9, Col. Plates VI–IX, Plates 47–59). There is no document relating to this commission, and the sequence of the sculptures must therefore be established by reference to the building history of the Chapel. Designed as the Chapter House of the convent of Santa Croce, the Pazzi Chapel (Figs. 19, 20) was commissioned from Brunelleschi by Andrea de' Pazzi in 1429 or 1430. In 1433 the income from 3000 florins was allocated to work in the Chapel, and part of the ambulatory or cloister was demolished to make way for the new structure. Work was in progress in 1433, when Eugenius IV dined in a room overlooking the site of the new Chapter House. In 1442 the income from 12,000 florins at 4% was made available for a six-year period for work in the Chapel, and in 1445 the will of Andrea de' Pazzi provided that the income from 16,000 florins should be used to complete the building. When Brunelleschi died in 1446, the Chapel was incomplete, and it was still unfinished in 1451, when the will of Andrea de' Pazzi's eldest son obliged his heirs

to contribute to the cost of its construction. In the Catasto returns of the Pazzi family a sum of 16,500 florins is mentioned in connection with the Chapel in 1457, but no provision is made for it in 1469. A date 'a di 11 ottobre 1459' is painted in fresco on the base of the drum of the cupola, and a second date '1461 a di 10 di luglio' is inscribed on the cupola of the portico. It has been deduced from this evidence that the bulk of the work undertaken in the Chapel before Brunelleschi's death dates from a four-year period between 1442 and 1446. The portico of the Chapel did not in its present form constitute part of Brunelleschi's scheme, and is perhaps due to Giuliano da Majano.

The enamelled terracotta sculptures in the Chapel fall into two clearly defined groups. The first consists of twelve roundels of Apostles on the Chapel walls (Col. Plates VI–VIII, Plates 47–58), which must have been part of Brunelleschi's original scheme for the interior, and the second of four large roundels of the *Evangelists* in the pendentives of the cupola, which must have been installed after 1459, the enamelled terracotta decoration of the small cupola in the portico (Col. Plate IX), which must date from after 1461, and the roundel of *St. Andrew* (Plate 59) over the entrance to the Chapel. Only the first of these two groups of works concerns us here.

The problem of equipping his architectural interiors with a component of relief sculpture was one with which Brunelleschi had a long-standing concern. In the Old Sacristy of San Lorenzo, which was completed in 1428, provision was made for four large roundels in the pendentives and four further roundels on the same level above the windows and the altar arch, all of which must have been designed for sculpture. At some date in the late fourteen-thirties, probably after 1437 but before 1443, the pendentive roundels were filled by Donatello with pigmented stucco reliefs of scenes from the life of St. John the Evangelist, and the intervening roundels with reliefs of the four Evangelists. In the Pazzi Chapel provision was also made for sculpture, this time for four large circular reliefs beneath the cupola and for twelve smaller circular reliefs on the walls, placed beneath the cornice and above the blind *pietra serena* arches with which the wall surfaces were articulated. Eight of these frames were on the altar and entrance walls and four were on the lateral walls. The *oculi* above the altar arch, the entrance and the arches on the walls were conceived as windows, not as they had been at San Lorenzo as frames to receive reliefs. This had the effect of ensuring that the sculptures in the roundels would be more legible than they had been at San Lorenzo, since they would be nearer to the eye and would be better lit.

If the reconstructed history of the Old Sacristy and of its sculptures is correct, we must assume that after its completion in 1428 the four pendentive roundels and the four wall roundels remained void, and that in the late fourteen-thirties, against Brunelleschi's wishes, the filling of the vacant frames was entrusted by Cosimo de' Medici to Donatello. In the Pazzi Chapel, on the other hand, throughout his lifetime and for some years after his death, Brunelleschi remained in charge. The objections to Donatello's reliefs in the Old Sacristy were two-fold, first that their perspective structure violated the plane of the wall surface, and second that their discordant local colouring (of which traces are still visible) disrupted the tranquil architectural forms. When, therefore, the filling of the frames in the Pazzi Chapel came to be considered, it was decided that the roundels must be composed in such a way as to reinforce, not to disturb, the architectural harmony, and that polychromy should be avoided and a bichromatic system be introduced. The result was twelve roundels which have in common first that the palette is confined to white and blue with surface gilding, and second that the figures are seated frontally, on horizontal lines of cloud, thereby extending the effect of verticality that is implicit in the pilasters on either side and in the protracted *pietra serena* window frames beneath.

When we enter the Pazzi Chapel, we see to the left of the altar roundels of *St. Matthew* and *St. Peter* (Col. Plate VI, Plates 54, 47), to its right *St. John the Evangelist* and *St. James the Great* (Col. Plates VII, VIII, Plates 55, 51), on the right wall *St. Andrew* and *St. James the Less* (Plates 53, 50), on the entrance wall, from left to right, *SS. Simon, Thaddeus, Thomas* and *Philip* (Plates 49, 56–58), and on the left wall *St. Matthias* and *St. Bartholomew* (Plates 52, 48). With one exception the treatment of the figures is uniform. The odd-man-out is the *St. Peter*. Like the other figures, he is shown frontally seated on a ledge of cloud, but the particularised vestment, the archaic classicising head, the grooved halo, and the pedantic handling of the keys balanced against a volume of epistles suggest that this is either an early relief prepared by Luca before the modelling of the other figures, or a relief glazed by Luca but modelled by Brunelleschi.

There has been widespread disagreement on the date of the Apostle roundels, which were assigned by Marquand to the years in which Luca was working on the Cantoria and by Bode to the years 1470–8. Since their style is manifestly incompatible with that of Luca's late works, they were ascribed by Bode in large part to his nephew, Andrea della Robbia. There is no evidence to substantiate so late a dating. The lost contract for the roundels probably dates from 1440–2, and it is likely that the earlier of them precede the first of the Duomo lunettes. It cannot, however, be presumed that all the roundels were modelled and glazed simultaneously.

There are indeed differences of style throughout the series which would be inexplicable if this were the case, and they may have been phased over as much as fifteen years. The most primitive is the *St. Bartholomew*, where the cloak is drawn up to reveal the ankles and falls in stiff folds between the knees. More varied, but still predominantly frontal, is the *St. Andrew*, with which must be grouped the beautiful *St. James the Great*, the *St. James the Less* (where the head recalls that of Christ in the *Resurrection* lunette), the *St. Matthias* and the *St. Philip*. If we suppose that the transition from the upright frontal Christ of the *Resurrection* to the more rhythmical figure of Christ in the *Ascension* represents a change in Luca's style, we might predicate that the two Apostle roundels in which the knees are frontal and the upper part of the body is turned, the *St. Matthew* and the *St. John the Evangelist*, date from the period of the *Ascension* lunette, that is from the late fourteen-forties, while three of the four reliefs on the entrance wall, in which the knees are turned decisively to the left and the principle of verticality is less strictly observed, would come at the end of the sequence, about 1450. With the exception of the *St. Peter* and of one later roundel, the *St. Thomas*, there is no reason to suppose that any other artist than Luca della Robbia was responsible for the designing or modelling of the figures. On the walls of the Pazzi Chapel the integration of sculpture and architecture is complete. The intellectual calculation through which its ideal space and its ideal figure decoration were produced is evident, but it is of secondary importance beside the emotive effect of the Chapel as a whole. No early Renaissance interior is so elevated, unselfconscious and serene. While its conception is due to Brunelleschi, it owes its specifically devotional character to the seriousness and sensibility of Luca della Robbia.

Concurrently with or immediately before the *Resurrection* Luca seems to have undertaken a commission for a work fully in the round. This is a group of the *Visitation* in San Giovanni Fuorcivitas at Pistoia (Cat. No. 10, Col. Plate V, Plate 60, Fig. 25). It was completed by October 1445, when a member of the congregation presented to the Sodality of the Visitation a sum for the purchase of oil to burn night and day before the group. It has been questioned whether the figures now in the church are the group to which this document relates and not a later substitution, but there can be no doubt whatever that they are by Luca della Robbia and were executed precisely at this time. The two figures are visually segregated from each other, the Virgin standing in full length facing to the right and St. Elizabeth kneeling in left profile in front of her. The upper and lower halves of the figures were fired separately, and the point at which they join is through the right forearm of the Virgin and the left elbow of St. Elizabeth. One of the most beautiful features of the group, the right hand of the Virgin placed on the Saint's shoulder, is fired in one with the upper section of the figure of the Saint. The lower halves of both figures are damaged and have been made up, and the edge of the robe of St. Elizabeth on the extreme right, over and beyond the feet, is new. Irregular pitting in the surface glaze seems to have been caused by air bubbles in the course of firing. The head of the Virgin, with its rippling hair and delicately modelled ear, recalls the outer figures in the relief of *Cithara Players* on the Cantoria. It is, however, to the classical moment of the *Resurrection* relief that the group belongs, and the geometrical expedient whereby the two figures are set in a right-angled triangle, with the Saint leaning forward towards the Virgin, who stands in front of her, exemplifies the same principle of classical design.

The death of Brunelleschi in 1446 represents the great caesura in Luca della Robbia's career. Had he, too, died in 1446, when the Cantoria and the *Resurrection* lunette were in place and the Pazzi Chapel roundels were more than half complete, he would still rank among the greatest Early Renaissance sculptors. But in practice Brunelleschi's death seems to have removed not just a stimulus but a constraint, and thereafter, confronting other problems in conjunction with other architects, Luca developed the decorative potentials of his medium to a point which could not have been imagined before that time.

V THE COMMISSIONS OF PIERO DE' MEDICI

On three occasions in his life of Luca della Robbia Vasari mentions Piero di Cosimo de' Medici. He was, so Vasari believed, 'fra i primi che facessero lavorare a Luca cose di terra colorita,' and was responsible for two major commissions: for the enamelled terracotta ceiling of the Cappella del Crocifisso at San Miniato al Monte and for the decoration of his own study in the Palazzo Medici. The architect of both the Chapel and the study was Michelozzo, with whom Luca was associated from 1446 in the Cathedral.

Our knowledge of Piero de' Medici as an artistic patron is sadly incomplete. Before April 1438 he was in touch with Domenico Veneziano, who wrote him from Perugia a celebrated letter soliciting a contract for 'qualche famoso lavorio' and describing himself as 'tenuto et hublighato' to Piero for some earlier favour. Piero was also in touch with Fra Filippo Lippi, one of whose paintings he turned down. He seems to have exercised strict supervision over the commissions he awarded. In a letter written to him from Venice in 1441, Matteo de' Pasti explains that in a work for Piero on which he is engaged, he is using 'oro masinato che io dipingo come ogni altro colore,' which has enabled him to introduce 'verdure . . . tutto tochate d'oro masinato.' The subject seems to have been a Petrarchan *Triumph*, and the artist asks how Piero would like the seated woman in the centre to be dressed. Should she be clad in a 'camora di picciolato o pur in un manto, come a me piacesse?' He is anxious, moreover, to start work on the companion *Triumphs*. 'Si che caramente vi priegho,' he enquires, 'che mi vogliate mandare la fantasia degli altri, or cioè ch'io li conpischa.' Something of the same attention must have been given to the design and detail of the *desco da parto* of the *Triumph of Fame* in the New York Historical Society, which Piero ordered in 1449 to commemorate the birth of his son, Lorenzo il Magnifico. His taste for gilding was notorious. In an insinuating letter of 1457, Filippo Lippi, taking the same line as Matteo de' Pasti, describes a panel of *St. Michael* with armour painted in silver and gold. What we know of Piero as a collector derives from an inventory of 1456, which includes, in addition to the rich household effects we might expect, thirty-one examples of damascened

Islamic metalwork and a quantity of Islamic glass. Nearest his heart, however, lay his collection of manuscripts, and Filarete (whose *Trattato di Architettura* is dedicated to him) describes how, when stricken with arthritis, he 'took great pleasure in whiling away time by having himself carried into his study . . . There he would look at his books as if they were a pile of gold.' The study to which he was transported was decorated by Luca della Robbia.

The two churches which gained most signally from Piero's benefactions were the Santissima Annunziata and San Miniato al Monte, and it was at San Miniato that contact with Luca was first made. The crypt of the church contained the miraculous Crucifix of San Giovanni Gualberto. In 1447 it was proposed by a 'Cittadino grande' (who is not named in the document, but can only have been Piero de' Medici) that an altar and tabernacle for the Crucifix should be built in the nave of the church. The tabernacle, it was promised, would be costly and of splendid appearance. The proposal was considered by the Arte di Calimala, which had rights over San Miniato, and was agreed subject to one condition, that the only arms on the tabernacle be those of the Guild. Evidently this was not what the 'Cittadino grande' had in mind, for after twelve months of discussion, in June 1448, the earlier decision was reversed. It was agreed that Piero de' Medici's arms might appear on the tabernacle, provided that in some appropriate place the arms of the Calimala were also shown. The only recorded payments in connection with the tabernacle are to the bronze sculptor Maso di Bartolomeo for two copper eagles standing on bales of cloth, the emblem of the Arte di Calimala, which were begun in January and cast in April 1449 and which still stand above the arch of the tabernacle at the front and back. There are no payments to Michelozzo, the architect of the chapel, or to Luca della Robbia.

The Cappella del Crocifisso (Cat. No. 11, Fig. 18) is one of Michelozzo's most distinguished creations, and a work on which no expense seems to have been spared. Only in the Medici church of San Lorenzo do we find architectural carving of such resplendently high quality. But its effect (as Piero de' Medici must from the first have wished) is due not simply to its architecture but also to its polychromy. Above the columns is a coloured marble frieze inlaid with the personal impresa of Piero de' Medici, and the internal ceiling and external roof are decorated in enamelled terracotta. The roof (Plate 62) is covered with a scale pattern in the form of horizontal rows of glazed tiles, which are alternately white, dull-green, and mauve, and the coffered ceiling (Plate 61) is decorated with twenty-four recessed blue octagons, framed with white leaf-and-dart and egg-and-dart mouldings and surrounded by a flat band with a leaf design. Linking the octagons are small squares, each with a bronze star, and in the centre of each octagon is a rosette, from which there radiate gold rays painted on the blue ground. The capitals of the two columns and the two pilasters supporting the ciborium depend from the antique, and the enamelled terracotta decoration of the roof and ceiling derives from Tuscan Romanesque ornament, of which the choir screen at San Miniato was a pre-eminent example. A precedent for the scale pattern on the roof occurs about 1175 on the choir screen of Sant'Agata near Scarperia, and carved slabs there and in the Pieve at Fagna offer analogies for the rosettes and for other features in the framing of the ceiling. These churches in the Mugello must have been well known both to Piero de' Medici and to Michelozzo, who had undertaken work at Trebbio, Caffaggiolo and Bosco ai Frati, and it is likely that the design of both roof and ceiling was due to the patron and the architect, and was translated into terms of enamelled terracotta by Luca della Robbia.

In the study in the Palazzo Medici the same tripartite collaboration was involved. The earliest account of it is by Filarete, who in his *Trattato* describes first the chamber of Piero de' Medici ('la qual camera è degnissima, perchè è molto hornato di quello, che a una degnia camera si richiede; che non sarebbe rifiutata da qualunque gran signiore sia') and then, adjacent to it, Piero's study ('uno studietto ornato di degnissimi libri e altre cose degne e così il suo studietto hornatissimo il pavimento, e così il cielo, di vetriamenti fatti a figure degnissime; in modo che a chi v'entra, da grandissima admiratione. El maestro di questi invetriamenti si fu Luca della Robbia; così per nome si chiama; il quale è degnissimo maestro di questi invetriati'). A later account is supplied by Vasari, who tells us in the second edition of his *Lives* that the room had a vaulted ceiling in enamelled terracotta decorated with 'varie fantasie' and an enamelled terracotta pavement ('il pavimento similmente'). It was a cool room, he adds ('molto utile per la state'), and was technically remarkable since both the ceiling and the floor seemed to be made of a single piece of enamelled terracotta. The room was destroyed after the sale of the Palazzo Medici in 1659 to the Riccardi,

and all that now survives from it is twelve roundels with the *Labours of the Months* in the Victoria and Albert Museum (Cat. No. 12, Col. Plates X–XII, Plates 63–71).

Filarete's *Trattato di Architettura* was completed in 1464, and his description of the study is evidently an eye-witness account. He paid his last recorded visit to Florence in 1456, and we are bound therefore to suppose that the decoration of the study was finished by that time. In the fourteen-fifties, work in the Palazzo Medici went ahead rapidly, and by 1457 the Medici family was living in the palace. The paintings executed by Pesellino and Uccello for the palace probably date from the mid-fifties, the Sala Grande was decorated by Antonio Pollajuolo in 1460, and the chapel was frescoed by Benozzo Gozzoli in 1459–60. Luca della Robbia's work in the study was of a rather different character in that it was structural, and there is no difficulty in supposing that it was carried out at the date Filarete's description would suggest, in the middle of the decade and in any event before 1456.

About the lost pavement there is little that can usefully be said. The mid-fifteenth century majolica pavements that survive in whole or in part, in the Carracciolo Chapel of San Giovanni Carbonara in Naples, in Sant' Elena in Venice, and in San Petronio (1487) and San Giacomo at Bologna (1488–94), provide no valid analogy for the pavement of the *studietto*. Robbia tile designs exist in the chapel of St. Lawrence of the Collegiata at Empoli, the chapel of San Bartolo in Sant' Agostino at San Gimignano, the Guerra chapel in San Lorenzo at Montevarchi, and the Sforza chapel in the Madonna della Neve at Santa Fiora, and it is suggested by Marquand that the first of them may reproduce the enamelled terracotta pavement of the Palazzo Medici. Though the pavement at Empoli includes a pattern of polychrome cubes like those used by Luca in the Chapel of the Cardinal of Portugal, it is difficult to believe that its comparatively weak leaf decoration, its floreated rosettes and its fictive textile fringe are not the invention of Andrea della Robbia. Vasari's account, moreover, seems to indicate that the pavement was figurated. With the ceiling, on the other hand, we are on firmer ground. The twelve roundels in London show varying degrees of curvature, and from them we can infer that the *Labours of the Months* were disposed in three rows of four roundels each. The first four and the last four roundels were oriented on the axis of the side walls, and in the centre were the months of May, June, July and August oriented lengthwise on the axis of the end walls of the room. The surface covered by the roundels would have been of the order of twelve by sixteen feet, and, when allowance is made for the factor of curvature, the room must have been about ten feet wide and a little over thirteen feet long. To judge from Luca della Robbia's other enamelled ceilings, the roundels would have been unified by heavy architectural mouldings, probably in white enamelled terracotta. Outside the roundels there are traces of flat enamelling in porphyry and in bright green.

In the context of Luca's work the ceiling is exceptional in almost every respect. The figures in the roundels are not modelled, but are drawn in white and dark blue on a blue ground (Col. Plates X–XII, Plates 63–71). They are thus the only figurated paintings in Luca's entire oeuvre. Each scene is circular, and round it runs a flat band in light and dark blue in which the hours of light and darkness are shown. The name of the month is inscribed in white at the base of the nocturnal section, and the hours of daylight are given in black letters in the light-blue area above. At the top, to left of centre, there appears the sun, depicted in yellow as a human head with flowing hair, beneath the sign of the zodiac appropriate to the month, and in a corresponding position in the dark-blue section is a white crescent moon. The whole representation is framed in white leaf-moulding. The iconography of the Labours of the Months with zodiacal signs surrounded by borders showing the hours of light and darkness seems to be confined to miniatures, and is of northern origin. It occurs, for example, in a German codex of 1445, the Passauer Kalendarium, now in the Landesbibliothek at Cassel, and was known in Florence by 1469 when it is found in a Book of Hours, at Holkham, illuminated for Clarice Orsini on the occasion of her marriage to Lorenzo il Magnifico. The paintings in the Holkham manuscript are by Francesco di Antonio del Cherico. The roundels from the *studietto* and the illuminations in the calendar of the Holkham manuscript do not correspond, but it is probable that both have a common source in a northern manuscript in Piero de' Medici's collection.

In the fifteenth century, humanists concerned with their classical heredity were faced with one disturbing fact: that however rigorously they might apply classical principles to contemporary society, daily life had almost nothing in common with life in Greece or Rome. No matter what philosophical doctrines they adopted, what social attitudes, what political beliefs, the conditions of urban living were unrecognisably diverse. In one area and one only could the present be linked firmly to the past, the countryside. Sacrifices were no longer made to Mars Silvanus, spoiled olives were no longer fed to discontented slaves, sick oxen were no longer dosed with raw eggs in a wooden spoon, but agricultural methods, the rotation of the crops, viticulture, and harvest practices remained essentially unchanged. For that reason, interest focused on two classical texts on agriculture, first on Columella's *De Re Rustica* and then, a little later,

on Cato's *De Agri Cultura*. The *De Re Rustica*, written about 65 A.D., was unknown until a manuscript of it was discovered by Poggio Bracciolini. He had it copied, and sold the copy to Giovanni di Cosimo de' Medici; a note to that effect appears at the end of the book, which is now preserved in the Laurenziana. A second copy figures in 1465 in the inventory of Piero de' Medici, and this too is in the Laurenziana; Piero de' Medici's name appears in ink on the last page. In all there are some twenty fifteenth-century manuscripts of the *De Re Rustica*, most of which precede the first printed edition of 1472. So it is in no way surprising that Columella should have supplied the basis for the *Labours of the Months* made by Luca della Robbia for Piero de' Medici. That can be established from the nature of the labours that are shown. In conventional cycles of the Labours of the Months the month of January is represented by a scene of feasting or by a man warming himself at a fire. In Luca's roundel of January, however, we see a woodman felling trees and cutting vine-props (Col. Plate X). This labour is described by Columella. 'It is also a fit time for making vine-props of even stakes,' he writes, 'and it is also equally suitable for cutting down trees for buildings, but both these operations are better carried out when the moon is waning, from the 20th to the 30th of the month, since all wood so cut is considered not to be attacked by decay. One workman can cut down, strip and sharpen a hundred stakes a day.' March, Columella tells us, 'is an excellent time for pruning vines,' and it is the pruning of vines that is depicted in the roundel for this month (Plate 64). April and May are normally represented by courtly scenes of hawking and hunting. In April, however, according to Columella, 'it is correct to begin the first training of the vines, while the eyes which are creeping forth can be struck off with the finger,' and this work is again illustrated in the roundel (Plate 65). In May, Columella tells us, 'cutting of the hay must be begun. A good labourer cuts a *jugerum* of meadowland.' The scything of grass is represented in Luca's roundel (Col. Plate XI). In June the corn is cut, and in July 'within thirty days of the cutting of the corn, the straw which has been cut is gathered into heaps.' This is portrayed in the scene of threshing depicted by Luca (Plate 67). In December, 'according to those who practise husbandry with unusual care, the soil ought not to be disturbed with any iron tool, unless you trench it for the sake of the vines . . . Whatever can be done outside this kind of work is included in the following list: the gathering of olives . . .' In orthodox Labours of the Months December is represented by the killing of pigs, but in Luca's roundel we see a peasant trenching the ground with a long-handled spade (Plate 71), and in November olive-picking is shown (Col. Plate XII). The decoration of Piero de' Medici's *studietto* was, therefore, a humanist cycle of Labours of the Months, depending in part from contemporary practice and in part from the antique.

In one respect the description of the roundels as glazed paintings is a misnomer, since the technique in which they are rendered has more in common with the silverpoint drawings produced in Florence in the middle of the fifteenth century than it has with paintings. There is indeed one group of drawings, mainly of academic nudes in Florence and Berlin, in which the method used to define the figures, through modelling in silverpoint on a prepared ground, does, in a superficial way, recall the handling of the roundels, and an effort has been made to ascribe the roundels and the drawings to one hand. This theory is untenable. In the drawings the forms are more pinched and the action is less well articulated than they are in the medallions. Alternatively it has been claimed that the roundels were designed not by Luca della Robbia but by Domenico Veneziano. This theory, as we shall see, is also untenable, though the influence of Domenico Veneziano on the roundels is very strong.

In all twelve scenes the source of light, the sun, is on the left, and the lighting is worked out with this in mind. Thus in the roundel of January the trees on the right, the figure of the woodman in the centre, and the pile of vine-props on the left are all shown with their left sides strongly lit and their right sides in shadow. This careful system of illumination, where directed light acts as a unifying agent in the composition, was explored by Domenico Veneziano, who uses it in the predella of the Santa Lucia altarpiece and most notably in the *Stigmatisation of St. Francis* in Washington, which is lit from a single light source, the seraph, on the right. It was Domenico Veneziano, moreover, who in the middle of the fifteenth century devised a method of so notating the components of his landscapes, that they present themselves to the spectator in the way in which in nature they strike the eye. In the tondo of the *Adoration of the Magi* in Berlin the shrubs in the middle distance are portrayed in a pointilliste technique and in the *Stigmatisation of St. Francis* the trees are depicted in somewhat the same way. This practice is taken over in the roundels. Similarly the treatment in the roundel of *June* of the man bending down as he reaps a field of wheat must remind us of the bands of light and shadow along the back of the kneeling King in the *Adoration* in Berlin. Should we on this account be justified in inferring that the roundels were designed by Domenico Veneziano, not by Luca? The answer must be negative, since all of the twelve roundels are constructed in a manner that is typical of Luca della Robbia.

Thinking back, as we must necessarily do, to the only narrative reliefs by Luca della Robbia that are properly authenticated, the *Scenes from the life of St. Peter* in the Bargello (Plates 34–36), we shall find that the same compositional devices are employed in the roundels as in the reliefs. There is the same insistence on geometry. In *February*, *March*, and *April*, the horizontals and verticals are established by the line of the horizon and the trunks of olive trees or the supporting trellises of vines. This thinking is common, in one form or another, to all of the twelve scenes. Not unnaturally the division of the picture space is more elaborate in the roundels than it had been fifteen years before, but in *January* and *July*, where the figures are posed diagonally across the field, or *May*, *November*, and *December*, where the field is bisected by the long handles of the scythe and trenching spade and by a ladder propped against the olive tree, there can be no doubt that the same mind is once again at work. The poses and indeed the types of certain of the figures, especially the youths who scythe the grass and trench the ground, also recall those of the executioners in the second of the St. Peter scenes. The only admissible conclusion is that the roundels were designed and painted by Luca della Robbia.

Their spatial structure is remarkably sophisticated. In *January* a receding line of trees on the right and three sticks in the foreground serve to establish a vanishing point in the centre of the scene. The device of the three sticks on the left is closely similar to that used by Uccello in the foreground of the Oxford *Hunt*. In *February* the vanishing point falls on the horizon, and the recession is established by three olive trees, in the foreground, the middle ground, and the distance. In *March* the extent of the area depicted is indicated by a receding trellis and in *April* the same device is used once more. In *May* and *June*, representationally the most ambitious of the scenes, there is no perspective element, and the extent of the dense wood and the depth of the cornfield are indicated optically. Recourse is had to the same expedients in the three other scenes, *August*, *October*, and *December*, in which a deep expanse of ground is shown.

What effect the roundels made when they were installed in the ceiling of the *studietto* we can only guess. But they record first a contact with country life that is more sentient, more practical, and more direct than that revealed by any other work of art produced in Florence in the fifteenth century, and second a remarkable responsiveness to visual experience. As Piero de' Medici, seated in his study, glanced up at them, they would have given him, as they give us, the reassuring sense that the present and the past are one.

VI FUNERARY COMMISSIONS

The concept of personal commemoration inspired some of the greatest Florentine Quattrocento sculptures, and on two occasions it impinged on Luca della Robbia and his work. It did so first in the tomb of Benozzo Federighi, Bishop of Fiesole, now erected in Santa Trinita (Cat. No. 13, Col. Plates XIII, XIV, Plates 72–77), and second at San Miniato al Monte in the Chapel of the Cardinal of Portugal (Cat. No. 14, Fig. 30, Col. Plates XV–XVII, Plates 78–80).

When Federighi died in 1450, he was buried in the chapel of his family in the church of San Pancrazio. Though his monument was not formally commissioned till 2 May 1454, it seems to have been planned by Federighi before his death and to reflect his modest character and conservative taste. On his appointment as Bishop of Fiesole in the spring of 1421 he had set about embellishing the cathedral. The artistic scene in Florence at the time was dominated by Gentile da Fabriano, and the first painter Federighi patronised, Benedetto di Nanni da Gubbio, was Umbrian. He was responsible for a cycle of nine scenes from the life of the patron of Fiesole, S. Romolo, in the tribune of the crypt and for three altarpieces. In 1426, on the Bishop's instructions, the sacristy of the Cathedral was decorated by a secondary artist from Prato, Arrigo di Niccolò, and about 1440 an altarpiece for the high altar, bearing Federighi's arms, was painted by Bicci di Lorenzo. For two aspects of his tomb Federighi is likely to have been responsible: that it is surrounded by a floreated border in enamelled terracotta, and that it contains behind the effigy reliefs of the Dead Christ, the Virgin and St. John, of a type which occurs on a number of Florentine Gothic tombs, notably on that of his predecessor as Bishop of Fiesole, Tedice Aliotti, in Santa Maria Novella.

The contract for the monument does not survive, but it is known, from later litigation, to have stipulated that the tomb should be carved in relief in marble, should be contained in a frame with foliage of gold and polychrome enamelled terracotta roughly four and a half braccia square, and should show the body of the Bishop and other figures and ornaments. It was to follow a design prepared by a certain Giovanni di ser Paolo. The interest of Federighi's nephew, Federigo di Jacopo Federighi, seems to have been limited to the financial aspect of the commission, and there is a presumption that the drawing by Giovanni di ser Paolo (son of a notary of the Wool Guild, who was a partner in Domenico and Federigo Federighi's firm) represented the monument in a form agreed by Luca della Robbia and the Bishop.

The church of San Pancrazio was modernised in 1752–5, and in January 1753 the Federighi monument was moved from its original position on the wall of the north transept and transferred to a corridor leading to the side entrance to the church. When the church was secularised in 1808, it was moved again, and was re-erected in 1809 in San Francesco di Paola. Finally, in 1896, it was set up to the position in which it stands today, in the second chapel to the left in the left transept of Santa Trinita. What we have now, however, is no more than the upper section of the tomb. A drawing of it in the *Sepoltuario* of Giovanni di Poggio Baldovinetti (Fig. 32), made when it was still in the corridor of San Pancrazio, shows that it was originally supported on two paired pilasters rising from a shallow step. Between the pilasters were three slabs of red marble, and on the front of the step were circles of marble or enamelled terracotta inlay. Though paired pilasters, as we know from the Cantoria, formed part of Luca's architectural repertory, there is no parallel for their employment in such a context before the tomb of Orlando de' Medici in the Santissima Annunziata, which was designed in the Rossellino studio, probably by Bernardo Rossellino, and which cannot have been begun before 1456, more than a year after the Federighi tomb.

The contract enjoined that Luca della Robbia should be paid 200 florins for his work and should procure the marble, for the cost of which he would be responsible. When the tomb was completed in 1456 (as we know it to have been from a Catasto return prepared by Luca in the following year) trouble began. A sum of 80 florins due to be paid to Luca by the Federighi at a rate of eight florins a month seems to have been withheld, and in February 1458 Federigo Federighi, through his brother Domenico, formally charged the artist with non-completion of the contract. The nub of the disagreement was the quantity and therefore the value of the marble used. When the Federighi insisted that the monument should be set up forthwith, the artist refused to comply, apparently on the ground that once it was let into the wall the depth of the marble slabs could no longer be properly assessed. The case was put out to arbitration—the arbitrator once more was Luca della Robbia's old colleague and associate Buggiano—and it was finally agreed that the true value of the marble was 40 florins and the comprehensive fee for the tomb that originally agreed, 200 florins. This contrasts with the figure of 'fl. 125 o circa' which Federigo Federighi in a tax return of September 1458 declared as his estimated liability. The comprehensive figure of 240 florins is considerably lower than the sums paid to Mino da Fiesole for the Conte Ugo monument in the Badia (400 florins) and to Antonio Rossellino for the tomb of the Cardinal of Portugal (425 florins), and is explained by the fact that the tomb was from the first planned as a deep relief. The closest analogy is with another relief tomb, the Lazzari monument of Antonio and Bernardo Rossellino at Pistoia, which cost in all 220 florins.

In looking at the tomb as it is installed in Santa Trinita (Plate 72), we must bear in mind that it was intended to be seen not at eye level but at a height of five to six feet from the ground, and that the surface is no longer in the state in which it was designed to be. Buggiano, in his arbitration report of 24 September 1459, instructed the two parties to pay three lire each for gilding on the mitre, the pillow, the edge of the chasuble and the bier-cloth, the hair and wings of the angels holding the epitaph, the haloes of the Dead Christ, the Virgin and St. John, and the three seraphim above them. 'Traces of gold still to be seen which accented the embroidered patterns but which is now happily almost worn away' were observed by Cruttwell in 1902 and have since disappeared. Marquand also claimed to have found 'traces of colour ... on the eyebrows and eyes of the angels,' as well as remains of gilding. When the monument was pigmented and gilded as it was meant to be, the contrast between the figurated surface and the enamelled terracotta frame would have been less marked.

The form of the sarcophagus seems to owe something to that in Bernardo Rossellino's Bruni monument, which was probably commissioned in 1444 and was certainly completed before work started on the Federighi tomb, and the epitaph in a circular wreath makes use of a motif introduced in Ghiberti's *Arca of the Three Martyrs*. The sense for the placing of the angels on their ground, however, differs from that of Ghiberti. The heads are more erect, the bodies are arranged diagonally, with their feet in the lower corners of the slab, and the same diagonal is reasserted by the upper edges of their wings (Plates 76, 77). One of the most attractive features of the carving is the treatment of the feet of the angels, one partly concealed by drapery and the other free. The head of the Bishop, turned towards the spectator, is depicted fully in the round (Plate 73), and seems to have been based on a death mask. The differences between the lunette of the *Dead Christ with the Virgin and St. John* on the Peretola tabernacle (Plates 40, 41) and the three figures on the Federighi monument (Plates 74, 75) are very great. Whereas the earlier relief was carved under the strong influence of Masaccio, the later is less expository and more contained. In so far as they have any reference to painting, these noble figures recall the late work of Fra Angelico.

The enamelled terracotta frame of the Federighi monument consists of a continuous frieze of lozenges, surrounded by white cord which starts at the centre of the base and terminates in the centre at the top. The sides contain six lozenges, and at the corners are four circles, two at the bottom filled with flowers and two at the top containing a reduced version of the Federighi arms (eight plates *argent* on an *azure* ground). Each of the ovals contains a bunch of flowers or fruit. On the base there are two ovals containing palm and olive branches, outside them two ovals with pink roses, and outside those again two ovals with sheaves of lilies. The other fruit or flowers represented are pomegranates, pine- and fir- or cedar-cones, and white and blue field flowers. At the point of juncture of each oval are four small flowers, two turned outwards and two reversed. The linear formulation of the flowers, and especially of the bunches of roses and lilies, depends directly from the style evolved by Ghiberti for the outer and inner jambs of the north door of the Baptistry (Figs. 37, 38). In the frieze Luca introduced two technical experiments: first, it was planned as a mosaic of enamelled terracotta, in which the pieces, sometimes very small, were glazed and laid down separately; and second, the ground within the ovals and outside each bunch of flowers was covered, before firing, with gold powder or gold paint and was then glazed. The effect may be less brilliant than was intended—the gold in the background is evident only on close inspection, and its presence has indeed been denied by certain scholars—and perhaps for that reason the technique was used again in only one later work.

It has been claimed that the cartoon for the frame of the Federighi monument was supplied to Luca by the painter Baldovinetti. There are flowers in abundance in Baldovinetti's work—in the Caffaggiolo altarpiece in the Uffizi of about 1453, in the mosaic over the north door of the Baptistry of the same year, in the somewhat later San Giorgio *Annunciation*, in the frame of the frescoed *Nativity* in the Santissima Annunziata (1460), and in the *Annunciation* at San Miniato al Monte—but nowhere are they painted with such cursive freedom and nowhere do they show such uninhibited inventiveness. The attribution rests on a double misestimate, of the capacity of Baldovinetti and of the artistic personality of Luca della Robbia. It would now be generally accepted that Baldovinetti, for all his elegance, was a less original and less distinguished painter than was at one time supposed, while Luca della Robbia developed in the fourteen-sixties, in the Chapel of the Cardinal of Portugal, into one of the great decorators of his time. The Federighi monument is the first work in which his talent as a decorator is fully manifest.

In his life of Jacopo da Portogallo, Vespasiano da Bisticci tells how the young Cardinal, sensing that death was near, 'drew up his will enjoining with papal authority that he should be buried in the church of San Miniato al Monte in Florence, of the Olivetan Order. He wished that a chapel should be constructed and endowed, where Mass would be said every morning (as it is now), and to leave it the vestments and other things pertaining to the divine office. . . . Thus he arranged everything in death as he had done in life.' The Cardinal died in Florence on 27 August 1459, and the planning of the memorial chapel, by Alvaro, Bishop of Silves, was begun without delay. Its architect was Antonio Manetti, and by June 1460 cornices in *pietra di macigno* were being carved to Manetti's design. Manetti himself died in November of the same year, but such progress had already been made that the whole structure, including the roof, was finished by June 1462. The tomb of the Cardinal, on the east wall of the chapel, was commissioned from Antonio Rossellino in 1461 and was completed five years later (Fig. 30). Antonio and Piero del Pollajuolo were entrusted with the altarpiece and the frescoed decoration of the altar wall, which was carried out in 1466–7, and frescoes of the *Evangelists* and *Fathers of the Church* beside the windows and in the spandrels and an *Annunciation* above the throne on the west wall were executed between 1466 and 1473 by Baldovinetti. The commission to Luca della Robbia for the ceiling of the Chapel (Cat. No. 14, Col. Plates XV–XVII, Plates 78–80) precedes the commissions for the paintings, and no longer survives in the original, but a reliable transcription gives its date as 14 April 1461 and the artist's fee as 150 florins. The progress of the work can be traced through a number of interim payments in the Cambini account books, from which we learn that Luca received payments of 20 florins on 9 April and 13 May 1461. Further interim payments must have been made between this date and 6 July 1462, when the balance of 40 florins was paid. It has been inferred from the documents that work on the ceiling was not started in earnest before March 1462. This may be correct if the term 'in earnest' connotes simply the installation of the roundels and adjacent decoration, but work on the components of the ceiling, which are of exceptional delicacy and elaboration, is likely to have been begun in the spring of 1461.

It has been said that the Chapel of the Cardinal of Portugal represents 'precisely the kind of integration of the arts to which Brunelleschi objected in the Old Sacristy,' but this is no more than a half truth. Brunelleschi's objection in the Old Sacristy was to pigmented reliefs and doorways which disrupted the internal architecture of the building. The chapel at San Miniato, on the other hand, is an Albertian structure. The ceiling was planned from the first to receive a skin of enamelled terracotta, and the walls were conceived as receptacles for Rossellino's tomb and throne. After Manetti's death, control of the whole project seems to have been assumed by Antonio Rossellino, and the chapel developed as an inspired example of loosely co-ordinated collaborative enterprise. The tomb includes a vision of the Virgin with the Child in benediction supported by two flying angels, and above the effigy kneel two larger angels, one of whom carries a crown while the other originally held the palm of chastity. On Luca della Robbia's ceiling (Plate 78) this imagery is elaborated. In the centre is the Holy Ghost, surrounded by seven candlesticks representing the seven gifts of the Holy Spirit (Plate 79), and outside it are figures of the Cardinal Virtues, Fortitude, Temperance, Prudence, and Justice (Col. Plates XV–XVII, Plate 80). That the Virtues, like the figure sculpture of the tomb, form a commentary on the Cardinal's life is made clear by the fact that one of them, the *Fortitude*, carries a shield with his arms. The components of Rossellino's tomb speak the language of affectionate respect. The story that they tell is not one of civic virtue, like the Bruni and Marsuppini monuments, nor of successful ecclesiastical administration, like the Brancacci and Coscia tombs. They record the brief career of a youth who was judged by his contemporaries to have sacrificed privilege to sanctity, and who had entered heaven as of right. Here the austere *Virtues* of Donatello and Michelozzo would have been inapposite. Instead the *Virtues* on Luca's ceiling, two of them gazing at the tomb, welcome the soul through whom, in life, their precepts were exemplified.

The roundels in the corners abut on the *macigno* arches and on the roundel with the Holy Ghost, and are set against a background of enamelled terracotta tiles decorated with cubes in yellow, green and purple, which seem to be projecting from the surface of the vault. This form of decoration is classical. The most celebrated example of it occurs in the Casa dei Grifi on the Palatine, on a pavement and two walls, where it has been explained as an emblem of Numerius Fabius Pictor, the owner of the house. The house dates from shortly before 80 B.C. and was not rediscovered till 1911, but the motif is twice used as wall decoration by Piero della Francesca, and frescoes

XVII. *Temperance*. Detail from the Ceiling of the Chapel of the Cardinal of Portugal (Cat. No. 14). Enamelled terracotta. San Miniato al Monte, Florence

XVIII. *Angels*. Detail from the Chapel of the Cross (Cat. No. 15). Enamelled terracotta. Collegiata, Impruneta

XIX. *The Crucifixion*. Detail from the Chapel of the Cross (Cat. No. 15).
Enamelled terracotta. Collegiata, Impruneta

XX. *Stemma of the Arte dei Maestri di Pietra e di Legname* (Cat. No. 18). Enamelled terracotta. Or San Michele, Florence

XXI. *Stemma of the Arte dei Medici e degli Speziali* (Cat. No. 17). Enamelled terracotta. Or San Michele, Florence

XXII. *Stemma of the Mercanzia* (Cat. No. 16). Enamelled terracotta. Or San Michele, Florence

XXIII. *Heraldic centre of the Stemma of King René of Anjou* (Cat. No. 21). Enamelled terracotta. Victoria & Albert Museum, London

XXIV. *Border detail from the Stemma of King René of Anjou* (Cat. No. 21).
Enamelled terracotta. Victoria & Albert Museum, London

of the same type must therefore have been known in the fifteenth century. It was later absorbed into the lingua franca of the Della Robbia shop and recurs, among other places, in the Martini Chapel in San Giobbe in Venice and on a pavement at Empoli. The colouring of the cubes on the ceiling of the Chapel seems to have been determined by heraldic, not aesthetic, considerations, and the insistent purple (for *gules*) and yellow (for *or*) relate to the arms of Aragon.

It was central to Luca's conception that the concave roundels should appear to be recessed, and the frames are carefully contrived with this in mind. Outside runs a heavy moulding in white-enamelled terracotta. Inside this is a flat band of three concentric rows of blue scales, which become lighter as they approach the centre. Inside these again is a triple-moulded frame in white-enamelled terracotta, leading the eye towards the roundel within. In the central roundel (Plate 79) the dove is depicted from beneath in brilliant white enamelling, against concentric bands of blue. The modelled candlesticks are glazed in yellow, and between them, radiating from the centre, is a pattern of gold rays. Similar gold rays are painted on the four other roundels. In the *Virtues* (Col. Plates XV–XVII, Plate 80) Luca's figure style undergoes a change. The principle of verticality is rejected, and the form of the figures is adjusted to the circular fields. They are posed with unprecedented freedom, and three of them are twisted above the waist. In the green, yellow-spotted serpent held by *Prudence* and in the blowing hair of *Temperance* we sense a new preoccupation with linear design.

In the chapel it must have been apparent from the first that the technique which Luca practised would be seen in close association with marble sculptures and with frescoes and panel paintings. Perhaps for that reason, as he reviewed the potential of enamelled terracotta in this unfamiliar context, he became increasingly alive to its pictorial possibilities. This affected not only the design but also the physical structure of the figures. In the *Fortitude* there are two joins which are almost imperceptible, one beneath the long fold of the cloak and the other below the collar. The *Temperance* has a single join beneath the left forearm and through the fold of drapery at the back, while the *Prudence* and *Justice* were each glazed in three sections; in the former, joins are visible above the serpent and across the left wing above the elbow, and in the latter they appear round the shield, over the left shoulder, and below the waist.

The four *Virtues* at San Miniato are some of Luca della Robbia's supreme achievements as an imagist. The *Justice* (Plate 80), shown like the other figures to the

holding a sword and the other an orb, are set on the relief plane. On the sleeves and across the hips the folds of her thin dress are resolved with exquisite elegance. Facing this figure in the chapel is the *Prudence* (Col. Plate XV), depicted in right profile with the profile of a bearded man behind her head. In her left hand is a fore-shortened mirror and in her right the emblem of wisdom, the serpent. From a linear standpoint this is the most evolved of the designs; a scarf worn over her shoulders blows outwards to the left. The *Fortitude* (Col. Plate XVI) is a predominantly frontal figure, whose wings extend over the whole field and whose mace, held in the right hand, fulfils the same role in the composition as the sword held by *Justice*. The *Temperance* (Col. Plate XVII), perhaps the most immediately appealing of the reliefs, is once more in profile, and gazes down intently at the goblets balanced in her hands. The heads and especially the lips of all four Virtues have a tremulous expressiveness.

When Baldovinetti's lunettes round the windows of the chapel, immediately beneath the ceiling, were more brightly coloured than they are today, and when the *Virgin and Child* on Rossellino's monument was backed with ultramarine and heightened with gilding, and the Cardinal's robes and the curtain were gilded, as we know them to have been, the colours of the ceiling must still have been stronger and more resonant than any others in the chapel, and Luca's roundels were (as they still are today) the dominant works through which the message of the chapel was communicated. The sole occasion in which an attempt was made to profit from the lesson of the ceiling occurred in Venice after 1471, when the nave of San Giobbe was extended and a chapel was built for the Martini family in which the form of the ceiling (Cat. No. 71, Fig. 50) copies that at San Miniato. In this case, however, Antonio Rossellino was not present—he died in 1478—and Luca della Robbia, who may still have been alive, did not intervene personally in the decoration. The four large roundels, framed in fruit borders, sit in their space uneasily—those at the corners are cut in an arbitrary fashion at the base by the *macigno* cornices—knees, emerging from a curved line of cloud, looks downwards to her right. Her wings, heightened with gold, fill the whole width of the roundel, and her hands, one and in place of the beautiful imagery of the *Holy Ghost* and the four *Virtues* we are confronted by a figure of *God the Father in benediction* and four half-length *Evangelists* plagiarised in part from the pendentive roundels in the Pazzi Chapel. The roof that, through the power of Luca's transfiguring imagination, had become the vault of heaven is once again a ceiling and nothing more.

VII IMPRUNETA

In the middle of the fifteenth century the most important of the country benefices in the vicinity of Florence was that of Santa Maria Impruneta. It was rich in natural resources—its clay promoted a thriving trade in tiles and pottery and is traditionally supposed to have been used by Luca della Robbia and his descendants for their glazed sculptures, its forests were filled with timber, and fruit and other produce were distributed in Florence from its orchards and farms—and it was the principal pilgrimage centre within ready access of the city. It owed its popularity to a single cult, that of a painting of the Virgin which had been unearthed by a team of oxen ploughing in the neighbourhood and was thought to have been painted by St. Luke. The picture was miraculous, and in times of crisis it was brought to Florence: between 1417 and 1500 it was taken there on thirty-two occasions. Sometimes the motive was propitiatory—in 1450 it was invoked to cure a drought; sometimes it was a gesture of thanksgiving—for the victory of Anghiari in 1440 and the election of Pope Nicholas V in 1447; and sometimes it was political, as on two occaions in 1454. Relics attract relics, and in the early fifteenth century the church also acquired a piece of the True Cross, which was deposited by Filippo degli Scolari (Pippo Spano) before his death in 1426.

For this reason the post of *plebanus* at Impruneta was one of the most coveted in the archdiocese of Florence. Technically the church was under Buondelmonti patronage, but when, in 1434, the Priore of San Niccolò oltr'Arno, Messer Tommaso di Maso da Perugia, was elected as Piovano, the nomination was submitted for approval to the Pope. Five years later, in 1439, Tommaso di Maso was succeeded by Antonio degli Agli, who remained at Impruneta for nearly forty years and gave the church and the conventual premises their present form.

Born about 1400, Antonio di Bellincioni degli Agli was a central figure in cultural life in Florence in the second and third quarters of the fifteenth century. A distinguished Latin and Greek scholar, and a relation of Barnaba degli Agli, the benefactor of San Domenico di Fiesole, he was appointed in 1428 to a canonry in San Lorenzo instituted by Giovanni di Bicci de' Medici, and ten years later became Canonico di Libera Collazione at the Duomo. By virtue of his association with the Papal court in Florence, he was appointed a year later as pedagogue to a young Venetian, Pietro Barbo, who had come there in the Pope's train, and when in 1464 Barbo was in turn elected Pope, as Paul II, he raised the status of the Pieve to Propositura and offered preferment to his old master. Partly from affection for Impruneta and partly from lack of serious ambition, Degli Agli rejected it, refusing the Archbishopric of Ragusa and a Cardinal's hat. In 1466, on the death of Salutati, the Bishop of Fiesole, Degli Agli was appointed Bishop, but he remained in that post only till May 1467, and then returned to Impruneta. In the spring of 1470 a further occasion for preferment occurred, with the death of Ugo Giugni, Bishop of Volterra, and Degli Agli was in turn appointed to this post, which he retained until his death in 1477. But as Bishop of Volterra he remained, in the words of Vespasiano da Bisticci, 'molto alieno a ogni pompa', and continued to reside at Impruneta, paying only intermittent visits to his diocese.

When Cosimo de' Medici in 1439 founded the Accademia Platonica, Degli Agli was, as a matter of course, incorporated in it, and at a meeting of the Academy in the Duomo of Florence in October 1441 he recited a *capitolo* on friendship, notable mainly for its attack on the concept of sensual love. One of Degli Agli's associates at this time was the future confidant of Pius II, Jacopo Ammanati, who looked upon him as his mentor. With the departure of Eugenius IV and his court in the spring of 1443, the quality of intellectual life in Florence suffered a decline, and when an Archbishop was appointed whose mind had been formed in the restrictive climate of the Dominican Observant movement, religious thinking took an anti-humanistic turn. The Archbishop approved the study of classical literature only if the purpose of the study was 'la maggior gloria di Dio,' and Degli Agli adopted the same view. With the approval of Nicholas V, he took it upon himself to counter the scorn felt by humanists for Christian mythology by restudying its Patristic sources. The result was *Le Vite e le azioni dei Santi*, which attempted to distinguish history from myth and to restate it in terms acceptable to contemporary humanism. In the *De immortalitate animae* and the *De rationibus fidei*, Degli Agli falls back on the conventional compromise of expressing respect for Plato on the ground that he foretold the Incarnation. He prepared a carefully composed letter of consolation to Cosimo il Vecchio on the death of Giovanni di Cosimo de' Medici in 1453, and when Cosimo il Vecchio died in 1454, he wrote a letter of condolence to Piero de' Medici, referring particularly to the cult of Saints Cosmas and Damian for whom Cosimo had had such great devotion and whom 'nos omnes coluimus semper et colimus.' But he was at the same time an admirer of the young Marsilio Ficino ('et Marsilius Ficinus noster magna indole iuvenis adest testis'), and he seems to have acted as Ficino's spiritual adviser and also to have lent him money. Under Lorenzo il Magnifico Degli Agli's reputation remained high, and he was one of the nine scholars chosen to intervene at the banquet organised by Lorenzo in November 1474 to expound the *Symposium* of Plato. But his inclination as a humanist was to paddle rather than to swim, and he withdrew from the discussion. This was the man with whom Luca della Robbia came into regular, perhaps daily contact at Impruneta.

Our knowledge of Degli Agli's activities at Impruneta is hampered by an almost total lack of documents. The only surviving record is of a payment of four florins to Luca della Robbia on 20 November 1466, for unspecified work, made by the Camarlingo of the Compagnia di Santa Maria Impruneta; a careful search by Dr. Gino Corti has failed to reveal any further payments. The earliest work in the church must, however, have been undertaken soon after Degli Agli assumed control in 1439. Its scope was comparatively modest: to supply the miraculous image with an appropriate tabernacle. It was commissioned from an unidentified Michelozzan sculptor, and its form was rigidly conventional. It was flanked by fluted pilasters, supporting a narrow frieze and pediment and resting on a strip of strigillated ornament flanked by bearded profile heads imitated from those of the Parte Guelfa niche on Or San Michele. The only feature in it that is irregular arises from its function, and takes the form of a large central aperture springing from spiral colonnettes, in which the *Madonna* could be shown. It had a precedent in the altar in the Brancacci Chapel in which the *Madonna del Carmine* was housed. The Brancacci altar seems to have included a predella in low relief, Donatello's *Ascension with Christ giving the Keys to St. Peter*, in London, and the Impruneta altar also included a *schiacciato* relief in marble. Now separated from the tabernacle, it shows the landscape round Impruneta with a depiction of the discovery of the painting and of the building of the church. The relief has been ascribed to Luca della Robbia and to Filarete, but is more probably the work of a Donatello

imitator by whom at least two other reliefs are known.

Degli Agli is said to have spent twelve thousand gold florins on the improvement of the church at Impruneta and its adjacent buildings. The architect to whom he had recourse was Michelozzo, who built or reconstructed the two cloisters and incorporated the rather heterogeneous buildings into a square fortified structure complete with towers. The plan for the interior of the church was influenced by two contemporary Medici commissions. The first was the free-standing Chapel of the Crucifix constructed by Michelozzo in San Miniato al Monte in 1448–9, and the second the work that immediately succeeded it, the Chapel of the Annunciation designed by Michelozzo and executed by Pagno di Lapo Portigiani on the entrance wall of the Santissima Annunziata, which was dedicated in 1452. At some uncertain date, after 1452 and probably though not certainly before 1456, when Michelozzo left Florence for Milan, two similar Chapels were constructed at Impruneta (Cat. No. 15, Figs. 21, 22) in the corners of the nave to right and left of the high altar. One of them was dedicated to the cult of the Madonna and the other to that of the True Cross.

The Chapel of the Crucifix at San Miniato al Monte and the Chapel of the Annunciation in the Annunziata were luxury structures. In the rustic setting of Impruneta, conditions were very different, and in the interest of economy a number of changes were introduced. The most significant of them was that the polychrome marble frieze which ran round both the earlier chapels was omitted, and that provision was made instead for a frieze in enamelled terracotta. Luca was required in the first instance to produce an enamelled terracotta frieze and enamelled terracotta ceilings for the two Chapels. The ceiling at San Miniato was almost certainly designed by Michelozzo, but at Impruneta Luca was a free agent. The ceilings of the Chapel of the Madonna (Plate 82) and the Chapel of the Cross are uniform; they consist of twelve square tiles with elaborate white mouldings copied from those at San Miniato. In the centre of each is a yellow flower protruding from a fluted disc, which is in turn surrounded by a circular white frame. Outside this frame, in the corners of the containing square, are sprays of pine-needles and pine-cones which are contiguous with the outer moulding. The tiles are set in narrow bands of mauve and green edged with white. The reference of the pine-cones is to the title of the church, Santa Maria in Pineta.

In the frieze of the Chapel of the Madonna, Luca seems to have enjoyed the same autonomy. In the centre of each of the two faces is a relief of the *Virgin and Child* enamelled in white on a blue ground (Plates 84A, B). In both cases the composition is pyramidal; the Child is confined to the Virgin's containing silhouette, resting His head and hands on His mother's chest. The two reliefs seem to have been modelled separately and have a somewhat different character. In that on the front the Child is shown with wide-open eyes, and the Virgin wears a veil and looks downwards to her left. In that on the side the Child is represented in repose—the present relief is a modern reconstruction, but the original head is shown in pre-war photographs—the hair of the Virgin is more loosely modelled, her veil is dispensed with, and she looks down sadly at the Child with half-closed eyes. In type and structure the two reliefs conform to Luca's *Madonna* reliefs of the mid-fourteen-fifties and are related both to the *Bliss Madonna* in New York and to the more elaborate *Madonna with the Apple* in Berlin. Both are in low relief and are likely from the first to have been designed for reproduction. In the frieze each of the foliated strips (Plate 85) was modelled and fired in sections (there are six sections on the front and eight on the side of the tabernacle), and is so planned that the stems of the bunches of fruit extend horizontally in a single line and are tied with ribbon at the point of juncture of each section. In its full form—two sections on the side are abbreviated—each section showed four fruits, two above and two below the stem. Bunches of grapes, citrons, and quinces are represented, the sections with grapes alternating between sections with more brightly coloured fruits. The choice of fruit throughout the frieze is emblematic. The grapes represent the Eucharist, citrons were associated with the Virgin, and the quince was a common symbol of the Resurrection.

The church at Impruneta was severely damaged by bombardment in 1944, and though the altars and the enamelled terracotta sculptures were at once reconstructed, they must be looked at with this in mind (Col. Plates XVIII, XIX). In the Chapel of the Madonna both the frieze of fruit on the south face and the *Virgin and Child* in the centre were mutilated and have been extensively made up. Their original appearance can be assessed only from pre-war photographs. The *St. Paul* beside the tabernacle is substantially intact, but the right side of the *St. Luke* was pulverised and has been reconstructed; there is also local make-up elsewhere in this second figure. The Chapel of the Cross is less well preserved. In the ceiling, which is extensively made up, most of the interstices are painted in imitation of enamelling, and the upper half of the blue background on the left side of the altar wall is new. Both *Saints* sustained extensive damage, especially the *Bishop Saint*, a great part of whose robe and body is new. The nose of the *Baptist* has also been remade. There are local areas of damage in the pilasters of the enamelled terracotta tabernacle, the most conspicuous of which is on the right. In the *Crucifixion* relief the shaft of the Cross below the feet of Christ is restored in two places—the

grain of the wood, which is visible in the sections in enamelled terracotta, is not reproduced in those parts which are new—and sections at the back of the head of the Virgin and in the left arm of Christ have also been renewed. The illustrations in this book are made from old photographs or from new photographs of those parts which have not been seriously impaired.

Whereas the frieze of the Chapel of the Madonna was completed in the form originally planned, the corresponding frieze of the Chapel of the Cross was filled not with enamelled terracotta, but with two stucco reliefs showing small figures of putti adoring a central chalice with the Eucharist. In the war these two reliefs were destroyed, and there is now no means of determining for sure at what date they were made. A number of conflicting explanations for their presence have been advanced. It has been suggested that the frieze was originally filled with enamelled terracotta decoration like that of the Chapel of the Madonna opposite, and that this was removed and 'is probably still in existence hidden away in some French château or the cellars of some museum'. According to this theory the putative date of its removal would have been 1636, when the altar was modified by the Archduchess Maria Maddalena; the stucco frieze, with its eucharistic iconography, would also have dated from this time. It has also been suggested that only the front faces of the Chapels were decorated in enamelled terracotta, and that the relief on the side of the Chapel of the Madonna was transferred to that position from the front face of the chapel opposite. On technical grounds this is improbable. The stucco frieze has also been interpreted as a sketch model for an enamelled terracotta frieze which was not executed. Enlarged photographs from the available negatives of the frieze show that it must have dated from the fifteenth century. Probably it was designed as a definitive way of filling the frieze rather than as a model for the way in which the frieze was eventually to be filled.

The work at Impruneta is best understood if we accept that what confronts us there is not a single integrated scheme but an inorganic development prosecuted over a term of years. The first challenge was offered by the altar of the Chapel of the Madonna (Plate 81). Consisting as it did of a high marble ciborium and a wide marble predella, it must, on the completion of Michelozzo's superstructure, have looked ungainly and irregular. The means of reconciling it with the containing tabernacle that was adopted by Degli Agli and by Luca della Robbia was to place two enamelled terracotta Saints in deep relief beside the tabernacle and to set them on a blue enamelled terracotta ground. The space beside the tabernacle was limited, and this determined the size of the two figures, whose heads are on the level of the capitals of the interior arch. Both are portrayed frontally, with a slight inward axis, and the hand of the figure on the right, St. Luke, extends across the pilaster towards the miraculous painting. Both figures were enriched with surface gilding (now best preserved in the volume of epistles held by St. Paul) and stand on a section of porphyry-coloured ground. The type and drapery forms of the *St. Luke* recall those of the later roundels in the Pazzi Chapel and especially of the *St. James the Less* (Plate 50). These figures may have been produced about 1455–60.

There is no evidence as to the appearance at this time of the altar of the Chapel of the Cross. In addition to housing the relic of the True Cross it seems to have served as the Sacrament Altar of the church. At some uncertain date, probably after 1460, it was equipped with two figures of Saints corresponding with those on the altar opposite, on the left *St. John the Baptist* and on the right an *Episcopal Saint*, between them an enamelled terracotta relief of *Christ on the Cross with the Virgin and St. John*, and a predella of adoring angels flanking the ciborium (Col. Plate XVIII). The figures of Saints are clearly somewhat later in style than those on the first altar—the lower part of the robe of the *Bishop Saint* makes use of the curved rhythms that we find again in the roundels of the *Virtues* at San Miniato (Plate 80, Col. Plates XV–XVII) and the strongly modelled *Baptist* looks forward to the *St. James* in the left wing of the Pescia altarpiece (Plate 125A). The predella must date from the same time. The angels carry scrolls with eucharistic inscriptions presumably selected by Degli Agli (PROBET AVTEM SEIPSVM HOMO/ET SIC DE PANE ILLO EDAT and HIC EST PANIS VIVVS/QVI DE CELO DESCENDIT) and are once more related, in the freedom of their poses, their cursive drapery and their exquisitely modelled heads, to the roundels in the Chapel of the Cardinal of Portugal. The first of the inscriptions comes from St. Paul (1 Cor. xi, 28) and the second from St. John (vi, 59). As noted by Marquand, the latter occurs in the liturgy under the heading *Homilia Sancti Augustini Episcopi*, and it establishes that the Saint on the right of the altar is Augustine, not Zenobius.

The *Crucifixion* (Col. Plate XIX) is Luca della Robbia's greatest narrative relief. It is narrow in relation to its height (its dimensions were determined by the enframing tabernacle, and the height and width of the tabernacle were in turn determined by the marble tabernacle on the altar opposite), and it is spaced with sublime economy and confidence. The Christ, in a resolutely frontal pose broken only by the head, which is turned down compassionately towards the Virgin, is uncompromising in its classicism. Beneath the arms of the Cross, in a rear plane, are two lamenting angels, one with hands crossed on his breast, the other with arms flung desperately apart and one hand concealed by the figure on the Cross. Under them are lines of pale-blue cloud. Above Christ's head is the superscription, in majestic humanist lettering, and above this again the Cross bursts into leaf, the foliage forming a nest for the exquisitely rendered pelican. At the base the Cross is wedged into the rocky ground, and in a hollow under it is a grimacing skull. The Virgin stands in right profile, as though frozen into immobility, with hands clenched, gazing up towards Christ. St. John, also in profile and also with head upturned, strides strongly forward, his hands clasped in front of him.

If the relief was modelled, as is likely, soon after 1460, it takes its place among the great Crucifixion representations of the third quarter of the fifteenth century. The Christ is Brunelleschan—it recalls, and may have been inspired by, the wooden Crucifix of Brunelleschi in Santa Maria Novella—and the leafy extrusion from the Cross and the nesting pelican find their closest parallels in the *Crucifixion* of about 1450 by Fra Angelico in the Fogg Museum and in the painted Cross by Baldovinetti in the Annunziata. But the artist of whose presence we are most acutely conscious is Domenico Veneziano. The single precedent for the expressive use of profile in Luca's Virgin and St. John occurs in the predella of Domenico Veneziano's St. Lucy altarpiece, where the Saint and executioner in the *Martyrdom of St. Lucy* and the mother in the *Miracle of St. Zenobius* are treated in somewhat the same way. The possibility that Luca was also cognisant of Flemish paintings cannot be ruled out. Van der Weyden habitually depicts the Virgin with hands clenched in despair and invests St. John with the nervous forward movement that is shown here, and it is far from inconceivable that Luca, when he modelled this astonishing relief, was haunted by some recollection of a work by Van der Weyden of the date of the *Entombment* in the Uffizi or of an Eyckian *Crucifixion* like that in the Ca' d'Oro.

The tabernacle that surrounds the *Crucifixion* relief is based upon Luca's marble tabernacle from Santa Maria Nuova, and based on it so closely that at the time that it was made the point of reference could be in no doubt. The proportions are a little different (if the tabernacle was to conform in size to the tabernacle in the Cappella della Madonna it was inevitable that this should be so), and it is constructed wholly of enamelled terracotta. But as we read down it from top to bottom the elements remain the same. There is a pediment surrounded by a heavy moulding (which may originally have been intended for a figure of God the Father, though it is now void of figure sculpture); there is a guilloche frieze, adapted from that on the base of the tabernacle at Peretola (Col. Plate I) in which the small circles are filled with yellow flowers; there are decorated spandrels, in which the fluted circles at Peretola are replaced by blue discs and the leaf decoration round them is replaced by green enamelling; there are pilasters, not the fluted classical pilasters of Peretola but pilasters covered with white acanthus scroll-work on a background of which the sections in the centre and at the top and bottom are porphyry and those between are green and blue; and beneath, in place of the strip of enamelled terracotta decoration used at Peretola, is a base in three sections consisting of flat enamelled pine-cones framed in blue. Throughout, the colour and the ornament deny the substance of the architectural forms in a fashion which has no precedent in Luca's earlier works. Pilasters covered with surface decoration are a common feature in the work of Andrea della Robbia—they occur, for example, in 1479 in the Niccolini *Annunciation* and the Brizi *Incarnation* at La Verna as well as in other altar-pieces probably dating from the fourteen-seventies—

but the design is invariably less ambitious and the colour less rich and varied than it is here. Two factors speak decisively for Luca's authorship. The first is the modelling of the small reversed white flowers, which form an equivalent in relief for the flat reversed flowers in the border of the Federighi monument. The second is that the flat pine-cones are portrayed in a blue recess, which is lit, like the *Labours of the Months* from the Palazzo Medici, from a point high on the left. This device has no equivalent in Andrea della Robbia. The importance of the tabernacle for Andrea della Robbia and for the whole future of sculpture in enamelled terracotta none the less was very great. When Andrea designed the *Crucifixions* in the Cappella delle Stimmate at La Verna and in the Cathedral at Arezzo, and modelled the eucharistic angels in the predella of the La Verna *Madonna della Cintola*, his point of departure was Luca's decoration of the Chapel of the Cross.

VIII NON-FIGURATIVE SCULPTURE

In the fifteenth century it was an accepted practice that the holders of public office should leave traces of their tenure in the form of painted or carved *stemmi* or coats-of-arms. In Florence, in the Bargello, this was the prerogative of the Podestà, as it was also at Pistoia and Arezzo. Elsewhere, at Scarperia and Certaldo and San Giovanni Valdarno, the Vicars and Commissaries appointed by the Florentine state customarily left, in the Palazzo Pretorio, a record of their names, their arms, and the year in which they held their offices. When a carved coat-of-arms was needed for this purpose, it was, in the normal course, commissioned from a stonemason not from a sculptor. By and large the results were undistinguished, though occasionally they reached a level which has tempted recent students to ascribe them to known artists, in one case to Luca della Robbia (Cat. No. 62, Fig. 56). From the fourteen-sixties on, however, a change takes place, and as visitors to Scarperia or San Giovanni can see with their own eyes, the carved *stemma* was progressively replaced by a *stemma* in enamelled terracotta.

Luca della Robbia's first involvement with this class of commission dates from 1463, when the Mercanzia, who had purchased the tabernacle of the Parte Guelfa on Or San Michele three years before, agreed that a new statue should be commissioned for the tabernacle and that the *stemma* of the Parte Guelfa above the vacant niche should be replaced. It was stressed in the record of this decision that the treatment of the tabernacle must demonstrate that the reputation of the Mercanzia surpassed that of the guilds who occupied the other tabernacles on the building. A powerful committee, headed by Piero di Cosimo de' Medici, representing the Arte di Calimala, and including Leonardo Bartolini, Dietisalvi Neroni, Pandolfo di Giannozzo Pandolfini, and Matteo Palmieri, was appointed to implement this resolution. Action on the new statue was deferred, probably till 1465, when a commission seems to have been placed with Verrocchio for the bronze group of *Christ and St. Thomas* that still occupies the niche. The replacement of the *stemma*, on the other hand, presented an easier problem, and in January or February 1463 the commission for an enamelled terracotta *stemma* to fill

the stone roundel that had contained the emblem of the Parte Guelfa was awarded to Luca della Robbia. By September the roundel was practically complete (Cat. No. 16, Col. Plate XXII).

In awarding the commission, the officials of the Mercanzia aimed at securing a work which would dominate its setting, and this Luca della Robbia supplied. In practice the use of enamelled terracotta involved a double substitution, of purple for *gules*, the familiar red of the Florentine fleur-de-lys, and of white for *argent*, the colour both of the shield and of the corded bale of the Arte di Calimala at its base. The central shield is balanced against a fluted shell, and the border of fruit and vegetables is made in eight parts. It consists of sixteen bunches of fruit tied with blue ribbons and interspersed with white and violet flowers. In its comparatively shallow modelling it recalls the frieze of the Chapel of the Madonna at Impruneta, but whereas at Impruneta only three symbolic fruits are shown, here there is no repetition, and the sixteen bunches comprise sixteen different types of produce: citrons, beans, pomegranates, chestnuts, apples, artichokes, cucumbers, pine-cones, quinces, plums, grapes, poppies, oranges, figs, pears and olives. Though on the inner edge a number of the leaves overlap the leaf-and-dart moulding, nowhere does the frieze approach the baroque exuberance of Luca's later work. Its sculptural interest rests in the handling of the central emblem. Here, for the first and perhaps the only time, the seeded fleur-de-lys becomes a colossal, obstreperous natural form which assumes its own organic life. As we see it from the street below, it reads with unprecedented strength.

Three other stone roundels above the niches on Or San Michele were filled in the fifteenth century with *stemmi* in enamelled terracotta. None of them is exactly datable, but it is likely that the two designed and carried out by Luca della Robbia follow, and do not precede, the *stemma* of the Mercanzia. The first is the *stemma* of the Arte dei Medici e degli Speziali (Cat. No. 17, Col. Plate XXI, Plate 86). The armorial device of the guild was the Virgin and Child in a tabernacle supported by Annunciation lilies. It appears in this form on an escutcheon displayed on the façade of the residence of the guild in the Palazzo de' Lamberti, on the guild *gonfalone*, and elsewhere. The guild tabernacle on the south side of Or San Michele had been filled in 1399 with a seated *Virgin and Child* in marble by Niccolò di Pietro Lamberti, and the roundel above, like the roundel over the other tabernacles, almost certainly contained the painted *stemma* of the guild. The Arte dei Medici e degli Speziali was the body in which Florentine painters by rule matriculated, and for it Luca produced an overtly pictorial relief. Across the bottom of the roundel there runs a platform from which rises the tabernacle, an arched structure resting on two columns. The orthodox background of the emblem was *azure*, and outside the tabernacle are two clumps of three-stemmed lilies in green and white on a blue ground. The interior of the tabernacle is backed by a curtain with a pattern of yellow quatrefoils which are set against green fern leaves interspersed with blue, yellow-centred flowers. An analogy for the fern leaves occurs in the tabernacle of the Chapel of the Crucifix at Impruneta, and the roundel on Or San Michele may date from the same time. The Virgin, an emblematic not a devotional image, is seated on a blue-green bench spotted with yellow, and wears a blue cloak with a green lining over a violet dress with yellow neckband and green sleeves. Though pallid, her face is pigmented in a semi-naturalistic fashion, with dark-blue eyebrows, eyelashes and pupils, and both she and the Child have yellow hair. The vivid polychromy of the Virgin's robe would in itself suggest a dating in the fourteen-sixties, and this is corroborated by the egg-and-dart moulding of the tabernacle which, as Marquand observed, is related to mouldings employed in the Chapel of the Cardinal of Portugal and not to those in earlier works. This late dating is also confirmed by the drapery style, which recalls that of the *St. Augustine* on the bronze door in the Cathedral. If the relationship of the roundel to contemporary painting rested solely in its use of colour, this would be remarkable enough, but the connection seems to have been more deliberate. The Child is a variant in reverse of the Child in a celebrated panel painting by Domenico Veneziano, the altarpiece from Santa Lucia dei Magnoli, now in the Uffizi, while the Virgin, with her high-waisted dress, brocaded collar and flaxen hair, is related to the *Madonnas* by Domenico Veneziano in the Berenson Collection and in the National Gallery of Art in Washington. These connections are so specific as to compel us to take account of the possibility that Domenico Veneziano was, directly or obliquely, responsible for its design. For a number of reasons this is unlikely to have been the case. The internal evidence for dating the *stemma* in the middle of the fourteen-sixties is very strong, and it can hardly therefore have been designed by an artist who had died in 1461. Moreover, the works by Domenico Veneziano that it brings to mind were executed not during the fourteen-fifties but a decade earlier.

The third of Luca's roundels on Or San Michele, that of the Arte dei Maestri di Pietra e di Legname (Cat. No. 18, Col. Plate XX), is pictorial in a rather different sense. The guild was one with which Luca had a close personal association; he was elected to it in 1432 and played some part in its administration until a year before his death. Its tabernacle on the north face of the building had been filled in the second decade of the century with statues by Nanni di Banco of the Quattro Santi Coronati, and beneath it was a predella showing artisans engaged in building a stone wall, carving a spiral column, measuring a capital, and blocking out the statue of a child. The roundel shows the emblem of the guild, an axe, surrounded by implements depicted in the predella, a blue trowel for the builders or *muratori*, a hammer and chisels for the carvers or *scarpellini*, and calipers and a T-square for the architects. The enamelled terracotta roundel undoubtedly replaced an earlier painting; its design has a generic relationship to those of the few guild ceiling frescoes that are preserved. Interest is concentrated not on the implements, but on the large central circle and on the four subsidiary circles at the top, bottom and sides with their guilloche decoration in three shades of blue. The emblem of the guild was an axe *argent* on a field *gules*, and in the central circle placed diagonally is an axe with a white blade and yellow handle on a purple ground covered with foliated ornament. The emblems in the four subsidiary circles are also white, but are set on discs covered with pale-green arabesques. Between the smaller circles are large, paired, five-petalled flowers in blue surrounded by green foliage that overlaps the white edge of the guilloche bands. On their much larger scale the flowers of the *stemma* recall those inserted between the flower-filled lozenges of the Federighi monument. The method by which Luca gives life to this large roundel is indeed evolved from that used in the Federighi frame, in that the outlines of the flowers and foliage are incised and were filled before glazing with gold powder or gold paint. When the surface was less obfuscated than it is today, this must have lent the roundel exceptional depth and resonance. Vasari regarded the *stemma* as experimental, and if it were made, as is likely, about 1465, it would represent the climax of Luca's experiments in the treatment of unincidented surfaces. The care with which it was pigmented can be deduced from the fact that it was glazed in fourteen parts.

From public manifestos, which the *stemmi* on Or San Michele were from the first designed to be, the way lay open to the private manifestos of family armorial bearings which are still found today at the entrances to so many palaces. For Alberti the palace was the physical embodiment of the family for whom it was named or by whom it had been built. This view was general in the fifteenth century, and for that reason special care was taken to provide the palace with a carved *stemma* or *impresa* of high quality. There is no evidence that Donatello was involved in commissions of this kind, though he was widely credited in the nineteenth century with the *stemma* of the Martelli, but Desiderio da Settignano seems to have made something of a speciality of heraldic sculpture, and the proficiency with which he handled it is attested by the great Minerbetti *stemma* at Detroit. In this context the potential of enamelled terracotta was very great, and the first patron to recognise it was Jacopo Pazzi, a member of the family for whom Luca della Robbia had worked at Santa Croce.

Best known for his part in the Pazzi conspiracy of 1478, Jacopo de' Pazzi is the subject of a malign character sketch by Politian, who describes his gaming and swearing, his ambition, arrogance, and wastefulness. Written from the standpoint of the victorious Medici and inspired by Sallust's account of Catiline, Politian's *Conjurationis Pactianae anni MCCCCLXXVIII Commentarius* depicts him as a man who embodied in a supreme degree in his own person the pride of which his family was commonly accused. This view seems to have been general. Guicciardini stigmatised the Pazzi as 'troppo superbi e altieri,' and Machiavelli cites this as the reason why Jacopo and his nephews did not receive the honours that they seemed to merit. Jacopo de' Pazzi was not excluded from public office—he headed embassies to the Emperor and the King of Naples, served ten years as *Priore*, on three occasions was a member of the *Otto*, and in 1469 became *Gonfaloniere di Giustizia*— but his civic rewards were generally conceded to be less than his deserts. In France, on the other hand, he received the recognition that was denied him in Florence. When King René of Anjou visited Florence, as claimant to the throne of Naples, in 1442, he was entertained by Andrea de' Pazzi at the Loggia de' Pazzi at Montughi, and a long-standing relationship ensued with other members of the Pazzi family, Piero de' Pazzi, to whose son, Renato, René stood godfather, Antonio de' Pazzi, who later undertook an embassy to the Angevin Court, and above all with their brother, Jacopo de' Pazzi. Through the years Jacopo de' Pazzi received a succession of appointments at the Angevin court, first as *clavaire* at Marseilles, then as Conseiller du Roi, and then as Maître d'Hôtel du Roi. A document of 1468 refers to him as 'consiliarium et cambellanum nostrum fidelem dilectum.' In 1453 he became a member of the recently instituted Order of the Crescent. At one time he appears also to have acted for King René in collecting works of art. The only independent mid-century Pazzi commission of which there is a record is due to Piero de' Pazzi, who at about the time of King René's visit, probably in 1443, ordered from Castagno, for the altar wall of the chapel in the Castello di Trebbio in Val di Sieci, a fresco showing his two elder children, Niccolò and Orietta, proudly holding a vase and chaplet of flowers beside the Virgin's throne, beneath a circle, now void, which may have been painted with the Pazzi arms.

After Andrea de' Pazzi died in October 1445, control of the principal artistic project to which the Pazzi were committed, the Pazzi Chapel in Santa Croce, passed first to Antonio de' Pazzi and then to Jacopo, and when in October 1473 after the completion of the Chapel a brief of indulgences was promulgated, Jacopo de' Pazzi was named as the founder of the Chapel. It is to Jacopo, therefore, that the revision in the late fourteen-fifties of the principles governing the decoration of the Chapel must be attributed. The first decision affected its interior. In 1459 the cupola was at last complete, and the circular stone frames introduced by Brunelleschi in the pendentives could be filled. It was decided that they should be supplied with large figures of the four Evangelists (which were iconographically inapposite since two Evangelists, Saints John and Matthew, were already represented on the walls), that they should be enamelled with strong polychromy, and that, though glazed in the Della Robbia shop, they should be modelled not by Luca but by Donatello. At the same time Brunelleschi's intentions for the chapel were violated in another, more significant respect, in that an external portico was built on to the façade. This work seems to have been entrusted to Giuliano da Majano, who in the autumn of 1478, after the failure of the Pazzi conspiracy, entered a claim on the estate of Jacopo de' Pazzi for work undertaken in the Palazzo Pazzi, the Loggia de' Pazzi at Montughi, and the Pazzi Chapel. It is known from an inscription that the construction of the cupola in the middle of the portico was finished in July 1461. This change affected Luca della Robbia in two ways. In the first place he was constrained to fill the vacant roundel over the chapel door with a figure of St. Andrew (who, like two of the Evangelists, was already portrayed in the interior of the chapel) (Plate 59). In the second he was required to line the cupola with enamelled terracotta.

The design of the interior of the cupola (Cat. No. 9, Col. Plate IX) is, in the context both of the work of Luca della Robbia and of mid-fifteenth-century Florentine decoration as a whole, one of extreme complexity. The surface is filled with four concentric circles of sixteen circular white frames decorated with laurel wreaths. Inside the frames are blue fluted, concave circles and in the centre of each is a yellow flower. The roundels diminish in size as they reach the top of the cupola. The area between them is coloured in simulated porphyry and *verde antico*, and again contains a yellow flower. The intention of these devices was illusionistic. The eye is carried up to the Pazzi arms, two gold dolphins on a blue field decorated with five crosslets, displayed on a fluted violet circle in the centre of the cupola, surrounded by a frieze of flowers and fruit of greater richness and elaboration than any Luca had planned before. The fruit seem to have been selected from those shown on the Mercanzia roundel, but for reasons of effect are replicated, so that each of the eight sections contains only one type of flower or fruit. They are, moreover, modelled in greater depth and are not segregated in bunches but are continuous. It can be inferred from this that the interior of the cupola was designed and executed after the Mercanzia roundel, probably in 1465–70. When this brilliant scheme was new, it must have seemed that the immemorial custom of imposing the donor's arms upon a benefaction was carried to a new level of ostentation and pretentiousness.

Among Jacopo de' Pazzi's achievements, Politian records the supererogatory rebuilding of the Palazzo Pazzi. It has been argued that the reconstructed palace was completed by 1469, but it seems that the old Palazzo Pazzi was still standing in that year and that the new palace dates from the early 1470s. For the palace Luca designed two large heraldic roundels with the arms of Jacopo de' Pazzi and his wife, Maddalena de' Serristori (Cat. Nos. 19, 20, Plates 88, 89). In the nineteenth century, when the Palazzo Pazzi was known as the Palazzo Quaratesi, the two *stemmi* were in a room on the first floor, but they may originally have been intended for use either in the cortile of the old Palazzo Pazzi before it was rebuilt or in that of the new structure. The only evidence for dating is a crescent that appears under the arms of Jacopo de' Pazzi and proves that the two roundels must postdate his admission to the Order of the Crescent in 1453. They were planned as a pair; in the *stemma* with the Pazzi arms the border of fruit runs clockwise, in that with the Serristori arms it runs in the opposite direction. The borders, though continuous, have more in common with the Mercanzia *stemma* than with that in the cupola of the portico of the Pazzi Chapel. The *stemma* of Jacopo de' Pazzi was mutilated, supposedly by an angry mob after the Pazzi conspiracy of 1478, when Medici *palle* (now removed) were superimposed on the relief.

The last and most splendid of Jacopo de' Pazzi's heraldic commissions can be dated more precisely. It shows the arms of his patron, King René of Anjou (Cat. No. 21, Plate 87, Col. Plates XXIII, XXIV), surmounted by an escutcheon in pretence for the Kingdom of Aragon, the crown of which was offered to René by the Catalans late in 1466. The *stemma* must therefore have been made after this time. Almost twice as large as the preceding *stemmi*, it was designed for the Loggia de' Pazzi at Montughi, where it was set in an external wall at a great height from the ground. The claim made by Giuliano da Majano in 1478 against Jacopo de' Pazzi's estate includes a reference to work at Montughi of which we have no other record, and it may be that Luca's *stemma* formed part of the same scheme. The shield proper is surmounted by a crowned helmet closed, from which rises the crest, a fleur-de-lys *or* between two dragon wings. Behind the shield and helmet is the ermine-lined mantle of Anjou. Above the crest, in tree-trunk capitals, are the initials of René of Anjou and his second wife, Jeanne de Laval; below the shield is a collar inscribed LOS : EN : CROISSANT : ; and on either side is a gold brazier with pierced rim, from which there issue purple flames. From the inner handles of the braziers hangs a band with the motto DARDANT DESIR, and on the base of the brazier on the left are the five crosslets of the Pazzi arms. Round the heraldic relief runs a border of purple (used throughout for *gules*) figured with a white fillet raguly (for *argent*). Though the arms are those of René of Anjou, they relate also to the Pazzi family, in that the flaming brazier was likewise a Pazzi emblem. To describe the roundel in conventional heraldic terms is, however, to give no impression of the visual effect made by the dragon wings, the open ermine cloak, and the purple flames ascending over the green ground. It has been suggested that a drawing of the coat-of-arms was supplied by the Anjou court, probably by the herald of the Order of the Crescent, and this may have been so, but no northern model can explain either the vitality of the design or the tactile qualities of the relief, which are personal to Luca della Robbia. The devices whereby movement is suggested in the rising flames are the same as those used in the flowing hair of *Temperance* in the Chapel of the Cardinal of Portugal, the relation of the wings to the containing circle is anticipated in the *Justice*, and the confident integration of the heraldic shield in the whole scheme has a precedent in the *Fortitude*. This extraordinary work is Luca della Robbia's decorative masterpiece.

The heraldic roundel is recessed within a frame in fourteen sections which contains the most ambitious fruit border in Luca's entire oeuvre. Though the effect is once more continuous, it represents twenty-eight bunches of fruit attached to a central branch by a white band. Seven types of fruit are shown—pine-cones, pears, lemons (or oranges), quinces, figs, grapes and cucumbers —and there are four bunches of each. An exceptional feature of this border is its size. The fruits are larger, richer and more voluptuous than the living fruit from which they depend, and there is no reason to doubt that they were in large part modelled personally by Luca della Robbia.

In Imperial Rome there is a perceptible development from the generalised fruit garlands suspended from bucranes which occur on so many Augustan friezes and cinerary altars to exactly rendered branches of orange and lemon trees such as we find on a Trajanic relief in the Lateran Museum. A rather similar development separates the garlands in the frieze of the tabernacle at Peretola (Col. Plate I) from the fruit border of the *stemma* of René of Anjou. Some indication of the spirit that infused Trajanic carvings of fruit and vegetables is provided by a verse section on gardening in the tenth book of Columella's *De Re Rustica*, with its apostrophe of cultivable fruit and vegetables, the 'prickly artichoke', the Punic tree (pomegranate), 'the twisted cucumber and swelling gourd,' damsons and apricots, panniers piled high with plums, Persian and Gallic peaches, and Chalcidian, Caunian, and Lydian figs. In Florence in the fifteenth century there was also a sophisticated interest in horticulture, and especially in the growing of fruit. Filarete, in a passage that abuts on that describing the study of Piero de' Medici, mentions a fish pond in the garden 'round which are planted a great many fruit trees from different regions, namely figs, pears, apples, plums, cherries, damsons, and other similar fruits,' and about 1470 we find in the *Memorie* of Benedetto Dei a careful list of seven categories of melon, seven types of fig, seven sorts of mushroom, and six kinds of pear. In the *Zibaldone*, Giovanni Ruccellai likewise describes the garden of his villa, with its bay trees, its figs and plums and juniper, and its white and pink rosebushes trained on trellises, which, when they were in flower, appeared so beautiful that he was unable with his pen to describe the consolation that the eye received in looking at them. The part which discriminating natural depiction might play in Renaissance sculpture had been sketched out by Ghiberti at the end of the first quarter of the fifteenth century on the inner and outer jambs of the north door of the Baptistry (Figs. 37, 38). With marble sculptors Ghiberti's message fell on deaf ears; the most aspiring piece of naturalistic marble carving, Bernardo Rossellino's doorway in the Siena Palazzo Pubblico, looks dull and academic beside the vivid modelling of the first door. For sculpture in enamelled terracotta, on the other hand, the lesson of Ghiberti was of decisive consequence. The euphuistic chasing of bronze casts gave way to clay shaped directly in the artist's hands, and when the element of colour was added to that of form, the age-old sense of wonder at the riches of the natural world received in the new medium its supreme embodiment.

IX THE MADONNA RELIEFS

One of the factors that distinguish Florentine sculpture in the fifteenth century from that produced in any other centre is the popularity of the half-length *Madonna* relief. To judge from the number of examples that survive, there can have been few prosperous houses or oratories in Florence in which a relief of the Virgin and Child, sometimes in marble, more often in the reproductive medium of painted stucco or terracotta, was not to be found. From the fourteen-twenties on, this type of sculpture was produced commercially, moulded in sculptors' workshops and pigmented in painters' studios. By this means the *Madonnas* of Donatello and other artists were given general currency. Though Luca's reliefs of the Virgin and Child are among his most profound and cogitated works, it is against the background of this activity that they must be judged. They were produced over a period of almost fifty years for a market which at the outset was dominated by Ghiberti and Donatello and at the close was glutted with reproductions of works by Desiderio da Settignano, Antonio Rossellino, Verrocchio and Benedetto da Majano. But the philosophy behind them was rather different. They were from the first divisible into two classes, works designed for reproduction (and after about 1440 for reproduction in enamelled terracotta) and works that were and that remained unique.

The first shop which attempted to match the demand for these devotional images with supply was that of Ghiberti. From it there emerged, in the fourteen-twenties, three small *Madonna* reliefs in terracotta couched in the idiom of the first bronze door. In one, now at Rochester (New York), the head of the Child is based on that of Christ in the panel of *Christ teaching in the Temple*; in another, formerly in the Silten collection, the headdress of the Virgin and the type and modelling of the Child recall the panel of the *Adoration of the Magi*; and in a third, a tondo in Berlin, a Child like that in the Silten *Madonna* is shown reaching forwards like the Judas in the *Betrayal of Christ*. The first and third of these reliefs are unique, and the second exists in only two versions. They were followed, seemingly in the middle of the fourteen-thirties, by two *Madonna* reliefs that exist in so many versions as to be

literally innumerable. In these the Virgin is shown in half-length supporting the Child on her left arm. In one she holds His left foot with her right hand and His right foot rests on her wrist; in the other the Child's left foot touches the back of the Virgin's right hand and His left leg is extended along her wrist. Both reliefs are moulded in one with a raised base, and were intended to stand, not to be hung. Generally the base shows two putti with a wreath and two blank shields (which would have been filled in for the purchaser of the relief), but in three versions of the second composition the base is decorated with a mould made from the Eve on the Porta del Paradiso. Probably these two reliefs continued in production after Ghiberti's death, through the sixties and seventies of the fifteenth century.

About 1430 Donatello entered the field. He did so with a masterpiece in marble, the *Pazzi Madonna*, from which, soon after it was made, coarse stucco derivatives were produced. Also in the fourteen-thirties he modelled a bronze plaquette of the *Virgin and Child* and a circular gilt bronze relief of the *Virgin and Child with two Angels*, now in Vienna, from both of which pigmented stucco replicas were made. It was, moreover, Donatello who first experimented in a systematic fashion with modelled reliefs planned as raised paintings. Two of these, one in the Louvre, and the other, much damaged, in East Berlin, survive. Concurrently he produced reliefs designed for reproduction, like the *Verona Madonna*, which was modelled in Padua but must have been sold extensively in Florence, and a bronze roundel of the *Virgin and Child with four Angels*, made as a gift for Giovanni Chellini but diffused in the form of stucco copies throughout Tuscany. Other artists engaged in the second quarter of the century in producing reliefs in multiple versions for private devotion were Nanni di Bartolo and Buggiano.

Luca della Robbia was certainly involved in the making of *Madonna* reliefs before 1428, when he produced a bronze relief of which the original is lost but which is known through a dated stucco replica in the Ashmolean Museum (Cat. No. 22, Plate 90A). The dominant influence in this work, and especially in the two adoring angels at the sides, is that of Ghiberti, but the triangular formulation of the group and the wide face of the Virgin are already typical of Luca della Robbia. Not long after, perhaps about 1430, he seems to have evolved another composition for reproduction, this time rectangular, in which the Virgin in half-length supports the standing Child (Cat. No. 23, Plate 90B). Here the type of the Virgin and the fluent, rather ingratiating pose of the Child closely recall the Oxford roundel. This relief is known only in coarsely moulded versions in Berlin and in the Musée Jacquemart-André.

The panels of the Cantoria provide the only criteria of judgement for Luca's *Madonna* reliefs from the fourteen-thirties. The first (Cat. No. 24, Plate 92), in Berlin (D.D.R.), is in pigmented terracotta, but is modelled not moulded. It has no background, and its shallow base, cut away across the corners, is already in a form that is preserved in Luca's later *Madonna* reliefs. The Virgin is set frontally, with her head turned to the right towards the Child; with her right hand she holds the Child's right foot. The modelling of her head and hair is smooth and confident, and her cloak falls over her right arm naturalistically, as though it were fabric and not clay. What, however, puts Luca's authorship beyond all doubt is not this figure but the Child, whose pinched, almost emaciated features closely correspond with those of the seated child with right arm raised in the right foreground of the *Players on the Cithara* (Plate 9). The marble relief was carved before 1434, and the Berlin *Madonna* must date from the same time.

Throughout the fourteen-thirties Luca was closely associated with Buggiano, and there are four stucco or terracotta reliefs, all of them known through multiple examples of inferior quality, which have been variously given to Buggiano and to Luca della Robbia (Cat. No. 25). The first work by Buggiano that we know, a marble *Madonna and Child* set in the back of the altar of the Old Sacristy of San Lorenzo, dates from 1432. One of the stucco reliefs (Berlin, I. 1724, Fig. 26) was manifestly made by the same sculptor. It shows the Virgin in right profile looking down at a Child inflated like a rubber tire, placed diagonally across the corner of the composition. In the marble relief the disproportionately large haloes of both figures are severed by a moulding, and in the stucco they protrude beyond the frame. This is an unattractive composition, but it must have been well known, since versions are found at Villamagna and Berlin, as well as in the Rijksmuseum and in the Musée Jacquemart-André in Paris. The second relief (Berlin, I. 146) is more ambiguous. It shows the Virgin with her head turned in somewhat the same way, with the Child standing on her right sheltering beneath her cloak. In this composition the Child is more strongly classical and recalls indeed the child on the extreme right of Luca della Robbia's *Tambourine Players* (Plate 17). But an attribution to Luca is ruled out by the formal inco-

herence of the design, and we must suppose that this, too, is by Buggiano, and was made shortly before 1440, when he was cognisant of the Cantoria reliefs. In the third relief (Berlin, I. 64, Plate 91A), the Virgin has a generic resemblance to the Virgin in the two previous stuccos and faces three-quarters to the right, while the Child stands to the right with legs apart and head upturned towards her. The design has the organic character that the other reliefs lack, and the head of the Child recalls those of the children in the *Players on the Psaltery* (Plate 5). This relief was very popular; versions of it, none of them of first-rate quality, are found in Berlin, the Musée Jacquemart-André, the Norton Simon Foundation, the Bargello and the Museo Bardini. The problem of the fourth relief (Berlin, I. 142, Fig. 27) is more difficult. It is a noble, indeed distinguished composition in which the Virgin is represented frontally, and the Child moves across her body as though in surprise, with His body and left leg disposed in a continuous diagonal. The nature of the composition is consistent with Luca's imaginative processes, but the types of the figures are difficult to reconcile with his, and the closest parallel for the head of the Child occurs in a late work by Buggiano, a marble putto head in the spandrel of the Cardini Chapel in San Francesco at Pescia. Regardless of their authorship, these stuccos represent an effort to meet the need for reproductive *Madonna* reliefs made by artists in the circle of Brunelleschi.

It has already been suggested that Luca's first experiments with enamelling must have been conducted while work on the Cantoria was in progress. In this connection two *Madonnas*, closely interrelated in design, are of particular importance. The first, formerly in Berlin (Cat. No. 26, Plate 91B), is recorded only in unflattering photographs. Modelled in terracotta, it was not designed for reproduction and portrayed the Virgin in rather more than half-length looking down towards the Child, who wore a tunic and was shown with raised right hand touching her chin. The head of the Virgin was tipped slightly backwards like two of the heads in the *Players on the Psaltery* (Plate 5), and her freely modelled hair was bound by a fillet like those worn by the *Psaltery Players*. The curly-haired Child recalled, more superficially, the right-hand child in the foreground of the same relief. The surface was covered with white glaze which had 'crawled', leaving the terracotta visible, and had then been covered with paint. The conclusion that this was an early trial in enamelling is inescapable. Despite its failure, Luca was not unnaturally reluctant to abandon the invention in this relief, and from it he prepared a second version, now at Copenhagen (Cat. No. 27, Plate 93), where the Child is represented nude and the glazing is successful; it is enamelled in white on a blue ground. The dating of the two reliefs is necessarily arbitrary, but the probability is that they were made in the middle of the fourteen-thirties, about 1435–7.

If defective glazing is, as it appears to be, a clue to the dating of the earliest enamelled terracotta reliefs, we are bound also to regard as a work of about 1438 the so-called *Friedrichstein Madonna*. It derives its name from a lost version in the Kaiser Friedrich Museum in Berlin and exists in a second version in the Albright-Knox Art Gallery at Buffalo (Cat. No. 28, Col. Plate XXV). Modelled in one with its ground and its surrounding frame, it shows the Virgin and Child in a window, represented in perspective in white glaze, round which is a flat frame decorated with vivid green strips on a white ground with blue discs at the corners. The class of composition to which it relates is that of the Virgin in artificially constructed interior space, which was initiated about 1430 in the *Pazzi Madonna* of Donatello and was pursued, in a marble relief with blue glass inlay in the Bargello, by a disciple of Michelozzo. In sentiment and pose and especially in the treatment of her cloak, the Virgin recalls the Virgin in the Copenhagen *Madonna*, and the folds of drapery under the Child's thigh are related to the tunics of the dancing figures in the *Trumpeters* (Plate 2). Stylistically, therefore, there is a presumption that the relief is a work of the late fourteen-thirties. The jarring colour in the frame anticipates the glazing of the tabernacle at Peretola. Technically the *Friedrichstein Madonna* is an inexperienced work. Photographs of the version in Berlin reveal a number of firing cracks in the left arm of the Child, across the Virgin's shoulder, and on her right hand, and in the relief at Buffalo, also as a result of faulty firing, the glaze has flaked on the Child's dress over His thigh, on the upper surface of the Virgin's left hand, and in the surrounding white frame. The two reliefs seem to have been made from a single mould and represent an early attempt by Luca to rival in enamelled terracotta the pigmented terracotta reliefs of Ghiberti and Buggiano. At a much later date the difficulties which are so clearly evident on the surface of the relief at Buffalo were overcome, and Luca learned to produce moulded reliefs for reproduction of which each example was of consistently high quality.

In close proximity to the *Friedrichstein Madonna* Luca seems to have evolved a second composition, known, from a later version in enamelled terracotta, as the *Corsini Madonna* (Cat. No. 29, Plate 94A). From the examples that survive—mainly in painted stucco, though a small version in stone was inserted over the lintel of a *pietra serena* doorway in Santa Maria Nuova—we must suppose that it was very popular. It shows the Virgin and Child in a circular concave field, and at the time it was produced, about 1440, it represented a strikingly progressive solution of the geometry of the tondo form. The version illustrated here is exceptional in that it is rectangular.

Since Luca's *Madonnas* were first studied, it has been recognised that the only means of dating them is afforded by their relationship to larger compositions which include figures of the Virgin and Child. That the resulting chronologies have been so various and so erratic is due in the first place to the misdating of one large lunette, that from San Pier Buonconsiglio, now in the Palazzo di Parte Guelfa, which was regarded by Bode as an early and by Marquand as a very early work, and in the second place to the fact that Bode and Marquand included among Luca's early works another relief, of the *Madonna and Child between two Angels*, the so-called Via dell'Agnolo lunette, which stood over the door of the former convent of the Santucce and is now in the Bargello (Cat. No. 69, Fig. 45). As long ago as 1915 it was pointed out that the building history of the convent was inconsistent with the early dating ascribed to the relief, and that it was made between 1470, when permission to establish the convent was granted by Sixtus IV, and 1495, when the premises were made over to San Pier Maggiore. The lunette is not a late work by Luca but a relatively early work by Andrea della Robbia.

In these circumstances the best course is to proceed at once to the only *Madonna* lunette by Luca della Robbia that is exactly datable. Now in the Galleria Nazionale delle Marche (Cat. No. 30, Fig. 24, Plate 95), it originally stood over the entrance to the church of San Domenico at Urbino (Fig. 23). An interim payment for it of four florins was made by Fra Bartolomeo da Urbino, the painter Fra Carnevale, on 19 June 1450. The payment was made through Maso di Bartolomeo, with whom Luca was associated both at San Miniato al Monte and in the commission for the bronze sacristy door in the Cathedral, and it was Maso di Bartolomeo who constructed the doorway of which the relief formed part. It shows the Virgin and Child in the centre on a blue ground and at the sides, segregated from the main group, SS. Dominic, Thomas Aquinas, Albertus Magnus, and Peter Martyr. From old photographs it can be seen that the architrave of the doorway established the front plane of the relief and created a platform on which the book held by St. Peter Martyr and the feet of the Child appeared to rest. The back plane was established by the stone moulding, which was cut decisively by the heads of the Virgin and of the two forward Saints and less emphatically by the heads of the two Saints behind. The action of the relief, when it was still *in situ*, therefore took place in illusionistic space between the projecting lintel and the arched frame above.

The lunette was gravely damaged before 1914 and was then extensively made up. The make-up has since been removed, and the impression left by the heads of the Saints is still animated and authoritative. The Dominican Order attached particular importance to authenticity in iconography, and the features here are more sharply individualised than those in the immediately antecedent *Ascension* lunette in the Cathedral. Thus the St. Thomas Aquinas (Plate 95) is recognisably related to the portrait type employed by Fra Angelico in the cloister of San Marco, and the Albertus Magnus corresponds with the half-length inserted by Angelico under the *Crucifixion* fresco in the Sala del Capitolo. The Virgin, on the other hand, is seriously impaired; the nose and upper lip are lacking, there are fractures across the face, and much of the glaze is missing on the right side and from the veil across the shoulder and right arm. The Child is better preserved, but only the two ends of His scroll are original. The lunette recalls the compositional procedure of the roundels in the Pazzi Chapel in the emphatic vertical of the frontal Virgin and the horizontal of the scroll set parallel to the lintel beneath. The main focus of interest is the Child, Whose right foot rests in the exact centre of the relief. His left shoulder is retracted, and the upper part of His body is contained within the Virgin's silhouette. It has been suggested that the Urbino lunette originally had a naturalistic frame of flowers or fruit. The structure of the doorway, however, proves very clearly that it cannot at any time have had a frame, and the presence of a polychrome surround would indeed conflict with its austere Michelozzan imagery.

A second enamelled terracotta lunette of the same type by Luca survives in the Bode Museum in East Berlin (Cat. No. 31, Plates 96, 98–100). When it was purchased for the Kaiser Friedrich Museum in 1905, it was stated to have come from the doorway of a private chapel in the Mugello, and it is therefore known as the Mugello lunette. It shows the Virgin and Child with two angels, and is ten centimetres lower and eighty centimetres narrower than the lunette at Urbino. The further shoulders of the angels are retracted, their heads project, and the outer edges of their wings are contiguous with the edges of the relief. This indicates that the relief was originally set, like the Urbino lunette, above a doorway of which the lintel would have served as a balustrade severing the figures and the stone frame would have reinforced the back plane of the relief. The style of figures is more strongly Michelozzan than at Urbino—they recall the unglazed terracotta lunette modelled by Michelozzo about 1437–8 for the doorway of Sant' Agostino at Montepulciano—and there is a presumption that the doorway for which the relief was made was designed by or in the style of Michelozzo. It was, moreover, a small doorway, since the structure of the figures suggests that they were intended to be seen only a little above the level of the eye.

In the careful description of the Mugello published in 1748 by Brocchi there is no reference to the relief, nor is it mentioned in the account of the Della Robbia reliefs in the Mugello prepared by P. Lino Chini in 1876. It must therefore originate from an oratory that is not described in either book. This may have been the Michelozzo chapel adjacent to Il Trebbio, the width of whose doorway with its lintel supports corresponds almost exactly with that of the lunette. The original lunette over the doorway has been dismantled and replaced by a stone lunette dating from the present century. In 1451, under the division of the property of Giovanni di Bicci de' Medici, Il Trebbio became the property of Pierfrancesco di Lorenzo de' Medici. In 1645 it was sold by the Grand-Duke Ferdinand II to Giuliano Serragli, and three years later was bequeathed by Serragli to the Filippini in Florence. After the eviction of the Filippini, the castle passed to Prince Marcantonio Borghese, by whom a great part of its contents was dispersed. The lunette may have been removed from Il Trebbio at this time.

The posing of the three main figures, and especially of the Virgin, gives the lunette a sense of movement which distinguishes it from the lunette at Urbino. The two main figures are less schematic, and the Virgin's veil, which covers the Child's right shoulder and right knee, is modelled with exceptional finesse. This time it is the Child's right hand, raised in benediction, that marks the centre of the relief. From this we might deduce that the relief was a little later than the lunette at Urbino but was probably made before Michelozzo left Florence in 1456. It is generally assumed that his work at Il Trebbio dates from soon after 1451 (though a considerably earlier date for it has also been advanced), and the Mugello lunette can thus be tentatively looked upon as a work of about 1450–5.

The third of Luca della Robbia's *Madonna* lunettes, that in the Palazzo di Parte Guelfa (Cat. No. 32, Plates 97, 101), was made for a position over an external doorway in the church of San Pier Buonconsiglio, from which it was removed in 1884. From 1446 till 1474 the rector of the church was Messer Lionardo di Francesco de' Falladanzi da Orta, who held the post jointly with the incumbency of San Miniato fra le Torri. A charitable man of some wealth, he is recorded as a benefactor both of San Miniato fra le Torri, for which in 1449–50 he commissioned the high altarpiece by Castagno now in Berlin, and of San Pier Buonconsiglio, in which he founded the Chapel of St. Paul. He was responsible as well for donations to the hospital of Santa Elisabetta (1450) and to the Certosa di Galluzzo. It may well have been Falladanzi who commissioned both the lunette at San Pier Buonconsiglio and a lost *Madonna and Child* in enamelled terracotta by Luca which stood over the entrance to San Miniato fra le Torri till 1785.

The lunette has an enamelled terracotta surround. As it was originally set up (not as it is set up today) there ran round its upper edge a white enamelled frame with leaf-and-cord moulding. Outside this was a wide floreated frame on a white ground, and outside that again was a double leaf-and-dart and egg-and-dart white enamelled moulding. Looking at the floreated frieze alone—it is one of the few friezes in Luca's work which is symbolical, containing as it does two flowers specifically associated with the Virgin, the lily and the rose— we may well be reminded of the frieze of fruit on the Cappella della Madonna at Impruneta, and Impruneta is recalled once more by the two flying angels who flank the Virgin, where the rhythmical poses and the torsion of the figures on their flat ground repeat those of the small angels in the predella of the Cappella della Croce. This might suggest a dating, give or take a little, of about 1460. The type of the Virgin is no longer Michelozzan, and her body, turned freely in space, and the linear resolution of her mantle bring to mind the fluid rhythms of the *Virtues* in the Chapel of the Cardinal of Portugal. The Child, set diagonally across the Virgin's body, with His left leg extended and His right knee drawn up, seems to depend from the antique, and anticipates the Child introduced by Verrocchio into the Pistoia altarpiece. By comparison with the Mugello lunette, this is a less human and less satisfying work.

One independent *Madonna* has always been linked to the Urbino lunette. This is a *Virgin and Child* in the gallery of the Spedale degli Innocenti (Cat. No. 33, Col. Plate XXVI). The basis of the connection is part structural and part typological. The Virgin is once more set parallel to the relief plane, and the Child, Who is seated on her left arm, holds His cartellino flat across her chest. On this occasion it is the Child's left foot that falls in the centre of the base, which is similar in shape to that in the Copenhagen *Madonna* but is glazed in blue and carries an inscription in white letters: QVIA RESPEXIT DOMINVS HVMILITATEM ANCILLE SVE. At the corners are roses and fern fronds. The form of the Virgin's head corresponds closely with that in the lunette, and the nose and upper lip enable us to reconstruct in imagination the missing parts of the Urbino relief. On this occasion the Virgin's cloak is fastened by a jewel at the throat. In the Urbino lunette the Child extends His scroll to onlookers below, and in the Innocenti *Madonna* the Virgin points with the forefinger of her right hand to the verse from the *Magnificat* on the base. The glaze is the same resonant, thick glaze that appears again in the lunette of the *Resurrection*, and it is likely that the *Madonna*, one of Luca's most beautiful and moving works, dates from shortly before the Urbino lunette, that is from about 1445–50.

In the following half-decade, the period of the Mugello lunette, Luca seems to have produced a second independent work of the same elevated quality, the *Altman Madonna* in the Metropolitan Museum, New York (Cat. No. 34, Col. Plate XXVII). Whereas in the *Innocenti Madonna* the figure of the Virgin was fired in one, in the *Altman Madonna* the head and body were fired separately, and reveal an incomparable subtlety of modelling, which makes this one of Luca's most personal and most deeply felt reliefs. The type of the Virgin corresponds with that of the Mugello lunette, though the folds of veil over her head are more capricious and more decorative, and she looks down to our right, in the direction to which the Child's gesture of benediction is addressed. The Child holds His scroll in His left hand, and its end falls on the shallow, pale-blue base. The illusion is created that the Virgin is about to speak, and once more its communicative character is induced not simply by the modelling, but by glazing of great richness and sensibility. The *Altman Madonna* seems to have been made about 1455.

Closely related to it is a *Madonna and Child* in San Michele at Lucca (Cat. No. 35, Plate 102), where the Virgin's retracted left shoulder again recalls the Mugello lunette. This beautiful relief is moulded in one with its protruding porphyry base. There is no reference in any early source to a *Madonna* made by Luca for Lucca, and nothing is known of the history of the relief before the nineteenth century, when it was shown in the lunette of a doorway of the oratory of Santa Lucia beside San Michele. The relief may from the first have been intended to be shown externally, and it is not impossible that it is identical with the *Madonna* by Luca della Robbia which was removed from the entrance to San Miniato fra le Torri in Florence in the late eighteenth century.

Not long after the *Altman Madonna*, probably in the half-decade 1455–60, Luca produced two *Madonnas*, which are paragons of sculptural inventiveness. Both reliefs show the Child holding a symbolic apple—the significance of this genre motif is the same that is borne by the figure of Eve beneath some of the *Madonna* reliefs of Ghiberti—and in the earlier of them, in Berlin (Cat. No. 36, Plate 103), the Child's body follows the left arm of the Virgin, His head is turned upwards and His eyes look out to the right. His right hand is raised to His parted lips, and His left hand is pressed against the Virgin's chest. The apple which He holds falls over the exact centre of the base. The upper part of His body is bent slightly back, and the Virgin caresses His thigh with her right hand. There are traces of surface gilding on the edge of the mantle and on the dress. The veil over the Virgin's head is treated with great freedom, and the juxtaposition of the solids of the two heads looks

XXV. *The Friedrichstein Madonna* (Cat. No. 28). Polychrome enamelled terracotta. Albright-Knox Art Gallery, Buffalo (N.Y.)

XXVI. *Madonna and Child* (Cat. No. 33). Enamelled terracotta. Galleria dello Spedale degli Innocenti, Florence

XXVII. *Madonna and Child* (Cat. No. 34). Enamelled terracotta. Metropolitan Museum of Art, New York (Altman Collection)

XXVIII. *Madonna of the Apple* (Cat. No. 37). Enamelled terracotta. Museo Nazionale, Florence

XXIX. *Madonna and Child in a Niche* (Cat. No. 40). Enamelled terracotta. Metropolitan Museum of Art, New York

XXX. *Madonna in a Rose-Garden* (Cat. No. 39). Enamelled terracotta. Museo Nazionale, Florence

XXXI. *Saint Ambrose*. Detail of the Bronze Door of the North Sacristy (Cat. No. 47). Duomo, Florence

XXXII. *Bust of a Lady* (Cat. No. 54). Enamelled terracotta. Museo Nazionale, Florence forward to Raphael's *Madonna della Sedia*. The second *Madonna of the Apple*, in the Bargello in Florence (Cat. No. 37, Col. Plate XXVIII), is not a variant of the Berlin composition, but an independent solution of the same artistic problem. This time the Child hides the apple possessively against the Virgin's dress. Her reflective head is posed frontally, and the Child looks up with an expression that connotes playfulness rather than surprise or doubt. The most significant difference between the two reliefs is in their form. The Berlin *Madonna* extends to right and left beyond the base, whereas in that in the Bargello the body is slightly lengthened and is pinched in across the thighs, so that the width of the bottom of the figure is roughly equivalent to that of the front face of the chamfered plinth.

The years after 1460, the period of the San Pier Buonconsiglio lunette, produced another half-length relief, in the Musée Jacquemart-André in Paris (Cat. No. 38, Plate 104). In this the type of the Virgin follows that in the lunette, as does the dressing of her hair and the cloak which falls from the crown or back of the head. The legs of the Child are disposed in somewhat the same way, but His head is turned frontally. His right hand is raised in benediction, and with the left He covers himself with the Virgin's cloak. Elegant as it is, this is a more artificial and less touching invention than those in the *Madonnas* that precede it.

About 1464 the pose of the Child in the Jacquemart-André *Madonna* and the San Pier Buonconsiglio lunette was reversed, and was adapted by Luca for the upper left panel of the bronze door of the North Sacristy (Plate 113). In close relationship to the *Madonna* on the door stands a relief, the *Madonna in a Rose-Garden* in the Museo Nazionale (Cat. No. 39, Col. Plate XXX), which shows the Virgin turned slightly to the right on a violet seat. Behind is a rose hedge, and her eyes follow the action of the Child, Who turns back to pick a rose with His left hand. In His right hand, once more at a point in the exact centre of the relief, He holds an apple. The figures are white and the background blue, but the foliage and the white roses with yellow stamens are coloured naturalistically. Another small plant with white flowers is represented on the left, and the shallow base is dull green. This is a poetical, beautifully modelled relief. The iconography of the Virgin and Child accompanied by a climbing rose bush makes its first appearance in Tuscany in the middle of the fourteen-twenties in the *Madonna* by Gentile da Fabriano at New Haven, and was developed by Domenico Veneziano in two *Madonnas* in Washington (where the climbing roses fill the whole background of the scene) and Bucharest (where the Virgin is seated in full length in front of a rose hedge). Luca della Robbia's relief may have been inspired by the Bucharest *Madonna* or some similar lost

work. In the Bucharest *Madonna*, however, the Virgin picks a rose for the Child, while in the enamelled terracotta relief the symbolic flower is plucked by the Child.

From about 1450 Luca della Robbia seems to have resumed his experiments with reliefs designed for reproduction. The prerequisite for this was that they should be shallow and suitable for moulding. Their quality is sometimes very high. This is the case with the *Bliss Madonna* in the Metropolitan Museum in New York (Cat. No. 40, Col. Plate XXIX), of which a second version, rather less well finished, exists in the Boston Museum of Fine Arts (Fig. 28). Here the Virgin and Child are set in a shallow niche. The turquoise-blue enamel of the interior of the niche is decorated with gold striations, and the front face is also covered with decorative gilding, and has two circles in the spandrels for coats-of-arms. The Child presses His head against the Virgin's cheek (in this the relief recalls the *Madonna of the Apple* in Berlin) and throws His arms about her neck, and the Virgin's right hand rests on the base. In the version in Boston the niche is blue and turquoise-blue, and the spandrels are decorated in green. The design seems to have been inspired by the great *Madonna* by Fra Filippo Lippi of about 1460 in the Museo Mediceo.

The Berlin *Madonna of the Apple* is recalled once more in two other reliefs of about 1459–60, in the frieze of the Cappella della Madonna at Impruneta (Plates 84A, B). These are enchantingly intimate reliefs, which lack only the volume of reliefs by Luca modelled in greater depth. Both are eminently suitable for moulding, and gave rise to a large number of reproductions or variants, turned out from the Della Robbia studio in large part by Andrea della Robbia.

A more important prototype is the so-called *Genoa Madonna* (Cat. No. 41), of which at least four examples produced by Luca della Robbia or under Luca's supervision survive. Perhaps the finest is at Detroit (Plate 105). The theme of the Virgin and the frightened Child had been treated by Donatello at Padua in a relief, the *Verona Madonna*, which may well have exceeded any other fifteenth-century *Madonna* in popularity. Though made in North Italy, versions of it were known from an early time in Tuscany, and it is from one of these that the *Genoa Madonna* depends. The uncompromising imagery of the *Verona Madonna* was, however, alien to Luca's temperament, and in his relief the tragic implications of the theme are no more than hinted at. Once more the planes are compressed for ease of reproduction, and the prevailing flatness is redressed by gilding in the haloes, on the hair of the two figures, and on the tunic of the Child. Dating soon after 1450, the *Genoa Madonna* is the first example in Luca's work of successful mass production. The account book of Neri di Bicci recalls his framing in April 1464 what is described as 'una Nostra Donna invetriata, die quelle di Luca della Robbia.'

It is generally vain to look for the originals of pigmented stuccos, since the intention behind them from the start was reproductive, and it is vain to look for originals of such works as the *Genoa Madonna*. Similarly there is no identifiable original of the latest of these works, the so-called *Rovezzano Madonna* (Cat. No. 42), an enchantingly lyrical design whose conception is developed from that of the *Madonna in a Rose-Garden*. It is in extremely low relief, and shows a Virgin of Humility in profile to the right. Across her lap she holds the Child, Who reaches outwards to touch the stem of a triple lily plant. The composition contains features of great beauty, none more exquisite than the Child's two outstretched arms and the long line of the Virgin's extended leg, and it enjoyed great popularity, sometimes in its pristine state, sometimes in a more descriptive adaptation by Andrea della Robbia with flying angels at the back and the Child's fist grasping the lily stem. The original must have been a very late work by Luca made in the fourteen-seventies. Two of the best versions are those in Sant'Andrea at Rovezzano, from which the relief derives its name, and in the Hyde Collection at Glens Falls (Plate 106). Another composition of the same type in which the Virgin, once more a Madonna of Humility, faces to the left and the Child looks up into her face (Cat. No. 43) exists only in the form of copies, in Berlin, the Victoria & Albert Museum (Plate 107), and elsewhere.

In the history of Quattrocento sculpture Luca della Robbia's *Madonnas* occupy a place like that of the *Madonnas* of Giovanni Bellini in the history of painting, in that they enable us to follow the responses of one artist to the formal and emotional challenge of a single theme. Conceived on a level of unwavering seriousness, they partake of the mimetic nature of the Cantoria carvings, and their inventiveness is the by-product of an art that was rooted in real life. The angels who diffidently bow their heads, like servers at the Mass, before the Oxford *Madonna of Humility*; the Child in the *Corsini Madonna* pulling at the Virgin's veil with a possessive arm; the Virgin in the *Friedrichstein Madonna* gazing at the Child with half-closed eyes; the Virgin of the two *Madonnas* at Impruneta clutching the Child against her breast as though protecting Him from harm; the Virgin of the *Altman Madonna* looking on in reluctant acquiescence as the Child's mission is affirmed; the majestic *Madonna* in the Innocenti pointing to the inscription that asserts her own humility; the nervous, playful Child of the *Madonna of the Apple* in Berlin—all these proceed from observation, but observation raised to a new power. If they repeatedly remind us of the sixteenth century rather than of the fifteenth—Raphael from childhood must have known the lunette at Urbino, and in Florence must have encountered others of Luca's reliefs—it is because the process by which they were evolved, the making of life studies and their distillation in a statement at once compact and humanly communicative, was the same process that was introduced in painting by Raphael, Andrea del Sarto and their contemporaries. The statements made in the *Madonnas* are expressed with such finality as to leave us unaware that any problem has been posed or any question asked. This result could not have been achieved in any other medium than that which Luca used, whereby an image that must initially have contained descriptive elements is universalised through the pure white enamelling of the figures and their celestial blue ground.

X LUCA DELLA ROBBIA AS A BRONZE SCULPTOR

The first commission to Luca della Robbia for a work in bronze dates from 1446, when he received, jointly with Michelozzo and Maso di Bartolomeo, a contract for the bronze door of the North Sacristy of the Cathedral. He must, however, have practised as a bronze sculptor before this time, possibly in the fourteen-twenties when he may have worked in the studio of Ghiberti. The context of the first work by him in bronze to have survived is Ghibertesque. It was made for the tabernacle for Sant' Egidio, now at Peretola (Cat. No. 5, Col. Plate I, Plate 37), where the two angels beside the tabernacle door support, at shoulder height, a wreath not unlike that in the centre of Ghiberti's *Arca of the Three Martyrs*, containing a gilt bronze roundel of the Holy Ghost. On the tabernacle the roundel is replaced by a modern cast, and the original is now in the Bargello. The dove is represented not on a flat background, but against a naturalistic sky indicated by a succession of raised horizontal clouds, for which the closest parallel occurs once more in Ghiberti, in the horizontal clouds between the flying angels over the head of Christ in the *Baptism of Christ* on the Siena Baptismal Font. The dove, on the other hand, plunging down towards the tabernacle door, is treated geometrically in a fashion that has a precedent in the Campanile reliefs. The surface of the roundel is divided by a vertical through the exact centre of the field, on which the head and the foreshortened body of the dove seem to have been aligned, and is divided a second time by a horizontal, once more in the centre, which determines the placing of the tips of the two outstretched wings.

No doubt Luca, at this and at an earlier time, produced other small-scale bronze reliefs. The only two of which we have a record are also generically Ghibertesque. The first shows the Virgin seated on clouds with the Child in her lap, surrounded by six flying angels (Cat. No. 45), which seem, in their staid fashion, to depend from the angels modelled by Ghiberti for the *Arca di San Zenobio*. The composition is known from upwards of nine versions in stucco and terracotta, sometimes circular, and sometimes, as in a version in the Louvre (Plate 94B), a circle impressed within a square, all of which seem to have been made, at first or second

hand, from a single superior original. The known versions are unequal in quality, and it was inferred by Marquand from their uniformity that they were modern (as, indeed, some of them may be). In some cases, as we might expect, they show traces of gilding or pigmentation, and there is every reason to suppose that they were made commercially. The prototype must have been well known, since it is recorded by a Pisanello follower in a drawing in the Ambrosiana in Milan, in which certain details have been modified. In a later variant of the composition, known through versions at Budapest and Leipzig, the Virgin and Child alone are represented on a flat ground relieved by garlands. As Bode was the first to recognise, the medium of the lost original is revealed by a slight undulation of the surface, which is exactly analogous to that on the gilt bronze roundel from the Peretola tabernacle. The angels on the back of the *Arca di San Zenobio* were modelled and chased by Ghiberti between 1439 and 1442, and the lost original of Luca's composition seems also to date from soon after 1440. The poses of the main figures once more have the schematic character which the reliefs of the same date in marble might lead us to expect. The two forearms of the Child are linked to form a diagonal through the composition, and the Virgin's right forearm is set horizontally, as is the Child's stiffly extended leg, which has a parallel in a *Virgin and Child with two Angels* by Fra Filippo Lippi (Metropolitan Museum of Art) datable to about 1438.

At either side of the Virgin in this relief, beneath the clouds, are two small cherub heads. Similar heads appear again beneath the clouds in a second circular relief (Cat. No. 22), known through versions in the Ashmolean Museum (Plate 90A) and the Louvre. In this the Virgin, like the Virgin in Donatello's *Madonna of the Clouds*, is represented as a Madonna of Humility seated in the sky, and is planned as a triangle superimposed on the circular field. Behind are two angels, one with hands clasped in prayer and the other with hands crossed on his breast, with their heads lowered in deference to the Child. The pose of the central group is less accomplished and less open than that of the other relief, and the type of the Virgin and the robes of the angels here recall the earliest of the Cantoria carvings. If, as is likely, the lost bronze original of this relief is by Luca della Robbia, it must have been produced shortly before 1430. Confirmation that this is so is supplied by two inscriptions incised on the back of the Oxford stucco, the first indicating the shop in which the squeeze was made and the second the date at which it was produced ('formato adj 17 di gennaio 1428'). Together these two reliefs suggest that before starting work on the Cantoria and for some years afterwards Luca, like Donatello, produced small bronze reliefs which enjoyed some popularity.

Luca's Cantoria, moreover, included a component of bronze sculpture. It took the form of a pair of gilt bronze angels holding candlesticks seated on the balustrade (Cat. No. 46, Plates 108–111). They are described by Vasari in the second edition of the *Lives* (they were, he writes approvingly, 'condotti molto pulitamente'), are mentioned in the seventeenth century by Baldinucci, and make their last appearance in 1677 in Bocchi's guide to Florence. They remained in position on the Cantoria until the upper section was dismantled in 1688, and thereafter all trace of them was lost till 1890, when they were identified in the Piot collection in Paris. They are now in the Musée Jacquemart-André. Though their source is not open to dispute, they have none the less given rise to a long and continuing controversy among scholars, some of whom regard them as the work of Donatello (one of these aberrant students indeed prepared a drawing showing them seated uneasily on the Donatello Cantoria), while others believe that one is the work of Donatello and that the other is by a member of Donatello's shop, and others again regard them as the work of a North Italian Donatellesque sculptor. The poses of the two figures are complementary. One, from the right of the balustrade, is shown with the left leg extended and the right knee drawn up, looking over his left shoulder, while the other, from the left of the balustrade, has his right leg extended and his left drawn up and rests the base of his candlestick on his left thigh. Both are winged, both wear wreaths, and across their thighs run garlands of leaves and flowers which would, if the angels were less playful and less negligent, have been hung on the front face of the Organ Loft. Not only is there no evidence whatever that Donatello's Cantoria at any time included two bronze candle-bearing angels, but the authenticated works produced by Donatello in the fourteen-thirties and forties include a number of putti which are wholly incompatible in type and style with these. Since there is no reference to bronze angels in the documents relating to Luca della Robbia's Cantoria, we must suppose that they were made after the Organ Loft was set in place. In type the angel with head turned over his right shoulder recalls the central head in the *Choral Dancers* relief (Plate 14), while the angel with head turned over his left shoulder is related to the foreground figure to the right of centre in the same scene. The resemblances extend beyond the heads of the angels to their tubular arms and to the treatment of their hair. Their poses, moreover, are foreshadowed in a figure in right profile on the extreme left of the *Choral Dancers*, which has its left leg extended and its right knee sharply raised. In Fra Filippo Lippi's dated *Madonna* of 1437 from Tarquinia Corneto, now in the Galleria Nazionale di Palazzo Barberini, the Child, with right knee bent, left leg outstretched and His distended face pressed to the Virgin's cheek, is related to the angels from Luca's Cantoria. When the angels were in their original position, the horizontal of their two forearms would have corresponded with the upper moulding of the front face of the balustrade. Though the two angels were undoubtedly modelled by Luca, it cannot be assumed that he was necessarily responsible for casting, chasing, and gilding them. Bronze casting for the Cathedral in the fourteen-forties, other than that involved in commissions to Ghiberti and Donatello, was entrusted in the main to Michelozzo, and it cannot be ruled out that Luca's models were cast by Michelozzo (with whom he was associated from 1445 in the contract for the bronze door of the North Sacristy) or by Maso di Bartolomeo (who was a party to the same commission).

The story of Luca's single documented work in bronze, the door of the North Sacristy of the Cathedral (Cat. No. 47, Col. Plate XXXI, Plates 112–121), covers a span of over thirty years. In March 1437 bronze doors for the two sacristies were commissioned from Donatello. The first was to be completed by April 1439, and the second by April 1441. The cost of the two doors was estimated respectively at one thousand one hundred and nine hundred florins. The commission had evidently been under discussion for some months, and we know that at the end of February 1437 a model for one of the doors stood in the Sala dell'Udienza of the Opera del Duomo. By the end of March Donatello had received an advance payment of two hundred and fifty florins in respect of the first door. At the end of April the services of a stonemason, Nanni di Miniato called Fora, who had worked on Luca della Robbia's Cantoria, were made available for unspecified work in connection with the door, and on 30 June a small quantity of bronze was purchased for Donatello's use. Thereafter, until 1445 when the contract was amended, there is no further reference to the commission. The surviving documents vouchsafe nothing about Donatello's door. We do not know what its panels would have represented or how they would have been articulated, but we may be confident that its programme would have been initiated by the authorities of the Cathedral, not, as has been suggested, by the artist. The two bronze doors in the

Old Sacristy of San Lorenzo, on which Donatello must have been engaged in the late fourteen-thirties, are considerably smaller than the projected door for the Cathedral, and each of them consists of ten square reliefs with confronting martyrs or apostles. The iconography of these figure reliefs would have been inapplicable to the Duomo, but it may well be that the form of the doors in San Lorenzo reflects that of the abandoned doors for the Cathedral.

When Luca della Robbia's Cantoria was set in place in 1438 and the enamelled terracotta lunette of the *Resurrection* was installed beneath it in 1445, the only feature lacking in what must, from the first, have been regarded as a sculptural complex, was the bronze sacristy door. Donatello had left Florence in 1443 for Padua, where he was engaged on three commissions for bronze sculptures. There was little or no prospect of his return to work in Florence, though in October 1445 he paid a visit to his native city and while there appraised, jointly with Luca della Robbia, the lavabo carved by Buggiano for the sacristy. In June 1445, therefore, after the *Resurrection* had been erected and before the reappearance of Donatello, the consuls of the Arte della Lana cancelled the contract for one of the two doors, that of the North Sacristy, and authorised the Operaii of the Cathedral to allot it to another artist. The choice of Michelozzo as Donatello's successor must already have been made, and on 1 July Michelozzo was awarded the contract. This arrangement was subject to one proviso, that if by the end of August Luca della Robbia agreed to certain terms proposed by the Operaii, the door would be allocated jointly to both sculptors. By 28 February 1446, when the formal contract was drawn up, a third artist was also associated with the project, the bronze sculptor Maso di Bartolomeo. The contract for the second bronze door, that of the South Sacristy, was retained by Donatello, who is described as late as 1459 as 'intagliatore e chondottore de le porte de la sagrestia.'

Under the decision of 1 July 1445, Michelozzo was constrained to execute the door 'secundum designum factum.' It has been argued that this design was that prepared by Donatello, and that Donatello was indeed responsible not only for the frame but for the relief style of Michelozzo's door. This theory is vitiated by the fact that neither the door frame nor the reliefs reflect in any way the stylistic preconceptions of Donatello. We are bound to assume that the 'designum factum' was a new design prepared by Michelozzo in the first half of 1445, and that Michelozzo, not Donatello, was the author of the model referred to in the contract of 1446 as being in the hands of the sculptor and his 'sociis intagliatoribus.' The fee was to be one thousand one hundred florins (the same fee as for the cancelled door of Donatello), ex-

clusive of damascening, which would be paid for separately. Each of the two wings was to contain five square reliefs with double frames. The flat area between the inner and the outer frames was to be damascened in gold and silver or in silver only, and at the corners of the rectangles were to be heads of Prophets, twelve in each wing. The ten square reliefs were to show, at the top the Virgin and Child and St. John the Baptist, and beneath the Evangelists and the Doctors of the Church. These figures were to be seated, and each was to be accompanied by two standing angels in half-relief. Over each seated figure there was to be a tabernacle in half-relief decorated with damascening. The backs of the two wings were to comprise five squares of bronze, with double frames like those of the panels on the front but without figures or other decoration.

For a short time the project went ahead without impediment. There is a reference to the purchase of bronze for the door on 24 December 1445, and on 10 January of the following year two thousand libri of bronze were obtained from the shop of Ghiberti. Visits in search of bronze were paid by Maso di Bartolomeo to Lucca, Pisa, Pistoia and Arezzo. On 25 February 1446, a trial casting seems to have taken place, and at the end of 1446 or in January 1447 the frames for the two doors were definitively cast. At this point, however, the door frames were set aside, and the surplus bronze, from which the reliefs were presumably to have been cast, was made available for a grille in the Chapel of St. Stephen, which then served as the Chapel of the Sacrament. The door frames were the subject of some trivial payments later in 1447, and in December 1451 we hear of them again, when a small sum was paid to Maso di Bartolomeo for partial replacement of the roof of the workshop 'dove noi faciamo i telai della porta di sagrestia di Santa Maria del Fiore.' A similar payment was made to Michelozzo 'pro suo tertio monte unius tecti facti in apotheca dicti Michelozzi sub quo laborata fuerunt et facta telaria dicte porte.' Throughout these years there is no record of any payment made in respect of the bronze door to Luca della Robbia.

In April 1461 the project was activated once more. Maso di Bartolomeo was dead, and a contract was drawn up with his brother, Giovanni di Bartolomeo, who was to receive two hundred florins for cleaning the frames of the door. If they were defective, the defects were to be made good with wax and bronze supplied by the Operaii. In this task Giovanni di Bartolomeo enjoyed the services of two assistants, Silvestro di Guglielmo and Simone del Bianco. Payments to Giovanni di Bartolomeo run through 1462 and 1463, and from one of them we learn that he also provided the square bronze plates for insertion in the frames at the back of the door. The completed door frames were formally accepted on 17 December

1463, by the Operaii and, in the absence of Michelozzo, who was no longer in Florence, by Luca della Robbia.

On 4 August 1464, a final contract was drawn up for the completion of the door. It takes note of the fact that 'circha ad anni 20 che mai non vi s'è su lavaroto né fatto alchuna cosa', that the door frames had been cleaned by Giovanni di Bartolomeo, that Maso di Bartolomeo was dead, that Michelozzo was no longer in Florence, and that Luca della Robbia was the sole survivor of the original contractors, and it entrusts the completion of the doors to Luca, for a fee of seven hundred florins (one thousand one hundred florins less the four hundred florins paid to Michelozzo and Maso di Bartolomeo). Luca's task was to 'fare compiere a storiare dette porti e ogni altra e qualunque cosa come nella prima allo-ghagione si contiene.' In May 1465 pieces of wood were supplied as a ground for three wax models, and later in the year two of the reliefs were cast. The other reliefs were cast between this date and October 1467, when bronze for the casting of 'l'ultime due istorie della porta della sagrestia' was procured from Verrocchio. Verrocchio was working at the time on the bronze candlestick for the Sala dell' Udienza of the Palazzo della Signoria, now in the Rijksmuseum, and the bronze purchased from him may have been the residue left over from this work. Other small payments were made to Luca between 1468 and 1472, but there is no record of the payment of any substantial part of the seven hundred florins due under the contract of 1464. The latest document, of 27 June 1475, records a payment of one hundred and thirty florins. This, it was recognised, was substantially less than the fee agreed, but the work produced was not in complete conformity with the models supplied, and Luca had for this reason renounced his claim to the full sum. Models for the hinges of the door were made by Domenico di Domenico Pagni da Prato before December 1474, and the doors seem to have been installed at the beginning of 1475, thirty-eight years after they had first been planned and thirty years after they were begun.

The contract of 1464 states in explicit terms that up to that time no payment of any kind in respect of the door had been made to Luca della Robbia. This must affect our view of the twelve Prophet heads in the frame. Their authorship has been the subject of widely divergent views. Reymond regarded the twelve lower heads as the work of Michelozzo. Cruttwell considered that the four heads above the panels of SS. Luke and Mark could be given 'with little hesitation' to Michelozzo. Bode believed that 'freilich ist das nüchterne, für die Wirkung der Reliefs sowohl wie der Köpfe in der Einrahmung derselben wenig günstige architektonische Gerüst und die Einteilung zweifellos die Erfindung von Michelozzo.' In the judgement of Marquand 'none of the heads are

by Michelozzo but all show the fostering care of Luca della Robbia.' Though they were cast separately, they form an integral part of the framing of the door, and in 1463, when the frames were accepted as complete, these heads must have been in their present state (Figs. 33–35). They must, therefore, be regarded as works by Michelozzo or Maso di Bartolomeo, or as replacements by Giovanni di Bartolomeo made when the doors were chased. While nothing in the heads is wholly inconsistent with the modelled relief by Luca that approximates to them most closely in date, the *Resurrection* in the Duomo, the resemblances are not so strong as to permit us to ignore the documentary evidence. Two of the heads, at the bottom of the left wing, are still in the rough, and suggest that the remaining twenty-two, no matter what their authorship, must owe a good deal of their definition to Giovanni di Bartolomeo. Like the protruding heads of Prophets on Ghiberti's first bronze door, the heads emerge from quatrefoils, but whereas Ghiberti's quatrefoils are shown complete in the centre of each wing, and are docked of one lobe at the sides, on Michelozzo's door the sixteen central quatrefoils each lack one lobe and the eight quatrefoils at top and bottom lack two. The types are more consistently classical than those used by Ghiberti, and seem to derive in the main from sarcophagus reliefs. Thus the third head from the bottom on the left of the left wing may depend from a Battle sarcophagus of the type of that in the Campo-santo at Pisa (Fig. 34) and the third head from the bottom on the right of the right wing may be drawn from a Muse sarcophagus. Other heads appear to have been based on Roman portrait busts; these include the male head second from the bottom in the left wing (Fig. 33) and the somewhat similar male head at the top left corner on the right. These two heads may be by Michelozzo. Others are less incisive and are likely to be by Maso and Giovanni di Bartolomeo. It may be relevant to recall that if Maso di Bartolomeo had had his way, the courtyard of the Palazzo Medici would have been decorated in 1452 not with the roundels we know today, but with a frieze of classicising heads.

One of the curious aspects of the door is the emphasis throughout the early documents on damascening. The technique was known in Florence—it is, for example, used decoratively on Ghiberti's *Arca of the Three Martyrs*, and is used again, illusionistically, in the *Medici Crucifixion* of Donatello—but nowhere was it employed as decoration on the scale that was envisaged here. A small section of damascening occurs in the right wing beneath the relief of *St. Mark* and above that of *St. Jerome*. Worked in silver inlay, the damascening takes the form of a diamond-shaped pattern with, in the centre of each field, a small quatrefoil (Fig. 31). It has been suggested either that the remainder of the damascening was not executed, or that it was executed and has been cleaned away. In the absence of incisions in any other area than that subjected to test damascening, the first explanation must be correct. The surface of the door could not have been damascened until it had been cleaned, and it is likely that the present damascening dates from after 1463. The little inlay that survives is sufficient to establish the difference between the austere but richly ornamented door conceived by Michelozzo and the undifferentiated bronze door that we see now.

The principal distinction between the reliefs as they were planned and the reliefs as they were executed lies in the absence of the damascened tabernacles in half-relief by which the central figure in each scene would have been emphasised if the tabernacles were mere canopies, or isolated if they went down to the ground. It is likely that the tabernacles were abandoned when it was decided that the damascening of the border should be discontinued.

The square format of the reliefs (Plates 112–121, Col. Plate XXXI) was chosen with a central tabernacle in mind. The absence of the tabernacle is specially noticeable in those reliefs where the figures are posed frontally (*Virgin and Child, St. John the Baptist, St. Luke*) or where the height of the figure leaves an awkward void (*St. Jerome*). The tabernacles originally planned may have been related to those behind the Saints in the stained-glass windows of Ghiberti, though they were intended to protrude from the surface of the reliefs. The absence of a vertical element in the compositions is redressed in the case of the *Four Evangelists* by placing the symbols above shoulder height. Though the diagonal posing of certain of the figures (e.g. *St. Matthew, St. Mark*) and the dual axis of others (e.g. *St. Ambrose, St. Augustine*) are inspired by the *Evangelists* and *Fathers of the Church* on Ghiberti's first bronze door, the horizontal relationship established between the Saints and the attendant angels lends the reliefs an adventitious narrative interest.

The contract of 1445 throws no light on whether the 'designum' prepared by Michelozzo included a scheme for the reliefs. The only one of the present reliefs which might refer back to such a scheme is the *St. Gregory the Great* (Plate 121), where the heavily modelled central figure depends from the figure of the same Saint on Ghiberti's door. The angels wear dalmatics, not the classical dress used in the other reliefs, and the relationship between them and the central figure is rigid and unrhythmical. The four flanges (which are common also to Luca's panels) are left in the rough and project from the surface of the relief. The model for this panel may have been the work of Maso di Bartolomeo. The remaining nine reliefs are by Luca della Robbia. One of his concerns was to make effective use of the width as

well as of the height of the bronze field, and the means by which he does so leaves little doubt that the nine reliefs were modelled when they were commissioned, in and after 1464, and not at any earlier time. The Virgin is seated in a low chair and looks down to the right at the Child, Whose pose is an inversion of that adopted for the enamelled terracotta lunette for San Pier Buonconsiglio. In the register beneath, the two Evangelists, John and Matthew, face towards the centre of the door. In the middle register in the left wing is a frontal figure of St. Luke and in the right wing is a figure of St. Mark turned to the right. These ill-adjusted reliefs may have been transposed during the assembly of the door. The three *Fathers of the Church* for which Luca was responsible are more assured and elegant. St. Ambrose is shown with his knees turned slightly to the right and his body twisted above the waist; his hands rest on two open volumes held by the angels at the sides. St. Jerome is turned to the left, pointing to a passage in an open book, and St. Augustine, in the lowest relief in the right wing, is writing in a volume supported on his right thigh and reading from a volume opposite. The style principles underlying these three figures are those of the *Virtues* at San Miniato al Monte.

The most appealing feature of Luca's nine reliefs is not, however, the central figure, but the angels at the sides. In the uppermost relief on the left the two angels, bending forwards with hands clasped in prayer, are recognisably related to those of the Pescia altarpiece. Opposite, the angels beside St. John the Baptist stand with hands crossed on their breasts. In the two reliefs beneath, the inner angel holds out an inkwell and the outer angel reads the words written by the Evangelist. In the *St. Mark* they look wonderingly at the Saint's contemplative head, and in the last three scenes they are participants in a continuum of action centring on the Saint. The limitation of the reliefs, and therefore of the door, is that for Luca della Robbia in old age bronze was an uncongenial medium. Like enamelled terracotta it depended upon modelling, and if the reliefs are translated back in imagination into the clay or wax in which they were originally conceived, we need have no difficulty in believing that the sculptural thinking they embody is as distinguished as that in larger works of the same time. But Luca lacked the time and patience to chase the surfaces in such a way as to ensure that the reliefs retained their spontaneity. The only panels which bear evident traces of meticulous and lively surface working are those of the Virgin and Child and of Luca's name saint St. Luke.

The apathy with which the door was greeted by the Operaii can be readily explained. When it was designed it was in competition only with Ghiberti's first bronze door and with the still unfinished Porta del Paradiso.

When it was completed, however, Donatello's doors had stood in the Old Sacristy for over thirty years, and on the south door of the Baptistry was that paragon of technical accomplishment, Vittorio Ghiberti's surround for the bronze door of Andrea Pisano. By these standards the bronze door in the Cathedral must have seemed archaic and unenterprising, and to Luca, busy as he was with the great *stemmi* and the Chapel of the Cardinal of Portugal, it may well have appeared in the same light.

There is a possibility, indeed a presumption, that Luca della Robbia, if he produced bronze reliefs from the middle of the fourteen-twenties, modelled the bronze angels for the Cantoria, and was responsible for nine of the ten bronze reliefs on the door of the North Sacristy, also undertook the making of bronze statuettes. One statuette, a *David with the head of Goliath* in the Metropolitan Museum of Art, New York (Cat. No. 57, Fig. 36), has been ascribed to him. The precedents for this sturdy, thick-necked figure in Luca's authenticated works are not strong enough to carry absolute conviction, nor does the Goliath head find satisfactory parallels in the independent heads on the bronze door or in the small figures cast by Maso di Bartolomeo for the grille of the Cappella della Cintola in Prato Cathedral. It appears to be the work of an unknown bronze sculptor operating in Luca's orbit, perhaps Pasquino da Montepulciano, by whom no authenticated works in bronze are known.

XI THE LATE WORKS

Desultory payments to Luca della Robbia for the bronze doors of the Cathedral continue till the summer of 1469, and the final payment, of 27 June 1475, suggests that the task of cleaning and chasing the bronze reliefs must have been in large part delegated to other hands. In enamelled terracotta we are confronted with the task of distinguishing the works made by Luca at this time from those made by his nephew, Andrea della Robbia. At Luca's death in 1482 Andrea was aged forty-six or forty-seven, and had behind him twenty-seven or more years of independent activity. It was assumed by earlier scholars that throughout this time he operated in the main as an assistant of his uncle. On certain major commissions the two artists may indeed have worked together, but if the documents are to be trusted this was an exception rather than the rule, and when we first encounter a documented work by Andrea della Robbia, the *Madonna of the Stonemasons* in the Bargello, which is datable to the year 1475,[1] its only link with Luca is through its technique. The Virgin is shown seated to below the knees, as she is in pigmented reliefs by Antonio Rossellino, and the Child reminds us of Verrocchio. Whereas Luca in his *Madonnas* employs a multiplicity of receding planes, Andrea disposes the right arm of the Child and the right hand and wrist of the Virgin on the surface of the relief. This difference is so fundamental that whenever we find *Madonnas* in which the arms of the Virgin and Child are shown on a single plane, we must accept the probability that they are by Andrea della Robbia.

One example is a *Madonna* at Nynehead (Cat. No. 64, Fig. 41), which is sensitively modelled, but in a fashion that indicates the presence of Andrea della Robbia not of Luca—it was probably made about 1465—and another is the *Demidoff Madonna* at Toledo (Cat. No. 65, Fig. 42), where the two arms once more are flat. It appears in recent books as Luca della Robbia, but was recognised by Cruttwell for what it was, a relief by Andrea of about 1460. The Child once more is Verrocchiesque. A third relief of the same class is the circular *Madonna delle Cappuccine* in the Bargello (Cat. No. 66, Fig. 43), where the floreated frame is a typical product of Andrea's shop and the relief of the Virgin and Child with two angels is, as Cruttwell and Reymond recognised, also typical of Andrea della Robbia. The relief is likely to belong in the half decade 1460–5. From the second half of the same decade comes the full-length *Frescobaldi Madonna*, formerly in Berlin (Cat. No. 68, Fig. 46), where the flaccid forms and the descriptive detail once more offer evidence of Andrea della Robbia's hand. The sole basis for dating any of these works is that the largest of them, the so-called *Via dell' Agnolo Lunette* in the Bargello (Cat. No. 69, Fig. 45), must, for reasons indicated in an earlier chapter, have been modelled and glazed soon after 1470.

Marquand describes Andrea's studio by the respectable nineteenth century term 'atelier', but it was (in a sense in which most painters' studios in the fifteenth century were not) a shop. One letter written by Andrea della Robbia survives.[2] It was addressed in June 1471 to a contact in Mantua and refers to a head in the workshop which had been reserved eight months earlier for the Marquess of Mantua by his agent Pier del Tovaglia. A small down-payment on it had been made, otherwise it would already have been resold, and Andrea now proposes to market it, but can make another if Federigo Gonzaga would still like one. This may have

---

1. No. 75. Marquand (1922, i, pp. 18–21, No. 7). The relief was commissioned by the Consuls and Council of the Arte dei Maestri di Pietra e di Legname on 5 March 1475 (o.s. 1474), to replace an existing statue or relief of the *Virgin and Child* in the Udienza of the Guild. For the relevant document see Marquand, *loc. cit.*, from Florence, Archivio di Stato, Deliberazioni dell'Arte de' Maestri di Pietra e di Legname, Arti II, Cod. 3, c. 27.
2. The letter is printed by A. Bertolotti (1890, pp. 12–13),

and was overlooked by Marquand. I am indebted for the reference to Professor Middeldorf. The document reads:

A di 28 di Giugnio 1471

Charissimo mio Elglie più di mesi otto che io ebbi fatta la testa ch io tolsi afare per il Singniore e perche io mi sono stato a bada di Pier del Tovaglia che è venuto due volte a Mantova poi che la testa fu fatta, e perchè la prima volta mi disse che ne ragiono chosti e maj non trovò chine been a little bust of the Baptist of which a number of variants survive.

At least from the fourteen-fifties there is evidence of the export of works by the Della Robbia. A document of 28 May 1454 lists, as part of a miscellaneous cargo despatched to Lisbon from Pisa 'sette casse di lavori di terra chotta envetriata, del marchese di Valenza.'[3] There is little room for doubt that this work, possibly a shield of arms, was made in the Della Robbia shop. Another instance, which is more fully documented, enables this export trade to be linked firmly to the activity of Andrea della Robbia.[4] In 1462 Guillaume Filastre was named Bishop of Tournai, and a year later he was despatched by Philip the Good to Rome. His secretary was a Florentine merchant in Bruges, Angelo Tani (the same Tani who commissioned the Memlinc Last Judgement at Danzig), and Filastre seems, possibly for this reason, to have stopped in Florence. While there, his attention was drawn to the novel technique of enamelled terracotta, and then or later he ordered a sepulchral monument from the Della Robbia kiln. When the tomb was completed in 1469–70, the transport of its component parts to Pisa was supervised by Tani and their shipment from Pisa to Ecluse was undertaken by another merchant with connections in the Netherlands, Tommaso Portinari (the donor of Van der Goes' Portinari Altarpiece). The tomb was erected at Saint-Omer, and the pieces of it that survive were made under the supervision of Andrea della Robbia. In the fourteen-sixties Andrea must also have received public commissions in Florence. One of them was for the stemma of the Arte della Seta on Or San Michele (Cat. No. 70, Fig. 49), whose emblem was that early symbol of trade unionism, a closed door. In the centre of the roundel is a white shield, supported by two putti, and the doorway is depicted in white with a violet surround and violet nails, rings and bolt. Vasari, no doubt deliberately, ignored this work. Its frame, with bunches of fruit widely spaced on a white ground, is typical of Andrea della Robbia, while the two children are conceived quite differently from the Child in Luca della Robbia's stemma of the Arte dei Medici e degli Speziali nearby. Their limbs are attenuated, their

sapesse nulla, e di poi scrissi una lettera chostì penso nolla abbiate avuta. Ora a questo dì di nuovo venne Pier del Tovaglia chostà e ramentalgli la detta testa che mi sapesse dire quelle n'avessi a fare: siamo a quello medessimo si che i o detto a Piero più volte che io l'arei venduta; ma perche o uto un fiorino però l o tenuta infino a ora: avisatemi quello abbia a fare della testa, che io avevo detto a Pier del Tovaglia, io la vendero, e lui mi disse vendila e rifanne un altra quando tella chiederanno; non m'è paruto dovere e pero nollo fatto piu presto potete mavissate o pensato infino aora che voi non siate stato nella terra: e avisate el Signor Messer Federigo se io o affare chose piaccia alla sua signoria sono apparecchiato: non mi distendo più. Iddio sia vostra guardia.

Vostro

Andrea di Marcho della Robbia in Firence.

Bertolotti assumes that the letter refers to a portrait of Federigo Gonzaga. Its terms, however, make this improbable. Piero del Tovaglia was the agent in Florence of Lodovico Gonzaga. No reply is recorded.

3. Florence, Archivio dello Spedale degli Innocenti, Estranei, n. 219, Francesco e Carlo di Niccolo Cambini a compagni di Firenze, Ricordanze segnate F, 1453–1455, c. 35c. I am indebted for this document to Dr. Marco Spallanzani. Other material relating to the export outside Italy of works from the Della Robbia shop is published by G. Corti (1970 and 1973, and in Corti/Hartt, 1962). Dr. Spallanzani informs me that a consignment of merchandise dispatched to Pisa for shipment to Naples on 20 September 1477, included 'una chasetta d'ase d'albero, entrovi una Vergine Maria di terra chotta invetriata,' destined for Marino Tomacello, a member of the Aragonese court (Florence, Archivio di Stato, V. Serie Strozziane, n. 30, Ricordanze rosse, segnate D, di Filippo e Lorenzo Strozzi di Firenze, 1475–1477, c. 177r.). Other evidence of the traffic in Della Robbia ware under the auspices of Andrea della Robbia is found in Venice: the components of the ceiling of the Martini Chapel in San Giobbe seem to have been glazed in Florence and to have been assembled, in a perfunctory fashion, at their place of destination. Similarly, four enamelled terracotta roundels were made in Florence in the shop of Andrea della Robbia for one of the funerary chapels in the church of Monteoliveto at Naples (Marquand, 1922, i, pp. 114–15, No. 76). These may be the source of the tradition that a royal tomb for Naples was executed by Luca della Robbia. The tomb is recorded in the Libro di Antonio Billi (Frey, 1892 (ii), p. 46: 'Fecie a Napoli il sepolcro dello infante, fratello di Alfonso, e altre cose') and by the Anonimo Magliabechiano (Frey, 1892 (i), p. 80: 'Fece anchora a Napolj il sepolcro dell'infante, fratello del re Alfonso, e altre cose assaj'). The commission is referred to in the first edition of Vasari (Vasari-Ricci, i, p. 250: 'A Napoli fece la sepoltura dello Infante fratello del Re Alfonso, et Duca di Calavria, della quale grandissima parte ne lavorò in Fiorenza') and with some emendations in the second edition (Vasari-Milanesi, ii, p. 175: 'Per Napoli ancora fece, in Fiorenza, la sepoltura di marmo all'infante fratello del duca di Calavria, con molti ornamenti d'invetriati aiutato da Agostino suo fratello'). As noted by Fabriczy (1888, p. 174), Luca della Robbia predeceased the two brothers of Alfonso, Duke of Calabria, of whom one, Cardinal Giovanni, died in 1484, and the other, the Infante Carlo, in 1486.

4. Du Teil, 1912.

poses are flat, and their lips are parted in the ingratiating half-smile that one learns to accept as a hall-mark of Andrea della Robbia's work.

From the mid-fourteen-seventies on Andrea della Robbia's development can be followed in considerable detail. About 1475 he was working for San Michele Arcangelo at Faenza, for which he executed the lunette of *St. Michael* in the Metropolitan Museum,[5] and in or before 1477 he made the great *stemma* of Federico Manfredi, Bishop of Faenza, and two other *stemmi* for the Cathedral.[6] Two years later he embarked on what were to prove his masterpieces, the altars for La Verna. The restoration of La Verna had been entrusted by Eugenius IV to the consuls of the Arte della Lana, who became protectors, governors and defenders of the sanctuary and its neighbourhood, and though in 1472 the newly constructed church and convent buildings were damaged by fire, by the end of the decade the decoration of the churches was under way.[7] The altarpieces were allotted to Andrea della Robbia, partly no doubt because his work conformed to Franciscan Observant taste, partly because he was himself inscribed in the Arte della Lana, and partly because enamelled terracotta could withstand the rigours of the climate on the holy but inclement mountainside. For La Verna he produced the beautiful altarpieces of the *Incarnation* and *Annunciation* (ca. 1479) in the Brizi and Niccolini Chapels of the Chiesa Maggiore,[8] the *Crucifixion* in the Cappella delle Stimmate (1480–1),[9] the *Madonna della Cintola* in Santa Maria degli Angeli (ca. 1486),[10] and the *Ascension* on the high altar of the Chiesa Maggiore.[11] To these years

belongs the public commission in Florence by which Andrea della Robbia is best known, the reliefs of *Orphans* on the Spedale degli Innocenti, which were installed in their roundels in 1487.[12] Through these works, many of which were executed in his uncle's lifetime, Andrea della Robbia established the vogue of enamelled terracotta as a vehicle for popular religious images, and developed a new equation between style in enamelled terracotta and style in painting which was to persist after his own death in 1522. It is against the background of this buoyant, vigorous activity that the late work of Luca della Robbia must be seen and judged.

It led him in the first place to experiment with the enamelled terracotta altarpiece. The only work from the years between 1470 and Luca's death in 1482 that is approximately datable is a *Madonna and Child between SS. James and Blaise*, now in the chapel of the Palazzo Vescovile at Pescia (Cat. No. 48, Plates 124, 125). Designed in the form of a triptych, with the two Saints in the wings and the Virgin and Child with two angels in the centre, its three sections are framed with flat strips containing a design of alternating blue and violet rosettes in white circles on a green ground. In the lower corners are small roundels with the *stemmi* of the Ospitalieri of San Jacopo at Altopascio and of the Capponi family. On top is a moulded cornice, and beneath is a frieze of fruit in five sections running the whole width of the altarpiece.

Though it bears the arms of the Ospitalieri of San Jacopo, the altarpiece was not commissioned for Altopascio, but for the small church of San Biagio at Pescia, where it is described in 1772. A dependency of San

5. O. Raggio, 1961. For a fuller account of Andrea della Robbia's activity see Pope-Hennessy, 1979.

6. Marquand (1922, i, pp. 41–43, No. 28). The *stemmi* commemorate the founding of the new Cathedral in 1474, and seem to have been installed before November 1477, when the Bishop was expelled from Faenza.

7. On La Verna see particularly Lazzeri, 1913; Secondo Pugliaro, 1931; A. Lensi, 1934; P. Gualberto Matteucci, 1964 (i) and (ii); Pierotti, 1913; Mencherini, 1914.

8. The sole evidence for the date of the two altarpieces is an inscription on the balustrade of the Cappella Brizi which reads: ISTAM CAPPELLAM FECIT FIERI JACOBVS BRITII DE PIEVE SANTI STEPHANI A.D. MCCCCLXXVIIII. The Niccolini and Brizi Chapels seem to have been constructed concurrently or in close association, and there is no documentary support for Marquand's contention that the *Annunciation* is the earlier of the two altarpieces.

9. The *Crucifixion* bears the arms of Tommaso degli Alessandri, and seems to have been inaugurated on 16 August 1481. For a reference to Andrea della Robbia possibly in connection with this work see Pierotti, *op. cit.*, p. 162.

10. Rights over Santa Maria degli Angeli were granted to Domenico Bartoli, his brothers and his descendants, at a Provincial Chapter of the Franciscan Observants held at Bosco ai Frati in May 1486. The altarpiece carried the arms of Domenico Bartoli and his wife Maddalena Ruccellai.

11. The altarpiece was transferred from the high altar to the Ridolfi Chapel in 1601. It is dated by Marquand (1922, i, p. 145, No. 92) at the beginning of the decade 1500–1510, but is likely to have been made somewhat earlier. The choir of the Chiesa Maggiore at La Verna was constructed in 1495.

12. For this see G. Morozzi (1964). The misdating of the Innocenti roundels to the mid-fourteen-sixties is a central source of confusion in Andrea della Robbia's early chronology. Both Marquand (1922, i, pp. 10–18, No. 6) and Cruttwell (1902, p. 139) advance a dating ca. 1463–6, in the belief that the roundels were made before the financial crisis which overtook the Hospital at the end of the following decade. The documentary evidence shows conclusively that they were commissioned after the crisis had been overcome, and immediately before Ghirlandaio's altarpiece for the church of the Hospital (1488).

Jacopo at Altopascio, to which the friars from Altopascio moved during the winter months, San Biagio bore the Capponi arms on its façade. The connection of the Capponi with Altopascio was very close, and after 1446 four successive members of the family were in control of the convent of the Ospitalieri. The *juspatronatus* of Altopascio was, however, formally granted to the Capponi by Sixtus IV only in 1472, and it is unlikely that the altarpiece was commissioned before this year. Stylistically the central panel is closely linked to the bronze door, the Child recalling the Child in the uppermost panel in the left wing and the two angels the angels beside St. Mark. The Virgin is represented without a headdress, and at first sight the central panel reads as though it were a sculptural enlargement from the small *Virgin and Child with Saints* by Pesellino in the Metropolitan Museum of Art. The frontal figures of the two Saints shown in isolation at the sides recall the lateral Saints in the Chapel of the Cross at Impruneta, but are modelled with greater sensibility, and the more cogitated of the two, St. Blaise, is shown gazing compassionately at the Child. No traces of surface decoration appear on the dresses of either Saint, but in the centre the cloak of the Virgin seems originally to have been enriched with elaborate gilded decoration along the inner and outer edges and the cushion beneath the Child was treated in the same way. In conjunction with the porphyry throne, this must originally have lent the triptych something of the character of the *Bliss Madonna* in New York. The modelling of the Virgin's head looks back to that of the *Virtues* at San Miniato al Monte and has the same emotive quality, and the modelling of the Child, so tender and compact, likewise leaves no doubt that the relief is autograph.

Painted altarpieces were commonly provided with predellas, and a number of Andrea della Robbia's altarpieces in enamelled terracotta were provided with predellas too. It seems that Luca della Robbia late in his career also experimented with enamelled terracotta predella panels. One of these is a small *Adoration of the Magi* in the Victoria & Albert Museum (Cat. No. 49, Plate 122), where the Virgin and Child resemble the central group in the Pescia altarpiece. This panel was copied by Andrea in predellas at Montepulciano, Assisi, and L'Aquila, but in Luca's version the sense of interval throughout the frieze-like composition is more classical, the modelling of the drapery is more confident, and the spatial content is more firmly defined. A companion relief of the *Nativity* was likewise copied by Andrea at Montepulciano, Assisi and L'Aquila, and is also evidently much superior to its derivatives.

With painters, above all with painters in the circle of Fra Filippo Lippi, the scene of the Virgin adoring the Child was very popular, and it is to this class of representation that the great *Incarnation* altarpiece of Andrea della Robbia at La Verna belongs. Luca della Robbia himself treated it on one occasion in a relief now at Nynehead (Cat. No. 50, Plate 123). It shows the Virgin almost in profile with her cloak pulled forwards so that she and the Child are linked in a triangle or pyramid. The figures, flanked by two lily plants, are strongly modelled and self-contained. In both respects Andrea della Robbia's *Incarnation* differs from Luca's relief. The modelling is less full and confident, and the scene is far from private; it presumes, indeed solicits, the presence of an onlooker. What cannot be established with any confidence is the chronological relationship between the two reliefs. The Nynehead relief was regarded by Marquand as an extremely early work, but it can hardly have been made before about 1465 and may well be even later. There is no means of establishing whether it precedes Andrea della Robbia's *Incarnation* or reflects his style.

The practice of Andrea della Robbia is certainly reflected in two pictorial reliefs modelled by Luca about 1475. Both are circular. The first is a large *Adoration of the Shepherds* in the Victoria & Albert Museum (Cat. No. 51, Plate 126), which may have been inspired by Antonio Rossellino's marble *Adoration of the Shepherds* in the Museo Nazionale. The view that this is a late work by Luca, not a work by Andrea della Robbia, is substantiated by the composition, which is based on a central vertical established by the stable and the shoulder and side of the Virgin seated within it and the horizontals of the ground and roof, as well as by the modelling of the Virgin's head, which is of consummate sensibility. A dog in the foreground looks back to those in the *Story of Jacob and Esau* on the Porta del Paradiso. Had this beautiful relief been modelled a decade earlier, it would have been completed with a frame of fruit modelled by or under the direction of Luca della Robbia. As it is, it is enclosed in a conventional frame decorated with white roses moulded in Andrea della Robbia's shop.

The second pictorial relief is the Foulc *Virgin adoring the Child* in the Philadelphia Museum of Art (Cat. No. 52, Plate 127). It shows the Virgin in right profile kneeling beside the Child, whose birth is celebrated by four flying angels with a cartellino at the back. The type of the Child corresponds with that in the Capponi altarpiece at Pescia. The effect of this delicate relief is weakened by a heavy frame with swags of fruit, which is said to have been purchased by its former owner from a separate source, and is a late work from the shop of Andrea della Robbia.

Some of the most ambiguous works of the fourteen-seventies are four roundels of Virtues in frames of fruit (Cat. Nos. 72–75, Figs. 51–53), one of them, the *Faith*, formerly in the Heilbronner collection, another, the *Prudence*, in the Metropolitan Museum of Art, and a third, the *Temperance*, in the Musée de Cluny. A fourth roundel, the *Justice* in the Musée de Cluny, was rightly separated from them by Marquand. All four roundels are said to have a Pazzi provenance, which cannot, however, be confirmed, and it was at one time claimed that they were made for the ceiling of the Pazzi Chapel. The roundels in Paris and New York are exceptionally refined, but are autograph works of about 1480 by Andrea della Robbia. The fourth is probably, but not certainly, a late work by Luca.

Two other works of some distinction are now commonly given to Andrea della Robbia, but seem to have been modelled by Luca about 1470. The first is a *Relief Bust of a Lady* in the Museo Nazionale (Cat. No. 53, Plate 128). The head is represented frontally, turned slightly to the left, and the hair is parted in two artificially supported tresses which have the same linear subtlety as the hair of *Temperance* in the Chapel of the Cardinal of Portugal, and serve, like the wings of the *Virtues* at San Miniato, to fill out and reinforce the circular blue ground. The form of the head, with a veil edged with pearls that covers the ears and a jewel on the crown, and of the neck, decorated with a necklace and a pendant pearl, is of great accomplishment, as is the pigmentation of the eyes and eyebrows and the white enamelling. There is no equivalent in the work of Andrea della Robbia for the bold modelling of the light-blue surcoat, with its padded shoulders, for the full neck of the green dress, or for the beautifully rendered edge of the chemise. The type is reminiscent of portrait busts by Desiderio da Settignano, and the relief represents the point at which the graphs of the two sculptors most nearly meet.

The second work dating from about 1470 is a *Bust of a Lady* also in the Museo Nazionale (Cat. No. 54, Col. Plate XXXII). Modelled fully in the round, and made in two sections, one the body, the other the head and neck, it has a hole in the head seemingly destined for a gilt wood or metal halo, and seems to represent a female saint. The freely modelled hair is glazed yellow, like the hair of the Virgin in the *stemma* of the Arte dei Medici e degli Speziali on Or San Michele, and the blue cloak is fastened with a white flower at the throat. Above its green lining can be seen the top of a mauve dress. The modelling of the face is related to that of the heads of the *Virtues* at San Miniato. In the Bargello it is shown alongside a *Bust of a Boy* in enamelled terracotta by Andrea della Robbia (Cat. No. 76, Fig. 60), and the distinction between the descriptive modelling of

Andrea's bust and the resolute forms of Luca's is very marked.

Possibly but not certainly, Luca in the last decade of his life continued to produce heraldic reliefs. The criteria for differentiating these from heraldic reliefs by Andrea are almost wholly subjective, though we know one *stemma*, that of Lorenzo and Francesco Davanzati on the Campanile at Pistoia, which is datable to the year 1490 and is therefore by Andrea della Robbia,[13] and one heraldic roundel with the arms of Federico Manfredi, Bishop of Faenza, which forms one of a group of commissions executed for Manfredi before 1477 by Andrea. There are, however, certain reliefs datable to the seventies of the fifteenth century which are conceived more boldly than the early heraldic designs of Andrea della Robbia. One of these is the *stemma* of Giovanni di Francesco Tornabuoni on the Palazzo Pretorio at San Giovanni Valdarno (Cat. No. 79, Fig. 57), where the lion rampant *or* and *vert* was regarded by Marquand, possibly correctly, as of a quality that could be explained only by Luca's intervention. This *stemma* dates from 1478-9. Associable with this is a Martelli *stemma* of uncertain provenance in the Rijksmuseum, Amsterdam (Cat. No. 80). Without some knowledge of the source from which it comes, no date can be given to this work. An earlier *stemma* of Ruberto Leoni of 1463 at San Giovanni Valdarno (Cat. No. 81, Fig. 58) seems to have been made in Luca della Robbia's shop, whereas a *stemma* of some distinction in the Palazzo della Stufa (Cat. No. 82, Fig. 59), tentatively given by Marquand to Luca, is undoubtedly a work of Andrea della Robbia.

* * * *

So Luca della Robbia, his work accomplished, sinks slowly out of view. He remained an active member of the Arte dei Maestri di Pietra e di Legname, paying his annual dues till 1481 and receiving small sums for his works as *sindacho* in 1471 and 1476 and as an intermittent member of the council from 1474 till 1480. Much of his business seems to have been conducted through his nephew Simone, who bought and sold land on his behalf and may, in the fourteen-seventies, have been incorporated in Luca's studio. Simone seems at some uncertain point to have matriculated in the Arte dei Maestri di Pietra e di Legname, where he served, in a surrogate capacity or in *propria persona*, as consul in 1474, 1478 and 1480,[14] and after the difficulties over Luca's will were settled, he became a business partner of his brother, whose firm is described in 1491 as

13. Marquand, 1922, i, p. 107, No. 72.
14. Florence, Archivio di Stato, Arti, Maestri di Pietra e Legname, 3 (Matricole, 1388–1518), c. 142r., 148r., 149v.

'Andrea di Marcho della robbia et fratellj de firenze.'[15] We catch a brief glimpse of him in 1497 disbursing money in connection with the installation of Andrea's roundels on the Loggia di San Paolo.[16] Luca's dependence on Simone della Robbia must go back at least to 1471, when the 'providus et discretus vir Lucas olim Simonis Marci della Robbia, scultor' named him as his universal heir. In his will Luca humbly recommends his soul to Almighty God, to the Virgin Mary 'et toti celestis curie Paradisi' and enjoins that his body shall be buried in whatever place his heir shall deem appropriate. When he died, on 20 February 1482, the choice inevitably fell upon the church with which his forebears had been associated, and we read in the *Libro dei Morti in Firenze*: 'Adi 23 di decto. Lucha della Robbia, riposto in Sancto Piero Maggiore.'

Luca della Robbia's was a domestic reputation. He did not work in Padua or Siena, like Donatello; he was not enticed to Rome; and even Filarete, while familiar with his name and with his work in the Palazzo Medici, was wholly unaware of the kind of artist that he was. In the account of his ideal palace, he describes a chimney-piece, carved from a beautiful, heat-resistant stone, which was incised 'di mano di buono maestro il quale si chiamava Luca della Robbia' with figures of Vulcan, Mucius Scaevola 'quando s'arse il braccio' and Tubal-cain, and in the centre 'Fetonte in sul carro di Febo,' beneath a frieze showing the invention of fire by the Egyptians. At his death, Luca della Robbia was the last survivor of the heroic generation of Florentine Early Renaissance artists. When he died, Ghiberti had been dead for almost twenty-seven years and Donatello for sixteen, and it was he alone who could recall the spirit of enquiry and experiment, the puritanical self-discipline whereby Renaissance style was forged. The biographer of Brunelleschi, expressing his disquiet at the changes Antonio di Manetti Ciaccheri introduced at San Lorenzo, cites the authority of Luca della Robbia, who 'lamented when they were being done, as he saw that he had made them in order to detract from Filippo's fame, since who-ever came there would think that, like the other things, they were Filippo's work.'

Luca's development differed from that of his contemporaries. Never did he, like Donatello after his return from Padua, relapse into an eccentric, introverted style of old age, couched in a language no one, save a handful of sophisticated patrons, could apprehend. Never did he, like Ghiberti after 1429, focus with obsessive concentration on a single illustrative project, in which, in miniature, a whole repertory of aesthetic thinking was compressed. He was an instinctive classicist, but his art grew directly from things seen, and it was from this dual relationship to the antique on the one hand and to the real world on the other that it drew its individuality and strength. 'His works in terracotta,' writes Pater, 'only transfer to a different material the principles of his sculptures. They have the impress of a personal quality, a profound expressiveness, what the French call *intimité*, by which is meant some subtler sense of originality . . . what we call *expression*, carried to its highest intensity of degree.' Luca della Robbia was an innovator in the sense first that he extended the expressive range of marble sculpture, and second that he invented a new medium and over decades, with absolute consistency, explored its communicative possibilities. He possessed at the same time a capacity for self-renewal which places him apart from other artists of his day. The stages by which the neo-classical naturalist of the Cantoria became the heroic fresco painter of the lunettes in the Cathedral, the staid decorator of the Pazzi Chapel, and acquired the linear mastery of the *Virtues* in the Chapel of the Cardinal of Portugal and the *Stemma of King René of Anjou*, are the more impressive in that they were not predictable. With no great artist of the fifteenth century is contact easier or more direct, and if Luca remains a popular sculptor it is for the selfsame reason that ensured his success in his own time, that his imagination functions within the limits of ordinary life, and that his personality evinces a tenderness and a compassion that sounds in all of us a responsive chord.

---

15. This term is used in a document of 20 August 1491, recording payment for the tondi of the *Evangelists* in Santa Maria delle Carceri at Prato (Marquand, 1922, i, p. 112, No. 74).

16. Marquand, 1922, i, p. 136, doc. 11.

Appendix 1

TAX RETURNS

Abbreviated summaries of the tax returns prepared by Simone di Marco della Robbia and by Luca della Robbia are printed by Cruttwell (1902, pp. 285–6, 300–6) and Marquand (1914, pp. xxxii–xxxix). The present texts have been transcribed afresh by Dr. Gino Corti, and are here published *in extenso*.

A. Portata al Catasto of Simone della Robbia 1427

Florence, Archivio di Stato. Catasto, 59 (S. Giovanni, Chiavi, 1427), c. 976r–979v:

156   Gonfalone Chiavi, Quartiere S. Giovanni
Questa è la rechata di Simone di Marcho della Robbia e de' figliuoli, prestanziati in decto gonfalone in fiorini quatro soldi quactordici e danari cinque a oro.... f. 4 s. 14 d. 5

In prima una chasa da llavoratore, con palchi, sala, camera e terreno, posta nel popolo di Santa Maria dal Tartigliese, Valdarno di sopra, contado di Firenze, nel borgho del Tartigliese, nella strada publica, confinata da primo decta strada, a II via, a III Niccholò di Giovanni del Bellaccio, a IIII Marcho del Bello del Bellaccio.

Item una chasecta posta dirietro alla sopradecta casa, che se ne fa stalla da bestie, posta nel decto popolo e luogo, confinata a I via, a II Filippo di Firenze del Pancia, a III via, a IIII le rede di Piero Teri, co' gli infrascricti pezi di terra, cioè.

Uno pezo di terra lavoratia, di staiora cinque a grano, posto nel decto popolo, luogo decto alla Tavolaia, a I via, a II Marcho del Bello Bellaccii, a III Filippo di Firenze del Pancia, a IIII Simone di Marcho sopradecto.

Item uno pezo di terra vignata, di staiora tre a grano, con uno poco d'orticello, posto nel decto popolo e luogo, a I via, a II Niccholò di Giovanni del Bellaccio, a III e a IIII Antonio di Salvestro di ser Ristoro.

Item uno pezo di terra lavoratia, di staiora cinque a grano, posto nel decto popolo a luogo, confinato a I via, a II Antonio di Salvestro di ser Ristoro, a III della chiesa di Santa Maria dal Tartigliese, a III di Simone di Marcho sopradecto.

Item uno pezo di terra lavoratia, di staiora due a grano, posto nel decto popolo e luogo, a I Niccholò di Giovanni del Bellaccio, a II, III e a IIII e beni della chiesa di Santa Maria dal Tartigliese.

Item uno pezo di terra lavoratia, di staiora cinque a grano, posta nel decto popolo, luogo decto a Ristone, [c. 976v] confinato a I via, a II ser Piero di ser Martino, a III e a IIII Antonio di Salvestro di ser Ristoro.

Item uno pezo di terra, di staiora uno a grano, posto nel decto popolo, loco decto al Coltolino, a I fossato, a II Filippo di Firenze del Pancia, a III decto Filippo, a IIII Antonio di Salvestro di ser Ristoro.

Item uno pezo di terra lavoratia, di staiora quatro a grano, posto nel decto popolo, loco decto a Ristone, a confinato a I fossato, a II Antonio di Salvestro di ser Ristoro, a III le rede di Piero Teri, a IIII le rede di Dino di Pero cartolaio.

Item uno pezo di terra lavoratia, di staiora secte a grano, posto nel decto popolo, luogo decto al Mezule, a I Locto di Maffio, a II Antonio di Salvestro di ser Ristoro, a III e a IIII le rede di Ghoro tintore.

Item uno pezo di terra lavoratia, di staiora secte a grano, posto nel decto popolo, loco decto ala Vecchiese, a I via, a II le rede di Lucha di Iachopo, a III le rede di Niccholò Fagni, a IIII Francescho di Rinieri da San Giovanni.

Item uno pezo di terra rovinata e caduta pel fiume d'Arno, posta nel decto popolo, loco decto la via della Fossa, a I decta via, a II ser Giovanni di ser Bartolo Gherardini e altri, a III [gap]

Item uno pezo di terra pasturata, di staiora quatro a grano, posto nel decto popolo, loco decto al Borro alla Rovinata, a I le rede di Ceccho di Pagno, a II Marcho del Bello Bellaccii, a III lo spedale dal Tartigliese, a IIII via.

Item uno pezo di terra pasturata, di staiora tre a grano, posto nel decto popolo, loco decto al Borro al Chastelluccio, a I Bastiano di Ceccho, a II le rede di Ceccho di Pagno, a III e a IIII Niccholò di Giovanni del Bellaccio.

Item uno pezo di terra boschata e con quercie, di staioro uno a grano, posto nel decto popolo e luogho, a I Filippo di Firenze del Pancia, a II decto Filippo, a III Andrea [c. 977r] di Romolo dal Tartigliese, a IIII Piero di Biagio dal Tartigliese.

Item uno pezo di terra boschata, di staiora uno a grano, a I e II Filippo di Firenze del Pancia, a III Andrea di Romolo, a IIII lo spedale dal Tartigliese.

Item uno pezo di terra boschata e con quercie, di staiora tre a grano, posto nel decto popolo, loco decto al Poggiuolo, a I

Filippo di Firenze del Pancia, a II le rede del Bellaccino, a III le rede di Dino di Pero cartolaio, a IIII Filippo di Firenze del Pancia.

Item uno pezo di terra boschata, posto nel decto popolo, loco decto Monte Mione, di staiora uno e mezo a grano, a I Piero di Vicho, a II e III Antonio di Salvestro di ser Ristoro, a IIII Marcho del Bello Bellaccii.

Item uno pezo di terra boschata, di staiora uno e mezo, posto nel decto popolo, loco decto al Borratino, a I e II Filippo di Firenze del Pancia, a III Antonio di Salvestro, a IIII Marcho del Bello Bellaccii.

Item uno pezo di terra vignata, di staiora uno e mezo a grano, posto nel decto popolo, loco decto Monte Mione, a I via, a II Niccholò di Giovanni del Bellaccio, a III lo spedale dal Tartigliese, a IIII Antonio di Salvestro di ser Ristoro.

Item uno pezo di terra boschata, di staiora uno a grano, posto nel decto popolo e luogo, e I via, II, III e IIII di Piero di Biagio dal Tartigliese.

Rendono tucte la sopradecte terre ogni anno, l'uno anno pe' l'altro ristorando,

staia sexanta di grano
barili dieci di vino
staia dieci d'orzo
staia dodici di sagina
staia sei di miglio
staia sei di panicho
libre dieci di lino grosso
uno paio di chapponi
libre 250 di carne di porco
serque cinque d'uuova [sic]

Lavora le sopradecte terre soprascricte [c. 977v] Marcho di Berto dal Tartigliese, dèbaci dare fiorini dieci . . . . . . f. 10 –

Item abbiamo in sul decto podere:
uno paio di buoi, di stima . . . . di f. dieci
una asina, di stima. . . . . di f. tre
cinque porci grandicielli . . . . . . } di stima in tucto di f. dieci
una troia con secte porcellini . . }
delle quali buoi e bestie n'abbiamo avere la metà.

Item una caseeta posta in Chastello San Giovanni, Valdarno di sopra, luogo decto via di Rachasoli, confinata a I decta via, a II rede di Lucha di Iacopo, a III Franceschо di Lucha, a IIII chiasso. La decta casetta tiene a pigione Franceschо di Lucha Salti da Chastello San Giovanni, e debbaci dare di pigione l'anno fiorini uno d'oro. . . . . .f. 1 –

Item uno pezo di terra vignata e parte lavoratia, di staiora quatro a grano, posto nella corte di Chastello San Giovanni, Valdarno di sopra, loco decto alla Fossa Corboli, confinato a I via, a II e III Antonio di Girolamo, a IIII Checcho di Macteo spadaio.

Item uno pezo di terra vignata, di staiora due a grano, posta nella decta corte, loco decto Fossato ala Villa, a I e II via, a III e a IIII Messer Palla di Nofri degli Strozi.

Item uno pezuolo di terra, che non è se none macchie di pruni, di meno d'uno staiorо, posto nella decta corte, luogo

decto nel Fondale, a I via, a II beni della pieve di Chastello San Giovanni, a III e a IIII ser Masso di ser Piero di ser Masso.

E. sopradecti tre pezzi di terra tiene a ficto da noi Antonio di Cente da Chastello San Giovanni, e danne di ficto lire sedici piccioli . . . . .L. XVI –

[c. 978r]
Item uno podere con chasa da signore e da llavoratore, con terre lavoratie, ulivate, arborate, vignate e con pergole e con alberi fructiferi e non fructiferi, posto nel contado di Firenze, nel popolo di San Tommè a Baroncelli, loco decto a Baroncelli, confinato a I le rede di Franceschо di Duccio Mellini, via in mezo, a II Filippo di Simone e il fratello, fossatello in mezo, a III Maso Davizi, a IIII via.

Item uno pezo di terra lavoratia e alborata, apartenente al decto podere, di staioro uno a grano, posto nel decto popolo, loco decto al Canpuccio, a I e II via, a III e IIII le rede di Conte Peruzi, fossatello in mezo.

Item uno pezo di terra lavoratia, apartenente al decto podere, di staioro uno a grano, posto nel decto popolo, loco decto Ritortole, a I via, a II e III le rede di Conte Peruzii, fossatello in mezo, a IIII le rede di Franceschо Mellini, fossatello in mezo.

Rende el sopradecto podere, l'uno anno ristorando l'altro,

staia trenta di grano
barili quaranta di vino
libre dieci di lino grosso
fructe fiorini due
due paia di chapponi
serque dieci d'uuova [sic]

Lavora el sopradecto podere Bartolo di Iacopo, vocato Bartolo della Dina.

Item una chasa posta nella città di Firenze, nel popolo di San Piero Maggiore, nella via che si chiama degli Albertinegli e riesce nella via di San Gilio, [c. 978v] confinata da primo via degli Albertinegli, a II dello spedale di Santa Maria Nuova, a III delle rede di Maso e Ugho degli Alessandri, a IIII via di San Gilio. La decta chasa à tenuta e tiene la metà una monna Nera vedova, pe'll'amore di Dio, già sono anni venti e più, e mai non ce ne à dato nulla; l'altra metà abbiàno apigionata del mese d'aprile proximo passato a Ugholino di messer Giovanni, e non se ne è facto pacto niuno. Crediano ce ne darà fiorini tre l'anno o circa, però che non vale tucta decta casa fiorini sessanta . . . . f. tre . . . . f. III –

Item debbe avere Simone proprio dalle infrascricte persone le infrascricte quantità, cioè da:

Corso di Giunta tintore, che à fallito . . . . .L. XXVIIII
Bernardo Baldovini, che è nelle Stinche . . . . .L. XV
Mino di Borgianni tintore, fiorini tre . . . . .f. III
Lone di ser Mactio, conciatore . . . . .L. XIIII
Iacopo e Antonio di Bartolo Malfasciati di Val di Sieve, fiorini octo d'oro . . . . .f. VIII
Simone di Benvenuto schardassiere . . . . .L. V

Item dee avere ser Giovanni di Simone proprio da:
Messer Francescho di Sandro Chanbini, per carte, fiorini quattro lire cinque soldi sedici............f. 4 L. 5 s. 16
Francescho e Giusto di Cino di Cino da Citina Vecchia e monna Bartolomea loro madre fiorini sexanta: dare, 'gli pe' lla metà volentieri.....................f. 60 d'oro
Monna Papera figliuola fu di Lenzone di Simone [c. 979r] ghalighaio e donna del decto ser Giovanni, per resto di dota, fiorini centodieci d'oro....................f. 110
ser Bonacchorso di Piero Bonacchorsi..............f. 3

Incharichi

Simone di Marcho sopradecto, d'età d'anni............84
monna Margherita donna del decto Simone, d'anni.......65
Marcho di Simone, d'anni.......................42
ser Giovanni di Simone, d'anni.....................33
Lucha di Simone, d'anni...........................27
monna Papera, donna del decto ser Giovanni, d'anni......26
Pulisena, figliuola di ser Giovanni [added later:] naque adì primo di sectembre 1427

Abbiàno a pigione una chasa con sale, palchi, camere, terreno, corte, cucina e volta e pozo, nella quale noi abitiano, dentrovi nostre masseritie, posta nel popolo di San Piero Maggiore, nella via di San Gilio, confinata a I via decta, a II Stefano di Salvi, a III Simone di Salvi, a IIII rede di Giovanni di Salvi. La decta chasa è delle rede di Giovanni di Salvi; paghianne di pigione fiorini dicianove d'oro al'anno ....f. XVIIII

Item abbiàno a dare agl'infrascricti huomini a persone le infrascricte quantità di dinari, cioè a:
sindachi del gonfalone delle Chiavi..............f. XIII
Comune di Firenze, pe' prestanzoni............f. XV
Lorenzo e Bernardo di Benino, linaiuoli........f. LXX
Tommaso Bartoli ritagliatore e compagni.......f. LXX
Macteo Rondinegli e conpagni ritagliatori.......f. XXX

[c. 979v]
Item doviàno dare a:
la ghabella del vino, per una promessa..........f. XXX
Bernardo de' Bardi a conpagni orafi ....f. XV
Pagholo di ser Giovanni speziale.............f. XVIII
Priore Risaliti e conpagni ritagliatori...........f. VIII
Francescho di Pierozo della Luna.............f. LXI

Item dee avere monna Papera, donna del decto ser Giovanni, dalle rede di Benedecto di ser Francescho del maestro Piero fiorini dugento o circa, per resto della sua dota, e quali s'ànno a piatire però sono in dif⟨e⟩renza, de' quali n'à a dare al decto ser Giovanni fiorini centodieci, chome detto è di sopra in questa scricta. Se si rischoteranno, gli raporteremo alla vostra signorìa.

Item mi truo⟨vo⟩ io Giovanni sopradecto tanti tra libri e inbreviature che gli stimo fiorini XXV.

[c. 980v]
[*note by a Catasto officer:*]
    Gonfalone Chiavi, adì 10 di luglio [1427]
Simone di Marcho della Robia e filgl[i]uoli..f. 4 s. 14 d .5
        Messa a libro, 532.

B. Portata al Catasto of Simone della Robbia 1430

Florence, Archivio di Stato. Catasto, 409 (S. Giovanni, Chiavi, 1430), c. 230v–231 v:
        Sustanze e incharichi di
Simone di Marcho della Robia, à di chatasto fiorini 1 –

2 chase poste nel borgho e nel popolo di Santa Maria al Tartagliese, cho' molti pezi di terra e cho' molti chonfini, chome apare per suo scritta partitamente. Lavora le sopradette terre e pezi e tiene le chase Marcho di Bennte [*sic*] dal Trartagliese [*sic*]; à di presta fiorini 12 e uno paio di buoi e una asina.
Rende

grano	staia	60	a s. 18 lo staio	lire	54	—	—
vino	barili	10	a s. 26 il barile	lire	13	—	—
orzo	staia	10	a s. 10 lo staio	lire	5	—	—
sagina	staia	12	a s. 6 lo staio	lire	3	s. 12	–
miglio	staia	6	a s. 10 lo staio	lire	3	—	—
panicho	staia	6	a s. 10 lo staio	lire	3	—	—
carne	libre	250	a L. 5 il cento	lire	12	s. 10	–
lino	libre	12	a s. 1½ libra	lire	—	s. 15	–
capponi	paia	1	s. 20 il paio	lire	1	—	—
uova	serque	5	a s. 2 la serqua	lire	—	s. 10	–

1ª troia con VII porcelini stimati ....f. 2 –
Somma lire 96 s. 7: a 7 per cento ......f. 347 s. 17 –

1ª chasetta posta in Chastel San Giovanni di Valdarno di Sopra, chon più chonfini, che none apare per suo scritta. Tiella [a] pigione Francesco di Lucha Salti per fiorini 1 l'anno: a 7 per cento.....................f. 14 s. 6
[c. 231 r]

3 pezi di terra posta nella chorte di Chastel San Giovanni, chon più chonfini, chome per suo scritta partitamente si chontiene. E sopradetti 3 pezi tiene a fitto Giuliano d'Antonio di Girolamo, danne l'anno di fitto lire 14 piccioli: a 7 per cento.....................f. 50 –

1° podere chon chasa da singniore e da lavoratore e chon più pezi di terra e chonfini, chome partitamente si chontiene. Lavoralo Antonio di Lorenzo chiamato Grazia.
Rende:

grano	staia	30	a s. 18 lo staio	lire	27	— —
vino	barili	40	a s. 26 il barile	lire	52	— —
frutte	fiorini	2	a.s.———	lire	8	— —
capponi	paia	2	a s. 20 il paio	lire	2	— —
uova	serque	10	a s. 2 la serqua	lire	1	— —
lino	libre	10	a s. 2 libra	lire	1	— —

Somma lire 91 s. –: a 7 per cento.......f. 325——

1ª chasa posta nel popolo di San Piero Maggiore, nella via degli Albertinegli, chon più chonfini, chome per suo scritta partitamente si chontiene. Abiàne di pigione da certe pinzochere fiorini 3 l'anno: a 7 per cento f. 42 s. 17 –
    Danari di monte dichono in Lucha mio figl⟨i⟩uolo di monte di prestanzoni, i' Lucha f. 150: a 50 per cento...................................f. 75 —
le paghe di detti fiorini......f.———......f. 9 —
de' avere il detto Lucha d'inchanti f. 12......f. 12——

Danari à 'vere Marcho mio figliolo

per 4 debitori, che 'l primo chominicia Andrea di Naldo a fiorini 26, e finiscie a Filippo di Cristofano a fiorini 5: in tutto f. 58 s. 7 d. 3 [a] fiorino . . . . f. 58 s. 5 –
per VI debitori, che sono debitori di ser Giovanni mio figl⟨i⟩uolo, che 'l primo chomincia ala Chamera del Chomune a fiorini 14, e finiscie a Iachopo e Antonio di Bartolo a fiorini 8: in tutto f. 134 lire 6 s. 10 d.–. f. 100——

    Somma f. 672 s. 2 a oro.

[c. 231 v]

Incharichi

per 5 creditori ànno i sopradetti, che 'l primo chomincia a' sindachi del ghonfalone delle Chiavi a f. 12 e finiscie a Luigi di Marcho Bartoli e conpagni a f. 22 s. 21 a 9 [a] fiorino: in tutto. . . . . .f. 75——
Tràsene f. 12 à dare a' ghonfalone, restono. . . . .f. 63——
Dicie tenghono una chasa a pigione nella via di San Gilio e nel popolo di San Piero Magiore, nella quale abito⟨no⟩ cholle maserizie, la quale è di Simone di Salvi di Filippo, e dàne l'ano f. 19: a 7 per cento
f. 271 s. 8 –

Bocche

Simone di Marcho della Robia, d'anni 87
monna Margharita donna del detto Simone, d'anni 68
Marcho di Simone, d'anni 43
ser Giovanni di Simone, d'anni 36
Lucha di Simone, d'anni 30
monna Antonia donna di detto Marcho, d'anni 20
Filippo figliolo del detto Marcho, d'anni ½ (cancelled with marginal note: morto)

    Sono 7 bocche . . . . .f. 1440 (corrected in: f. 1200)
    Somma tutto lo 'ncharicho f. 1534 s. 8 a oro
    Somma la prima facia del mobile in questo, c. 230
                       f. 364 s. 3 –
    Somma la seconda facia, c. 231. . . . . f. 672 s. 2 –
    Somma tutto il mobile. . . . . .f. 1036 s. 5.–
    Manchagli.
    Conposto in soldi otto, c⟨i⟩oè s. 8.

C. Portata al Catasto of Simone della Robbia 1433

Florence, Archivio di Stato. Catasto, 499 (S. Croce; Chiavi, 1433: campione delle portate), c. 692r–694r:

Sustanze di
Simone di Marcho della Robbia e figl⟨i⟩uoli, ànno s. 16 d. 3.

Una chasa posta nel popo⟨lo⟩ di S. Maria al Tartagliese, da llavoratore, e una altra chaseta allato a quella, che dicie se ne fa stalla, cho' suoi vocaboli e chonfini.

19 pezi di terra lavoratia vigniata, posta nel popolo di S. Maria al Tartagliese, chon diversi chonfini chome dà per la sua schritta. Lavora dette terre Stefano di Ciecho dal Tartagliese.
À un bue vecchio.

À 5 porci grandiciegli ⎫ Stimiamo d'achordo ogni ⟨co⟩sa
À una asina ciecha ⎭   f. 4 –
Rendono, ristorando l'uno anno l'altro:

grano. . . . . .staia 60 per s. 18 lo staio	lire 54 –
vino . . . . .barili 10 per 2. 26 barile	lire 13 –
horzo. . . . . .staia 10 per s. 10 lo staio	lire 5 –
saggina . . . . .staia 12 per s. 6 lo staio	lire 3 s. 12
miglio . . . . .staia 6 per s. 10 lo staio	lire 3 –
panicho . . . . .staia 6 per s. 10 lo staio	lire 3 –
lino . . . . .libre 12 per s. 2 libra	lire 1 s. 4
charne . . . . .libre 250 per s. 100 libra	lire 12 s. 10
huova e polli nel secondo, in tutto . . . . .lire 1 s. 10

    Somma detta rendita lire 96 s. 16: a lire 4 per fiorino, f. 24 s. 4: a f. 7 per cento, f. 345 s. 14 d. 4
                      f. 345 s. 14 d. 4

Una chasa posta in Chastel San Giovanni, Valdarno di Sopra, chon suoi vochaboli e chonfini. Stavi a pigione Francho di Lucha, danne l'anno f. 1 d'oro: a f. 7 per cento
           . . . . .f. 14 s. 5 d. 9
                 364.0.1

[c. 692v]
Un pezo di terra posta nella chorte di Chastel San Giovanni, chon suoi chonfini. Dicie non ne chavano nulla. . . . . .f.——

Una chasa posta nel popolo di San Piero Magiore, via degli Albertinegli, chon suoi vochaboli e chonfini; della metà s'à di pigione lire 10 pìccioli: a f. 7 per cento f. 36 s. 3. ——
Del 'altra metà non se n'à nulla perché vi sta una vedova per l'amor di Dio.

Un podere chon chasa da signiore e da lavoratore, chon terre lavoratie vigniate alborate ulivate, posto nel popolo di San Tommè a Baroncielli, chon suoi vochaboli e chonfini, chon due pezi di terra posti in detto popolo, cho' loro chonfini. Lavora Lorenzo di Silmiano e Antonio suo figliuolo; à di presta fiorini 15.
Rende in parte l'uno anno per l'altro:

grano. . . . . .staia 30 per s. 18 lo staio	lire 27 –
vino . . . . .barili 40 per s. 26 barile	lire 52 –
frutte. . . . . .fiorini 2————————	lire 8 –
chapponi nel secondo paia 2 per s. 20 paio	lire 2 –
huova nel secondo serque 10 per s. 2 serqua	lire 1 –
lino nel secondo libre 10 per s. 2 libra	lire 1 –

    Somma detta rendita lire 91: a lire 4 per fiorino, f. 22 s. 15: a f. 7 per cento . . . . .f. 325 ——
                361. 3. 0

[c. 693r]
Un podere chon chasa da lavoratore, chon terre lavoratie ulivate alborate vigniate, posto nel popolo di S. Andrea a Luiano, chon suoi vocaboli e chonfini.
Lavora detto podere Lariano d'Antonio. Ànno un paio di buoi di fiorini 20 d'oro.
Rende l'anno in parte:

grano . . . . .staia 24 a s. 19 lo staio	lire 23 s. 16 –
horzo . . . . .staia 3 ⎫ per s. 10 lo staio	lire 3 –
fave . . . . .staia 3 ⎭	
spelda . . . . .staia 6 per s. 6 lo staio	lire 1 s. 16 –

vino . . . . barili 6 per s. 34 barile lire 10 s. 4 –
olio . . . . barili 2 nel primo barili 3, per s. 100
　　　　　　　　barile lire 15 –
charne . . . . libre 100 per s. 100 il cento lire 5 –
chapponi . . . . paia 1 per s. 20 paio lire 1 –
huova . . . . serque 60 per d. 2 l'uno lire – s. 10 –

　　Soma detta rendita lire 60 s. 6: a lire 4 per fiorino,
　　f. 15 s. 1 d. 6: a f. 7 per cento . . . . f. 215 s. 7 d. 3

Un pezo di terra lavoratia e ulivata, posta in detto popolo,
chon suoi chonfini, non dà alchuna rendita, dicie gli chostò
f. 16 d'oro . . . . f. 16————
　　　　　　　　241. 7. 3

Truovasi Marcho suo figl⟨i⟩uolo in sula botegha di
guadangno d'arte di lana, che dicie in Agnolo di ser Martino,
per saldo fatto, fiorini 160 . . . . f. 160————
　　　　　　　　401. 7. 3

[c. 693v]
f. 300 di monte di prestanzoni dichono in Lucha di Simone:
a f. 45 per cento . . . . f. 135 ————
f. 200 di monte chomune, in lui: a f. 33⅓
per cento . . . . f. 66 s. 13 d. 4
f. 35 d'achatti e d'altri danari: a f. 20 per cento f. 7 .————
f. 5 s. 18 d. 5 d'achatti: a f. 80 per cento . . . . f. 4 s. 16 –

　　　　　　　Paghe sostenute
f. 16 di paghe di f. 150 di prestanzoni, di ⎫
1427 a ogi, al 1431　　　　　　　　　　 ⎪
f. [lacuna] di paghe di f. 150 di prestanzoni ⎬ a d. 4 per
da 1431 a ogi　　　　　　　　　　　　　 ⎪ fiorino
f. [lacuna] di paghe sostenute dal '31 in qua ⎪ f. – s. 5 d. 4
di. f. 200 di monte chomune　　　　　　 ⎭

　　　　　　　Debitori
Iachopo e Antonio di Bartolo . . . . . . f. 8 –
Rede di Marcho di Berto dal
Tartagliese . . . . f. 10 –
gli Otto della Ghuardia, in nome di
ser Giovanni suo figliuolo . . . . f. 17 s. 10 a oro
Rede di messer Francesco di Sandro f. 4 lire 5 s. 16 piccioli
Vannozo Serragli, overo Papi detti . . . f. 13 lire 2 –
Agniolano di Lorenzo . . . . f. 3 lire 2 –

　　Soma detti debitori f. 55 lire 11 s. 16: stimagli . . f. 25 ——
　　　　　　　　238. 14. 8

　　　　　　　Incharichi
Una chasa tenghono a pigione dalle rede di Simone di Salvi
di Filippo, posta nel popolo di San Piero Maggiore, chon suoi
chonfini, dove abitano, e diànne l'anno f. 19 d'oro: a f. 7 per
cento . . . . f. 271 s. 8 –

[c. 694r]
　　　　　　Incharichi
Agniolo di ser Martino . . . . f. 26 s. 10 a oro f. 26 s. 10
Bernardo de'Bardi e conpagni　 f. 15 –　　　　　f. 15 –
Antonio di Ghezo e conpagni . . f. 20 –　　　　　f. 20 –
Priore Risaliti e compagni . . . . . f. 9 –　　　　　f. 9 –
Lorenzo di Benino di Ghucio . . f. 13 –　　　　　f. 13 –
Bernardo di Filippo G⟨i⟩ungni
e compagni . . . . f. 7 –　　　　　f. 7 –

Mariotto di Francesco di ser
Segnia . . . . f. 4 s. 10　　f. 4 s. 10
Agniolo di ser Martino e com-
pagni . . . . f. 6 –　　　　f. 6 –
il Chomune di Firenze . . . . f. 15 –　　　　f. ————
　　　　　　　　101. 0. 0

Truovasi Marcho suo figl⟨i⟩uolo debito in su la bottegha
d'Angnolo di ser Martino dov'è chompagno, per saldo fatto,
f. 84 s. 10 . . . . f. 84 s. 10 –
　　　　　　　　185. 10. 0
　　　　　　　Bocche
Simone di Marcho . . . . d'anni 89
monna Margherita sua
donna . . . . d'anni 70
Marcho di Simone . . . . d'anni 46
monna Antonia sua donna　 d'anni 20
Checcha di Marcho . . . . d'anni 1
Iachopo di Marcho . . . . . . d'anni 1
ser Giovanni di Simone . . . d'anni 39
monna Nanna sua donna . . d'anni 19
Lucha di Simone . . . . d'anni 33———— f. 1800 -
　　Somma tutte le sustanze . . . . f. 1365 s. 5 –
　　Somma incharichi e bocche . . . . f. 2256 s. 18 –
　　　　Manchagli . . . . f. 891 s. 13 –
Chonposto d'achordo in s. 10.

D. Portata al Catasto of Luca della Robbia 1442

Florence, Archivio di Stato. Catasto, 627 (S. Giovanni,
Chiavi, 1442), c. 233r–v:

109　　　Quartiere San Giovanni, gonfalone Chiavi

Dinanzi da voi, signiori uficiali della chonservazione e
aumentazione della nuova graveza della città di Firenze, si
raporta le sustanze e benini [sic = beni] di Lucha di Simone
di Marcho della Robia, aprestanziato nella presente istri-
buzione della cinquina nel chonfalone delle Chiavi i' soldi
19 danari 1 a oro.

In prima la terza parte per non diviso chom Marcho e ser
Giovanni mie' frategli, di II chase poste nel borgho e nel
popolo di Santa Maria al Tartagliese in Valdarno di sopra,
chon più e più pezi di tera e più chonfini chom'apare nella
scritta del secondo chatasto, che dicieva in Simone di Marcho
mio padre. Lavoralo a mezo Piero di Lucha; rende in parte:
　　grano istaia sesanta . . . . istaia 60
　　vino barili dieci . . . . barili 10
　　oorzo [sic] istaia dieci . . . . staia 10
　　sagina istaia dodici . . . . staia 12
　　miglio istaia cinque . . . . staia 5
　　panicho istaia sei . . . . staia 6
　　charne libre dugentocinquanta . . . . libre 250
　　lini libre dodici . . . . libre 12
　　chaponi paia dua . . . . libre [sic] 2
　　uova serque dieci . . . . serque 10

[in Catasto officer's hand]: rende il sichondo chatasto il
tutto lire 96 soldi 6, gonfalone Chiavi a c. 230; tóchane
per la ⅓ parte lire XXXII soldi 2

E di tutta questa rendita mi tocha il ⅓ . . . . f. 8 s. – d. 6

La terza parte d'una chasetta posta nel popolo di San Piero Magiore, nella via degli Albertinelli, tiella a pigione Michele zoppo, chalzolaio, e danne l'anno di pigione fiorini tre: tochamene fiorini 1 d'oro l'anno . . . . f. 1 s. ———

Danari di monte

La terza parte di fiorini cinquantuno di monte di 5 interi, ischritti in Simone di Marcho m⟨i⟩o padre; àsene avere le paghe di magio passato in qua . . . . f. 2 s. 10 d. 4

La terza parte di f. 42 s. 13 d. 8 a oro di prestanzoni d'otto per cento cholla ritenzione, di Simo⟨ne⟩ detto ischritti

f. – s. 16 d. 6

12. 7. 4

[c. 233v]

La terza parte di f. 117 di monte chomune, in Simone detto; àsene avere le paghe di magio pasato in qua . . . . f. 1 s. 9 s. 3

La terza parte di f. 25 s. 13 d. 9 a oro di cinque achatti di f. sesantamila de' chontadini, iscritti in Simone detto, chome veranno le tratte . . . . f. ———

E più f. IIII d'oro paghai del balzello, ischritti i' Lucha detto, e quali paghai fuori del termine . . . . f. ———

E più lla ⅓ parte della 48ª ventina . . . . f. ———

E più f. trecento di monte di prestanzone d'otto per cento, dichono i' Lucha detto . . . . f. 18 s. ———

E più f. quatrocentoventitre, cioè f. 423, di monte chomune, che dichono i' Lucha detto . . . . f. 15 s. 17 d. 3

Ed io Lucha torno in chasa cho' Marcho di Simone mio fratello.

Lucha sopradetto, d'età d'anni 43.

12. 7. 4
35. 6. 6
47. 13. 10
Adì 24 di gennaio [1442/43] f. 1.

E. Portata al Catasto of Luca della Robbia 1446

Florence, Archivio di Stato. Catasto, 681 (S. Giovanni, Chiavi, 1446), c. 403r-v:

176   Quartiere S. Giovanni, Gonfalone Chiavi

Susstanze e 'ncharichi

Lucha di Simone di Marcho della Robbia, à di di⟨e⟩cina . . f. 1 e di dissipiacente . . . . f. uno s. 10

E di chatassto 1427 fiorini uno per chonposizione; diciea in Simone di Marcho della Robbia e ne' figliuoli . . . . . . f. uno

Una chasa da llavoratore, possta nel popolo di Santa Maria al Tartagl⟨i⟩ese di Valdarnno di sopra, nel borgho del Tartagl⟨i⟩ese, chonfinata a I isstrada, a II via, a III Nicholò di ⟨Gi⟩ovanni Bellacci, [a] IIII Marcho del Bello Bellacci.

Una chasetta possta dirieto a detta chasa, fàssene istalla da besst⟨i⟩e, in detto popolo, a I via, [a] II Filippo di Firenze del Pancia, [a] III e a IIII rede di Piero Teci.

XVIIII pezzi di terra chon dette chase: el primo chonfina a[I] via e II Marcho del Bello Belacci e III Filippo del Pancia, IIII loro medesimi; l'ùtimo chonfina a I via, e a II e a III e a IIII Piero di Biagio del Tartigl⟨i⟩ese, chome appare pe' lla isscritta sua. Lavoratore Marcho di Berto del Tartigliese.

Rende l'anno in parte: [c. 403v]

grano	staia	60
orzo	staia	10
saggina	staia	12
migl⟨i⟩o	staia	6
panicho	staia	6
vino	barili	10
lino grosso	libre	10
capponi	paia	1
uova	serque	5
carne	libre	250

Della sopradetta rendita toccha a mme la terza parte, perché nosstro padre morì e llasciò tre figliuoli, e siàno divisi. El sopradetto podere è oggi in buona parte nel fiume d'Arno ed è istatato [sic] già è più tenpo; el perché nel 1444 l'afittamo a Piero di Chimento per staia 60 di grano l'anno, delle quale ne toccha in mia parte istaia 20.

Danari di monte

fiorini 910 o circa di monte chomune in mio nome
fiorini 103 o circa di monte chomune i' nome di Simone di Marcho della Robbia mio padre.

Boche

Lucha detto, d'anni 46. [c. 403v]
[on bottom of page, by a Catasto officer:]
Rechò Lucha adì 28 [=February 1446/47]

F. Portata al Catasto of Luca della Robbia 1451

Florence, Archivio di Stato. Catasto, 717 (S. Giovanni, Chiavi, 1451), c. 464r

223   Quartiere Sancto Giovanni, Gonfalone Chiavi

Sustanze di

Lucha di Simone di Marcho della Robbia intagliatore. Disse el primo chatasto in Simone di Marcho mio padre, èbbene . . . . f. 1 s. ———

Ebbi di decina nel 1447 . . . . f. 1 s. 13 d. 4 a oro

Fu' ridotto per gli sgravi . . . . f. 1 ———

Una meza chasa per non divisa cho' figl⟨i⟩uoli di Marcho della Robbia mie' nipoti, la quale tegnamo per nostro abitare, posta nel popolo di San Lorenzo, nel ghonfalone del Lione ad Oro, nella via Ghuelfa, chonfinata da I via, da secondo mona Antonia donna che fu di Cristofano da Schopeto, da 3° ser Antonio da Quarto prete, da 4° el chapitolo de' chanonici di Santa Maria del Fiore. Pàghasene a detti chanonici pel livello lire dieci soldi otto l'anno. Detta chasa chomperamo da Lippo di Biagio da Peretola adì 31 d'aghosto 1446, per pregio di fiorini dugento venti, charta per mano di ser Iachopo da Romena.

Una chasa da lavoratore, posta nel popolo di Santa Maria a Tartagliese di Valdarno di sopra, chonfinata da primo strada, da secondo via, da 3° Nicholò di Giovanni Bellacci, da 4° Marcho del Bello Bellacci.

Una chasetta posta dietro a detta chasa, che sse ne faceva stalla e oggi è rovinata.

19 pezi di terra chon detta chasa: el primo chonfina da primo via, da secondo Marcho del Bello Bellacci, da 3° Filippo del Pancia, da 4° loro medesimi; l'ultimo chonfina da primo via, da secondo 3° 4° Piero di Biagio da Tartagliese.

Lavoravale nel primo chatasto Marcho di Berto da Tartagliese; rendevano in parte:

grano	staia	60
orzo	staia	10
saggina	staia	12
miglio	staia	6
panicho	staia	6
vino	barili	10
lino grosso	libre	10
chapponi	paia	1
uova	serque	5
carne	libre	250

Della detta rendita me ne tocha la terza parte, e ll'altra alle rede di Marcho della Robbia mio fratello, e ll'altra alla redità giacente di ser Giovanni della Robbia mio fratello, chome per le loro scritte vedrette.*

El sopradetto podere è oggi buona parte nel fiume d'Arno ed è stato già più tempo; il perche nel 1444 l'affittamo a Piero di Lucha di Chimenti per istaia 60 di grano l'anno, de' quali me ne tocha per la mia terza parte staia venti di grano.

G. Portata al Catasto of Luca della Robbia 1457/58

Florence, Archivio di Stato. Catasto, 829 (S. Giovanni, Chiavi, 1457/58), c. 115r–116r:

389   Quartiere S. Giovanni, gonfalone Chiavi

Lucha di Simone di Marcho della Robbia. Primo chatassto disse in Simone di Marcho mio padre, ebbe........f. 1——
O di valsente.............................f. 1 s. 7 d. 9
e di cinquina.............................f. – s. 14 —

Susstanze

Al'27 d'Antonio e Niccholò di messer Nicholò da Rabatta, gonfalone Ruote, 25.

Una meza chasa pe'non divisa cho'figl⟨i⟩uoli di Marcho mio fratello, per mio abitare, possta nel po⟨po⟩lo di San Lorenzo, gonfalone del Lione ad Oro, in via Guellfa, chonfinata da primo via, da secondo mon'Antonia donna fu d'Iachopo da Schopeto, da 3° Piero Sassetti, da 4° el

†......
......
el ¼ a Simone della Robbia al '69, 579, tutto

---

* on fol. 462, in the tax return of Marco di Simone's children and heirs, their ages are given: Andrea 15, Simone 14, Paolo 12, Francesco 8, Margherita 7. The house in via degli Albertinelli is stated to have been sold for 40 florins on August 6, 1451.

† This marginal note (in a Catasto officer's hand, as the other ones) is almost lost because paper is torn out here; not reproduced in Catasto 831, c. 177v.

chapitolo di Santa Maria del Fiore. La quale chonperamo Marcho di Simone mio fratello ed io Lucha da Lippo di Biagio da Peretola adì 31 d'agossto 1446 per pregio di florini 220, charta per mano di ser Iachopo da Romena. Pàghasene l'anno d'avillare a' chap⟨i⟩tolo di Santa Maria dell Fiore...................lire 10 s. 8....f. ————

Al'27 di Simone di Marcho dalla Robbia, gonfalone Chiavi, 528, per rendita di lire 29 s. 3 d. 8.

La terza parte d'un podere posso nel popolo di Santa Maria al Tartigelse [= Tartigliese] di Valdarno di sopra, ci⟨o⟩è una chasa da llavoratore chon 19 pezi di terra chon detta chasa, chonfinati cholle rede d'Antonio di Salvesstro di ser Risstoro e chon Andrea Bellacci e cholle rede d'Antonio di Firenze e chon Santa Maria del Tartagelese [= Tartagliese] e chon Berto di ser Amideo e chon Francesscho di Bartolomeo Baldovini e cholle rede di Marcho del Bello Bellacci e cholla istrado [*sic*] e chol fiume d'Arno e chon atri [= altri] chonfini e cho'lloro medesimi. Lavoràvalo nel primo chatassto Marcho di Berto dal Tartigl⟨i⟩ese. Oggi detto podere è buona parte in Arno, el perché è sstato a ffitto anni 13 a sstaia 60 di grano l'anno. Tochamene i'mia parte isstaia 20. Tiello a ffitto al presente Batissta di Giovanni. Siché di detta rendita mi toccha la 3ª parte, e ⅔ a'figliuoli di Marcho di Simone mio fratello e rede di ser Giovanni, chome pe'lloro isscritta vedrete.

*Al'69 Chia⟨vi⟩, a Lucha della ⟨Robbia⟩ la ½ per rendita ...... A Andrea ⟨della Robbia⟩ per la ¼ parte. A Simone de⟨lla Robbia⟩, al'69, Chiavi, per rendita ....

Grano......isstaia 20   per L. 29 s. 3 d. 8 pìccioli————
f. 104 s. 4 d. 7

[c. 115v]
Truovomi el [= in] sul monte, nel quartiere di San Giovanni, isscritti in me Lucha di Simone di Marcho, fiorini 1203 soldi 6 danari 9, e io ne piglio le paghe.......f. 240 s. 13————

O pagate tutte le mie graveze insino al quinto..f. ————

Truovomi di pag⟨h⟩e guadagnate d'agosto in qua fiorini 203 ....f. 2————

†Adì 20 di settembre 1458 .... co' llui in f. 75 per .... e per ogni altro avessi dato dal⟨le⟩ possessioni in fuori .... i creditori non s'ànno loro a sba⟨ttere⟩ .... ser Domenicho ⟨da Chati⟩gnano.

E più ò una sepoltura di marmo, la quale ò fatta già è più d'un anno a fFederigho d'Iachoppo Federighi, della quale siàno a ppiato alla Merchatantìa: no'ne posso ragionare allchuna chosa insino a tanto non è terminata. Quando sarà chiarita, sarò dinanzi del vosstro uficio.......f. 75————

Boche
Lucha sopradetto, d'età d'anni 58.........f. 200————

Incharichi
Sbattesi detto avillaro chome fu fatto nel'57.

O a dare ogn'anno al chapitolo di Santa Maria del Fiore, pe'lla metà della [*sic*] avillaro della chasa dove io abito in detta chasa, lire 5 solidi 4......a fiorini 7 per cento, monta ....f. 18 s. 11 d. 6

Creditori
Non si sbattono perché nella compositione di così fu d'achordo, chome appare di sopra

E ppiù resto a dare a detto chapitolo per detto avillare, chome appare a libro loro, lire 15.........f. ————
E più ò a dare a tTaddeo di Lucha di Taddeo saponaio, per danari chontanti presstatomi più tenpo fa e 'n più volte e più tenpi, fiorini 75...................f. ————

---

* See note † on previous page.

† This note has been transcribed putting together what remains both in Catasto 829 and in Catasto 831, c. 177r.

[c. 116r]
[all the following in a Catasto officer's hand:]

Sustanze

Somma la prima facc⟨i⟩a delle sustanze di questa scritta
f. 104 s. 4 d. 7
Somma le sustanze della seconda faccia, ché el resto di detta
facc⟨i⟩a sono incharichi.................f. 329 s. 13——
433. 17. 7
Abatti per incharicho di fiorini 5 per cento per mantenere
chase e possessioni e per incharicho di bocche una, chome
appare in questo, nella seconda facc⟨i⟩a di questa scritta
f. 218 s. 11 d. 6
Resta il valsente, abattuto gl'incharichi......f. 215 s. 6 d. 1
Tócchagli di chatasto, a soldi X a oro per cento. f. 1 s. 1 dd. 7
E per una testa, soldi sei a oro ....f. – s. 6 d. –
[c. 116v]   1. 7. 7
Rechò e' detto adì 28 di febraio 1457 [= 1458 *s. c.*]

H. Portata al Catasto of Luca della Robbia 1469

Florence, Archivio di Stato. Monte Comune, 100 (Catasto
del 1469, S. Giovanni, Chiavi, 2°), c. 925r–v:

Quartiere di San Giovanni
ghonfalone Chiavi

Lucha di Simone di Mar⟨c⟩ho della Robbia, ghonfalone
Chiavi, ebbe di catasto 1427, dise ⟨in⟩ Simone di Mar⟨c⟩ho
e figl⟨i⟩uoli, in detto ghonfalone delle Chiavi......f. 1 ——
Ebbe di valsente 1451, dise in Lucha di Simone, ghonfalone
Chiavi ....f. 1. 7. 8
Ebbe di ventina 1468, in detto Lucha, ghonfalone detto
....f. 1. 15. 2

Sustanze

Una meza casa per non divisa con Andrea e Simone di
Mar⟨c⟩ho miei nipoti, posta nel popolo di San Lorenzo,
ghonfalone Lion d'Oro, da primo via, secondo Piero Sassetti,
3° Berto di Rondone legniaiulo, 4° capittolo di Santa Maria
del Fiore. La quale comperamo io Lucha e Mar⟨c⟩ho mio
fratello, padre di detto Andrea e Simone, da lLippo di
Biagio da Peretola adì XXI d'aghosto 1446, per pregio di
f. 220, carta per ser Iacopo da Romena. La quale abittiamo
familiaremente per nostro uso ....f. ——

Una meza casa per non divisa con Andrea e Simone di
Mar⟨c⟩ho miei nipoti, da lavorattore, posta nel popolo di
Sancta Maria al Tartagliese, Valdarno di sopra, nel borgho
del Tartagliese, confinata da primo strada, secondo via, 3°
Nicolò di Giovanni Bellaci, 4° Mar⟨c⟩ho del Bello Bellaci.

XVIIII pezi di terra con detta casa, per non divisi con Andrea
e Simone sopradetti, da primo via, secondo Mar⟨c⟩ho
del Bello Bellaci, 3° Filippo del Panc⟨i⟩a, 4° loro medesimi.
L'ùtimo confino [*sic* = confina] a [primo] via, secondo, 3°,
4° Piero di Biagio dal Tartagliese.

Um pezo di terra per non divisa con detti Andrea e Simone,
posta in detto popolo, comperamo da Firenze di Zelone di
ser Firenze soto dì 27 di febbraio 1468, carta per ser Piero

di ser Andrea da Campi, per pregio di fiorini nove soldi X.
E lla detta casa con detti dic⟨i⟩annove pezi di sopra
nominati dicono nel catasto del '57 pe' ⅔ in figl⟨i⟩uoli e
rede di Simone di Mar⟨c⟩ho della Robbia, ghonfalone
Chiavi. E sopradetti pezi di terra ne ttoccha a me Lucha
sopradetto la metà della detta rendita, e ll'altra metà a
Andrea e Simone di Mar⟨c⟩ho miei nipoti. Lavoragli
Marcho di Chimenti dal Tartagliese; rendono l'anno di
fitto:

ghrano staia . . . . .staia	60	di detta rendita tocha a me	
carne, um porcho. . . .libre	200	Lucha la metà, cioè grano staia 30, carne libre 100,	
um paio di chapponi. .paia	1	f. 9———	
uova serque cinque. .serque	5	capone e uova [gap]	
		f. 156. 8. -	

Dal'58, da Zelone di ser Firenze uno pezzo di terra per
f. 9, che s'ag⟨i⟩ugnie in ne'beni leghati di sotto.

Due pezi di terra per non divisi con Andrea e Simone detti,
con detto podere, sono nell'anno 1457 in figl⟨i⟩uoli e rede
di Simone di Mar⟨c⟩ho come di sopra, da primo [e] secondo
via, 3° rede di Conte Peruzi, fosatello i' mezo. L'alltro pezo
à da primo via, secondo, 3° rede di Conte Peruzi, fossatello
i'mezo, 4° Piero di Francescho Mellini. Lavoral⟨i⟩ ogi
Francescho di Bartolomeo da Baroncelli; rende a me Lucha
di Simone, per la partte mi tocha, a mezo chon Andrea e
Simone miei nipoti: [c. 925v]

ghrano staia . . . . .staia	15		
vino bar⟨i⟩lli. . . . . . .barili	20	per la mia metà	
chapponi. . . . . .paia	½	f. 152. 4. 3	
uova serque . . . . .serque	2½		

Lavoransi dette terre con um bue di lire XXXIII, delle
quali ne tocha a me Lucha sopradetto lire XVI soldi X.

E più mi truovo in sul monte, nel quartiere di
San Giovanni, c. 431, f. 1463, cioè fiorini
millequattrocentosesantatre, dicono in mio
nome propio.
E più mi truovo del monte del '66, in
detto quartiere, c. 471, in detto nome,
f. novantaquattro s. XIIII d. VI
}f. 373. 17. 3

E più mi truovo di paghe ghuadagniate f. XIII, dicono in me
Lucha di Simone, in detto quartiere. . . . . .f. 3. 13. 4

Beni alienati

Una casetta posta in Castello San Giovanni, luogho detto
via da rRicasoli, da primo via, secondo rede di Lucha di
Iacopo, 3° Francesco di Lucha, 4° chiasso. Venduta a
Francesco di Lucha Salti da Castello San Giovanni, per
fiorini otto.

Due pezi di tterra lavoratìa e soda, posta nelle corti di
Castello San Giovanni, da primo via, secondo, 3° Antonio
di Girolamo, 4° Checcho di Matteo spadaio. L'ùtimo da
primo via, secondo beni della pieve di Castel San Giovanni,
3°, 4° ser Massìo di Piero di ser Massìo. Venduta [sic] a
Ghualtieri d'Agniolo da Castello Francho, speziale, per
fiorini XXXIIII adì XXIIII d'aprile 1432, come apare per
la sua schritta del suo 3° catasto.

Um poderetto posto nel piviere di Santa Maria Inpruneta,

popolo di Santo Andrea a lLuiano, da primo via, secondo,
3° G⟨i⟩achi di Tomaso da Luiano, 4° beni della pieve.
Vendutto a 'Ntonio di Ghuido di ser Tomaso, adì XII di
maggio 1445, per fiorini 100, per ser Agniolo di Piettro da
tTerranuova.

Incharichi

Ho a dare ogni anno al capittolo di Santa Maria del Fiore per
la metà dell'avillaro della casa dove abittiamo, lire cinque
soldi IIII.

Bocche

Lucha, d'anni................. 70

Rendita f. 74. 16. 3 decima f. 7 9. 8

[*by a Catasto officer hand :*]
Somma le sue sustanze.......................f. 700. 2. 9
Abatti 5 per cento............f. 7. 12. 3
Abatti per una bocha ....f. 200 —
Avanzali, chome si vede, f. 492. 10. 6: a soldi X per cento,
gli tocha di chatasto f. due s. VIIII d. IIII.......f. 2. 9. 4

[c. 926v]
Rechò e' detto, 15 aghosto [1469]

I. Portata al Catasto of Luca della Robbia 1480

Florence, Archivio di Stato. Catasto, 1021 (S. Giovanni,
Chiavi, 1480), c. 420r–v:*

246   +Quartiere di San Giovanni, ghonfalone Chiavi

Lucha di Simone della Robbia ebbe di chatasto 1469 in
Lucha detto e in detto ghonfalone.....f. 2 [L.] 0 s. 5. d. 4
E di sesto, in detto nome............f. 2 [L.] 3 s. 19 d. 2

Sustanze

Dal'70,894, da Lucha detto, per suo uso.

Una meza casa per non divisa con Andrea e Simone di Mar⟨c⟩ho miei nipotti, posta nel popolo di San Lorenzo, ghonafalone Lion d'Oro, da primo via, sechondo Piero Sassetti, 3° le rede di Bertto di Rondone legnaiuoli, 4° chapittolo di Santa Maria del Fiore. Conperai io Lucha e Mar⟨c⟩ho mio fratello e padre di detti Andrea e Simone, da lLippo di Biagio da Peretola adì XXI d'aghosto 1446, per pregio di fiorini dugentoventi, cartta per ser Iacopo da Romena. La quale abittiamo.

Al'95, gonfalone Chiavi, a n° 37, a Andrea suo nipote, i'nome d'una chasa per uso.

Dal'70 come di sopra, per rendita di f. 10. 18. 11.

Una meza casa per non divisa con Andrea e Simone miei nipoti, da llavorattore, posta nel popolo di Santa Maria al Tarttagliese di Valdarno di sopra, nel borgho del Tartagliese, da primo strada, secondo via, 3° Nicholò di Giovanni Bellacci, 4° Mar⟨c⟩ho Bellaci.

Dic⟨i⟩annove pezi di tterra con detta casa, per non divisi con detti miei nipoti, da primo via, secondo Mar⟨c⟩ho Bellaci, 3° Filippo del Panc⟨i⟩a, 4° loro medesimi; l'utimo confinatto da primo via, da secondo, 3°, 4° Piero di Biagio dal Tarttagliese.

Al'95 a non soportanti, cioè Marcho di Chimenti dal Tartagliese per f. 100 larghi, ⟨in no⟩me di ¾ di podere, che .... a chonto di Simone di Marcho

---

* This document being in bad state of preservation, the transcription of certain parts, especially marginal notes and figures, has necessitated reference to its copy, in *Monte Comune*, 102, c. 446r–v.

Um pezo di terra per non diviso con detti miei nipotti, in detto popolo, comperamo da Firenze di Zelone di ser Firenze sotto dì 27 di febbraio 1468, cartta per ser Piero di ser Andrea da Campi, per f. 9 s. X a oro, cioè fiorini nove soldi 10 a oro.

Dal'70 come di sopra, per un pezo di terra per rendita di f. o. 12. 8

E delle sopradette terre n'è oggi buona parte inn Arno, chome chiaro vi mostrerò. Lavora le sopradette terre Francesco di Chimenti di Mar⟨c⟩ho dal Tarttagliese; danne l'anno di fitto per la partte mia:

ghrano staia ....staia	30
carne ....libre	100
capponi mezo paio .....paia	$\frac{1}{2}$
uova serque ....serque	$2\frac{1}{2}$

Um podere per non diviso con Andrea e Simone detti, [con] casa da signore e dda llavorattore, posta nel popolo di San Tomaso a Baroncelli, da primo via, secondo Piero di Francesco Mellini, terzo Filippo di Simone e'l frattello, fossattello i 'mezo, 4° rede di Tommaso Davizi.

Dal'70 come di sopra, per rendita di f. 10. 13. 2.

Due pezi di terra per non divisa con detti e con detto podere, da primo via, secondo, 3° rede di Conte Peruzi e fossattello in mezo. L'altro pezo da primo via secondo, 3° rede di Conte Peruzi, fossattello in mezo, 4° Piero Mellini.

Lavora 'l detto podere Lucha di Franchesco Gr⟨i⟩lloni; rende per la metà:

ghrano................staia	15
vino.................barili	6
capponi ....paia	$\frac{1}{2}$
uova ....serque	$2\frac{1}{2}$

Lavoransi dette terre o detto podere con um bue di lire XXXIII, tochane a me Lucha lire XVI soldi X..f. 152. 4. 3

Incharichi
Ho a ddare ogni anno al capittolo di Santa Maria del Fiore, per la metà del'avillaro della casa dove abitto, lire cinque soldi IIII.

Bocche
Lucha, età d'anni 82

[c. 421r]
[the following in Catasto officer's hand:]
Somma il valsente .... f. 317. 12. 3
Abatti 5 per cento per la conservazione de' beni..f. 15. 17. 3
Resta il valsente netto f. 301. 15: a 7 per cento, fanno d'entrata f. 21. 2. 4.
Abattesi f. 9. 10 per la metà d'uno avillaro pàgono per la casa al chapitolo di Santa Maria del Fiore, che sono di rendita di soldi 13 danari 6. Resta l'entrata netta, tràttone s. 13 d. 6..................................f. 20. 9. -
Avanzagli f. 20 s. 9: tocchagli per la schala, a 7 per cento, fiorini uno s. otto d. sette a oro...................f. 1. 8. 7
Arbitrio, soldi dieci di fiorini larghi ....s. 10

Tocchagli a fiorini larghi...............f. 1 lire 3. 9. 4

della Robia, in questo c., fatta la vendita per ser Giovangualberto di Giovanni di Giovanni Pieri, sotto [dì] primo dì febraio 1492. f. 156. 8.——

Al'95, gonfalone Lion Nero, n° 93, a Domenicho di Piero Mellini, per rendita di f. 10. 13.

Appendix 2

WILL OF LUCA DELLA ROBBIA AND SUBSEQUENT LITIGATION

Luca della Robbia's will is published in an abbreviated form by Gaye (i, pp. 184–5), Cruttwell (1902, pp. 304–5) and Marquand (1914, pp. xxxvii–viii). The present complete text has been transcribed by Dr. Gino Corti. The consequential documents of November 1482, which have also been trancribed by Dr. Corti, are unpublished.

Florence, Archivio di Stato. Notarile ante-cosimiano, G 525 (ser Agnolo di Cinozzo, testaments, 1442–1489), c. 120r-v:

[publicavi ut hic et restitui dicto Simoni heredi]
[*marginal note:*] 1470 die XVIIII februarii [= 1471 s.c.]

In Dei nomine amen. Anno Domini ab eius salutifera incarnatione millesimo quadringentesimo septuagesimo, indictione IIIIᵃ et die XVIIII mensis februarii. Actum Florentie, in refectorio fratrum Sancti Marci de Florentia, presentibus fratre Honofrio Andree Honofrii de Florentia, fratre Allessandro Filippi de Florentia, fratre Antonio Angeli dell'Aione, fratre Stefano Stefani, fratre Marcho Pieri Succhillo, fratre Zenobio Mattei et fratre Sante Bardini de Calavria, omnibus fratribus ecclesie Sancti Marci de Florentia, testibus ad infrascripta omnia et singula proprio hore infrascripti testatoris vocatis, habitis et rogatis.

Cum nichil sit certius morte et nil incertius eius hora, hinc est quod providus et discretus vir Lucas olim Simonis Marci della Robbia, scultor, civis florentinus et de populo Sancti Laurentii de Florentia, sanus mente, sensu, corpore, visu et intellectu, nolens intestatus decedere sed de suis bonis legitime providere, suum quod dicitur nu[n]cupativum testamentum sine scriptis, facere procuravit et fecit seu condidit in hunc modum videlicet.

In primis quidem animam suam omnipotenti Deo eiusque gloriose Virgini Matri Marie et toti celestis [*sic*] curie Paradisi humiliter et devote recommendavit; et sepulturam corporis sui elegit eo loco et cum illis funeris expensis prout videbitur infrascripto suo heredi.

Item reliquit et legavit Opere Sancte Marie Floris de Florentia et nove constructioni murorum civitatis Florentie et nove fabrice dicte Opere, inter omnes, libras duas florenorum parvorum.

Item iure legati reliquit et legavit domine Checche, eius nepoti et filie olim Marci Simonis della Robbia ad presens vidue, florenos auri centum, quos solvi et dari voluit per infrascriptum Simonem eius heredem.

Item dicens et asserens dictus testator qualiter ipse habet duos nepotes ipso fratre, videlicet Andream et Simonem, fratres et filios olim Marci Simonis della Robbia, eius nepotes ex fratre carnali, et qualiter ipse Lucas tempore vite sue docuit artem suam sculture dictum Andream et adeo quod ipse Andreas per se solum ut magister potest exercere artem dicti Luce, et eidem Andree in [c. 120v] vita ipsius Luce reliquit omne creditum dicti Luce et adeo quod ipse Andreas hodie, mediante industria dicti Luce et eius documentis, habet artem lucrativam, adeo quod usque in hodiernum diem satis superlucratus est et hodie superlucratur et in futurum actus sit superlucrari cum ipsa arte et eius exercitio et potest facilime et honorifice se et familiam suam nutrire, et dictum Simonem nichil docuit in vita sua quia exercuit aliam artem. Et considerans quod omnia bonia [*sic = bona*] ipsius Luce non sunt sufficientia nec tante extimationis quanta est industria dicti Andree, quam ipse Andreas habet mediantibus documentis dicti Luce, idcirco voluit, ut dictus Simon habeat aliquid ex bonis dicti Luce et ne possit tam a dictum [*sic = dicto*] Simone quod [*sic = quam*] ab omnibus intelligentibus de ingratitudine reprehendi, idcircho in omnibus et singulis aliis suis bonis mobilibus et immobilibus, iuribus, nominibus et actionibus, presentibus et futuris, sibi universalem heredem instituit, fecit et esse voluit dictum Simonem olim Marci Simonis della Robbia, eius nepotem ex fratre carnali.

Et hanc suam dixit et asseruit esse et esse voluit suam ultimam voluntatem et ultimum testamentum, quam [et quod] valere voluit iure testamenti, et si iure testamenti non valeret, valere voluit iure codicillorum, et si iure codicillorum non valeret, valere voluit iure donationis causa mortis vel alterius cuiuscunque ultime voluntatis, qua et quibus magis, melius et efficacius valere poterit et teneret. Capsans, irritans et annulans omne et quodcunque aliud testamentum et ultimam voluntatem a se hinc retro factam manu cuiuscunque notarii vel alterius cuiuscunque persone, licet in eo vel eis vel aliquo ipsorum essent apposita aliqua verba precisa, derogatoria vel penalia, de quibus dixit se ad presens non recordari et penitere, et presens testamentum et ultimam voluntatem omnibus aliis prevalere. Rogans prefatos testes religiosos ut sint testes omnibus predictis, et me notarium infrascriptum ut de predictis omnibus et singulis publicum conficiam instrumentum.

Ego Angelus olim Cinozi notarius rogatus subscripsi.

Florience, Archivio di Stato. Notarile antecosimiano, S 503 (ser Bastiano Serforesi, 1481–1488):

fol. 6^v: [*13 November 1482*]
Compromissum Andree et Simonis della Robbia

Item dictis anno indictione et die XIII mensis predictis [*sic*]. Actum in populo Sancti Micaelis Vicedominorum, in apoteca Iuliani infrascripti, presentibus testibus testibus [*sic*] Ioanne Dominici Antonii, populi Sancti Laurenzii, et Guglielmo Caroli Gugl[i]elmi, populi Sancti Pieri Maioris, legnaiuolis etc. Andreas olim Marci dela Robbia, civis Florentinus, ex parte una, et Simon eius frater carnalis, ex alia, omnes eorum lites etc. generaliter etc. remiserunt in

    Iulianum Leonardi de Maiano   } presentes,
    Franciscum Ioannis Francisci, alias Francione } et
    Franciscum Dominici, alias Monciatto, absentem,

tanquam in eorum et cuiuslibet eorum arbitros etc. Dantes etc. omnibus in concordia etc. auctoritatem etc. laudandi etc. per totum diem XX presentis mensis etc. Cum pacto quod in dicto compromisso veniant et venire intelligantur omnes contractus et scripture liquidate et non liquidate, pertinentes ad divisionem domus eorum habitationis et omnes differentie quas haberent procedentes ad dictam divisionem dicte domus et ad dictam domum etc. Et cum pacto quod omne aliud compromissum hactenus per eos factum, ex nunc intelligatur et sit revocatum et anullatum etc. Promittentes etc. Sub pena florenorum centum etc. Obligantes etc. Rogantes etc.

ibidem, fol. 7^r–8^v: [*14 November 1482*]
Laudum Andree et Simonis dela Robbia

In Dei nomine amen. Nos Iulianus olim Leonardi de Maiano, Franciscus olim Ioannis Francis**c**i alias Francione et Franciscus Dominici alias Monciatto, legnaiuoli, cives Florentini etc., arbitri et arbitratores, amici comunes et amicabiles compositores, nominati electi et assumpti ab Andrea olim Marci dela Robbia, ex parte una, et a Simone eius fratre carnali, civibus Florentinis, ex alia, ut de compromisso in nos facto publice constat manu ser Bastiani notarii infrascripti. Et viso dicto compromisso per dictas partes et quamlibet earum in nos facto et contentis in eo. Et visa auctoritate potestate arbitrio et balia nobis vigore dicti compromissi a dictis partibus et qualibet earum nobis data concessa et attributa. Volentes ac cupientes tollere decidere et fine bono terminare omnes et quascunque lites, questiones, discordias et differentias que sunt vel erunt vel in futurum quomodolibet esse possent inter dictas partes et quamlibet earum, ad concordiam reducere et pro posse conservare. Primo namque auditis et intellectis, discussis et diligenter examinatis iuribus utriusque partis et cuiuslibet earum, et omnibus et singulis auditis, visis et intellectis que dicte partes et quelibet earum et quilibet ex dictis partibus dicere proponere ostendere et allegare voluerunt. Et reperto esse litem et differentiam inter dictas partes occasione bonorum mobilium et immobilium dictarum partium et occasione divisionis dictorum bonorum, et habita diligenti et solemni informatione et colloquio in predictis et circa predicta et quolibet predictorum et dependentibus et connexis ab eisdem. Et visis auditis et consideratis que videnda et consideranda fuerunt: pro bono pacis et concordia dictarum partium et cuiuslibet earum, et super omnibus habita deliberatione solemni, Dei nomine invocato, pro tribunali sedentes, omni modo via iuribus, quo qua et quibus magis et melius possumus

et debemus, laudamus sentenciamus mandamus arbitramur decidimus diffinimus dividimus et declaramus inter dictas partes et quamlibet earum modo et forma inferius denotatis videlicet.

In primis, cum inveniamus et nobis constet quod quedam domus in quibus ad presens habitant dicte partes, et iam diu una cum Luca eorum olim patruo habitaverunt, inter ipsum Lucam et dictas partes comuni concordia fuerint divise et nunc inter ipsas partes sit lis et differentia de redividendo ipsas domos et quod male dividi possunt absque incommoditate dictarum partium ex eo quia unaqueque dictarum partium habet plures filios et deveniende sunt in maximam familiam, adeo quod non sufficiant ambabus pro habitatione commoda. Ideo dictis de causis et aliis iustis et rationabilibus causis moti que nos movere merito potuerunt et debuerunt et possunt et debent, et pro concordia pace et quiete dictarum partium et cuiuslibet earum et ne scandala inter ipsas aut earum filios in futurum suscitentur, laudamus sentenciamus damus concedimus et adiudicamus domum in qua ad presens habitat dictus Simon, et de qua est differentia inter ipsas partes occasione divisionis de qua supra fit mentio, posita Florentie in populo Sancti Laurentii de Florentia et in via que dicitur via Guelfa, cui a primo via dicta, a secundo Petrus de Sassettis, a tertio heredes Berti Rondonis, [a] quarto capituli Sancte Marie del Fiore, cum salis cameris volta puteo curia et horto et cum aliis suis hedificiis et cum omnibus suis pertinentiis adherentiis et circumstantiis et servitutibus suis usque in vias publicas, dicto Andree. Et sic eam hoc nostro presenti laudo, dicto Andree damus concedimus et adiudicamus ad habendum tenendum possidendum [fol. 7^v] usufructandum vendendum alienandum et quicquid sibi suisque heredibus deinceps placuerit perpetuo faciendum, et cum omnibus et singulis que infra predictos continentur confines, et cum accessibus et egressibus suis usque in viam publicam, et cum omnibus et singulis que dicta bona habent in se, super se vel infra seu inter se in integrum, omnique iure et actione usu dominio proprietate et possessione, adiacentiis coherentiis et servitutibus dictorum bonorum ipso Simoni modo aliquo pertinentibus. Pro quibus dictum Simonem et eius heredes et bona omnia mobilia et immobilia, iura et actiones, presentia et futura, obligata et ipotecata esse volumus et mandamus dicto Andree, pro tutela et defensione dicte domus et bonorum eidem Andree ut supra pro tutela et defensione dicte domus et bonorum eidem Andree ut supra adiudicatorum, hoc nostro presenti laudo sententia arbitrio et arbitramento in casu evictionis dictorum bonorum, tam pro sorte quam pro omnibus et singulis damnis expensis et interesse que fecisset aut substinuisset quoquo modo dictus Andreas vel eius heredes vel habentes ius et causam ab eo.

Item laudamus sentenciamus arbitramur et mandamus quod dictus Andreas auctoritate propria possit dicta bona intrare et de eis tenutam et corporalem possessionem aprehendere et tenere sine aliqua contradictione vel molestia, modis et formis inferius denotatis.

Item laudamus et condemnamus dictum Simonem ad dandum tradendum et consignandum dicto Andree dictam domum et bona ut supra contenta et confinata, liberam et expeditam, absque aliqua exceptione vel controversia iuris vel facti, infra tempus duorum annorum proxime futurorum modis et conditionibus inferius denotatis et descriptis. Et in reconpensationem et satisfactionem et raguaglio dicte domus de qua supra fit mentio, dicto Andree adiudicate, ipsum Andream vigore dicte nostre auctoritatis condemnamus laudamus sententiamus et arbitramur ad dandum et solvendum dicto Simoni florenos ducentos quinquaginta auri largos infra predictum tempus duorum annorum proxime futurorum ab hodie, absque aliqua exceptione cavillatione aut controversia non obstante etiam si diceretur quod dictus Andreas aliis de causis esset creditor dicti Simonis aut habere deberet ab eo, non possit fieri compensationem: ita quod effectus sit quod infra predictum tempus duorum annorum ad manus dicti Simonis deveniat dicta quantitas florenorum CCL largorum, adeo quod dictus Simon de tota dicta quantitate possit facere voluntatem suam prout sibi libere videbitur et placebit. Et in casu quod dictus Andreas vellet solvere dare et pagare dictum pretium dictorum florenorum ducentorum quinquaginta largorum antequam veniret tempus dictorum duorum annorum dicto Simoni, teneatur et debeat ipse Andreas notificare dicto Simoni in forma valida antea per sex menses quemadmodum ipse est paratus sibi solvere dictam summam et quantitatem dictorum florenorum CCL largorum, quam depositare teneatur adeo quod dictus Simon de dicto pretio cum tradiderit dictam domum dicto Andree liberam et expeditam, possit facere voluntatem suam ut superius diximus. Et sic condemnamus [fol. 8ʳ] in dicto casu dictum Simonem ad dandum tradendum et consignandum dictam domum dicto Andree, ut superius diximus, absque aliqua exceptione. Et in casu quod dictus Andreas dicto Simoni non solveret dictam summam et quantitatem dictorum florenorum CCL largorum infra dictum tempus duorum annorum, volumus quod dictus Andreas teneatur solvere dare et pagare dicto Simoni dicta de causa florenos auri XXX largos, ultra quantitatem predictam dictorum florenorum ducentorum quinquaginta largorum, ita quod in totum quantitas solvenda per ipsum Andream dicto Simoni in dicto casu sit florenorum ducentorum octuaginta largorum.

Item laudamus quod predicti Andreas et Simon, durante tempore dictorum duorum annorum vel quo dictus Simon habitabit morabitur et permanebit in dicta domo, non possint habitare dictam domum sive dictas domos nisi eo modo et forma et prout et sicut habitabant vivente dicto Luca eorum patruo et ante mortem dicti Luce, preter quam dictus Simon non possit aliqua in parte habitare per se vel per alios de sua familia hortum dictarum domorum, set quod dictus Andreas teneatur suis impensis claudere vel claudi facere hostium dicti

horti adeo quod dictus Simon illo aliqua in parte uti vel frui non possit ultra preter voluntatem dicti Andree.

Item laudamus quod in casu quod dictus Simon staret in dicta domo ultra dictum tempus duorum annorum ex eo quia aliqua de causa non solveretur sibi dictum pretium, non teneatur propterea ipse Simon solvere aliquod pretium pro pensione dicte domus et bonorum dicto Andree vel alicui altere persone pro eo recipienti.

Item laudamus et volumus quod hostium cuiusdam camere terrene per quod dicte partes vadunt et veniunt de una domo in aliam, claudatur impensis dicti Andree, adeo quod aliqua ex dictis partibus durante tempore dictorum duorum annorum vel quo dictus Simon stabit in dicta domo, aliquo modo dicto hostio uti non possit ad intrandum sive exeundum per dictum hostium.

Item laudamus quod quedam fenestra existens in camera sive anticamera dicti Simonis, claudatur expensis dicti Andree adeo quod dictus Simon ea uti non possit, et si ea uti vellet propter lumen, teneatur ipse Simon illam ferrare suis impensis et quando exibit se dicta domo, ferramenta inde extrahere et secum portare pro voluntate sua.

Item laudamus quod dictus Simon teneatur dare licentiam et curare ita et taliter quod iura que ipse habet in dicta domo occasione avillaris sive alterius cuiuscunque rei, transferantur et deveniant in dictum Andream prout et sicut et quando predicto Andree videbitur et placebit, impensis tamen dicti Andree in forma iuris valida.

Item laudamus sententiamus mandamus et arbitramur quod dicte partes [fol. 8ᵛ] et quelibet earum et quilibet ex dictis partibus faciant et observent et cum effectu executioni mandent omnia et singula in presenti laudo contenta et declarata, sub pena et ad penam in conpromisso inde facto contenta et declarata.

Latum datum et pronuntiatum fuit dictum laudum arbitrium seu arbitramentum et sententia et omnia et singula suprascripta in presenti laudo et sententia contenta, per suprascriptos arbitros et arbitratores pro tribunali sedentes in apoteca dicti Iuliani posita in via Servorum et in populo Sancti Micaelis Vicedominorum, sub annis Domini nostri Yesu Christi MCCCCLXXXII, inditione prima et die XIIII mensis Novembris, presentibus Nicolao Zenobii alterius Zenobii populi Sancti Petri Maioris, et Francisco Ioannis Toruccii sensale populi Sancte Felicitatis, et Ieronimo Dominici Stefani ceraiuolo dicti populi Sancti Micaelis, testibus ad hec vocatis habitis et rogatis.

Item dictis anno inditione die loco et testibus, predicte partes etc. audito etc. ratificaverunt emologaverunt etc.

PLATES

1. *Cantoria* (Cat. No. 1). Marble, made up in plaster. Museo dell'Opera del Duomo, Florence

2. *Trumpeters* (detail of Plate 1). Marble

3. *Dancing Girls* (detail of Plate 2)

4. *Dancing Girl* (detail of Plate 2)

5. *Players on the Psaltery* (detail of Plate 1). Marble

6. *Singing Girl Playing a Psaltery* (detail of Plate 5)

7. *Players on the Cithara* (detail of Plate 1). Marble

8. *Girl Listening to the Cithara Players* (detail of Plate 7)

9. *Boy Listening to the Cithara Players* (detail of Plate 7)

10. *Drummers* (detail of Plate 1). Marble

-11. *Boy Playing a Drum* (detail of Plate 10)

12. *Dancing Boy* (detail of Plate 10)

13. *Dancing Boy Holding a Rose* (detail of Plate 10)

14. *Choral Dancers* (detail of Plate 1). Marble

15. *Singing Girls* (detail of Plate 14)

16. *Players on the Organ, Lute and Harp* (detail of Plate 1). Marble

17. *Tambourine Players* (detail of Plate 1). Marble

18. *Boy Playing a Portable Organ* (detail of Plate 16)

19. *Boys Playing Tambourines* (detail of Plate 17)

20. *Cymbal Players* (detail of Plate 1). Marble

21. *Child Sounding Cymbals* (detail of Plate 20)

22. *Boys Singing from a Book* (detail of Plate 1). Marble

23. *Boys Singing from a Scroll* (detail of Plate 1). Marble

24. *Singing Boys* (detail of Plate 22)

25. *Singing Boys* (detail of Plate 23)

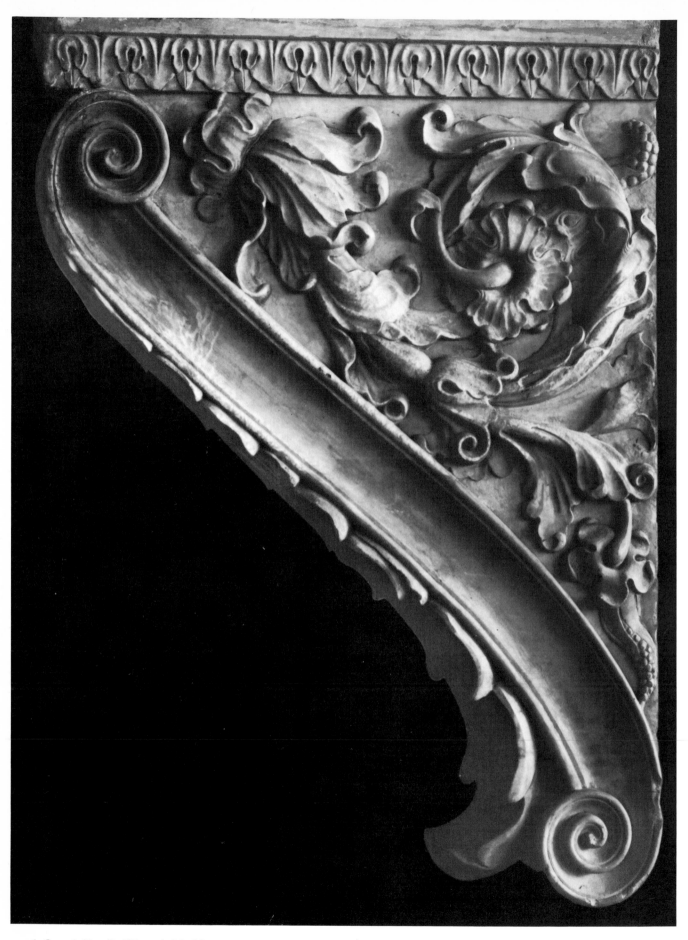

26. *Console* (detail of Plate 1). Marble

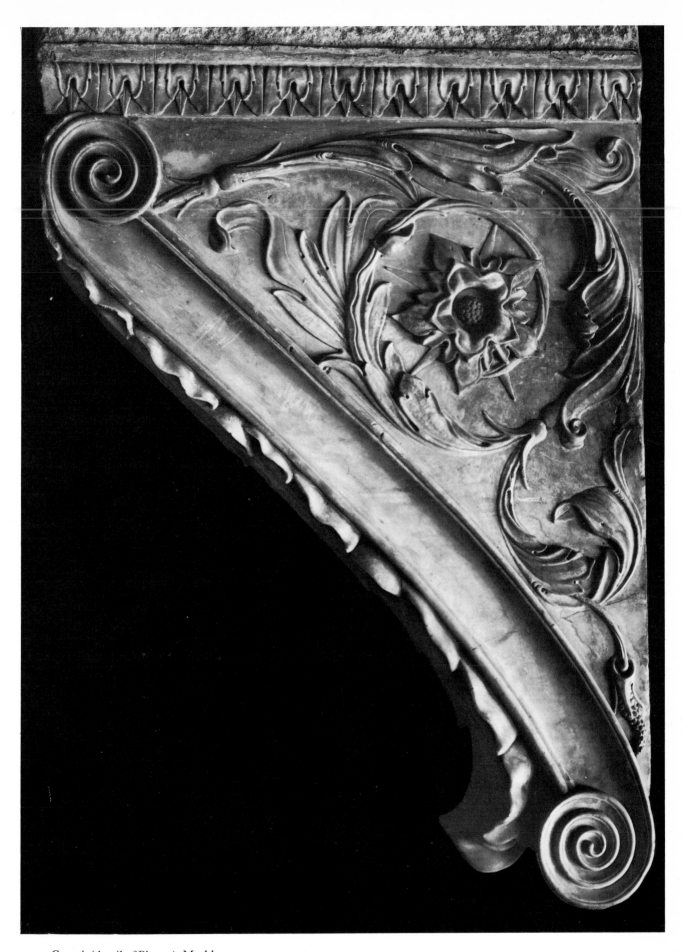

27. *Console* (detail of Plate 1). Marble

28A. *Soffit Relief* (detail of Plate 1). Marble

28B. *Inscribed Frieze* (detail of Plate 1). Marble

29. *Grammar* (Cat. No. 2). Marble. Museo dell'Opera del Duomo, Florence

30. *Philosophy* (Cat. No. 2). Marble. Museo dell'Opera del Duomo, Florence

31. *Poetry* or *Rhetoric* (Cat. No. 2). Marble. Museo dell'Opera del Duomo, Florence

32. *Arithmetic* (Cat. No. 2). Marble. Museo dell'Opera del Duomo, Florence

33. *Astrology* (Cat. No. 2). Marble. Museo dell'Opera del Duomo, Florence

34. *The Deliverance of St. Peter* (Cat. No. 3). Marble. Museo Nazionale, Florence

35. *The Crucifixion of St. Peter* (Cat. No. 3). Marble. Museo Nazionale, Florence

36. *St. Peter Freed from Prison* (detail of Plate 34)

37. *The Holy Ghost* (cf. Col. Plate I). Gilt bronze. Museo Nazionale, Florence

38. *Angel Supporting a Wreath* (detail of Col. Plate I).
Marble. Santa Maria, Peretola

39. *Angel Supporting a Wreath* (detail of Col. Plate I).
Marble. Santa Maria, Peretola

40. *The Mourning Virgin* (detail of Col. Plate I). Marble. Santa Maria, Peretola

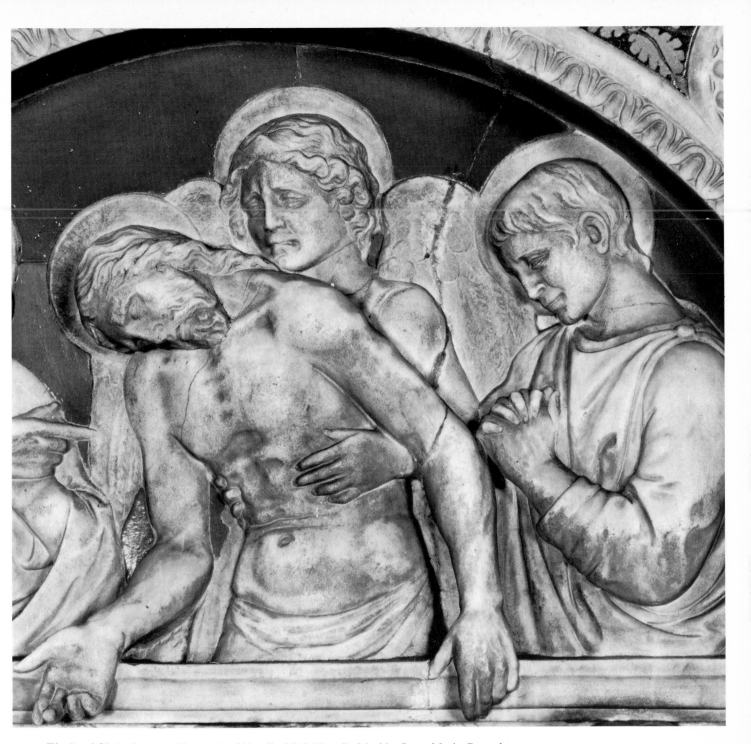

41. *The Dead Christ Supported by an Angel* (detail of Col. Plate I). Marble. Santa Maria, Peretola

42. *The Risen Christ* (detail of Col. Plate II). Enamelled terracotta. Duomo, Florence

43. *Sleeping Soldier* (detail of Col. Plate II). Enamelled terracotta. Duomo, Florence

44. *The Ascending Christ* (detail of Col. Plate III). Enamelled terracotta. Duomo, Florence

45. *Heads of Apostles* (detail of Col. Plate III). Enamelled terracotta. Duomo, Florence

46. *Angel with Candlestick* (Cat. No. 8). Enamelled terracotta. Duomo, Florence

47. *Saint Peter* (Cat. No. 9). Enamelled terracotta. Pazzi Chapel, Santa Croce, Florence

48. *Saint Bartholomew* (Cat. No. 9). Enamelled terracotta. Pazzi Chapel, Santa Croce, Florence

49. *Saint Philip* (Cat. No. 9). Enamelled terracotta. Pazzi Chapel, Santa Croce, Florence

50. *Saint James the Less* (Cat. No. 9). Enamelled terracotta. Pazzi Chapel, Santa Croce, Florence

51. *Head of Saint James the Great* (detail of Col. Plate VIII). Enamelled terracotta. Pazzi Chapel, Santa Croce, Florence

52. *Saint Matthias* (Cat. No. 9). Enamelled terracotta. Pazzi Chapel, Santa Croce, Florence

53. *Saint Andrew* (Cat. No. 9). Enamelled terracotta. Pazzi Chapel, Santa Croce, Florence

54. *Head of Saint Matthew* (detail of Col. Plate VI). Enamelled terracotta. Pazzi Chapel, Santa Croce, Florence

55. *Head of Saint John the Evangelist* (detail of Col. Plate VII). Enamelled terracotta. Pazzi Chapel, Santa Croce, Florence

56. *Saint Thaddeus* (Cat. No. 9). Enamelled terracotta. Pazzi Chapel, Santa Croce, Florence

57. *Saint Simon* (Cat. No. 9). Enamelled terracotta. Pazzi Chapel, Santa Croce, Florence

58. *Saint Thomas* (Cat. No. 9). Enamelled terracotta. Pazzi Chapel, Santa Croce, Florence

59. *Saint Andrew* (Cat. No. 9). Enamelled terracotta. Pazzi Chapel, Santa Croce, Florence

60. *The Virgin and Saint Elizabeth* (detail of Col. Plate V). Enamelled terracotta. San Giovanni Fuorcivitas, Pistoia

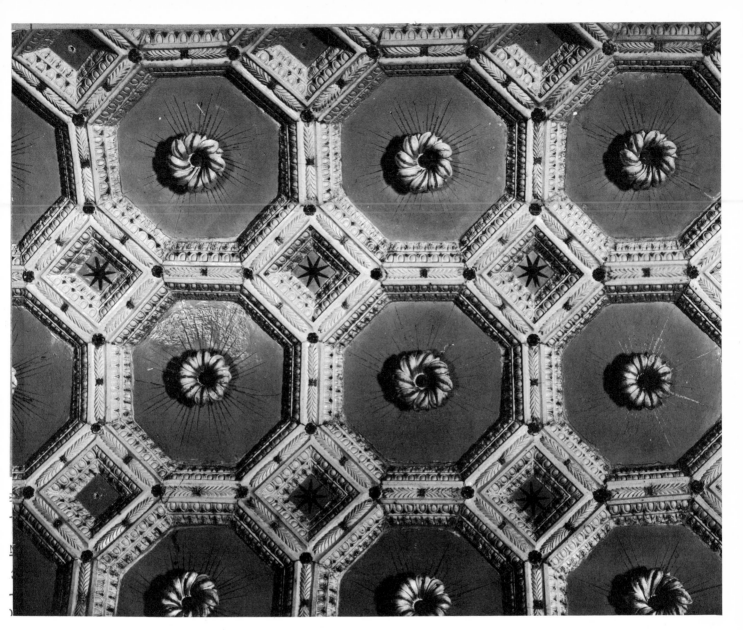

61. *Ceiling of the Cappella del Crocifisso* (detail of Fig. 18). Enamelled terracotta. San Miniato al Monte, Florence

62. *Roof of the Cappella del Crocifisso* (detail of Fig. 18). Enamelled terracotta. San Miniato al Monte, Florence

63. *February* (Cat. No. 12). Enamelled terracotta. Victoria & Albert Museum, London

64. *March* (Cat. No. 12). Enamelled terracotta. Victoria & Albert Museum, London

65. *April* (Cat. No. 12). Enamelled terracotta. Victoria & Albert Museum, London

66. *June* (Cat. No. 12). Enamelled terracotta. Victoria & Albert Museum, London

67. *July* (Cat. No. 12). Enamelled terracotta. Victoria & Albert Museum, London

68. *August* (Cat. No. 12). Enamelled terracotta. Victoria & Albert Museum, London

69. *September* (Cat. No. 12). Enamelled terracotta. Victoria & Albert Museum, London

70. *October* (Cat. No. 12). Enamelled terracotta. Victoria & Albert Museum, London

71. *December* (Cat. No. 12). Enamelled terracotta. Victoria & Albert Museum, London

72. *Monument of Benozzo Federighi* (Cat. No. 13). Marble and enamelled terracotta. Santa Trinita, Florence

73. *Head of Benozzo Federighi* (detail of Plate 72). Marble

74. *The Mourning Virgin* (detail of Plate 72). Marble

75. *The Dead Christ* (detail of Plate 72). Marble

76. *Angel Holding a Wreath* (detail of Plate 72). Marble

77. *Angel Holding a Wreath* (detail of Plate 72). Marble

78. *Ceiling of the Chapel of the Cardinal of Portugal* (Cat. No. 14). Enamelled terracotta. San Miniato al Monte, Florence

79. *The Holy Ghost* (detail of Plate 78)

80. *Justice* (detail of Plate 78)

81. *Altarpiece of the Chapel of the Madonna* (Cat. No. 15). Marble and enamelled terracotta. Collegiata, Impruneta

82. *Ceiling of the Chapel of the Madonna* (Cat. No. 15). Enamelled terracotta. Collegiata, Impruneta

83. *Altarpiece of the Chapel of the Cross* (Cat. No. 15). Enamelled terracotta. Collegiata, Impruneta

84A. *Madonna and Child* (Cat. No. 15). Enamelled
terracotta. Collegiata, Impruneta

84B. *Madonna and Child* (Cat. No. 15). Enamelled
terracotta. Collegiata, Impruneta

85. *Detail of Frieze of the Chapel of the Madonna* (Cat. No. 15). Enamelled terracotta. Collegiata, Impruneta

86. *Virgin and Child* (detail of Col. Plate XXI). Enamelled terracotta. Or San Michele, Florence

87. *Stemma of King René of Anjou* (Cat. No. 21). Enamelled terracotta. Victoria & Albert Museum, London

88. *Stemma of Jacopo de' Pazzi* (Cat. No. 19). Enamelled terracotta. Palazzo Serristori, Florence

89. *Stemma of Maddalena de' Serristori* (Cat. No. 20). Enamelled terracotta. Palazzo Serristori, Florence

90A. *Madonna and Child with two Angels* (Cat. No. 22).
Pigmented stucco. Ashmolean Museum, Oxford

90B. *Madonna and Child* (Cat. No. 23). Stucco.
Musée Jacquemart-André, Paris

91A. *Madonna and Child* (Cat. No. 25). Pigmented stucco.
Formerly Duveen Bros. Inc., New York

91B. *Madonna and Child* (Cat. No. 26). Terracotta covered
with pigmentation over traces of enamelling.
Formerly Kaiser Friedrich Museum, Berlin

92. *Madonna and Child* (Cat. No. 24). Pigmented terracotta. Bode Museum, Berlin (D.D.R.)

93. *Madonna and Child* (Cat. No. 27). Enamelled terracotta. Statens Museum for Kunst, Copenhagen

94A. *The Corsini Madonna* (Cat. No. 29). Pigmented stucco. Musée Jacquemart-André, Paris

94B. *Madonna and Child with six Angels* (Cat. No. 45). Terracotta. Louvre, Paris

95. *Saint Dominic and Saint Thomas Aquinas* (detail of Fig. 24). Enamelled terracotta.
Galleria Nazionale delle Marche, Urbino

96. *The Mugello Lunette* (Cat. No. 31). Enamelled terracotta. Bode Museum, Berlin (D.D.R.)

97. *The San Pierino Lunette* (Cat. No. 32). Enamelled terracotta. Palazzo di Parte Guelfa, Florence

98. *Angel* (detail of Plate 96)

99. *Angel* (detail of Plate 96)

100. *Madonna and Child* (detail of Plate 96)

101. *Madonna and Child* (detail of Plate 97)

102. *Madonna and Child* (Cat. No. 35). Enamelled terracotta. San Michele, Lucca

103. *Madonna of the Apple* (Cat. No. 36). Enamelled terracotta. Staatliche Museen, Berlin-Dahlem

104. *Madonna and Child* (Cat. No. 38). Enamelled terracotta. Musée Jacquemart-André, Paris

105. *Madonna and Child* (Cat. No. 41). Enamelled terracotta. Detroit Institute of Arts

106. *Madonna and Child with a Lily Plant* (Cat. No. 42). Enamelled terracotta. Hyde Collection, Glens Falls, N.Y.

107. After Luca della Robbia: *Madonna and Child* (Cat. No. 43). Enamelled terracotta. Victoria & Albert Museum, London

108. *Angel with a Candlestick* (Cat. No. 46). Bronze. Musée Jacquemart-André, Paris

109. *Angel with a Candlestick* (Cat. No. 46). Bronze. Musée Jacquemart-André, Paris

110. *Head of an Angel* (detail of Plate 108)

111. *Head of an Angel* (detail of Plate 109)

112. *Bronze Door* (Cat. No. 47). North Sacristy, Duomo, Florence

113. *Madonna and Child with two Angels* (detail of Plate 112)

114. *Saint John the Baptist with two Angels* (detail of Plate 112)

115. *Saint John the Evangelist with two Angels* (detail of Plate 112)

116. *Saint Matthew with two Angels* (detail of Plate 112)

117. *Saint Luke with two Angels* (detail of Plate 112)

118. *Saint Mark with two Angels* (detail of Plate 112)

119. *Saint Augustine with two Angels* (detail of Plate 112)

120. *Saint Jerome with two Angels* (detail of Plate 112)

121. Maso di Bartolomeo(?): *Saint Gregory the Great with two Angels* (detail of Plate 112)

122. *The Adoration of the Magi* (Cat. No. 49). Enamelled terracotta. Victoria & Albert Museum, London

123. *The Virgin adoring the Child* (Cat. No. 50). Enamelled terracotta. Parish church, Nynehead, Somerset

124. *Madonna and Child with Saint James the Great and Saint Blaise* (Cat. No. 48). Enamelled terracotta. Palazzo Vescovile, Pescia

125A. *Head of Saint James the Great* (detail of Plate 124)

125B. *Head of Saint Blaise* (detail of Plate 124)

126. *The Adoration of the Shepherds* (Cat. No. 51). Enamelled terracotta.
Victoria & Albert Museum, London

127. *The Virgin adoring the Child* (Cat. No. 52). Enamelled terracotta.
Philadelphia Museum of Art

128. *Relief Bust of a Lady* (Cat. No. 53). Enamelled terracotta relief. Museo Nazionale, Florence

CATALOGUE

Works by Luca della Robbia (Cat. Nos. 1–54)

1 Cantoria. Museo dell'Opera del Duomo, Florence.

Plates 1–28

Marble: overall 328 × 560 cm.
Singers from a Book: 103 × 65 cm.
Trumpeters: 101·5 × 94 cm.
Players on the Psaltery: 99·5 × 94 cm.
Players on the Cithara: 101·5 × 94 cm.
Drummers: 102 × 95 cm.
Singers from a Scroll: 103 × 64 cm.
Choral Dancers: 99 × 95 cm.
Players on the Organ, Harp and Lute: 100 × 95 cm.
Tambourine Players: 99 × 95 cm.
Cymbal Players: 99 × 93 cm.

All the reliefs in the upper register are carved in one with a leaf-and-dart and a strip of unincidented moulding along the bottom edge, except the *Players on the Psaltery*, which has only a leaf-and-dart moulding. The reliefs in the lower register include a flat moulding within the figurated field and an unincidented strip below; the *Players on the Organ, Harp and Lute* includes a similar strip above.

The figures in all ten reliefs are shown standing on fictive clouds. The four upper reliefs on the front are recessed within decorated frames. In the four lower reliefs on the front the figures are depicted in front of a flat background surrounded by a shallow moulding. This difference is due to the fact that the upper reliefs formed an integral part of the architecture of the Singing Gallery, whereas the lower reliefs were recessed on a rear plane between the five consoles which supported the structure.

SUBJECT

The ten figurated reliefs of the Cantoria illustrate Psalm 150, and were distributed as follows:

Laudate Dominum in Sanctis eius. Laudate eum in firmamento virtutis eius. Laudate eum in virtutibus eius. Laudate eum secundum multitudinem magnitudinis eius. Laudate eum *in sono tubae* (first relief on left in upper register). Laudate eum *in psalterio* (second relief from left in upper register) *et cythara* (second relief from right in upper register). Laudate eum *in timpano* (relief on extreme right in upper register) *et choro* (first relief on left in lower register). Laudate eum *in cordis et organo* (second relief from left in lower register). Laudate eum *in cymbalis benesonantibus* (second relief from right in lower register). Laudate eum *in cymbalis jubilationis* (relief on extreme right in lower register). Omnes spiritus laudet Dominum.

Unconvincing attempts have been made to relate the *Singing Boys* at the ends of the gallery to the first line of the inscription, which is otherwise unillustrated. Marquand (1914, pp. 8-9, 17) relates them to the word *Alleluia* with which the Psalm normally begins and ends.

HISTORY

In all early sources the structure now known as the Cantoria is referred to as an Organ Loft not as a Singing Gallery. It is so described by the Anonimo Magliabecchiano (Frey, 1892 (i), p. 80: 'Et infra l'altre sue opere in Firenze in Santa Maria del Fiore fece l'hornamento dell'organo maggiore, condotto con molta diligentia. Et sonuj tutte le storie a proposito, mostrando le fiure i loro effettj, che in esse s'intervenghono, benche per la loro alteza poco si vegghino le loro perfectionj') and in the *Libro di Antonio Billi* (Frey, 1892 (ii), p. 45). In the 1550 edition of Vasari's *Lives* (Vasari-Ricci, i, p. 249) the Cantoria is described as follows:

> . . . perchè diè materia di disporre gli Operai sopradetti ad allogarli l'ornamento di marmo dell'organo, sopra la sagrestia nuova di Santa Maria del Fiore: nel quale fece egli i cori della musica con diligenza et con sottil magisterio lavorati, dove sono alcune figure che cantano, et ancora che elle siano alte, vi si conosce il gonfiare della gola per lo alito: Et le battute in su le spalle, da chi regge la musica. Et in queste medesime istorie, andò imitando et suoni et balli, con tutti gli affetti simili, in cosa per cosa, finendo il tutto molto piu pulitamente, che non fece Donato stesso. Perchè si vede in quel di Donato più risoluta pratica e più maestrevole vivezza, che non fa perfezzione: et finita bontà in quel di Luca.

In the 1568 edition of the *Lives* (Vasari-Milanesi, ii, pp. 169-70) this account is elaborated:

> Perlochè i detti Operai, che oltre ai meriti di Luca furono a ciò persuasi da messer Vieri de' Medici, allora gran cittadino popolare, il quale molto amava Luca, gli diedero a fare, l'anno 1405, l'ornamento di marmo dell'organo, che grandissimo faceva allora far l'Opera per metterlo sopra la porta della sagrestia di detto tempio. Della quale opera fece Luca nel basamento, in alcune storie, i cori della musica che in vari modi cantano; e vi mise tanto studio e così bene gli riuscì quel lavoro, che ancora sia alta da terra sedici braccia, si scorge il gonfiare della gola

di chi canta, il battere delle mani di chi regge la musica in sulle spalle de' minori, ed in somma diverse maniere di suoni, canti, balli ed altre azioni piacevoli che porge il diletto della musica. Sopra il cornicione, poi, di questo ornamento fece Luca due figure di metallo dorate; cioè due Angeli nudi, condotti molto pulitamente, siccome è tutta l'opera, che fu tenuta cosa rara.

The 'gonfiare della gola di chi canta' seems to refer to the second figure from the right of the *Players on the Cithara*, and the 'battere delle mani . . . in sulle spalle de' minori' to the relief on the right side of the structure.

The appearance of the name of Vieri de' Medici in the second edition of the *Lives* is inexplicable. A powerful political figure in the last quarter of the fourteenth century, he was inscribed in the Arte del Cambio in 1348, was in active control of the Medici Bank in Florence and Rome till 1393, when he retired on account of old age or ill-health, and died on 13 September 1395. His sons, Nicola (1385–1454) and Cambiozzo (1391–1463), became insolvent in 1430, and can have played no part in the commissioning of the Cantoria. His nephew, Antonio di Giovanni di Cambio, died in 1397, two years before Luca della Robbia's birth. There is likewise no evidence of a connection between Luca della Robbia and Giovanni di Bicci de' Medici (d. 1429) or Averardo di Francesco de' Medici (d. 1434). For these members of the Medici family see Roover, 1963, p. 35 ff.

The last account of the Cantoria before its removal from its original position is by Bocchi-Cinelli (1677, p. 59):

Le figure dell'Organo che è sopra la *Sagrestia Vecchia* sono di mano di Luca della Robbia raro scultore, e mirabile, come alcune storie nel basamento de' musici, che cantano con tanta vivezza, che pare, che felicemente esprimano quello, per cui sono state fatte. I due Angeli di bronzo indorati furono condotti da Luca con tanta pulitezza, e con tanta leggiadria che con parole isprimere con [*sic*] si potrebbe.

In 1688, on the occasion of the wedding of the Gran Principe Ferdinando, son of Grand-Duke Cosimo III, to Violante of Bavaria, the upper parts of Luca della Robbia's and Donatello's galleries were removed on the initiative of Alessandro Segni. The supports and the four lower reliefs of Luca's Cantoria were left in position and a larger wooden gallery was constructed over them. The purpose of this change was to enable a larger choir to be used at the wedding ceremony, and the mistaken view that Luca's Organ Loft was itself intended as a Singing Gallery may date from this time. The gallery is described in this state in 1757 by Richa (vi, p. 149):

. . . e in alto l'Organo lavoro di Fra Ermenegildo di Lucchese degli Argenti (e non Bernardo, come scrive il Migliore) il qual Frate principiollo nel 1545, avendovi fatte le canne alte 20 palmi. I molti Fanciulli di marmo in atto di cantare, erano un adornamento della Cantoria, ma tolti via in occorrenza delle nozze del Gran Principe Ferdinando il quale volle, che s'ampliasse il palco, che di presente è di legno intagliato coll'Arme de' Medici, questi sono inoggi nell'Opera ben custoditi, insieme con quelli dell'altro Pergamo, che si dissero opera di Donatello, e della Robbia.

The six reliefs removed from the gallery and the reliefs from the upper section of Donatello's Cantoria were initially used for the parapets of two pulpits built under the side arches of the choir. They were then stored in the Opera del Duomo. The architectural elements from the upper part of Luca's Cantoria were used for repairs, while those of the Donatello Cantoria were preserved. For this see Follini-Rastrelli, ii, p. 408. In the early nineteenth century the carvings were removed to a 'stanza più decorosa' (for this and for the later history of the Cantorias see B. Marrai, 1900 (i), and the excellent account of G. Brunetti, in Becherucci/Brunetti, i, pp. 277–80). In 1822 the six figurated reliefs from Luca's Cantoria were transferred to the Uffizi by Senator Giovanni Alessandri. They were later moved to the cortile of the Museo Nazionale, where they were joined in 1867 by the four figurated reliefs and the architectural elements which had been removed from their original site in the Cathedral in 1841, and in 1870 by other architectural carvings from the Opera. In 1883 the carvings were transferred to the newly established Museo dell'Opera del Duomo. The only evidence for the architectural character of the gallery of the Cantoria at this time was that available in documents, and in 1891, when the Cantoria was reconstructed by Luigi del Moro, the six upper reliefs were separated by single pilasters (Fig. 3). It was objected by Reymond (1897 (i), p. 186 ff.) that this was stylistically implausible, and that paired pilasters must have been employed. In 1899 a damaged section of paired Corinthian pilasters was discovered in the Baptistry and was rightly identified as part of the upper section of the Cantoria. It contained, on the outer edges, the same moulding that runs along the base of the reliefs. The 1891 reconstruction was none the less preserved till 1939. In 1941 a section of the upper frieze and inscription, which was originally set over the *Players on the Cithara*, was discovered by Professor Rodolfo Sabatini, by whom a further reconstruction was prepared in 1954. This is the section bearing the words: IN VIRTVTIBVS EI⟨VS⟩ · LA⟨VDATE⟩ EV⟨M⟩ SECVNDVM.

DOCUMENTATION

The documents relating to the Cantoria are published by Poggi (1909, pp. 249–56, Nos. 1240–85) and are reprinted by Marquand (1914, pp. 17–24). A high proportion of these documents has been checked and retranscribed by Dr. Gino Corti, with results that add nothing to the history of the Cantoria but confirm the exemplary accuracy of Poggi's work.

The commission for the Cantoria has not been traced. The earliest document commonly associated with the Cantoria is a payment to Luca della Robbia of 10 lire 'de quodam marmore albo' on 4 October 1431 (Poggi, 1909, No. 1240). If this marble were intended for the Cantoria, the commission would have been placed in the course of 1431. The first occasion on which the 'lavorio del perghamo degli orghani' is specifically mentioned is on 9 April 1432, when Luca received a payment of 6 florins (*ibid.*, No. 1241), and it is thus possible that the commission was awarded between these two dates. On 11 July 1432, reference is made to an area in the Opera del Duomo which was to be set aside for work on the Cantoria (*ibid.*, No. 1243). An entry of 29 April 1432 (*ibid.*, No. 1242) records the transport to the Opera del Duomo of the 'cornices perghami locati ad faciendum Luce Simonis Marci della Robbia', which were to be carved by a stonemason in the employment of the Opera, Caprino di Domenico di Giusto da Settignano. A further payment of 40 lire was made on 23 December 1433 (*ibid.*, No. 1251), to Nanni di Miniato called Fora 'per sua faticha innavere fatto braccia 10 di chornice del perghamo che fa al presente Lucha di Simone della Robbia.' A payment to Luca of 20 March 1438 (*ibid.*, No. 1281), however, leaves no doubt that he was responsible for executing the five consoles (which were valued at 17 florins, 4 soldi, 2 denarii each), as well as 'otto venbris acchanalatis et basis et capitellis' (valued at a total of 45 florins, 14 soldi, 3 denarii), a 'cornice grossa cum litteris et cum dentellis' measuring 14⅛ braccia, 'una alia cornice grossa sine dentellis alinguazata' measuring 14⅘ braccia, 'unius fregi cum litteris' measuring 9¼ braccia, and another 'cornice' for an unspecified position measuring 6¼ braccia. The total cost of these architectural elements was 266 florins, 8 soldi. The architectural carving throughout the Cantoria is of uniformly high quality, and it is not possible to identify the sections entrusted to Nanni di Miniato and Caprino di Domenico.

On 22 October 1432 (*ibid.*, No. 1244) Luca received a further sum of 12 florins in respect of the Cantoria, and on 29 November (*ibid.*, No. 1245), the Capomaestro was authorised to hand over to him 'medietatem cuiusdam lapidis recise pro faciendo tabulas perghami.' A supervisory committee, composed of Niccolò di Ugo degli Alessandri, Matteo degli Strozzi, and Giovanni di Lapo Niccolini, was formed on 9 December 1432 (*ibid.*, No. 1246), to supervise work on the *Arca di San Zenobio*, the altar in the chapel of St. Zenobius, the new organs of Matteo da Prato, and Luca's Cantoria. On 23 January 1433, they disbursed 15 florins to Luca (*ibid.*, No. 1247), on 31 March a further 27 florins (*ibid.*, No. 1248), and on 12 November (*ibid.*, No. 1250) another 15 florins. Part payments were also made on 23 December 1433 (*ibid.*, No. 1251: 10 florins), 15 January 1434 (*ibid.*, No. 1253: 10 florins), 13 February 1434 (*ibid.*, No. 1254: 5 florins), 18 March 1434 (*ibid.*, No. 1255: 10 florins), 2 June 1434 (*ibid.*, No. 1256: 25 florins), and 9 June 1434 (*ibid.*, No. 1257: 50 florins). A key document is one of 26 August 1434, which records that four figurated reliefs, two large and two small, were complete (*ibid.*, No. 1258: 'Item [similis modum et forma] extimaverunt et extimationem fecerunt quatuor petia seu quatuor petiis storiarum cuiusdam perghami locati Luce Simonis Marci della Robbia, videlicet duo maiora et duo minora videlicet quodlibet petium maius fl. LX et quodlibet petium minus fl. XXXV, in totum in ipsa quatuor petia fl. au. CLXXXX'). Since the recorded payments made to Luca total 18 florins in 1432, 67 florins in 1433 and 100 florins in the first half of 1434, it can be inferred that up to that time he worked largely, if not exclusively, on the four reliefs. A further payment of 30 florins (*ibid.*, No. 1259) was authorised on 17 December 1434.

The composition of the supervisory committee changed with the banishment of Matteo Strozzi in November 1434, and on 24 January 1435 (*ibid.*, No. 1260) the commission to the previous committee was annulled. Strozzi was succeeded (*ibid.*, No. 1265) by Salvi di Neroni Dietisalvi. A sum of 10 florins was paid to Luca on 1 April 1435 (*ibid.*, No. 1261), and on 22 April 1435, the rate of remuneration for the reliefs was increased from 60 florins to 70 florins with provision for a

proportionate increase for the lower paid reliefs (*ibid.*, No. 1262: 'Prefati operarii ... considerantes quasdam storias marmoris factas ad instantiam opere per Lucam Simonis [marci] della Robbia, pro uno perghamo sibi per operarios dicte opere locato, et advertentes ad quoddam pretium alias factum per eorum antecessores quibusdam storiis dicti perghami per eum factis et considerantes dictum Lucam fecisse certas alias storias dicti perghami que nondum fuerunt extimate et in quibus maiorem laborem et longius tempus misit, et quod, in magisterio, dicte storie quas facit ad presens sunt pulcriores ac meliores, idcirco [...] deliberaverunt quod dicta opera teneatur et obligata eidem Luce dare [et solvere] pro qualibet storia facta et nondum extimata, et etiam pro qualibet storia fienda totius perghami, fl. septuaginta, et pro qualibet storia minori illud minus quod tangeret pro rata cuiuslibet storie'). This and the document dated 26 August 1434 are misinterpreted by Marquand (1914, p. 13), who translates 'maius' and 'minus' as 'major' and 'minor,' and infers that four scenes in the lower register were the 'minor' reliefs. The only admissible translation of these terms is 'larger' and 'smaller,' the small reliefs being those on the ends of the gallery.

Other payments to Luca in 1435 comprise 55 florins on 26 April (Poggi, 1909, No. 1263), 20 florins on 30 June (*ibid.*, No. 1266), 40 florins on 26 August (*ibid.*, No. 1267) and 40 florins on 7 December (*ibid.*, No. 1268). Payments in 1436 comprised 20 florins on 24 April (*ibid.*, No. 1270), 30 florins on 20 June (*ibid.*, No. 1271), and 40 florins on 10 October (*ibid.*, No. 1272). The site of the workshop was changed again in March 1437 (*ibid.*, No. 1273), and payments in that year consist of 50 florins on 9 April (*ibid.*, No. 1274), 30 florins on 30 August (*ibid.*, No. 1277), 40 florins on 30 October (*ibid.*, No. 1278), and 150 florins on 19 December (*ibid.*, No. 1279). On 30 April 1437, the Capomaestro, Battista d'Antonio, was instructed to have the figurated reliefs polished and to replace them in a suitable position so that they should not be damaged (*ibid.*, No. 1276: 'Item deliberaverunt quod Batista caput-magister poliri faciat omnes figuras que sunt miste cum marmore opere in laborerio dicte opere in terra per Lucam Simonis della Robbia, et postea reponi faciat in loco proheminenti ut non devastentur'). On 14 March 1438, it was arranged that the wall of the Sacristy should be broken through so that the consoles of the Cantoria could be installed (*ibid.*, No. 1280: 'teneantur rumpi facere certam partem pilastri sacristie in qua stare (debeant) becchatelli perghami marmoris facti per Lucam Simonis Marci della Robbia in quo poni (debent) orghana ecclesie prefate'). On 20 March, Luca was paid for parts of the architectural frame (*ibid.*, No. 1281, see above: 266 florins, 8 soldi), and further payments were made on 30 April (*ibid.*, No. 1282: 50 florins), 26 May (*ibid.*, No. 1283: 40 florins) and 28 August (*ibid.*, No. 1285: 42 florins, 8 soldi 'pro resto pergami').

If the first two of the large reliefs were assessed at 120 florins, the two small reliefs were assessed at 70 florins, and the remaining six large reliefs were assessed at 420 florins, the total cost of the figurated reliefs would have been 610 florins. The overall payments to Luca from 1432 to 1437 amount to 740 florins, and though they include a sum for a model made in 1434 in competition with Donatello for a stone head to fill the *gula* of the cupola (Marquand, 1914, p. 33, No. 5) it is reasonable to suppose that through this period he was engaged principally on the figurated carvings. Payments for the architectural parts of the Cantoria total 398 florins, and are confined to 1438, but it is possible that the surplus of 130 florins paid before the end of 1437 was also connected with this work.

EXECUTION

Considerable diversity is apparent in the figurated reliefs, and it is essential, for an understanding of Luca della Robbia's development, to establish the approximate sequence in which they were produced. This aspect was not investigated by Marquand, Bode or other earlier students of Luca della Robbia. Lisner (1960, pp. 8–11) identifies the *Tambourine Players*, the *Players on the Psaltery*, the *Trumpeters* and the *Players on the Organ, Harp and Lute* as the earliest of the carvings, to which the document of August 1434 relates. These views are elaborated in a careful, unpublished thesis by the same student (1955), in which it is argued (i) that the *Tambourine Players* was begun at the end of 1432 and finished not long afterwards, since its design is reflected in the dated *Madonna of Humility* by Domenico di Bartolo of 1433 in the Pinacoteca Nazionale at Siena, (ii) that the *Players on the Cithara* 'weist auf Lucas spätere Arbeiten voraus', (iii) that the *Boys singing from a Scroll* establish 'die späte Entstehung der Sängertafeln.' The criteria of judgement behind these opinions are entirely subjective, and it has been suggested by the present writer (1958, pp. 293–4) that the only satisfactory method of analysis is one that proceeds directly from the documents. Since two small reliefs on the Cantoria were completed by August 1434, and since two reliefs are smaller than the rest, it follows that the two end reliefs of *Singing Boys* are among the earliest of the carvings. His is contested by Seymour (1963, p. 109 ff.) on the ground that the small reliefs are incompatible in style with large reliefs to which he mistakenly ascribes an early date. This case is endorsed by Del Bravo (1973, p. 29 n. 20), who advances the theory that the present reliefs are replacements for two earlier reliefs. Del Bravo argues that 'i due rilievi minori già eseguiti il 26 agosto 1434 ... furono certamente rifatti perché nel documento del 22 aprile 1435 si prevede nuovamente l'esecuzione di storie minori.' Not only is there no reference in the abundant documentation on the Cantoria to the recarving or substitution of reliefs, but the document of 1435 refrains from placing an exact value on further small reliefs, presumably because no provision had been made for them and they would not therefore be required. The *Singing Boys* are thus, as their grouping, postures and morphology suggest, some of the earliest carvings on the Cantoria. This case is accepted by Brunetti (in Beccherucci/Brunetti, i, p. 277). Most closely related to these carvings are the central reliefs in the upper register, the *Players on the Psaltery* and the *Players on the Cithara*. The sequence of these carvings, all of which were completed by 1434, appears to be (i) *Cithara Players*, (ii) *Boys singing from a Book*, (iii) *Boys singing from a Scroll*, (iv) *Psaltery Players*. The two reliefs in the centre of the front face of the gallery depend from classical Muse sarcophagi (see below), and represent an earlier conception of the Cantoria than that embodied in the more vigorous carvings executed between 1434 and 1437.

The most ambitious and evolved of the reliefs are the *Trumpeters* and *Cymbal Players*. These must come towards the end of the series, and confirmation that this is so is provided by the fact that the *Trumpeters* is unfinished; five feet in the centre and on the right are left in the rough and the face, neck and hair of the dancing girl leaning forward to the right of centre have not been brought to completion. The superior reliefs, to which reference is made in a document of 1435 and which were the subject of increased valuations, are likely to have been the *Tambourine Players* and the *Players on the Organ, Harp and Lute*, and these must have been followed by the *Drummers* and *Cymbal Players*, where the emphasis on movement seems to reflect some knowledge of the Cantoria and Prato Pulpit reliefs of Donatello. From a figurative standpoint the most advanced of the reliefs is the *Choral Dancers* in the lower register. While the model for this relief was unquestionably made by Luca della Robbia, the articulation of the figures, the carving of the hair and eyes, and the incomplete realisation of the spatial structure suggest that it was carved in marble by a younger sculptor, whose style looks forward to the practice of the Rossellino shop.

The marble for the Cantoria seems to have been quarried and selected with great care. A document of 29 April 1435 (Poggi, 1909, No. 1264), recording a payment for marble to Nanni di Piero Ticci, states that 'maius tempus consumatur in charichando et scharichando marmore dicti perghami quam aliud marmor.' Some of the slabs none the less are flawed by grey veining.

The only names other than that of Luca della Robbia mentioned in documents in connection with the Cantoria are those of Caprino di Domenico di Giusto da Settignano, who was employed to work on the 'cornices perghami' on 29 April 1432 (ibid., No. 1242), and Nanni di Miniato called Fora, who on 23 December 1433 (ibid., No. 1251) was paid forty lire 'per sua faticha innavere fatto braccia 10 di chornice del perghamo che fa al presente Lucha di Simone della Robia.' It has been inferred from this that the initial contract with Luca (unlike that with Donatello) provided only for figurated reliefs, while the architecture of the Organ Loft was the subject of a separate contract by the Opera. If this were so, the arrangement must have been subject to some later change, since payments to Luca in 1437 and 1438 relate explicitly to the consoles and other architectural features of the Cantoria. Nanni di Miniato called Fora (for whom see Fabriczy, 1906 (i)) seems to have been working with Donatello and Michelozzo in Pisa in 1426–8 on the Brancacci and Aragazzi monuments, and was in Naples in 1433 involved in the erection of the Brancacci monument. He appears to have had a close connection with Matteo Strozzi, one of the members of the supervisory committee for the Cantoria, to whom at various times he offered two figurated reliefs, one with the story of Bacchus, discovered in the area of Pisa and Lucca, and reported in 1430 on the epitaph of the Tomb of the Dioscuri in Naples (for which see L. Correra, 1904).

The intervention of other artists in the pulpit is conjectural. It is possible that Buggiano intervened at certain points; the heads of the two children who peer out from right and left of the *Drummers* are, for example, closely reminiscent of Buggiano's style in the lavabo of the North Sacristy. In the

Tambourine Players the cursive, Neo-Attic drapery of the second figure from the right, as well as her hair and eyes, look forward to the later work of Agostino di Duccio (whose early works, however, are problematic and not strictly related to the Cantoria in style or technique). The principal problem arises with the *Choral Dancers*, where the execution shows some affinities to the right-hand figure in Bernardo Rossellino's Monument of the Beata Villana. This relief and a *Madonna* relief in the Museo dell'Opera del Duomo are conceivably earlier works by the same member of the Rossellino shop.

PIGMENTATION

Marquand (1914, p. 10) observes of the *Players on the Psaltery* that 'the background seems to have been coloured, possibly blue.' Schubring (1905, p. 19) believed that certain ornamental details in the reliefs were gilded and that the hair and eyes were pigmented or toned. A number of the reliefs in the Tempio Malatestiano at Rimini, which evidently owe their genesis to Luca's Cantoria reliefs, show extensive remains of blue pigmentation in the background and of local surface gilding. *In situ* the contrast between Luca's Cantoria and the strongly gilded and coloured Cantoria of Donatello must have been very marked. There is, however, no reference to the pigmentation or gilding of Luca's Cantoria in any document or later description.

EPIGRAPHY

The inscription on the Cantoria has received less attention than it deserves. While it does not aspire to the strict classicism introduced by Alberti at Rimini in the middle of the century (for this see Mardersteig, 1959) and contains, like the inscription on the Federighi monument, some of the imperfections of Early Renaissance lettering, it has much in common with the majuscule *formata* developed by Poggio Bracciolini (after 1408) and Niccoli (for the latter see S. Morison, 1943; for Early Renaissance lettering in general see Covi, 1963, with bibliography). Classical lettering becomes a regular feature of sculptural inscriptions after the mid fourteen-twenties, and the inscription on the Cantoria was preceded by the experiments of Ghiberti (on the *Arca of the Three Martyrs* of 1424–8 and the Dati tomb slab in Santa Maria Novella of 1425–7), and of Donatello (on the Coscia monument in the Baptistry of 1425 and the Pecci tomb slab in Siena of 1426). The forms of certain letters on the Cantoria, notably the A and the E, depart from those used by Ghiberti and Donatello. The inscription on the Cantoria differs from earlier inscriptions in two respects, first that it was intended to edify and not simply to inform, and second that its length was preordained and was not planned in relation to the space available. It is significant that the upper line (which is a modern replacement) was originally reconstructed with conventional contractions, which proved, on the rediscovery of one section, to be incorrect. Along with the fact that the letters were pigmented, the form of the inscription leaves no doubt that it was intended to be read by worshippers on the floor of the church in conjunction with the figure reliefs. The letters in the central frieze (where the inscription relates to the four scenes above) are considerably fewer than those in the top and bottom inscriptions; the capitals are therefore larger and the spacing is more generous. In the third line, the concluding verse (which is not illustrated) is contracted to OIS SPS LAVDET DNM. A peculiar feature is the rendering of the word LAVDATE, which is reduced to the letters LA with a curling sprig of foliage running across them. In the bottom line, where the letter L occurs at the end of one piece of marble and the letter A at the beginning of another, the sprig is confined to the first letter.

MUSICAL BACKGROUND

The available information about the organs of the Cathedral is printed by Poggi (1909, pp. cxxx–cxxxvii, Nos. 1319–1453). The need for a modern organ in the Duomo is mentioned in 1383 (*ibid.*, No. 1319). In 1388 it was agreed that a new organ should be ordered (*ibid.*, No. 1322), and an organ seems to have been supplied by a certain Fra Domenico da Siena (*ibid.*, No. 1323). A wooden casing was provided for it in 1411 (*ibid.*, Nos. 1325–8), and in 1413 it was covered with a blue curtain decorated with lilies. In 1422 and 1423 payments were made to Matteo di Paolo da Prato, apparently in connection with the repair or reconditioning of this organ (*ibid.*, Nos. 1330–5). The organ case was repainted by Giovanni di Guccio at this time (*ibid.*, No. 1332). In November 1426 (*ibid.*, No. 1336), the Operaii enjoined 'quod provisor opere teneatur actari facere organa chatredalis ecclesie florentine.' On 25 September 1432, it was decided 'quod Matteus, magister orghanorum, actet expensis opere orghana ecclesie maioris florentine que sunt pulvere et aliis rebus turpibus devastata' (*ibid.*, No. 1337). In November 1432, Matteo da Prato is again mentioned as 'magistro qui facit orghana opere' (*ibid.*, No. 1338), and in June 1433, 'el modello degli orghani' arrived from Prato (*ibid.*, No. 1340). The pipes were cast in 1434 and 1435. An organ case was ordered on 7 February 1435, from Agnolo di Lazzaro and Jacopetto (*ibid.*, Nos. 1343, 1345) and in April of the same year a payment of 100 florins was made to Matteo da Prato. At the time of the consecration of the Cathedral in 1436, the new organ was not ready and arrangements were made to have the previous organ repaired, once more by Matteo da Prato (*ibid.*, Nos. 1348, 1352). In February 1436, Antonio di Bartolomeo Squarcialupi became organist of the Cathedral. Work continued in the late fourteen-thirties on the organ case but no progress seems to have been made with the new organ. In September 1438, the Operaii, who were disquieted at the delay, put pressure on Matteo da Prato to complete the work, threatening him with imprisonment, and a new contract was entered into with Antonio di Migliore Guidotti (*ibid.*, No. 1366). Matteo da Prato was constrained to return to the Opera the money and the large quantity of lead and *stagno* with which he had been supplied, and it was agreed that the money should be refunded in instalments. Antonio Guidotti's work seems, however, to have proved unsatisfactory, and the organ was once more entrusted to Matteo da Prato and was declared in 1448 to be 'in bona perfectione et bene fulcitum' (*ibid.*, No. 1398). The surrounding casing was executed by Giovanni di Domenico da Gaiole, gilded by Luigi di Bartolomeo, and painted with a lily, two putti and an Agnus Dei by Andrea del Castagno. A casing was also made by Giovanni di Domenico da Gaiole for the old organ (which by this time was reinstalled in Donatello's Cantoria).

Matteo da Prato (for whom see C. Guasti, 1865) was a

figure of some distinction, who was responsible for organs in the Servi at Pistoia, in the Baptistry in Florence, at Or San Michele (1428), San Francesco at Lucca and the Badia (1440), and died in 1465. In 1434, he wrote a letter to the Opera reporting the completion of a relief on Donatello's Prato pulpit ('e pronettovi per gl'intendenti di questa terra, che dicono tutti per una bocha, che mai si vide simile storia'). It cannot be precluded that he advised on musical aspects of Luca della Robbia's reliefs. Two precedents have some relevance for the musical imagery of the Cantoria. These are (i) the *Music-making Angels* carved for the façade of the Cathedral, now in the Museo dell' Opera del Duomo, especially Jacopo di Piero Guidi's *Angel with Cymbals* (1383) and *Angel with Viol* (1388) and Piero di Giovanni Tedesco's *Angel with Portable Organ* and *Angel with Lute* (probably 1386–7), and (ii) the shutters of the Or San Michele organ (1429), which were painted by Francesco d'Antonio and show two groups of angels singing from scrolls (formerly Toscanelli collection, Pisa, now Accademia, Florence. For these see Salmi, 1929, pp. 18–24). In every case the reliefs depict contemporary musical instruments. Thus a portable organ, like that depicted in the *Players on the Organ, Harp and Lute*, is represented in a fresco by Lorenzo di Bicci of the *Marriage of St. Cecilia and Valerianus* in the sacristy of the Carmine; a cithara virtually identical with those in the *Players on the Cithara* is depicted by Agostino di Duccio in the Chapel of Isotta in the Tempio Malatestiano at Rimini, where a lute, a psaltery and tambourines similar to those portrayed by Luca also appear; and three trumpets, like those in the *Trumpeters*, are depicted on the Adimari cassone. It has been claimed (e.g. by Schering, 1913, p. 59) that the *Players on the Organ, Harp and Lute* depicts a musical ensemble. This is contested by Winternitz (1967), who relates the instruments solely to the words of the Psalm illustrated. The truth may lie between these two extremes. Thus it is demonstrable, from the Adimari cassone, that two different types of trumpet, in the same ratio of two to one, were played in association, while in the Tempio Malatestiano Agostino di Duccio shows a portative organ and harp played together, a lute and psaltery in association, and two types of drum synchronised. The form of the cithara, with large ears and projecting frets, is discussed by E. Winternitz (1961 (i)). About 1432 the papal choir consisted of nine to twelve singers, and the numbers depicted on the end reliefs of the Cantoria, five and four, or nine if the two groups are aggregated, may have some validity in relation to the choir of the Duomo in Florence at the time. The development of polyphonic singing and the composition of the plainchant choir in the Cathedral are discussed by Frank A. D'Accone (1971; see also D'Accone, 1961, for useful supplementary information). A suggestive article by G. Croll (1968) deals with Dufay in Florence, where he arrived in June 1435, and proposes a possible equation between his musical style and the decoration of the Cantoria.

CLASSICAL SOURCES

The classical sources of the Cantoria reliefs are not discussed by Marquand or Cruttwell, and are the subject only of parenthetical reference by Lisner (1955, p. 195), who relates the seated central figure in the *Players on the Organ, Harp and*

Lute to an Apollo or Orpheus representation, with specific reference to reliefs at Pisa and Leningrad. The study was first opened in a brilliant article by C. Del Bravo (1973), who established (i) Luca della Robbia's use of Greek medallic sources, (ii) the dependence of the *Choral Dancers* from the Neo-Attic vase at Pisa, and (iii) the relation between the central figure in the *Players on the Tambourine* and a Daedalus sarcophagus in the Louvre. The article is vitiated by the mistaken assumption that the sarcophagus reliefs known to Luca della Robbia were those now in the Camposanto at Pisa, which have no more than a tangential relationship to the panels of the Cantoria. I am indebted to Ruth Rubinstein for drawing attention to the importance for Luca of the Woburn Muse sarcophagus. For the sarcophagus reliefs and other classical sculptures mentioned in this book in connection with the Cantoria see the following works:

Mansuelli, i, Nos.:

1 *Decorative Carving.* The relief, which was discovered with the Ara Pacis sculptures and reached Florence from the collection of Cardinal Ricci at Montepulciano, represents the type of Augustan decorative carving which was adapted for the consoles of the Cantoria.

15 *Maenads in ecstasy.* This fragmentary relief reached the Uffizi in 1783 from the Villa Medici. For other versions of the composition see Caputo, 1948. The style has some relevance to that of the *Choral Dancers.*

59/60 *Boy with a goose* (Fig. 9). One of the two versions of this statuette was seen by Vasari in the Pitti and was known, in the third decade of the fifteenth century, to Masaccio. The types of the children and their poses are related in reverse to those of the left-hand child in the foreground of the *Players on the Cithara.*

149 *Sacrificial scene* (Fig. 7). It is not known when this relief arrived in Florence. It is of Hadrianic not Flavian origin (see Toynbee, 1934, p. 244), and the figures on the right holding up a wreath may have inspired the central figures in the *Drummers* on the Cantoria.

161 *Dionysiac scene.* The relief was formerly in the Palazzo Riccardi; its antiquity has been questioned. The maenad figure on the left (Fig. 11) represents the type from which the central dancer in Luca's *Trumpeters* depends.

247 *Erotes.* From the Palazzo Riccardi. This late second or early third-century relief provides a parallel in reverse for the left-hand foreground figure in the *Cymbal Players.*

M. Wegner, 1966, Nos.:

228 Vienna, Kunsthistorisches Museum (Inv. I. 171). The sarcophagus (Fig. 4) was at Santa Maria Maggiore in the sixteenth century, and was also known in the fifteenth century (drawings in Ambrosiana and elsewhere). There can be little doubt that it was studied by Luca della Robbia.

231 Woburn Abbey (Fig. 5). From the Villa Giustiniani. A drawing after the sarcophagus appears in the Codex Coburgensis. Also known to Luca della Robbia. The elbow of the second figure from the left is exposed, as it is in the *Psaltery Players*, and is not covered by a cloak as in Wegner No. 215 (Villa Medici).

F. Matz, i, Nos.:

44 Hever Castle. Known from the fifteenth century, when it
was drawn by an artist sometimes identified with Gentile
da Fabriano, it presents loose analogies for the *Cymbal
Players*.
61 Rome, Palazzo Colonna. Known to Dal Pozzo, earlier history unrecorded. Loose analogies for the *Cymbal Players*.

F. Matz, ii, No.:

100 Woburn Abbey (Fig. 6). The sarcophagus reached
Woburn in 1815 from the Villa Aldobrandini, where it is
recorded in 1603. Earlier history unknown. Known to
Francesco di Giorgio (?), Aspertini and other fifteenth-
century artists. The relief is the source (i) of the left hand-
child in the foreground of the *Players on the Psaltery*, (ii)
of the foremost musician in the *Trumpeters*.

F. Matz, iv, No.:

Beilage 130. Modena, Galleria Estense. Parallel for dancing
figures in the *Trumpeters*.

C. Robert, i, Nos.:

21 Adonis sarcophagus (Lateran). Loose parallel for the central figure seated on a stool in the *Players on the Organ,
Harp and Lute*. For the form of the stool see G. M. A.
Richter, *The Furniture of the Greeks, Etruscans and
Romans*, London, 1966.
35 Daedalus sarcophagus (Louvre, Paris). Recorded only
since the pontificate of Pius IV (1559–65). Two figures
with garlands at the corners of the front (Fig. 10) are
rightly identified by Del Bravo as a typological source
for the central figure in the *Players on the Tambourine*.
47 Endymion sarcophagus (Rome, Palazzo Rospigliosi).
From St. John Lateran. Close parallel for the child on the
left of the *Players on the Organ, Harp and Lute*.

C. Robert, ii, No.:

196 Garland sarcophagus (Rome, Palazzo Barberini). Parallel
for head of central child in the *Cymbal Players*.

2 **Five Reliefs.** Museo dell'Opera del Duomo, Florence.
                                                    Plates 29–33
Marble: individual dimensions below.

Five reliefs carved by Luca della Robbia for the north face of
the Campanile are described by Vasari (Vasari-Milanesi, ii,
pp. 169–70): '. . . prima che fusse dagli Operai di Santa Maria
del Fiore richiamato a Firenze: dove fece per lo campanile di
quella chiesa cinque storiette di marmo, che sono da quella
parte che è verso la chiesa (le quali mancavano, secondo il
disegno di Giotto), accanto a quelle, dove sono le Scienze ed
Arti, che già fece, come si è detto, Andrea Pisano. Nella prima,
Luca fece Donato che insegna la grammatica; nella seconda,
Platone ed Aristotile per la filosofia; nella terza, uno che suona
il liuto per la musica; nella quarta, un Tolomeo per l'astro-
logia; e nella quinta, Euclide per la geometria. Le quali storie,
per pulitezza, grazia e disegno, avanzarono d'assai le due fatte
da Giotto, come si disse; dove in una per la pittura Apelle
dipigne, e nell'altra Fidia per la scultura lavora con lo scar-

pello. Perlochè i detti Operai, che oltre ai meriti di Luca
furono a ciò fare persuasi da messer Vieri de' Medici, allora
gran cittadino popolare, il quale molto amava Luca, gli diedero
a fare, l'anno 1405 [*sic*], l'ornamento di marmo dell'organo.'
Vasari's claim that the Campanile reliefs preceded the Cantoria is in conflict with documents which show that the commission dates from 30 May 1437 (Poggi, 1909, No. 325). An
interim payment of 30 florins was made on 2 December 1438
(*ibid*., No. 326), and a final payment of 70 florins on 10 March
1439 (*ibid*., No. 327), both payments recorded in two separate
accounts by the Operaii. The total payment for the five reliefs
was 100 florins.

Luca della Robbia's reliefs occupied their original positions
on the north face of the Campanile till 1965, when they were
transferred to the Museo dell'Opera del Duomo (Beccherucci/
Brunetti, i, p. 276). The original sculptural programme for the
lowest register of the Campanile made provision for twenty-
one reliefs, carved by or under the supervision of Andrea
Pisano. They comprised (West face) *The Creation of Adam,
The Creation of Eve, The Labours of Adam and Eve, Jabal,
Jubal, Tubalcain*, and *Noah*, (South face) *Gionitus (Astronomy),
The Art of Building, Medicine, Hunting, Weaving, Phoroneus
the Lawgiver*, and *Daedalus*, and (East face) *Navigation, Her-
cules and Cacus, Agriculture, Theatrica, Phidias (Sculpture),
Apelles (Painting)* and *Architecture* (*ibid*., p. 234). No provision was made for reliefs in the hexagonal frames on the
north face. Access to the Campanile from the street was gained
by a doorway on the east side (for this see M. Trachtenberg,
1971, pp. 73–4). This seems originally to have been a low
doorway designed by Andrea Pisano, was later enlarged, and
finally, about 1360, was expanded to its present form by
Talenti. The Talentian doorway extended to the area of the
hexagons, and two of the reliefs (*Phidias* and *Apelles*) were
therefore moved to the north face of the Campanile. No provision was made for a continuation of the cycle on the north
face, perhaps because this area was obscured by a raised passage or bridge leading from the Cathedral to an upper storey
of the tower. The bridge survived till after 1397, and was
probably demolished in the early fifteenth century, when a
number of documents (*ibid*., pp. 204–5), the earliest dating
from 1397 and the latest from 1431, refer to the cleaning up of
the area between the Duomo and the Campanile. The commission to Luca della Robbia arises directly from these
changes, and had as its objective the filling of the five vacant
hexagonal frames on the north wall. The five reliefs represent:

GRAMMAR. Marble: $81 \cdot 5 \times 68 \cdot 5$ cm. In the exergue at the base
is a fluted disc, of a type which recurs in the spandrels of the
Peretola tabernacle. The figure on the left is identified by
Vasari as the mid-fourth century grammarian Aelius Donatus.
Schlosser (1896, pp. 63, 72) identifies him as the later Latin
grammarian Priscian, author of the influential *Institutiones
Grammaticae*. For the sources of the open door motif in
antique sarcophagi, and its continuation in Renaissance
funereal symbolism, see Bialostocki (1973), pp. 7–32.
Schlosser (*loc. cit*.), however, notes that the window is 'das
Symbol dieser Disciplin, die das Propyläum aller übrigen ist.
Ebenso auf dem Fresco der spanischen Kapelle und im
Ambraser Codex.'

PHILOSOPHY. Marble: 83·5 × 69 cm. In the exergue is a flower and leaves. The subject is described by Vasari as 'Platone ed Aristotile per la filosofia.' This explanation has been generally accepted, since the dresses in both cases are classical. Schlosser (1896, p. 73) misidentified the relief to which Vasari refers as the fourth in the series, and interpreted this relief as *Logic and Dialectic*. The treatment of the two disputing figures has a close parallel in the panels of confronting Martyrs and Apostles on the two doors by Donatello in the Sagrestia Vecchia of San Lorenzo. The doors are not documented, but are generally assumed to date from ca. 1437–43 (see Janson, 1957, with bibliography). The relationship is discussed by Bode (1900, p. 4), who denies a connection, postulated by Reymond (1897 (ii), pp. 24–26), with the bronze doors of Donatello and refers the motif instead to 'mittelalterliche Vorbilder', and by Herzner (1976 (ii)).

POETRY (?). Marble: 81·5 × 69 cm. In the centre of the rocky foreground is seated a bearded male figure playing a lute. To the left is a group of birds (eagle, hawk, duck, goose, heron, stork) and to the right a group of animals (boar, lion and lioness, wolf, and two others). Two more birds appear in the trees above and behind the central figure. The relief is said by Vasari to represent 'uno che suona il liuto per la musica,' and is commonly interpreted as Orpheus. Winternitz (1960, pp. 410–19) observes that 'zur älteren Bildtradition, Orpheus als Weisen oder Magier darstellend, gehört noch Luca della Robbias Marmorrelief am Campanile des Florentiner Doms,' and relates the representation to a passage in Dante's *Convivio* (Trattato II, cap. 1, i, Florence, ed. 1934, pp. 97–8): 'si come quando dice Ovidio che Orfeo facea con la cetera mansuete le fiere, e li arbori e le pietre a se muovere: che vuol dire che lo savio uomo con lo strumento de la sua voce fa(r)ia mansuescere e umiliare li crudeli cuori, e fa(r)ia muovere a la sua volontade coloro che non hanno vita di scienza e d'arte; e coloro che non hanno vita ragionevole di scienza alcuna sono quasi come pietre.' It is argued by Schlosser (*loc. cit.*) that since music was, presumably, already represented in the fifth of Andrea Pisano's reliefs, Orpheus must here represent Poetry, in this case as an attribute of Rhetoric, as described by Vincent of Beauvais and Honorius of Autun. He is followed by Brunetti (Beccherucci/Brunetti, i, p. 276). For other Renaissance euhemeristic interpretations of Orpheus, including observations culled from Leonardo Bruni and Gemisthus Pletho (who was in Florence at the time Luca was carving the reliefs), see Walker, 1953.

ARITHMETIC. Marble: 81·5 × 69 cm. In the exergue is a foliated design with two flowers. Schlosser (*loc. cit.*), d'Ancona (1902, p. 272) and Marquand (1914, pp. 37–38) identify the figures as Euclid and Pythagoras for Geometry and Arithmetic. The iconography of the relief is referred by Horne (1915, pp. 5–6) to a passage in *De Arithmetica Opusculum* of Filippo Calandri (Florence, 1491):

'Numero e decto ogni collectione dunita; et scriueuansi enumeri apresso degliantichi con uarii caracteri latini & in uarii modi: ma dua nesono piu facile & alpresente in uso: luno e del notargli con proprii loro characteri che uulgarmente son decti figure dabaco: & laltro con leda della mano: Vero e che ilmodo del notare e numeri con decte figure dice Lionardo pisano hauer nel. Mcc. incirca rechato dindia in Italia: et decti cara[c]teri: o uero figure essere indiane: a presso deglindi hauere imparato lacopulatione desse: Ma ilmodo del significare enumeri con le dita della mano essere cosa antica apresso de latini: come ancora testifica Juuenale & san Hieronymo. Et accioche delluno et dellaltro modo sabbia optimo documento: prima porreno in che modo ciascuno numero con ledita sipuo significare da uno per insino a dieci mila: di poi come si debbino scriuere.' Horne infers that the relief represents the two methods of calculating numbers which were in use in Italy in the fifteenth century. The gesture of the figure on the right, however, may be oratorical rather than enumerative (see, for example, Chomentovskaja, 1938), and the object he holds in his left hand is ambiguous.

ASTROLOGY. Marble: 81·5 × 69 cm. In the exergue is a garland· Vasari identifies the figure as Ptolemy and the subject as Astrology. Schlosser (*op. cit.*, pp. 63, 73), followed by d'Ancona (*loc. cit.*), identifies the figure as Tubalcain, and considers it 'von einer schwächeren Hand zu sein; es fällt auch durch die Grösse der Figur und dadurch, dass es ein bereits behandeltes Thema wieder aufnimmt, aus der Reihe der übrigen etwas heraus.' Marquand (*op. cit.*, pp. 38–9) accepts this explanation but defends Luca's authorship. Horne (*loc. cit.*) explains the subject as Astrology and the figure as Pythagoras on the basis of passages in Boethius (*Boetii Opera*, Venetiis per Joannem & Gregorium de Gregoriis, 1499, f. 23) and of its description in a fifteenth-century manuscript dialogue by John Hothby (Florence, Bibl. Naz., Cod. Magliabecchiano Cl. xix, No. 36, f. 81t., *Dialogus Johannis ottobi anglici in arte musica*). The latter reads: 'Si fabros uiuentes cum malleis ferreis atque ipso pitagora constituere potuissemus superuacaneum esset qualisquidem maluissem si fierj potuisset quam talibus uti figuris: nam ipsi quoque florentinj olim ingeniosissimj in turrj sua marmorea, que templo pulcerimo iminet, fabros pithagoram malleos ipsos cum incudine, si istud fierj potuisset, potius constituissent quam talem sculpturam insculpsissent.'

The fourteenth-century reliefs were carved to a homogeneous programme, illustrating the Creation of Man and the mechanical and some liberal arts, and derived in the main from *Genesis*, Isidore of Seville and Brunetto Latini (for this see Becherucci/Brunetti, i, pp. 233–8). Luca della Robbia's five reliefs form a fifteenth-century extension of this scheme. Marquand (1914, p. 34) infers from the payments for the carvings that 'Luca della Robbia was not compelled to complete a definite scheme, but was free to select his own subjects.' This statement is correct in so far as the five supplementary reliefs do not strictly form part of the fourteenth-century programme, but wrong in so far as it assumes Luca to have been solely responsible for the subject matter of the new reliefs. No iconographic programme for the reliefs proposed to date is wholly satisfactory.

The fourteenth-century reliefs in the lowest register of the Campanile were traditionally ascribed to Giotto, and it is questioned by Cavallucci and Molinier (1884, p. 24) whether 'Luca se servait-il en cette occasion des dessins de Giotto qui ne devaient pas être encore perdus, ou tâcha-t-il simplement de mettre son oeuvre en harmonie avec les autres sculptures qui ornaient le Campanile.' The possibility that use was made of fourteenth-century designs can be discounted, but in the relief style of certain of the carvings an attempt is made to approximate to the earlier reliefs. Thus, in the *Poetry or Rhetoric* use is made of a rocky foreground extending to the base of the hexagon, like that employed in many of the earlier reliefs, and the foliage of the trees extends over the moulding, as it does in *The Creation of Adam* and *The Creation of Eve*. Similarly the *Astrology* looks back to the frontal figure of *Jubal* and to the careful description of metallurgical technique in the *Tubalcain*, and the *Grammar* makes use of some of the same expedients as the relief of *Medicine*. In all other respects Luca's reliefs are works of striking independence and originality.

3 The Deliverance of St. Peter. Museo Nazionale,
   Florence (No. 219).   Plates 34, 36
   The Crucifixion of St. Peter. Museo Nazionale,
   Florence (No. 201).   Plate 35
Marble: (a) 69 × 78 cm. (b) 69 × 68 cm.

On 15 November 1435 (Poggi, 1909, No. 1065) the Operaii of the Duomo instructed Brunelleschi and Ghiberti jointly with the officials of the sacristy to prepare plans for the installation of altars in the chapels in the three tribunes of the church ('ordinationem novorum altarium novarum tribunarum, eo modo et forma prout eis et duabus partibus eorum videbitur'). 'Certi altari di legniame' (*ibid.*, No. 1066) were installed in 1436 in preparation for the consecration of the church by Eugenius IV, and in the winter of 1436-7 protective grilles were ordered for the fifteen new chapels and were provided with locks and keys. As early as 1428, it had been decided (*ibid.*, No. 898) that the central chapel in the central tribune should be dedicated to St. Zenobius, and in March 1439 (*ibid.*, No. 1075), the titles of the fourteen remaining chapels were decided on. The intended dedication of the five chapels in the central tribune was (*left to right*) to St. Andrew, St. Peter, St. Zenobius, St. Paul and St. James the Less. At a later date this sequence was changed, the chapel of St. Paul becoming that of St. John the Evangelist, the chapel of St. Andrew becoming that of St. Paul, and the chapel of St. James the Less becoming that of SS. James and Philip. At the date of Luca della Robbia's intervention in the planning of the chapels these changes had not been effected, and the three central chapels in the central tribune were therefore those of (*left*) St. Peter, (*centre*) St. Zenobius, (*right*) St. Paul. In March 1439 (*ibid.*, No. 1076), Bernardino di Marco Salviati and Francesco Cambi degli Orlandini were nominated by the Operaii to supervise the construction of three altars ('super ordinando et construi et fabricari faciendo et compilando tria altaria in cupola magna ecclesie catedralis civitatis Florentie, illius qualitatis et eo modo et forma et prout et sicut eis videbitur et placebit'). Though they were not itemised there can be little doubt that the three altars were those for the three central chapels. On 6 April 1439, the execution of two altars was allotted to Donatello (*ibid.*, No. 1078: 'E piu gli fu alloghato per insino a dì 6 d'Aprile 1439 a fare 2 altari di marmo nella tribuna di santo Zanobi in certo modo e disegno:

non v'à avuti danari alchuno e non gli à cominciati') and six days later a similar agreement was entered into with Luca della Robbia (*ibid.*, No. 1079: 'A Lucha di Simone della Robbia per insino a dì 12 d'Aprile 1439 fu allogghato a fare 2 altari in marmo nella tribuna di santo Zanobi secondo cierto disegnio, à avuto in presta f. XX d'oro'). It is assumed by Poggi (*ibid.*, p. CXIV) that in these documents four separate altars are involved. A further document of 20 April 1439, however, (*ibid.*, No. 1080) reveals that the altars allotted to Luca della Robbia were those of SS. Peter and Paul, and that the second was to be made from a wax model by Donatello ('Secundum vero altare sit in capella titulata sub vocabulo santi Pauli apostoli, illius longitudinis et largitudinis prout supra dicitur de alio superiori, et secundum modellum eis dandum, quod factum fuit de cera per Donatum Nicholai Betti Bardi, quod est in dicta opera, videlicet super quatuor colonnis et in parte intus cum forma ovale cum storiis et figuris circum circha santi Pauli predicti.'). The reference to Donatello's responsibility for the model of the altar of St. Paul suggests that two altars only were planned. The same document records the projected dimensions of the altar of St. Peter ('in capella titulata et sub titolo santi Petri apostoli, in dicta ecclesia, unum altare marmoris longitudinis et largitudinis secundum modellum lignaminis, videlicet in largitudine brachiorum trium cum septem octavis alterius brachii vel circha et cum illis mensuris sibi dandis et cum tribus conpassis in facie anteriori, uno videlicet in qualibet testa, in quibus sint storie santi Petri predicti, prout dabuntur et designabuntur ei et a parte posteriori prout alias deliberabitur'). An interim payment was made to Luca for the two altars on 23 November 1439 (*ibid.*, No. 1085: 'A Lucha di Simone di Marcho della Robbia, maestro di schultura, fior. XX per parte di suo maestro di due altari di marmo con fighure fa per la chiesa maggiore'). There are no later documentary references to either altar. The two reliefs of *Scenes from the Life of St. Peter*, now in the Bargello, were correctly associated with the St. Peter altar by C. F. von Rumohr (ii, pp. 290-1, 363-4), by whom they were discovered in the Opera del Duomo. It is likely that they were originally to have been accompanied by a third relief of *St. Peter enthroned*.

Each of the two altars was to be completed by Luca della Robbia in a period of fifteen months, and the unfinished state of the present reliefs suggests that work on them must have been broken off in the course of 1439. It is likely that the altars corresponded with that designed by Brunelleschi for the Sagrestia Vecchia of San Lorenzo, the base of which incorporates on the front two reliefs of *Prophets* on each side of a central grille, and on the back two reliefs of *Prophets* flanking a central *Virgin and Child*. The *Prophets* carved by Buggiano for the altar in the Sagrestia Vecchia are framed with half-columns which are closely similar to those framing Luca della Robbia's *Deliverance of St. Peter*, and the dimensions are in broad conformity; the left-hand relief on the altar measures, between the columns and including upper and lower mouldings, 65 × 47 cm. The varying widths of Luca's scenes are accounted for by the absence of enframing half-columns in that on the right.

Jacopo di Cione's altarpiece from San Pier Maggiore (Fig. 14), on which Luca based his *Crucifixion of St. Peter* (see above, p. 32), is documented to 1371 (see Gronau, 1945, and Steinweg). The predella panel of the *Crucifixion of St. Peter* is now in the Pinacoteca Vaticana, and the *Deliverance of St. Peter* is in the John G. Johnson Coll., Philadelphia. For Giovanni dal Ponte's predella from San Pier Scheraggio, now in the Uffizi (Fig. 15), see Toesca (1904) and Shell (1958).

4 Model for the Tomb of Count Hugo of Tuscany. Badia, Florence.

Knowledge of this commission is confined to a single payment published by Poggi (1903, p. 103):

> 1439 (s.c. 1440) Mercoledì a dì 3 di marzo. A spese straordinarie lire tre s. 7 d. 6 piccioli, per loro a Luca di Marco [*sic*] della Robbia, scarpellatore, portò e' detto in grossi, sono per sua fatica d'un disegno e d'un modello di terra fe' per fare la sepoltura d'Ughone.'
> (Giornale segnato B, 1435–1441, c. 285 v.)

Until 1439 the body of Count Hugo of Tuscany, the founder of the Badia (d. 1001), was preserved in a porphyry sarcophagus in the Cappella Maggiore of the church. In 1440 the remains were transferred to a newly constructed wooden sarcophagus in the Sacristy, for which a payment to 'Piero di Lorenzo dipintore nel Corso' was made on 18 August of that year (for this see *ibid.*, p. 102). The present wall monument of Count Hugo of Tuscany was commissioned from Mino da Fiesole on 25 June 1471, and was initially installed in the Cappella Maggiore of the church, being subsequently moved to the east transept. In the absence of other evidence there is no means of establishing whether the tomb designed by Luca della Robbia was a wall monument or a sarcophagus. According to Puccinelli (1664, p. 62 ff.) and Paatz (i, pp. 265, 297–8), a proposal made by Cosimo de' Medici before 1432 that the Gothic premises of the Badia should be replaced with a new building by Brunelleschi, was rejected by the monks. It is possible that the commission to Luca della Robbia, which was not proceeded with, was in some way connected with this scheme.

5 Tabernacle. Santa Maria, Peretola.

Col. Plate I, Plates 37–41
Marble and enamelled terracotta: 260 × 122 cm.

The tabernacle was commissioned for the Chapel of St. Luke in S. Egidio prior to 4 August 1441. Payments for the tabernacle (transcribed by Marquand, 1914, p. 65, from the Archivio del R. Arcispedale di S. Maria Nuova. Libro Debitori e Creditori 1441–1446, Segn. C, a c. 69) to a total of 98 florins were made to Luca between that date and 2 June 1442. Undated documents of 1442 (Libro Debitori e Creditori, 1441–1446, Segn. C, a c. 154) and 1443 (Libro Debitori e Creditori 1443–1490, a c. 15) record the overall cost of the tabernacle as 'fior. cientosette, lib. I, soldi 16.' The marble for the tabernacle was obtained from the Opera del Duomo (payment of 2 June 1442: 'lire quaranta, soldi 10 posto che l'opera di Santa Maria del fiore de avere in questo a c. 103, sono per 7 pezzi di marmo di lib. 5400 per soldi 15 per libbra e erano auti della detta opera che se n'havessi a far debitore detto Lucha').

Included in the 98 florins paid before 2 June 1442 is a sum of 30 florins paid to an assistant, 'Domenico di Cristofano che lavoro collui.' An earlier transcription of the latter document (Cavallucci/Molinier, 1884, pp. 187–8) reads: 'ad Ant. di Cristofano ch'e al lavoro collui.' The correct form of this name (Corti) is Agnolo di Cristofano. There is no other reference in the documents to Agnolo di Cristofano, who may have worked on the marble framing of the tabernacle.

The Cappella Maggiore of Sant' Egidio was known in the second half of the fourteenth and first half of the fifteenth centuries as the Cappella di San Luca, since the Compagnia di San Luca had its headquarters in the hospital of Santa Maria Nuova. The tabernacle was commissioned as a sacrament tabernacle ('un tabernacolo di marmo per tenere il chorpo di Christo nella cappella di Santolucha'). Its position in the Cappella Maggiore cannot be ascertained, but it is likely to have been set on the right wall. There is no record of the date at which the tabernacle was removed from the church and transferred to Peretola. The tabernacle is wrongly associated by Milanesi (in Vasari-Milanesi, ii, p. 176, n. 3) with a work which was at that time preserved in the Spedale di Santa Maria Nuova, and was first correctly identified by Liphart (see Bartolucci, 1885). The commission for the tabernacle forms part of a programme for the redecoration of the Cappella Maggiore of the church, which opened in September 1439 with a commission to Domenico Veneziano for frescoed *Scenes from the life of the Virgin*. These frescoes (on which Domenico Veneziano worked from 1439 till 1455, assisted in September 1439 by Piero della Francesca) appear to have been on the right wall. For the documentation of the frescoes see Herzen (1856), Milanesi (1862, p. 6) and Giglioli (1905, p. 206). The frescoes are fully discussed by Salmi (1947) and Wohl (1958, pp. 377–400). They appear to have been painted over in the course of a renovation of the Cappella Maggiore in 1594. A few fragments have been recovered.

The two Victory figures supporting a central wreath relate to a motif illustrated by Cartari (ed. 1647, p. 371) and derive either from a gold medallion of Constantine the Great (Gnechi, i, p. 20, No. 58), in which the wreath is held in place with the raised arms of the two figures and is not supported from beneath, or from a solidus of Constans (*RIC* viii, Trier 135), where it is also supported with the forward arms. In both cases the two figures are represented in profile. Other coins of the first half of the fourth century show figures of Roma and Constantinopolis holding up a wreath, seated in full face. Del Bravo (1973, p. 16) relates the Christ, the Angel and the St. John the Evangelist to a sarcophagus lid with the story of Pentheus in the Camposanto at Pisa (for which see Papini, 1912, ii, No. 62); this connection is too slight to be admissible.

The gilt bronze roundel inside the wreath was stolen and is replaced by a modern cast; the original has been recovered and is in the Bargello. The rectangular aperture beneath, now filled with a later relief of the *Blood of the Redeemer*, may originally have held a grille. Both at the top and bottom the curtain behind the Angels and the wreath are so disposed as to suggest recession in what is in fact a single plane. The brocaded curtain is likely to have been pigmented.

It is pointed out by Cora (1973, p, 174) that Luca would have been familiar with the important series of vases made by

Giunta di Tagio for the *spezeria* of Santa Maria Nuova in 1431–2. While these pieces and other Florentine majolica of the same date may afford a technical precedent for the enamelled terracotta inlay of the tabernacle, they offer no parallel for its tonality nor for the style of ornament used in the spandrels or in the roundels and spandrels of the base.

6 The Resurrection. Duomo, Florence.

Col. Plate II, Plates 42, 43
Enamelled terracotta: 200 × 265 cm.

The lunette of the Resurrection over the door of the North Sacristy of the Cathedral was commissioned on 21 July 1442. (Florence, Archivio dell'Opera del Duomo, II. 1. 88. Bastardello di deliberazioni e stanziamenti, 1441–1442, 32r.):

dicta die (21 July 1442). Item locaverunt Luce Simonis della Robbia scultori, ad faciendum in archo supra sacrestiam sui perghami Resurrexionem Domini in terra cotta invetriata prout videntur alia laboreria fieri et secundum designum factum et melius si melius fieri potest et promisit dare perfectam hinc ad unum annum et operarii promiserunt dare illud pretium fiendum per homines eligendos per consules et Operarios qui tunc temporis erunt cum hoc quod possit dare duos suspectos; que omnia etc. promixit actendere etc. sub pena lib. C. Presentibus Filippo Brunelleschi, Ridolfo (Lotti), Andrea Lazeri, Simone Laurentii et aliis.
(Transcription from Marquand, 1914, p. 75. Checked by Corti, whose transcription is less complete.)
An interim payment of 50 lire was made on 18 January 1445, when part of the relief was already installed in the lunette (Stanziamenti G, c. 31, transcribed by Marquand, *loc. cit.*). The record of the concluding payment on 26 February 1445, reads:

Luce Simonis della Robbia intagliatori l. CCCCXL sunt pro resto et integra solutione unius laborerii invetriati (in margine: in quo est Resurrexio Domini nostri) facti et positi in archo prima sacrestie, videlicet l. CXL pro sua industria et inventione ad inveniendum dictum laborerium et residuam pro suo magisterio dicti laborerii alias libras C quas iam habuit super dicto laborerio in quo est Resurrexio domini nostri Jesu Christo. (Stanziamenti G, c. 38, transcribed by Marquand, *loc. cit.*).

The composition of the relief is mistakenly stated by Marquand (1914, pp. 73–75, No. 18) to be 'more or less dependent on Ghiberti's Resurrection on the first Baptistry doors.' Though the placing of the sarcophagus parallel with the relief plane, the centralised figure of Christ, the trees at the sides and the sleeping soldiers in the foreground are common to both scenes, the classicism of Luca's scheme is in marked contrast to the International Gothic idiom of Ghiberti's. The figure of the Risen Christ does not float over the tomb, but stands firmly on a small segment of blue cloud, and the winding cloth is represented as a form of toga. The relief is the first significant Renaissance reinterpretation of the traditional Resurrection iconography (for this see Schrade, 1932, pp. 252–3).

The figures, sarcophagus, trees and foreground are white, and the flat background is a uniform blue. The clouds beneath Christ's feet and the small clouds in which the figures of the

angels terminate are pale blue. The figures were enriched with surface gilding, of which traces can be seen in the cruciform halo of Christ, in the wound on His right hand, in the rays which emanate from His body (better preserved on the left than on the right), in the hair and wings of the angels, and locally in the armour of the sleeping soldiers. A number of small pieces of flat blue glazed terracotta to the right of the tree on the right and below the upper angel on the right seem to indicate either that there was some miscalculation in the fitting of the pieces in the lunette or that the sections of the relief were at some time removed and awkwardly replaced.

7 The Ascension. Duomo, Florence.

Col. Plate III, Plates 44, 45
Enamelled terracotta: 200 × 260 cm.

Three documents relating to the commissioning and execution of the Ascension lunette over the door of the South Sacristy of the Cathedral are published by Rumohr (ii, pp. 364–5) and are reproduced, in Rumohr's transcriptions, by Cruttwell (1902, pp. 293–4) and Marquand (1914, pp. 76–78, No. 19). The first of these documents has been checked by Corti and reads:

Archivio dell'Opera del Duomo. Libro Alloghagioni. Registro segnato I, f. 54v–55r:
1446. Die XI mensis Ottobris.
Operarii antedicti, omni modo etc., protestatione premissa etc., locaverunt et concesserunt etc.
Luce Simonis della Robbia scultori, presenti et conducenti, ad faciendum: unam storiam terre cocte Invetriate illius materie qua est illa posita in arcu sacrestie que storia debet esse videlicet Ascensio [*corrected above*: Resurrectio] Domini nostri Yesu Cristi, cum duodecim figuris Apostolorum et Matris eius Virginis Marie et quod mons sit sui coloris arbores etiam sui coloris et secundum designum factum in quodam modello parvo, qui stare debet in Opera usque ad perfectionem dicti laborerii et melius, si melius fieri potest. Quam storiam debet perfecisse hinc ad otto menses proxime futuros, et posuisse super archum secunde sacrestie et pro qua storia et Magisterio debet abere [*sic*] et pro suo magisterio labore et industria illud quod declaratum erit per offitium Operariorum pro tempore in offito existentium. Que omnia etc., pro quibus etc., obligaverunt etc. Rogantes etc. Presentibus testibus domino Iohanne Spinellini preposito duomis [*sic*] et ser Ambroxio Angeli Angeni et Iohanne Francisci Zati.

On 23 December 1450, Luca was paid 'lib. 150 pro parte locationis sibi facte de calmo supra secundam sacrestiam' (Delib. dei Consoli e Operari, c. 17t), and on 30 June 1451, he received a further sum of 150 lire ('Luce Simonis della Robbia libras centum 50 pro parte solutionis unius storie per eum facte super archetto secunde sacristie') (Delib. cit., c. 47). A number of interim payments are transcribed by Mather and printed by Marquand (1928, pp. 145–6). Milanesi (in Vasari-Milanesi, ii, p. 202) summarises an otherwise unpublished record of 5 August 1451, in which the total sum due for the lunette is assessed by Bernardo Rossellino and Pagno di Lapo Portigiani at 500 lire. The gilding in the cruciform nimbus of Christ is better preserved than in the *Resurrection*, as are the surrounding rays. On the right hand side there is again evidence of miscalculation, and the relief is completed along the edge with an irregular strip of blue enamelled terracotta.

8 Two Kneeling Angels carrying Candlesticks. Duomo, Florence.   Col. Plate IV, Plate 46

Enamelled terracotta: 84 × 57 cm. each.

The two figures were commissioned in or before June 1448 (see below) for the Cappella del Sacramento (or 'capella corporis Christi') in the Cathedral. The Cappella del Sacramento was established in the chapel of St. Anthony the Abbot or of the Parte Guelfa, in the south tribune of the Cathedral, till 1446, when it was transferred to the chapel of St. Stephen in the north tribune, which served as the Cappella del Sacramento between 1446 and 1588 when it was moved to the chapel of St. Zenobius in the central tribune. A tabernacle was executed for the Chapel by Buggiano with the assistance of Giovanni di Domenico da Gaiole and was painted by Maestro Buto (see Poggi, 1909, p. cxvi, Nos. 1089–1101). The two *Angels* by Luca della Robbia, which were later placed in the South Sacristy of the Cathedral (for this see Paatz, iii, p. 524, n. 334) and are now on the altar of St. Zenobius, were commissioned to stand beside Buggiano's tabernacle. The exact relation between the three elements cannot be established, since the tabernacle has disappeared. The payments relating to the two *Angels* are as follows:

(i) A part payment to Luca della Robbia on 28 June 1448, of 40 lire 'pro duobus angelis de terra factis pro tenendo in capella corporis Christi,' and a payment to a painter Domenico di Francesco of 23 lire 'pro suo magisterio ad pingendum duos angelos qui retinentur in capella corporis Christi.' (Poggi, 1909, No. 1104).

(ii) a payment to a woodcarver, Giovanni di Domenico da Gaiole, on 1 February 1449, of 3 lire 'pro duobus pariis alarum factarum angelectis in capella corporis Christi.' (*ibid.*, No. 1106).

(iii) an appraisal of the two *Angels* on 5 August 1451, by Bernardo Rossellino and Pagno di Lapo Portigiani at a sum of 90 lire ('debere abere libras XC de dictis duobus angelis terre chotte sine aliquo colore qui retinentur in dicto loco, pro ornamento corporis Christi'). (*ibid.*, No. 1113).

The wooden wings of the *Angels* are now missing. The payment to Domenico di Francesco may refer to surface gilding or painting, traces of which, as is correctly noted by Marquand (1914, pp. 94–97, No. 23), are visible in the borders of the mantles in old Brogi photographs of both *Angels*. The index finger of the right hand of the *Angel* facing to the right is restored. The eyebrows and the edges of the upper eyelids are blue and the eyes grey-blue.

9 Decoration of the Pazzi Chapel. Santa Croce, Florence.   Col. Plates VI–IX, Plates 47–59

From the time Luca della Robbia's roundels in the Pazzi Chapel were first studied, it has been recognised that the building history of the chapel provided the only means by

which they could be dated or grouped. It is assumed by Fabriczy (1892, p. 216) and Paatz (i, pp. 536–41) that the new Chapter House was commissioned by Andrea de' Pazzi in 1429 and was begun by Brunelleschi between 1430 and 1433, was well advanced by 1443, when Eugenius IV was entertained in a room above or overlooking the new chapel, and was completed after Andrea de' Pazzi's death in 1445 by his son. Characteristic of this phase of study of the Chapel is the belief of Sanpaolesi (1953) that it was 'compiuto, all'interno, verso il 1440.' It was also believed at this time that the portico in front of the Chapel was integral to Brunelleschi's scheme. More recent investigation has shown that the construction of the Chapel was phased over a much longer period of time, and that the portico is an accretion to the Chapel probably made on the design of Giuliano da Majano. Examination of the building in 1962 (Laschi/Roselli/Rossi) revealed on the cupola of the Chapel proper the painted date 1459, and on the cupola of the portico the date 1461. The chronology outlined in the text is based upon re-examination of the documentary background of the commission by H. Saalman (1958, pp. 217–19, 136–7) and Bialostocki (1972, pp. 390–1). From an analysis of tax declarations it appears likely that the sum available for the building of the chapel in 1433 was the interest at 4% on a capital figure of 2,000 florins, not, as Fabriczy believed, the interest on an aggregate sum of 13,000 florins. In its early stages the building of the Chapter House seems to have been inadequately financed, and only in 1442 were additional funds (in the form of income at 4% from 12,000 florins of state loans) made available for a period of six years. The bulk of the work in the Chapel supervised by Brunelleschi must therefore have been confined to the period between 1442 and Brunelleschi's death in 1446. Thereafter progress seems once more to have slowed down. The building was still unfinished in 1469 and was not completed before 1473. The part played by Jacopo de' Pazzi in its completion is recognised by Richa (i, p. 110) and Moisé (1845, p. 295 n.1), who prints a brief of indulgence granted to the chapel on 8 October 1473: 'Cupientes igitur ut Cappella, seu Capitulum Sancti Andreae situm in claustro Fratrum Minorum Sanctae Crucis de Florentia, quam dilectus nobis in Christo Jacobus da Pactiis eques flor. fundavit.' The inscription round the altar refers to the Pazzi family in the plural, and not to any specific member of the family. The complex of enamelled terracotta sculptures in the Chapel comprises:

(i) The cupola of the portico. Width at base: 481 cm.

(ii) A roundel with a seated figure, variously interpreted as God the Father and, more plausibly, as St. Andrew, over the entrance door. Diameter: 134 cm.

(iii) Twelve roundels with seated figures of Apostles on the Chapel walls. These represent (altar wall, left to right) St. Matthew, St. Peter, St. John the Evangelist and St. James the Great, (south wall, left to right) St. Andrew and St. James the Less, (entrance wall, left to right) St. Simon, St. Thaddeus, St. Thomas and St. Philip, (north wall, left to right) St. Matthias and St. Bartholomew. Diameter: 134 cm.

(iv) In the pendentives of the cupola four roundels of the Evangelists. Diameter: 170 cm.

There are no documents relating to the sculptures, and the

earliest source by which they are noted is Albertini (1510: 'La chiesa di sca. Croce antiqua & molto grande & lunga bracc. 200 nella facciata dinazi marmores e sca Lodovico epo di bronze e mano di Donato ilquale co Luca de rubes & Desiderio faciono assai cose nel Capitulo bellissime de Pazi').

The enamelled terracotta sculptures in and outside the Chapel fell into two groups. The first consists of roundels on the Chapel walls, which must have formed part of Brunelleschi's original scheme for the interior. The roundels are likely to have been commissioned about 1442, though their production may have continued over a period of about ten years. There is no evidence as to the date at which they were installed. The date 1459 refers to the construction of the cupola, not to the construction of the pendentives on which it rests. The Evangelist roundels may, therefore, have been commissioned before 1459, but they are unlikely to have been installed till after that year. The decoration of the portico must have been undertaken after the completion of the cupola in 1461, and the roundel over the entrance is likely to date from the same time. The presence in the Chapel of two clearly defined groups of sculptures can be corroborated on technical grounds, in that the first group is bichromatic and the second polychromatic, making use not only of white and blue with surface gilding on the haloes, but also of green, purple and yellow. The palette of the Evangelist roundels corresponds exactly with that of the portico cupola; and the roundel above the entrance, though predominantly in white and blue, holds a green cross. There must thus, after Brunelleschi's death, have been a change in the aesthetic governing the decoration of the Chapel. Since St. Matthew and St. John the Evangelist appear in the Apostle roundels, it cannot be assumed that Brunelleschi's original intention was to commission roundels with the Evangelists for the pendentives.

Looking at the Apostle roundels in the interior of the chapel singly (Plates 47–58), in conjectural chronological order not in the sequence in which they are set round the walls, it may be noted that:

St. Peter. This relief differs from the eleven other Apostle roundels in the Chapel (i) by virtue of its viewing point, which is in the centre of the base, (ii) in its striated halo, (iii) in the archaic head, which differs markedly from that of the St. Peter in the Duomo *Ascension* lunette, (iv) in the imperfect glazing of the Saint's right hand, right knee and book. These points suggest that the relief may have been modelled by Brunelleschi not Luca della Robbia, and was glazed by Luca at an earlier time than the *Resurrection* lunette in the Cathedral.

St. Bartholomew. The relief is visualised from a much lower viewing point than the St. Peter. The somewhat tentative foreshortening on the thighs is especially evident in photographs (Alinari 3546) made from a central viewing point. The glazing has much in common with that of the St. Peter, and has crawled on the right shoulder and upper arm, the right hand, and robe. The knife, the tip of the nose and the toes of the left foot have been broken. This is the earliest work by Luca della Robbia in the Chapel, and like the St. Peter is likely, for technical reasons, to predate the *Resurrection* lunette.

St. Philip. In construction the relief is closely related to the

St. Bartholomew, but is a little later in date. There is a break or damage to the glaze on the nose.

St. James the Great. The confident pose, the idealised head and the quality of glazing correspond closely with those of the Christ in the *Resurrection* lunette, and this beautiful figure must have been made at the same time. The cloak, like the winding sheet of Christ, pulls away from the body, and the section of blue background beneath the right arm was modelled and glazed in one with the figure.

St. James the Less. The roundel closely conforms in style to the preceding relief. Slight damage appears on the nose and locally on the left hand.

St. Matthias. Closely related to the two preceding roundels.

St. Andrew. The robe, with its pattern of parallel folds, and the sweeping lines of the cloak have close analogies in the *Ascension* lunette. As with the St. James the Great the section of background beneath the right arm was modelled and glazed in one with the figure. The left side of the cross is broken, and seems originally to have extended to the edge of the roundel.

St. Matthew. The roundel, one of the finest of the series, seems to have been made in close proximity to the St. Andrew. The pose, in which the Saint is shown looking down towards the volume of gospels in his left hand, has a new amplitude. From this point the concavity of the roundels becomes somewhat deeper than in the earlier reliefs. Slight damage on the nose and chin of the angel.

St. John the Evangelist. The roundel belongs to the same group as the SS. Andrew and Matthew. The pose of the body is, however, less frontal, and contains an element of contrapposto. The eagle (head missing) is used to establish the notional depth of the cloud on which the Evangelist sits. Some damage in the hair over the right temple.

St. Thaddeus (sometimes wrongly identified as St. Paul). The contrapposto evident in the preceding relief is more pronounced, and the figure lacks the volume of the three previous Apostles. This and the two following roundels may have given rise to Bode's suggestion (1900, pp. 9–10) that Andrea della Robbia participated in the cycle.

St. Simon. The pose shares the characteristics of the St. Thaddeus, and the head is turned three-quarters left. The more linear style looks forward to that of the *Virtues* in the Chapel of the Cardinal of Portugal, and further to the early work of Andrea della Robbia, though, like the previous relief, this is certainly by Luca himself.

St. Thomas. The lower part shows a general correspondence with that of the St. Simon, though the folds of the dress and cloak are more broken and particularised. The Saint's head is turned down towards the girdle of the Virgin, which he holds in both hands. The type of the Saint, the descriptive modelling, and the idiosyncratic arrangement of the body suggest that we have here to do with a work of Andrea della Robbia of about 1460.

The *Evangelist* roundels in the pendentives of the cupola have been the subject of four main theories. The first, proposed by Liphart (in Burckhardt/Bode, ii, p. 350), is that the reliefs were modelled by Brunelleschi and glazed by Luca della

Robbia. On chronological grounds this view manifestly is untenable, since the roundels belong to a late not to an early phase in the decoration of the Chapel. The second, proposed by Reymond (1897 (ii), pp. 85–92), is that the roundels were made by Luca della Robbia in the decade 1470–80. The arguments against this view are well summarised by Marquand (1914, pp. 251–3). The third (for which see Janson, 1973) is that the roundels were made in the Della Robbia shop and provided a model for the roundels of the Evangelists executed for the Martini Chapel in San Giobbe, Venice. The fourth (for which see Pope-Hennessy, 1977) is that the roundels were modelled by Donatello about 1459–60 and were glazed in the Della Robbia shop, probably by Andrea della Robbia. It is likely that the roundels were installed not long after the cupola was completed, that is about 1460–1.

The enamelled terracotta sculptures in the portico of the Chapel are two in number:

St. Andrew (Plate 59). The Saint is seated against a background of concentric blue circles like those used in the four roundels on the altar wall in the interior of the Chapel. With his right hand he holds a green cross which recedes sharply into the picture space, and in his left hand he holds a book. Unlike the Apostles in the interior he has no halo. In style the relief is evidently later than the companion figures, and may date from about 1460–5.

Cupola. At the base are sixteen large medallions, framed with leaves of laurel on a white ground and containing blue fluted circles each with a yellow flower or rosette. Above are three further rows of sixteen medallions, diminishing in size as they approach the centre of the dome. The intervening areas between the roundels are filled with simulated red and green porphyry relieved with yellow flowers. At the top is a continuous frieze of flowers and fruit enclosing a violet fluted disc, on which is displayed a shield with the Pazzi arms (two dolphins hauriant, embowed, addorsed, *or*, on a field *azure* seme of five crosslets botonny, fitched, *or*).

On the front face of the Chapel is a frieze of putto heads modelled in terracotta. It has been suggested (G. Brunetti, 1958) that these are the work of Luca della Robbia. The basis of this attribution is provided by the cherub heads in marble in the interior of the Federighi Monument. An attribution to the Della Robbia workshop is very plausible.

10 **The Visitation.** San Giovanni Fuorcivitas, Pistoia.
Col. Plate V, Plate 60, Fig. 25
Enamelled terracotta: height of Virgin 184 cm., height of St. Elizabeth 115 cm., overall width 153 cm.

The documentary background of the group (for which see Marquand, 1914, pp. 27–33, No. 4, and Bacci) is as follows. On 11 October 1445, Monna Bice, widow of Jacopo di Neri de' Fioravanti, presented to the sodality of the Visitation of the Virgin to St. Elizabeth and to the prior of the church of San Giovanni Fuorcivitas, who was also rector of the sodality, an annual sum for the purchase of oil for a lamp which was to burn night and day before the figure of the Virgin of the Visitation in the church ('voluit in perpetuum die noctuque

ardere debeat unam lampadem ad onorem Dei et Virginis Marie coram figuras Virginis Marie sancte Elisabet visitationis earum, in ecclesia S. Johanni forcivitas'). In September 1507, there is a record of a small payment of 'lire tre per braccia sei di velo per metere alla figura di santa Lissabeta,' and in July 1512, a further payment was made 'per braccia XII di tela cilestra per fare una tenda a santa Elisabetta.' On 9 May 1513, it was reported that 'qualche divota persona vuole fare uno tabernaculo et ornamento alla nostra santa Helisabetta' for the sum of 'fior. tre larghi d'oro'. This offer was accepted, and on 24 April 1514, a payment was made to a painter, Scalabrino di Piero di Stefano 'posto lui per parte di dipintura del tabernacholo dell'altare.' In October of the same year a further payment was made to a second painter, 'Giovabatista dipintore per xonto del tabernacholo di santa Lisabetta.' Eleven years later, on 5 February 1523, a member of the Compagnia di S. Elisabetta, Niccolò di Giuliano Godemini, volunteered 'pagare alla detta Compagnia di Sancta Lisabetta lib. dugento di denari spiccioli della quali se ne debbe spendere lib. 50 den. in ornamento della cappella ovvero tabernaculo di sancta Lisabetta per detta e in detta Compagnia, e oltra dette lib. 50 spendere in ornamento e aconcime predetto in buona forma quella quantità di sua denari ch' a llei parra.' On 14 March 1525, 'Giuliano di mo. Bartolomeo scarpellino da Firenza' was paid 'lib. 50 den. de' denari di detta Compagnia per conto dello ornamento di detta cappella di sancta Lisabetta.' In 1546 and 1561 instructions were given that 'l'altare et la figura della Nostra Donna et santa Lisabetta' should be covered 'a maggior devotione di quella, eccetto che ne' giorni solenni e pascali.' Nothing survives of the original altar of the Visitation, which was demolished in the eighteenth century and replaced by the present altar.

It was inferred by Bacci from these documents (i) that though the endowment of 1445 specifically relates to 'figuras', this must have been an earlier *Visitation* 'tutto diversa della nostra,' and (ii) that the present group must date from the time of the reconstruction of the tabernacle and altar in the early sixteenth century. So far as concerns the documents, these inferences are unjustified, since the 1445 payment refers to a three-dimensional group, not to a relief or painting, and the sixteenth-century payments make no reference to the commissioning of a sculpture. The only valid deduction is that the payments relate to the veneration of a group which was in existence in 1445 and still served as a focus of devotion for the Compagnia di S. Elisabetta in 1561. This deduction would be doubtful only if the group now on the altar were, as maintained by Bacci, incompatible with the style of Luca della Robbia in 1445 and consistent with productions of the Della Robbia shop in the early sixteenth century. Bacci's argument is rejected by all recent students save Planiscig (who omits the group from both editions of his monograph on Luca della Robbia) and Procacci (1947, p. 23, No. 17), who observes that 'l'ipotesi del Bacci sembra esser giusta, per quanto non sia stato accettata dalla maggior parte della critica posteriore,' and ascribes the group to an unknown Tuscan sculptor of the early sixteenth century. It is argued by Horne (1915, p. 4) that 'the movement, the *atteggiamento* alone of the figures, so different in their subtle correlation to the almost archaic simplicity of Luca's early figures in marble, surely betrays the influence of Leonardo da Vinci.'

The group has had a chequered critical history. Traditionally ascribed in Pistoia to Fra Paolino, it was given by Bode (1878, p. 20) initially to Andrea della Robbia and is regarded as a work of Andrea by Reymond (1897 (ii), pp. 180–2) and A. Venturi (vi, pp. 593–4). Milanesi (in Vasari-Milanesi, ii, p. 197) refers to it as 'lavoro che non sappiamo a chi dei Della Robbia attribuire.' The attribution to Luca della Robbia is due to Marquand (1894, pp. 11–12; 1907, pp. 36–41; and 1914, *loc. cit.*), and is endorsed by Cruttwell (1902, pp. 96–97), who seems to have regarded it as a mature work, and Bode (1902, pp. 189–91), who thought it 'augenscheinlich ein Werk seiner späteren Zeit.' With the publication of the document of 1445, the question required to be reformulated, and allowed of two alternatives: (a) to regard the group as a work of Luca della Robbia of the mid-fourteen-forties, or (b) to regard it as a late work of Andrea della Robbia.

The arguments from technique and style in favour of the first of these alternatives are overwhelming. A firm point of reference is provided by the two candle-bearing *Angels* executed by Luca for the Cappella Corporis Christi in the Duomo in Florence in 1448. The two *Angels* are free-standing, and like the figures in the Pistoia *Visitation* are modelled in one with their shallow glazed base. The treatment of the drapery forms, of the Virgin's robe where it touches the ground and of the cloak of St. Elizabeth draped over her feet, is closely similar to that in the two *Angels*, and the modelling of the Virgin's hair closely resembles that of the *Angel* on the right. For ease of firing the upper halves of the two figures of the *Visitation* were glazed separately. The pigmentation of the irises is the same. The relief most closely related in style to the *Visitation* is the *Resurrection* lunette in the Cathedral, which was commissioned in 1442 and completed in 1445. If the robe of Christ is compared with the dresses of the Virgin and St. Elizabeth, it will be seen that the forms throughout are very similar. These analogies are so decisive that were there no putative date for the *Visitation*, it would be obligatory to ascribe it to Luca at this and at no other time. Marquand notes 'traces of gilding, crudely renewed and then removed in modern times, on the hair and borders of the garments.' There are likewise traces of surface pigmentation and gilding in the halo of Christ in the *Resurrection* lunette. As observed by Marquand, the quality of the glazing of the *Visitation* group resembles that of the two *Angels* in the Cathedral.

If the documents of 1507–14 referred to the making of a new group of the *Visitation*, we should expect this to have been commissioned from Andrea della Robbia and executed either by Andrea or by Giovanni della Robbia. The closest iconographical parallel in the late work of Andrea occurs in the relief of *The Meeting of SS. Francis and Dominic*, which was installed over the entrance to the Ospedale di San Paolo in Florence in 1493. The realistic treatment of this work is unlike that of the *Visitation*. One of the few works commissioned from Andrea in the second decade of the century which can be exactly dated on the basis of documents is the Acciauoli altarpiece in Santi Apostoli, for which payments are recorded in 1512. The standing angels to left and right of the tabernacle in this work have no resemblance to the figures in the *Visitation*. It would be wrong to assume, from the popularity in Florence of the *Visitation* altarpieces of Ghirlandaio of 1492 (Louvre, Paris, commissioned for Cestello) and Albertinelli of 1503 (Uffizi, Florence), that representations of the subject on a large scale were confined to the late fifteenth and early sixteenth centuries, and it is probable that the composition of Ghirlandaio's altarpiece derives from Luca della Robbia's group.

11 Roof and Ceiling of the Cappella del Crocifisso.
San Miniato al Monte, Florence.   Plates 61–62, Fig. 18

The ceiling of the Cappella del Crocifisso at San Miniato is ascribed to Luca della Robbia by the Anonimo Magliabecchiano (Frey, 1892 (i), p. 80: 'Et in San Miniato a Monte fece la volta della cappella et anchora lavoro nella cappella del cardinale di Portogallo, dove è sotterrato, di detta materia nella volta d'essa') and by Vasari (Vasari-Milanesi, ii, p. 175: 'e particolarmente al detto Piero de' Medici, nella chiesa di San Miniato a Monte, la volta della cappella di marmo, che posa sopra quattro colonne nel mezzo della chiesa, facendovi un partimento di ottangoli bellissimo').

The Cappella del Crocifisso (for which see Stegmann/Geymüller, ii, pp. 14–15; Berti, 1850, p. 65f.; Marquand, 1914, pp. 85–89; Paatz, iv, pp. 232–4, 278–80; and Caplow, pp. 444–50) was designed to house the miraculous Crucifix of San Giovanni Gualberto. The Crucifix was installed in the new chapel or ciborium in 1466, and in 1671 was transferred from San Miniato to Santa Trinita. The first reference to the Chapel occurs on 27 June 1447, when a document (Fabriczy, 1904, p. 53) records: 'Altare del Crocifisso possa essere ornato da un Cittadino grande che si offerirà fare un tabernacolo di grande apparenza e spesa; e questo se li concede con che non vi possa mettere altra arme che quella dell'Arte.' The guild referred to in this document is the Arte di Calimala, and the patron is Piero de' Medici. A document (*ibid.*) of 10 June 1448 reverses the earlier decision: 'Piero di Cosimo dei Medici nell' ornamento di marmo che fa alla cappella del Crocifisso possa farvi scolpire la sua arme, purchè nel luogo più conveniente vi metta quella dell'Arte, non ostante che altra volta fosse stato deliberato il contrario.' Payments to the bronze sculptor Maso di Bartolomeo for two copper eagles standing on bales of cloth, the emblem of the Arte di Calimala, run from 28 January to 22 April, 1449, when the eagles were being cast. It is assumed by Cruttwell (1902, pp. 90–91) that in addition to the external roof and the internal ceiling of the Chapel, Luca della Robbia was responsible for the inlaid marble frieze, which runs round the Chapel, and for the marble *impresa* of Piero de' Medici (a falcon and a ring with three feathers). This is incorrect, as is the assumption of Marquand that the commission to Michelozzo and Luca della Robbia proceeds from that to the same artists for the *studiolo* of Piero de' Medici in the Palazzo Medici. The Cappella del Crocifisso is the first work in which collaboration between Michelozzo and Luca can reasonably be presumed. It is concluded, almost certainly correctly, by Stegmann/Geymüller (ii, p. 15) that 'die reiche Kassettendecke in glasierter Terrakotta jedenfalls nach Michelozzos Zeichnung von Luca della Robbia ausgeführt.'

12 **Labours of the Months.** Victoria & Albert Museum, London.   Col. Plates X–XII, Plates 63–71
Enamelled terracotta: individual dimensions below.

JANUARY (7632–1861). Width 59·7 cm. Roundel in blue, white, yellow and black enamelled terracotta, bordered with a white leaf-moulding in low relief. The figurated area is bounded by a border in light and dark blue representing the hours of light and darkness. In the flat border are (*upper left*) the sun in the sign of Aquarius and (*lower right*) the moon. The border is inscribed with the words (*left*) DIES, (*right*) ORE 9¼, (*base*) IANVARIVS. Like the other roundels, this is concave and slightly curved. In the centre is a bearded man, with axe raised above his head, felling trees. Vertical and horizontal breaks and firing cracks. Lower right section of border made up.

FEBRUARY (7633–1861). Width 60 cm. In the flat border are (*upper left*) the sun in the sign of Pisces and (*lower right*) the moon. The border is inscribed with the words (*left*) DIES, (*right*) ORE 10½, (*base*) FEBRVARIVS. Horizontal breaks above and below. Some local restoration in moulded border. In the centre is a youth grafting fruit trees. He holds a knife in his left hand and a hammer and bundle of twine or bass in his right, and is engaged in making an incision in the branch of a small tree in the centre foreground.

MARCH (7634–1861). Width 59·7 cm. In the flat border are (*upper left*) the sun in the sign of Aries and (*lower right*) the moon. The border is inscribed with the words (*left*) DIES, (*right*) ORE 12, (*base*) MARTIVS. Horizontal breaks through the shins of the figure. Some subsidiary breaks. In the centre are two vines trained on vertical and horizontal supports and a bearded man with a pruning knife in his right hand pulls down a branch of the vine preparatory to cutting it.

APRIL (7635–1861). Width 58·4 cm. In the flat border are (*upper left*) the sun in the sign of Taurus and (*lower right*) the moon. The border is inscribed with the words (*left*) DIES, (*right*) ORE 13½, (*base*) APRELIS. Horizontal break through the right shin and left foot of the figure. Some subsidiary breaks. In the centre is a youth turned to the left, with a knife held in his mouth and a bundle of twine or bass in his belt, training the branches of a vine to a trellis. The light and dark blue of the border are proportionately inverted, the hours of darkness mistakenly filling 13½ hours.

MAY (7636–1861). Width 56·8 cm. In the flat border are (*upper left*) the sun in the sign of Gemini and (*lower right*) the moon. The border is inscribed with the words (*left*) DIES, (*right*) ORE 14⅔, (*base*) MAIVS. Outside the roundel are traces of enamelling in green and porphyry. Horizontal break through the centre. The roundel shows a youth turned to the left mowing grass with a scythe.

JUNE (7637–1861). Width 56·5 cm. In the flat border are (*upper left*) the sun in the sign of Cancer and (*lower right*) the moon. The border is inscribed with the words (*left*) DIES, (*right*) ORE 15⅓, (*base*) IVNIVS. Outside the roundel are traces of enamelling in porphyry. Firing crack through the centre. Moulded border left broken and repaired. Horns of moon perhaps restored. A clean-shaven man with a sickle in his right hand is shown bending forward in right profile reaping a field of wheat.

JULY (7638–1861). Width 56·2 cm. In the flat border are (*upper left*) the sun in the sign of Leo and (*lower right*) the moon. The border is inscribed with the words (*left*) DIES, (*right*) ORE 14⅔, (*base*) IVLIVS. Outside the roundel are traces of porphyry enamelling. Horizontal break beneath the armpits of the figure, and vertical break between this and the centre of the base. Border made up, especially on left. A clean-shaven man with a flail raised above his head is shown threshing corn.

AUGUST (7639–1861). Width 56·8 cm. In the flat border are (*upper left*) the sun in the sign of Virgo and (*lower right*) the moon. The border is inscribed with the words (*left*) DIES, (*right*) ORE 13½, (*base*) AVGVSTVS. Horizontal and vertical breaks. A yoke of oxen are seen ploughing. On the right a youth bends over the plough.

SEPTEMBER (7640–1861). Width 60·3 cm. In the flat border are (*upper left*) the sun in the sign of Libra, and (*lower right*) the moon. The border is inscribed with the words (*left*) DIES, (*right*) ORE (number eliminated by break), (*base*) SEPTEMBER. Extensive make-up on right side. A youth is shown gathering grapes. With his left foot resting on the vinetrunk, he reaches up to sever a bunch of grapes with a knife held in the left hand.

OCTOBER (7641–1861). Width 60·3 cm. In the flat border are (*upper left*) the sun in the sign of Scorpio and (*lower right*) the moon. The border is inscribed with the words (*left*) DIES, (*right*) ORE 10½, (*base*) OCTVBER. Central vertical break. A youth is shown striding to the right across a ploughed field sowing corn.

NOVEMBER (7642–1861). Width 60 cm. In the flat border are (*upper left*) the sun in the sign of Sagittarius, and (*lower right*) the moon. The border is inscribed with the words (*left*) DIES, (*right*) ORE 9⅓, (*base*) NOVEMBER. Broken diagonally across the lower half. Vertical and horizontal cracks above. A youth is shown seated in the fork of a tree picking olives.

DECEMBER (7643–1861). Width 59·7 cm. In the flat border are (*upper left*) the sun in the sign of Capricorn, (*lower right*) the moon. The border is inscribed with the words (*left*) DIES, (*right*) ORE 8⅔, (*base*) DECEMBER. Diagonal, vertical and horizontal breaks. A youth turned to the right with legs astride is shown trenching the ground with a long-handled spade.

The identification of the roundels as part of the ceiling of a room in the Palazzo Medici decorated by Luca della Robbia is due to Robinson (1862, pp. 59–63). The room is described by Filarete (printed in Oettingen, 1890, p. 678) in the following terms: 'Su la qual sala si è la camera di Piero, suo figliuolo di detto Cosimo. La qual camera è dignissima, perchè è molto hornata di quello, che a una degnia camera si richiede; che non sarebbe rifiutata da qualunque gran' signiore sia. Dopo questa è uno studietto hornatissimo; il pauimento, e così il cielo, di vetriamenti fatti a figure degnissime; in modo che a chi v'entra, da grandissima admiratione. El maestro di questi invetriamenti si fu Luca della Robbia; così per nome si chiama; il quale è degnissimo maestro di questi invetriati; et anche in iscultura si dimostra. Ora lasceremo stare gli

Fig. 1. Interior of the Duomo, Florence

Fig. 2. Donatello: *Cantoria*. Museo dell'Opera del Duomo, Florence

Fig. 3. Luca della Robbia: *Cantoria* (reconstruction of 1891). Formerly Museo dell'Opera del Duomo, Florence

Fig. 4. Roman, third century A.D.: *Muse Sarcophagus.* Kunsthistorisches Museum, Vienna

Fig. 5. Roman, third century A.D.: *Muse Sarcophagus.* Woburn Abbey

Fig. 6. Roman, third century A.D.: *Bacchic Sarcophagus*. Woburn Abbey

Fig. 7. Roman (Hadrianic): *Sacrificial Scene*. Uffizi, Florence

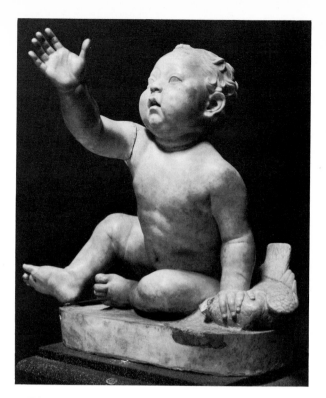

Fig. 8. *Classical Vase*. Camposanto, Pisa

Fig. 9. Roman, second century A.D.: *Boy with a Goose*. Uffizi, Florence

Fig. 10. Roman, third century A.D.: *Putto with Garland*, from the end of a *Daedalus Sarcophagus*. Louvre, Paris

Fig. 11. Roman, third century A.D.: *Maenad*, from a *Dionysiac Scene*. Uffizi, Florence

Fig. 12. Workshop of Nanni di Banco (Luca della Robbia?): *Head of a Seraph*, from *The Assumption of the Virgin*. Duomo, Florence

Fig. 13. Nanni di Banco (?): *Angel*, from *The Assumption of the Virgin*. Duomo, Florence

Fig. 14. Jacopo di Cione: *The Crucifixion of Saint Peter*. Pinacoteca Vaticana

Fig. 15. Giovanni dal Ponte: *Saint Peter Freed from Prison*. Uffizi, Florence

Fig. 16. Brunelleschi and Buggiano: *Altar*. Sagrestia Vecchia,
Duomo, Florence

Fig. 17. *The Lower Register of the Campanile*. Duomo, Florence

Fig. 18. Michelozzo: *Cappella del Crocifisso*. San Miniato al Monte, Florence

Fig. 19. Brunelleschi: *The Interior of the Pazzi Chapel*. Santa Croce, Florence

Fig. 20. Brunelleschi and (?) Giuliano da Majano: *The Exterior of the Pazzi Chapel*. Santa Croce, Florence

Fig. 21. Michelozzo and Luca della Robbia: *The Chapel of the Madonna*. Collegiata, Impruneta

Fig. 22. Michelozzo and Luca della Robbia: *The Chapel of the Cross*. Collegiata, Impruneta

Fig. 23. Maso di Bartolomeo and Luca della Robbia: *Façade*. San Domenico, Urbino

ornamenti di questo studio et anche della camera, che come è detto, sono degnissime.' The relevant passage in Vasari (Vasari-Milanesi, ii, p. 174) reads: 'Onde, il magnifico Piero di Cosimo de' Medici, fra i primi che facessero lavorare a Luca cose di terra colorita, gli fece fare tutta la volta in mezzo tondo d'uno scrittoio nel palazzo edificato, come si dirà, da Cosimo suo padre, con varie fantasie, ed il pavimento similmente; che fu cosa singolare, e molto utile per la state. Ed è certo una maraviglia, che, essendo la cosa allora molto difficile, e bisognando avere molti avvertimenti nel cuocere la terra, che Luca conducesse questi lavori a tanta perfezione, che così la volta come il pavimento paiono di non di molti, ma d'un pezzo solo.' Robinson (*loc. cit.*) suggested 'that these medallions originally formed part of the system of decoration of this celebrated cabinet; but there is, it is true, no positive evidence to that effect'. His view is recorded by Cavallucci and Molinier (1884, pp. 68–70: 'Que ces médaillons soient de Luca ou de son école, cela est possible; mais, nous le répétons, cela n'est point prouvé') and Stegmann and Geymüller (ii, p. 2), is rejected by Cruttwell (1902, pp. 129–30: 'The style of drawing has no connection whatever with the Robbia, or even the Florentine School. The medallions . . . were in the Marchese's Catalogue described, probably correctly, as of Pisan origin'), Reymond (1897 (ii), pp. 95–96: 'une oeuvre faite par un artiste italien, dans la seconde moitié du XVe siècle') and De Foville (1910, p. 61), and is accepted by Bode (1905, p. 67; 1902, pp. 148–9, with a well-argued refutation of Reymond), Lethaby (1906), Wallis (1903, p. xxx), Marquand (1914, pp. 89–94, No. 22), Maclagan and Longhurst (1932, pp. 31–34), Salmi (1936, p. 129), Planiscig (1948, pp. 38–39, 67, Nos. 56–67), and Pope-Hennessy (1964, i, pp. 104–12, Nos. 82–93).

The apartments of Piero de' Medici were situated on the first floor of the palace (for this see W. Bulst, 1970). The only available information about the dimensions of the *studietto* is that deduced from the ceiling roundels by Lethaby (*loc. cit.*) and repeated by Marquand (*loc. cit.*) and Pope-Hennessy (*loc. cit.*). Based on the curvature of the roundels, this shows that they were arranged in three rows of four each, the roundels in the central row being oriented axially to the end walls of the room (May, June, July, August) and those in the lateral rows (January–April and September–December) axially to the side walls. According to Lethaby's calculations, the entire surface covered by the roundels would have been of the order of twelve feet by sixteen feet. When allowance is made for the factor of curvature, the width of the room would have been nine or ten feet. The *scrittoio* of the Palazzo Ducale at Urbino is of approximately the same size. Somewhat larger dimensions (4 m. by 5·5 m.) are inferred by Heikamp and Grote.

The room was destroyed in the course of the rebuilding of the palace after its sale to the Riccardi (1659) (for this see F. Büttner, 1970). According to Robinson (*loc. cit.*) the roundels later 'formed part of the decorations of a fountain in a garden near Florence,' presumably the 'Casino del Marchese Riccardi' or Gualfonda gardens described by Bocchi-Cinelli (1677, pp. 557–9; for the history of Gualfonda see Ginori Lisci, 1953). They were purchased in the nineteenth century for the Museo Campana, and reached the Museum as part of the Gigli-Campana collection.

The date of the construction of Piero de' Medici's *studietto* cannot be established with complete precision. If we assume that the description given by Filarete was based on first-hand observation, we are bound to suppose that the room was complete when Filarete paid his last visit to Florence in 1456, three years before work started on the frescoes by Benozzo Gozzoli in the chapel. It is established that the Medici were already living in the palace in 1457 (for this see I. Hyman, 1977, p. 177). On the other hand, a reference to the *scrittoio* in a *terza rima* account of the palace in 1459, published by R. Hatfield (1970, pp. 235–6), makes no reference to Luca della Robbia's decorations. There is no reason to assume with Robinson (*loc. cit.*) that the decoration of the room was commissioned after the death of Cosimo il Vecchio in 1464, nor with Marquand (*loc. cit.*) that it dates from 1445–50 and was executed immediately before the Cappella del Crocifisso at San Miniato al Monte. This dating is repeated by Planiscig (*loc. cit.*). The Sala Grande of the palace was decorated by Antonio Pollajuolo in 1460, and the paintings made for it by Uccello and Pesellino probably date from the late fifties (in the case of Pesellino's from before 1457). A date 1450–6 is proposed by Pope-Hennessy (*op. cit.*, p. 107). The presence in the interstices of the ceiling of two colours (porphyry and a strong green) which do not recur in the San Miniato chapel and are characteristic of Luca's later works renders a dating before 1455 improbable. The patronage of Piero de' Medici is discussed in an interesting article by E. H. Gombrich (1966). The primary sources for Piero's relations with artists are Gaye (i, XLIX, pp. 136–7, and LII, pp. 141–2) and Milanesi (1869, pp. 78–82). For his intervention in the decoration of the chapel of the Palazzo Medici see Grote (1964).

The reasons for ascribing the roundels to the workshop of Luca della Robbia are affirmed by Lethaby, and are accepted by Bode, Marquand, Maclagan and Longhurst, Salmi and Planiscig. It does not necessarily follow that Luca was responsible for the drawing of the figurated area. Luca's responsibility for the twelve scenes is denied by Marquand (*loc. cit.*), on the ground that 'these flat-headed, long-limbed, stiffly draped figures are not like Luca's, nor do the compositions suggest his methods,' and by Salmi (1936, p. 75), who rejects them on grounds of their dissimilarity to a flat enamelled terracotta lunette of *God the Father between two Angels* in the Museo dell'Opera del Duomo. This argument is irrelevant, since the lunette (for which see Becherucci/Brunetti, i, p. 285, No. 150) is a documented work of 1488 by Andrea della Robbia. Salmi associated the designs with Domenico Veneziano, and ascribes them to the same hand as a group of drawings in the Uffizi, Florence, and the Kupferstichkabinett, Berlin (Berenson, 1938, ii, pp. 357–8, Nos. 2773–9F). The reasons for supposing that Luca della Robbia was responsible for the design as well as for the execution of the roundels are summarised in the text of this book.

The iconography of the Labours of the Months with zodiacal signs surrounded by borders showing the hours of light and darkness seems to originate in Northern miniatures. It occurs, e.g., in a German codex of 1445, the Passauer Kalendarium now in the Landesbibliothek at Cassel (2° Mss. astron. 1, for which see Hopf & Struck, 1930, pp. 116–18) and appears in Italy at a somewhat later date in an *Office of the Virgin* illuminated for Clarice Orsini, wife of Lorenzo il Magnifico, in the collection of the Earl of Leicester at Holkham. The Holkham manuscript is datable to the year 1469, and the calendar in it is likely to depend from a Northern manuscript in the Medici collection. The Holkham manuscript and the roundels of Luca della Robbia may thus have a common illuminated prototype. The manuscript is regarded by D'Ancona (1914, i, p. 62) as the earliest manuscript illuminated by Francesco di Antonio del Cherico, who was active in 1452–84 (see also M. Levi d'Ancona, 1962, pp. 108–16). The decorative motifs employed in manuscripts by Francesco di Antonio del Cherico (such as the title-page of the Biblioteca Laurenziana Livy, Plut. 63.22, for which see D'Ancona, 1914, ii, p. 879) include a number of elements, e.g. pine-cones, which are common also to Luca's decorative borders.

The points at which the iconography of the roundels departs from the conventional iconography of the Labours of the Months are the following: (i) January is represented by a woodman felling trees and making vineprops, not by a man warming himself at a fire or by a scene of feasting; (ii) April and May are represented by men training vines and mowing grass, not by courtly scenes of hawking and hunting; (iii) December is represented by a man trenching the ground with a long-handled spade, not by the killing of pigs. These and other scenes seem to depend from, or to be influenced by, passages in Columella's *De Re Rustica* (see Ash/Forster/Heffner). Some relevant passages in Columella are:

January. 'It is also a fit time for making vine-props of even stakes, and it is also equally suitable for cutting down trees for buildings; but both these operations are better carried out when the moon is waning, from the 20th to the 30th of the month, since all wood so cut is considered not to be attacked by decay. One workman can cut down, strip and sharpen a hundred stakes a day; he can also split, smooth on both sides and sharpen sixty oaken or olive-wood props.' (xi, ii, 11–12).

March. 'From March 1st to 23rd. is an excellent time for pruning vines . . . and it is the very best moment for engrafting vines and trees.' (xi, ii, 26).

April. 'It is also correct to begin the first training of the vines, while the "eyes" which are creeping forth can be struck off with the finger.' (xi, ii, 38).

May. 'During these days the cornfields must be weeded, and the cutting of the hay must be begun. A good labourer cuts down a *jugerum* of meadow-land.' (xi, ii, 40).

September. 'During these days the vintage takes place in most districts, different people having inferred from different signs that the grapes are ripe.' (xi, ii 67).

October. 'In the same regions the early-ripe cereals are sown, particularly two-grained wheat.' (xi, ii, 74).

December. 'During these days, according to those who practise husbandry with unusually scrupulous care, the soil ought not to be disturbed with any iron tool, unless you trench it for the sake of the vines.' (xi, ii, 95).

The *De Re Rustica* was known in the fifteenth century from a number of Florentine manuscripts deriving from an ancient manuscript discovered by Poggio Bracciolini. For the copies of Columella's *De Re Rustica* owned by Giovanni and Piero di Cosimo de' Medici (Bibl. Laurenziana, Plut. 53, 27; Plut. 63, 32, the former inscribed on the last page 'Liber Poggii, quem vendidit Joanni Cosmae de Medicis,' and the latter inscribed with the name of Piero de' Medici) see particularly F. Pintor (1960) and V. Rossi (1893).

13 Monument of Benozzo Federighi, Bishop of Fiesole. Santa Trinita, Florence.

Col. Plates XIII, XIV, Plates 72–77
Marble and enamelled terracotta: external frame (without cornice) 257·5 × 257·5 cm., width of frame 30·7/30·9 cm., height of cornice 14 cm., interior of niche 196 × 196 cm.

Earlier studies of the Federighi Monument are superseded by a comprehensive article by Dr. Hannelore Glasser (1969).

The tomb of Benozzo Federighi, Bishop of Fiesole (d. 27 July 1450) is described by Vasari (Vasari-Milanesi, ii, p. 176) in the church of San Pancrazio: 'Fece ancora per messer Benozzo Federighi vescovo di Fiesole, nella chiesa di San Pancrazio, una sepoltura di marmo, e sopra quella esso Federigo a giacere ritratto di naturale, e tre altre mezze figure. E nell'ornamento de' pilastri di quell'opera dipinse nel piano certi festoni a mazzi di frutti e foglie sì vive e naturali, che col pennello in tavola non si farebbe altrimenti a olio: ed in vero, questa opera è maravigliosa e rarissima, avendo in essa Luca fatto i lumi e l'ombre tanto bene, che non pare quasi che a fuoco ciò sia possibile.' It is recorded in San Pancrazio by Bocchi-Cinelli (1677, pp. 204–5). According to a document of 6 February 1458 (see below), the tomb was to be installed 'allato a una capella di Federighi.' The Federighi altar was the first altar to the left of the Cappella Maggiore on the left wall of the church (Paatz, iv, p. 574), and the Federighi Monument stood to its right. The position is described by Glasser (p. 1, n. 2) as 'on the north transept wall between the chapel of the Ridolfi (which was adjacent to the choir chapel) and the Federighi altar on its left.' San Pancrazio was modernised in 1752–5 (Paatz, iv, p. 565), and on 2 January 1753, the tomb was moved to a new position in a corridor leading to the side entrance to the church. A drawing of it at this time in the *Sepoltuario* of Giovanni di Poggio Baldovinetti (Bibl. Riccardiana, Fondo Moreni 339, f. 134) is published by A. Parronchi (1964) and Glasser (p. 9). The church of San Pancrazio was secularised in 1808, and in 1809 the monument was transferred to San Francesco di Paola (Paatz, v, p. 299). The date of its transfer is mistakenly given by Cruttwell (1902, p. 93) as 1783. At this time the paired pilasters and platform shown in the *Sepoltuario Baldovinetti* (Fig. 32) were eliminated, and the upper part of the tomb only was reinstalled. For the tomb in San Francesco di Paola see the earlier literature of Luca della Robbia and E. Marcucci (1883). In 1896 the upper part was transferred to the second chapel to the left in the left transept of Santa Trinita (Paatz, v, pp. 299, 371).

The tomb of Benozzo Federighi was commissioned by his nephew Federigo di Jacopo Federighi on 2 May 1454 (not, as stated by Marquand, 2 March 1455). The contract is lost, but its substance is reconstructed by Glasser from documents arising out of litigation in 1458–9. It is known to have stipulated that the tomb was to be carved in relief in marble ('una sepultura a rilevo, di marmo'), contained in a frame with foliage of gold and polychrome enamelled terracotta approximately four and a half braccia square ('con fogliame messo a oro e diversi colori invitriati intorno a uno quadro di braccia 4½ o circa'), and was to show the body of the Bishop and other figures and ornaments according to a design in the hand of Giovanni di ser Paolo ('suvi il corpo d'un vescovo di rilevo, di marmo, con altre figure e adornamenti come appare per uno disegno di mano di Iohanni di ser Paulo'). The tomb was to be completed and installed within ten months, and subject to a final appraisal was to cost the sum of 200 florins. The cost of the marble was to be deducted from the total sum. If the monument was not completed on schedule, Luca della Robbia was to refund the cost of the marble and to pay a fine of 25 florins. Of the sum due, 80 florins would be paid to the sculptor at the rate of 8 florins each month. The date for the completion of the tomb was 2 March 1455.

The tomb is mentioned in a Catasto return of Luca della Robbia of 1457/1458: 'E più ò una sepoltura di marmo, la quale ò fatta già è più d'un anno a federigho di Iachopo Federighi, della quale siano appiato alla Merchatantia: no'ne posso ragionare allchuna chosa insino a tanto non è terminato. Quando sara chiarita, sarò dinanzi del vostro uficio f. 75.'

On 6 February 1458 Luca della Robbia was formally charged by Federigo Federighi, through his younger brother Domenico, with non-completion of the contract ('E dixe e dice decto Domenico decto nome che per decto Federigho e per la parte sua tutte le predecte cose e ciascuna d'esse furon e sono state observate e adimpiute per la parte sua, e tutto quello e tanto quanto fu et era tenuto observare al decto maestro Luca. Et per decto maestro Luca decto mercato e tutte le predecte cose nè alcuna d'esse non furon nè sono state observate alcune cose nè quelle a tanto quanto era tenuto e doveva secondo la forma di decto obligo, e di tutte le predecte cose e di qualunche d'esse, et sempre à cessato ciò fare, contra ogni debito di ragione'). Luca was therefore required to hand over the completed monument within fifteen days ('che decto maestro Luca li debbe aver data e consegnata la decta sepultura in quindici dì proxime futuri, in quello modo e forma e di quella qualità e bontà che e come di sopra esso maestro Luca li fu et è tenuto di dare e consegnare come di sopra'). In a statement of 16 February, Luca della Robbia replies to these charges. The first of the points made in this document is a countercharge that the 8 florins per month due to the sculptor for ten months of work on the tomb had not been paid ('per la sua parte a decto Luca essi fiorini octo il mese diece mesi e non gliele avendo dati non può fare o tentare decta conventione et accordo di concludere et allegare, di che di sopra si fa mentione, per suo favore contra decto Luca, et intendandolo ciò non si può amettere di ragione'). The tomb had been completed a year or more before ('già fa un anno o più fu facta e compiuta interamente'). The sculptor was not, however, compelled to finance it from his own resources ('ne quella arebbe potuto nè dovuto fornire e compire di suo chè è povero homo, perche arebbe avuto di bisogno di spenderli e in lavoranti e altro circa quella, come richiedeva la natura della cosa e lavorio'). The pieces of the monument had not been set in the wall since it was necessary first to assess their value ('imperò che innanzi a decto muramento decta sepultura

dovendosi stimare come dice la scriptura'). Had it been set in the wall as Federighi required, no accurate assessment could have been made ('essendo murata non si potrebbe decta stima fare giustificatamente per difecto di misura et evidentia e di quello è permesso nel muramento bisogna nascondere di quella, come dovuto fu et è'). It is proposed by the sculptor that Andrea di Lazaro Cavalcanti (Buggiano) be appointed on his behalf to assess the value of the tomb, and that a second assessor be named by Federighi. Once the assessment has been made, Luca declares himself ready to instal the monument as soon as he has received the 200 florins due 'diputata decta valuta di decti marmi che sono circa di fiorini 40 salvo il calcolo della ragione.' A reply made on behalf of Federighi on 21 February contests these points, which were restated by the sculptor on 2 March. A tax declaration prepared by Federighi on 14 September 1458, lists among his liabilities a sum of 'fl. 125 o ca.' due to Luca della Robbia. It is suggested by Glasser that the artist's reluctance to instal the monument before it was assessed may have been bound up with the depth of the marble slab from which the relief was carved.

On 21 July 1459, Buggiano was appointed by both parties to decide in what respect if any the work was defective, and after it was installed to establish its worth ('ad videndum dictum opus jam factum si in aliquo est defectivum seu si quid in eo deficit et tale defectum declarandum antequam muretur et deinde, illo murato, ad existimandum et appretiandum ipsum laborerium et opus'). On 6 August he reported that the work was not defective in any respect, but that Luca should gild it in areas to be indicated by the assessor at a cost to be divided between both parties ('debeat dorare a mordente sepulchrum seu laborerium de quo ibidem fit mentio ubi et quomodo videbitur eidem Andree ad comunes expensas utriusque partis'). A final report was prepared by Buggiano on 24 September 1459, specifying a payment on each side of 'lire tre di piccioli' for gilding on the mitre, the pillow, the edge of the chasuble and the bier-cloth, the hair and wings of the angels holding the epitaph, the haloes of the Dead Christ, the Virgin and St. John, and the three seraphim above them. The value of the tomb was agreed at 200 florins, and the marble at 40 florins ('cioè tre tavole di marmo rosso e quatro cholonne quadre chon altri ornamenti e una cornice di sopra detto lavoro'). It is convincingly argued by Glasser that the three slabs of red marble must have intervened between the paired pilasters of the base, and registered either as a single area of red or as three red panels framed in white mouldings. The *Sepoltuario Baldovinetti* contains a drawing of the tomb of Orlando de' Medici in Santissima Annunziata in which the height of the architectural base of the tomb is much exaggerated, and it is possible that the pilasters of the Federighi Monument were also lower than is suggested by the Baldovinetti drawing. 'Traces of gold still to be seen which accented the embroidered patterns but which is now happily almost worn away' were noted by Cruttwell in 1902, and Marquand (1914, pp. 122–30, No. 33) records 'traces of colour . . . on the eyebrows and eyes of the angels, and of gilding on the nimbuses and other details.' In the Baldovinetti drawing the four pilasters rest on a shallow platform decorated with small circles, perhaps representing marble or enamelled terracotta intended to repeat in pattern the *palle* of the Federighi arms (as in the painted entablature in Lippi's Medici altarpiece in the Uffizi).

The enamelled terracotta frame is well described by Marquand (1914, p. 127): 'It is not composed, as M. Gerspach asserts, of twenty-eight pieces, corresponding to the ovals or circles into which the design is distributed, but each of these twenty-eight sections is subdivided into many small pieces, in some cases as many as thirty-eight in number. Each separate piece is coloured and glazed, and is set in very hard cement. In other words it is a mosaic, of the variety called *opus sectile*, the units of which are not marble but glazed terracotta. The ground against which the floral pattern is set is of gold, the technical character of which is noteworthy. Many years ago I made a note to the effect that this consisted of a gold enamel beneath a glaze. Since that time M. Gerspach has reiterated his statement that the gold was not protected by a glaze, but was exposed to the atmosphere without protection.' An analysis by Mather, printed by Marquand (*loc. cit.*), shows that the gold was applied in the form of paint to the terracotta, which was then covered with a yellowish glaze. The use of this technique is confirmed by a documentary description cited above ('con fogliame messo a oro a diversi colori invitriati'). The contention of Ballardini (1929) and Cora (1973, p. 175) that the enamelled terracotta frame is not fire-gilded rests on a misinterpretation of references to the gilding 'a mordente' of the marble reliefs. Kennedy (1938, pp. 81–87) judged the design of the frame to be 'too intricate for Luca's essentially naturalistic and uncomplicated ideas,' and regarded Baldovinetti as 'the only man in Florence who could have made the carefully shaded wash-drawings which were used by the painter of the mosaic.' There is, however, no close analogy for the bunches of flowers and fir-cones in Baldovinetti's work. The linear formulation of the flowers, and especially of the bunches of roses and lilies, seems to depend directly from the style evolved by Ghiberti for the outer and inner jambs of the north door of the Baptistry (designed 1423, probably cast 1424). Within the oeuvre of Luca della Robbia the only points of reference for the frame are supplied by the *stemma* of the Arte de' Maestri di Pietra e di Legname on Or San Michele (where the large flowers in the trapezoidal spaces round the edge closely resemble the small flowers which link the oval medallions on the Federighi monument) and the predella of the Tabernacle of the Cross at Impruneta (where the pine-cones and pine leaves resemble those on the Federighi tomb). As noted by Marquand, 'glazed gold leaf or gold powder like that in the border of the Federighi tomb' is also used on the Or San Michele *stemma* of the Arte dei Maestri di Pietra e Legname.

It is stated in a document of 1458 (see above) that the tomb was to depict the body of the Bishop, in marble, 'con altre figure e adornamenti come appare per uno desegno di mano di Iohanni di ser Paulo.' This is interpreted by Sanchez and Glasser (*op. cit.*) as a reference to Giovanni, son of Ser Pagholo dell'Arte della Lana, the notary of the Wool Guild, who was a partner in the bottega of Domenico and Federigo Federighi. The document may refer to a design for the entire monument or to a drawing for those 'adornamenti' which were not executed in marble.

The paired pilasters which supported the tomb have a close parallel in the paired pilasters supporting the tomb of Orlando de' Medici in Santissima Annunziata (where, however, the bases are segregated and not linked as they appear to have been in Luca's monument). Designed in the Rossellino studio, probably by Bernardo Rossellino, the Orlando de' Medici monument was commissioned on 11 December 1455, more than a year after the Federighi tomb, and there is no means of establishing the relative priority of the two designs. Paired pilasters are also used in the upper section of Luca's Cantoria. The form of the sarcophagus seems, as claimed by Glasser, to owe something to that in Bernardo Rossellino's Bruni monument (probably commissioned 1444, variously supposed to have been completed by 1446–7 or 1450–1). The epitaph in a circular wreath makes use of a motif introduced in Ghiberti's *Arca of the Three Martyrs* (conjecturally completed in 1428), where it is also supported by angels with bent arms, though the legs of the two figures, extended diagonally into the lower corners of the rectangle, follow those of Bernardo Rossellino. A connection is postulated by Glasser with the tomb of Eugenius IV (d. 1447) in San Salvatore in Lauro, Rome, where the body rests on a cloth formulated like that in the Federighi monument. According to this theory, 'it seems less likely that the Federighi tomb is a mutation which by coincidence prefigures Roman tomb types of the second half of the Quattrocento than that it was patterned after a Roman type of which few examples remain completely intact.' This is possible, but not wholly convincing. The case derives some substance from the fact that in the tomb of Eugenius IV the effigy is backed by three upright figurated reliefs. Representations of the Pietà, flanked in separate panels by the Virgin and St. John, occur on Florentine Gothic tombs, notably on the tomb chests of the Baroncelli monument in Santa Croce (1327–8) and on the tomb of Tedice Aliotti, Bishop of Fiesole, in Santa Maria Novella (after 1336).

14 Ceiling of the Chapel of the Cardinal of Portugal.
San Miniato al Monte, Florence.
Fig. 30, Col. Plates XV–XVII, Plates 78–80
Enamelled terracotta.

Earlier accounts of the Chapel of the Cardinal of Portugal are superseded by a volume based on rediscovered documents in the Archivio dello Spedale degli Innocenti, Florence (Hartt/Corti/Kennedy, 1964). The documents relating to the ceiling, and its iconography and structure, are well analysed by Hartt (*ibid.*, pp. 73–78). What is known of the initial contract with Luca is due to Manni (xvii, p. 153, reprinted in Hartt/Corti/Kennedy, p. 135):

'Altra scritta finalmente stipulata ne' 14 aprile 1461. ho veduta col famoso Luca di Simone di Marco della Robbia per i lavori da farsi di terra cotta della cupola di essa Cappella del Cardinale, per il prezzo di fiorini 150. larghi, ove esso Luca si soscrive.' The following payments were made to Luca della Robbia through the Cambini Bank of the Spedale degli Innocenti between April and August 1462:

(1) 9 April 1462: 'E adì VIIII d'aprile f. venti l., per lui a Lucha di Simone della Robbia, portò chontanti: sono per parte di lavori à fare; al giornale, a c. 109
...f. XX l. .

13 May 1462: 'E adì XIII detto f. venti l., per lui a Lucha della Robia, portò contanti, per parte di lavorìo, al giornale, c. 128   . . . f. XX l. .

(Hartt/Corti/Kennedy, pp. 138–40, Doc. 5)

(2) 6 July 1462: 'E dì VI di luglio f. quaranta l., per lui a Lucha di Simone della Robbia, porto contanti, per resto di f. 150 l. dovea avere per la chappella del Chardinale; al giornale, c. 162   . . . f. XL l. .

21 July 1462: 'E dì detto f. otto l., per lui a Lucha di Simone della Robbia, e per lui al detto Andrea d'Antonio da San Friano, portò contanti, per resto di f. 158 l... gli dà dello invetriato del ciello della chapella, d'achordo chol detto Lucha; al giornale, c. 170   . . . f. VIII l .   (ibid., p. 142, Doc. 7)

(3) 6 August 1462: 'E dì VI d'aghosto L. dicianove picc., per lui a Giovanni d'Andrea dipintore, portò contanti: sono per ònpere 13 stette e mettere oro al cielo di detta chappella; al giornale, c. 179   . . . f. III bol. 31.'   (ibid.)

On 27 September 1466, a sum of 50 florins given by the Bishop of Silves to Luca della Robbia through the Medici Bank on 30 October 1462 was reimbursed. The relevant document reads: 'E de' dare adì xxvii di settembre f. cinquanta d'oro l., portò mess. Alfomso Iannis comtanti: sono per tanti dise n'avea paghati el veschovo per mano de' Medici di Firenze sino adì 30 d'ottobre 1462 a Lucha di Simone della Robia, per parte di lavoro overo invetriato che disse avea fatto per la chapella.   . . . f. 51 s. 5.'   (ibid., p. 154, Doc. 15)

The respects in which the structure of these roundels differs from that of the roundels in the Pazzi Chapel is discussed above, pp. 48–9. Vasari praises the *studietto* of Piero de' Medici on the ground that the ceiling and floor appeared to be made from a single piece of enamelled terracotta, and the same emphasis on visual continuity is apparent through the ceiling of the Chapel. The colour and pigmentation of the roundels are of special subtlety, as is apparent, e.g., in the scale pattern outside the roundels, where the outer scales, in darker blue than those nearer the centre, are outlined against a manganese purple ground. Marquand (1914, pp. 175–80, No. 52) observes of the intervening spaces that 'the effect intended, that of a mosaic, would have been more successful had smaller units been employed, as the tiles, on some of which as many as a dozen cubes are represented, have separated and display but too clearly the economical method of construction.' It appears that the interstices between the rectangular panels which are evident in old photographs have since been corrected by relaying or inpainting. In the Casa dei Grifi (for which see A. van Buren, 1940), the motif of projecting cubes in three colours appears on a pavement and as wall decoration in two rooms. According to Pliny, *pavimenta scutulata* were introduced in Rome after 149 B.C.

15 **Chapels of the Madonna and of the Cross.**
Collegiata, Impruneta.
Col. Plates XVIII, XIX, Plates 81–85

The works by Luca della Robbia at Impruneta form part of the decoration of the two lateral chapels of (*left*) the Madonna and (*right*) the Cross. The Chapel on the left was constructed to house the miraculous painting of the Virgin and Child, for which the church was celebrated, and that on the right housed a relic of the True Cross presented by Filippo dei Scolari (Pippo Spano, d. 1426). The relic of the True Cross was removed by the French in 1800. For the history of the miraculous painting and of the church see particularly E. Casotti, 1713 and 1714; U. Ceccherini, 1890; R. Bianchini, 1932; and M. Cagnacci, 1969.

The parish and province of Impruneta were exceptionally well endowed. According to D. Herlihy (1968), only the Archbishop of Florence enjoyed a richer benefice than the *plebanus* of Impruneta. The church, however, owes its distinction to the sums (said to total twelve thousand florins) expended on it by Antonio di Bellincioni degli Agli, who was appointed as Piovano in 1439 and remained in office till his death in 1477. Degli Agli was credited with responsibility for the decoration of the church at Impruneta as early as 1471 in the *Theotocon* of the Dominican, Fra Domenico da Corella, in two lines of verse:

Allius hanc ornare volens antonio edem
Eximia pollens relligione pater.

These are transcribed by Casotti (1714, p. 16). Caplow (ii, p. 617) implies, without justification, that the tabernacles in the church were erected at the expense of the Buondelmonti family, as the church was, in the mid-Quattrocento, under Buondelmonti patronage. She adds that 'a date between 1453 and 1460 based on the date of the tabernacles and money spent by the abbot seems reasonable.' Degli Agli was not an abbot, and there is no information on the incidence of his expenditure. The principal sources for the career of Degli Agli are Vespasiano da Bisticci (i, pp. 295–7); S. Salvini (1782, p. 41); G. Mazzucchelli (I, i, pp. 185–6); A. della Torre (1902); G. Calamari (i, 1932, pp. 35–36); and A. d'Addario (1960, p. 400 f). For Degli Agli's relations with Marsilio Ficino see P. Kristeller (1937, p. 204) and Karl Markgraf von Montoriola (1926, p. 232). Degli Agli was buried in the church at Impruneta. For his tomb, which was erected by his niece Deianira, see Middeldorf (1976).

The structure of the two chapels at Impruneta depends from the Chapel of the Annunciation in the church of Santissima Annunziata in Florence, which was executed by Pagno di Lapo Portigiani from designs by Michelozzo, and was dedicated in 1452. The two chapels are given to Michelozzo by Fabriczy (1904, p. 42) with a conjectural dating about 1460. The only systematic analysis of them is that of Saalman (1966, p. 250) who infers from the presence of *foglie d'acqua* capitals in the second cloister, identical with those carved for San Barnaba in Florence after 1435, that Michelozzo was responsible for planning the conversion of the church premises as well as for designing the two altars. Saalman suggests, on the analogy of the Palazzo Communale at Montepulciano, that the work at Impruneta was undertaken from Michelozzo's designs by members of his workshop. It follows that Michelozzo's journeys to Milan and Ragusa have no evidential value in relation to the date of execution of the Impruneta chapels. The structure of the chapels represents a modified and coarser variant of that in the Annunziata. Caplow (i, pp. 453–5), on the other hand, ascribes the 'improvements' in them to the intervention of Luca della Robbia in their design.

The tabernacle containing the miraculous painting of the Madonna is rightly described by Stegmann and Geymüller (p. xiii) as a weak reflection of the Parte Guelfa niche on Or San Michele. It is ascribed by Middeldorf (1973) to Filarete. If by Filarete, it would have been carved before 1433. In a *supplica* submitted by the Piovano of Impruneta to the Priors of the Republic in 1423 the miraculous painting is described as being enclosed in a tabernacle in the wall. It is unlikely that this was identical with the present tabernacle, which seems to be the work of a secondary Michelozzan sculptor and to date from about 1440. The *schiacciato* marble relief of the discovery of the miraculous painting has been variously ascribed to Michelozzo (Cruttwell, 1902, p. 110; Reymond, 1897 (ii), pp. 67–83; Schubring), Pagno di Lapo Portigiani, Luca della Robbia (Procacci, 1947, p. 19, No. 12) and Filarete (Middeldorf, *loc. cit.*), as well as to an anonymous Donatellesque sculptor who was also responsible for a marble relief of the *Virgin and Child with four Angels* in the Victoria & Albert Museum (Pope-Hennessy, 1964, i, pp. 91–93). There is no connection between this relief and Luca della Robbia's authenticated works in marble. It is likely that the tabernacle and predella represent an initial attempt by Degli Agli to improve the facilities of the church, though it is also possible that they were commissioned by his predecessor, Tommaso di Maso da Perugia, who was appointed as Piovano in 1434. In either case the tabernacle and predella must precede, and were incorporated in, Michelozzo's Chapel of the Madonna, and determined certain aspects of the decoration of the Chapel of the Cross on the opposite side of the church.

The enamelled terracotta elements in the Chapel of the Madonna comprise (i) the frieze on the two exposed faces, each of which contains in the centre a relief of the Virgin and Child flanked by fruit, (ii) the ceiling, consisting of twelve coffers, each with a yellow rosette or flower in the centre of a blue fluted disc in a narrow circular white frame, surrounded by a heavy white moulded frame with pine-cones at the corners, and (iii) beside the tabernacle figures of (*left*) St. Paul and (*right*) St. Luke. The frieze of fruit recalls that surrounding the *stemma* of the Mercanzia on Or San Michele (1463), and the ceiling conforms to the palette of the cupola of the Pazzi Chapel portico (after 1461). It is, therefore, likely that the reliefs of the Virgin and Child and the figures of Saints likewise represent Luca della Robbia's style about 1460. Though an attempt is made by Cruttwell (1902, pp. 111–13) to ascribe the relief of the Virgin and Child on the side of the Chapel and the figure of St. Paul to Andrea della Robbia, there is no reason to question the attribution of the whole of the terracotta component of the Chapel to Luca della Robbia.

The enamelled terracotta elements in the Chapel of the Cross consist of (i) the ceiling, which corresponds with that of the Chapel of the Madonna, (ii) the tabernacle containing a relief of the Crucifixion, (iii) a predella with eight angels adoring the Eucharist, and (iv) figures of (*left*) St. John the Baptist and (*right*) St. Augustine. Until the demolition of the church through military action in the summer of 1944 (for this see Hartt, 1949, p. 58 f.), the frieze in the two faces of the Chapel of the Cross was filled with small figures of putti adoring a central chalice with the Eucharist in stucco. It is assumed by Cruttwell (p. 115) that this frieze was made in the middle of the seventeenth century in substitution for a frieze in enamelled terracotta which was removed. There can, however, be no reasonable doubt, from photographs taken before 1944, that the frieze dated from the fifteenth century. It has been variously ascribed to Luca della Robbia and Donatello. It is suggested by Procacci (*loc. cit.*) that 'si tratta certo di un abbozzo fatto per vedere l'effetto complessivo della decorazione a basso rilievo con l'architettura.' The relief of the Crucifixion was removed from the tabernacle on the altar in 1636 in compliance with the wishes of the Archduchess Maria Maddalena of Austria, and was replaced in its original position in 1924. Cruttwell (pp. 113–14) ascribes the *St. John the Baptist* to Luca and the *St. Augustine* to Andrea della Robbia, and suggests that the altar was planned as a Sacrament Altar and was later transformed into a shrine for the relic of the True Cross. While the inscriptions held by the angels in the predella (PROBET AVTEM SEIPSVM HOMO/ET SIC DE PANE ILLO EDAT and HIC EST PANIS VIVVS/QVI DE CELO DESCENDIT) leave no doubt that the intervening space was from the first designed to house the Sacrament, it is likely that the altar also incorporated the relic, and that the iconography of the upper part was determined by this fact. Both the *St. John the Baptist* and the *St. Augustine* are manifestly works of Luca della Robbia, as is the *Crucifixion* relief. There is no means of establishing whether the containing tabernacle was planned by Luca or by Andrea della Robbia. The groups of angels in the predella are autograph Luca. The anomalous, rather eclectic character of the tabernacle and the absence of enamelled terracotta decoration in the Chapel frieze suggests that work on the Chapel of the Cross may have been broken off, and was brought to its present state of relative completion only after some delay.

A document published by Mather (1918, p. 191, and in Marquand, 1928, p. 149) records a payment of four florins made to Luca by the Camarlingo of the Compagnia di Santa Maria Impruneta on 20 November 1466 ('Anno dato adj 20 di novembre 1466 lib. trentasette e per luj dal Chapitolo di Sca. Maria del Fiore lib quindicj per uno cherubino cioè l'arme di detto Chapitolo per mandare alla Pieve di Sco. Lorenzo a Signa e F. quatro larghi per luj da Filippo di Giovanni Vanni Kamerlingho della Compagnia di Sca. Maria Inpruneta messi a entrata a Libro segnato DD. c. 39 lib. 37', in Archivio del Rdo. Capitolo di S. Maria del Fiore, Libro Specchio di Livellari segnato A. 1437-1461, c. 136). It is inferred by Mather, probably correctly, that this payment relates to the decoration of one or other of the Impruneta altars. For the history and regulations of the Compagnia di Santa Maria Impruneta, founded in the fourteenth century, see C. Guasti (1866).

A tradition that the Della Robbia modelled in clay from Impruneta is recorded by Bianchini (*op. cit.*, p. 57, n. 1): 'Una vecchia tradizione vorrebbe che i "Della Robbia" avuto in dono dai fornacini dell'Impruneta, grande quantità di scelta terra, per i loro preziosi lavori, volessero compensarli prendendo in affitto una vecchia fornace in quel di Fabbiolle e che ivi abbiano modellati tutti i lavori che nella nostra chiesa si conservano.'

16 **Stemma of the Mercanzia.** Or San Michele, Florence.
Col. Plate XXII
Enamelled terracotta: diameter 180 cm.

The *stemma* of the Mercanzia is the only one of the three heraldic roundels executed by Luca della Robbia for Or San Michele that is exactly datable. The tabernacle over which it is set, in the centre of the east façade, was constructed about 1422 for the Parte Guelfa to house Donatello's statue of St. Louis of Toulouse. The statue was removed from its niche in or before 1459, and in December of that year the tabernacle was purchased from the Parte Guelfa by the Mercanzia. The documents (for which see Fabriczy, 1900, p. 253 ff., and Poggi, 1949, pp. 18–19) record the decision of the Mercanzia, on 29 March 1463, to commission a statue for the vacant niche and to install a *stemma* over it ('ad providendum expensis dicte Universitatis Mercatorum de ornamento statua et signo condecente et venerabili in dicto et circha dictum tabernaculum et ad locandum et faciendum et fieri faciendum in predictas et in [*sic*] circha predicta ea omnia et singula de quibus et prout et sicut dictis operariis videbitur et placebit'). Provision was made at this time for effacing the *stemma* of the Parte Guelfa above the tabernacle. The new *stemma* was commissioned from Luca della Robbia in January or February 1463, and was substantially complete by 28 September of that year. The document (for which see Marquand, 1893 (i), p. 154; Fabriczy, *loc. cit.*; Marquand, 1914, p. 183; and Poggi, *loc. cit.*) reads: '28 di Sett. 1463. Luce Marci della Robia intagliatore F. 25 a sold. 88 et den. 5 per fiorino pro parte solutionis et mercedis operis per eum facti de signo et arma et circa signum et arma dicte Universitatis per eum applicandum in circulo posito in facie Oratorii S. Anne site in Platea Orti S. Michaelis civitatis Florentie supra pilastrum dicte Universitatis positum in dicta facie contra Oratorium S. Michaelis in orto secundum ordinationem et commissionem operariorum ordinatorum et deputatorum de mense Januarii seu Februarii 1462 (s.c. 1463) per tunc officium sex Consiliariorum dicte Universitatis pro ornando et decorando dicto pilastro L. 110 sol. 10 d. 5 piccioli.'

The roundel shows a shield *argent* containing a seeded fleur-de-lys *gules* above a corded bale *argent*. The shield is displayed against a blue fluted shell, with grooved arrises, which is in turn surrounded by a white leaf-and-dart moulding and a wide border of flowers and fruit. The border is modelled and glazed in eight sections, and comprises sixteen bunches of flowers and fruit tied with blue ribbons and arranged clockwise round the circle. The fruit and vegetables are rightly identified by Marquand as (*clockwise from base*) citrons, beans, pomegranates, chestnuts, apples or quinces, thistles or artichokes, cucumbers, pine-cones, quinces, plums, grapes, poppies, oranges, figs, pears and olives, interspersed with white and violet-red flowers. Marquand (1914, p. 182) notes that 'the terracotta does not touch the dentils of the frame, as in the other medallions which Luca made for Or San Michele.' This may tend to confirm that the *stemma* precedes those of the Arte de' Medici e Speziali on the south and of the Arte de' Maestri di Pietra e di Legname on the north face of the building.

17 **Stemma of the Arte dei Medici e degli Speziali.** Or San Michele, Florence. Col. Plate XXI, Plate 86
Enamelled terracotta: diameter 180 cm.

The tabernacle on Or San Michele installed by the Guild is the second from the right on the south face of the building. It is dated 1399 and contains a marble *Virgin and Child*, the *Madonna delle Rose*, ascribed to Niccolò di Pietro Lamberti (cf. Paatz, iv, pp. 493, 527–8). There is no evidence as to whether a *stemma* was painted in the roundel above, but this is probable. In the absence of documents, the date of Luca della Robbia's *stemma* can only be conjectural. It is likely that the first enamelled terracotta *stemma* on Or San Michele was that of the Mercanzia, which replaced that of the Parte Guelfa above the central niche on the east face, and that this was followed by replacements in enamelled terracotta for two further painted *stemmi* of the Physicians and Apothecaries and the Stonemasons and Woodcarvers. If this sequence is correct, the present relief may date from ca. 1464–5. This dating receives some confirmation from the drapery style, which recalls that of the *St. Augustine* on the bronze door in the Cathedral, and from the vivid polychromy, which is related to that of the cupola in the atrium of the Pazzi Chapel (after 1461). Marquand (1914, pp. 130–2, No. 34) notes that the mouldings of the upper part of the tabernacle resemble those of the roundels in the Chapel of the Cardinal of Portugal.

18 **Stemma of the Arte dei Maestri di Pietra e di Legname.** Or San Michele, Florence. Col. Plate XX
Enamelled terracotta: diameter 180 cm.

The tabernacle of the Arte dei Maestri di Pietra e di Legname on Or San Michele is the second from the right on the north face of the building. It was filled, in the second decade of the fifteenth century, probably after 1413, with statues of the Quattro Santi Coronati by Nanni di Banco, who carved below it a predella showing four representatives of the Guild engaged (left to right) in building a stone wall, carving a spiral column, measuring a capital, and blocking out a figure of a child, possibly the Child Christ. The *stemma* of the Guild (which consisted of an axe accompanied by the tools shown in use in the predella) may have been painted above the niche at this time. The enamelled terracotta *stemma* by Luca della Robbia now above the niche is most readily explicable as a replacement for, or a free adaptation of, an earlier painted original. The reasons for supposing that the work is based upon an earlier painting are (i) that it shows a generic resemblance to, e.g., the ceiling fresco still preserved in the Residenza of the Arte de' Giudici e Notai, (ii) that the interior of the tabernacle containing Nanni di Banco's *St. Eligius* is decorated in inlay with a repeated pattern of tongs, the emblem of the Arte degli Orefici e Manischalchi, (iii) that the linked circles are based on a Cosmatesque motif used, e.g., on the floor of San Clemente and in the cloisters of St. John Lateran and San Paolo fuori le mura, which also appears in Tuscan Romanesque ornament. This would explain the decision to plan the *stemma* as a mosaic of flat enamelled terracotta elements, for which the only parallel occurs in the border of the Federighi monument. The pictorial character of the design is noted by Vasari (Vasari-Milanesi, ii, pp. 175–6: 'Dopo le quali cose, cercò Luca di trovare il modo di dipignere le figure e le storie in sul piano di terra cotta per dar vita alle pitture, e ne fece sperimento in un tondo che è sopra il taber- nacolo de' quattro Santi intorno a Or San Michele; e nel piano del quale fece, in cinque luoghi gl'istrumenti ed insegne dell'arte de' Fabbricanti, con ornamenti bellissimi'). Mar- quand (1914, pp. 132–4, No. 35) observes correctly that 'the outlines of the plants and flowers are incised, and the inter- spaces filled with gold beneath the glaze.' This technique is otherwise confined to the Federighi monument. In the absence of documents, the date of the roundel is conjectural. Technical considerations invalidate the case for an early dating ca. 1440, advanced by Bode (1902, pp. 146–7). Marquand (loc. cit.) argues from the relationship to the border of the Federighi monument that the stemma dates from 1455–60. This date is adopted by Paatz (iv, p. 495). A slightly later dating, ca. 1465, would also be admissible (see previous entry).

19 **Stemma of Jacopo de' Pazzi.** Palazzo Serristori, Florence. Plate 88
Polychrome enamelled terracotta: diameter 180 cm.

The shield in the centre contains the arms of Jacopo de' Pazzi (azure, semé of five crosslets, botonny fitched or, two dolphins, hauriant, embowed, addorsed, or, in chief a label of Anjou of four points gules, enclosing three fleurs-de-lys or. Azure kite- shaped shield set against a mottled violet disc. Below the shield a yellow crescent). The arms were defaced in or after 1478, and were replaced either with the Medici arms or with those of Franceschetto Cybo, who acquired the Palazzo Pazzi and the Villa Pazzi at Montughi at the end of the fifteenth century. The arms added in substitution for those of Pazzi have been removed. The border was glazed in eight sections, and shows (from base) grapes, oranges, pine-cones, apples, grapes, cucumbers, pine-cones and apples. According to a document transcribed by Mather and published by Marquand (1914, pp. 161–2), the marriage of Jacopo de' Pazzi and Maddalena de' Serristori took place in 1446. A. Moscato (1963, p. 35) implies that the stemmi were made for the grande sala on the first floor of the Palazzo Pazzi between 1458 and 1469. Saalman (1964 (i)) rejects Moscato's view that the palace was built between 1462 and 1469, and argues that though the site to the south of the old palace was acquired from Piero de' Pazzi in 1462, the palace itself was still stand- ing in 1469, and that the new Palazzo Pazzi by Giuliano da Majano therefore dates from the fourteen-seventies. For the subsequent history of the palace see Ginori-Lisci (1972, ii, pp. 545–50), who observes that 'le rudimentali palle aggiunte allo stemma simboleggiano la vittoria dei Medici.' In the fifteenth century the palace passed first to Cardinal d'Estoute- ville and then to Franceschetto Cybo, remaining Cybo property till 1564, when it passed to Senatore Lorenzo Strozzi. From 1760 till 1843 it was known as the Palazzo Quaratesi. This and the companion stemma were purchased by Conte Umberto Serristori in the nineteenth century.

20 **Stemma of Maddalena de' Serristori.** Palazzo Serristori, Florence. Plate 89
Polychrome enamelled terracotta: diameter 180 cm.

The shield in the centre contains the Serristori arms (azure, a fess argent between three mullets of eight points or a label of Anjou of four points gules, enclosing three fleurs-de-lys or). It is set against a fluted green roundel, round which runs a border of fruit and leaves on a white ground set between white egg-and-dart mouldings. The border was glazed in eight sections, the joins between them being concealed by over- lapping leaves. The roundel forms a pair to that with the stemma of Jacopo de' Pazzi (Cat. No. 19), also in the Palazzo Serristori.

21 **Stemma of King René of Anjou.** Victoria & Albert Museum, London (6740–1860).
Col. Plates XXIII, XXIV, Plate 87
Enamelled terracotta: diameter 335·3 cm.

The roundel (for which see Pope-Hennessy, 1964, i, pp. 112– 15) shows in the centre a shield bearing the arms: quarterly of five, three in chief and two base, (1) Kingdom of Hungary (ancient), (2) Anjou-Naples (the arms of the Duchy of Anjou with a label for the Kingdom of Naples), (3) Kingdom of Jerusalem, (4) Duchy of Anjou, (5) Duchy of Bar. Overall, an escutcheon in pretence for the Kingdom of Aragon. The shield is surmounted by a closed crowned helmet or, from which rises the crest, a double fleur-de-lys or between two dragon wings. The helmet and shield are placed on an ermine- lined mantle of the arms of Anjou. Above the crest are the letters IR in tree-trunk capitals. Below the shield are the insignia of the Order of the Crescent, a collar inscribed LOS: EN:CROISSANT:. Upon either side is a golden brazier with pierced rim. From the braziers issue manganese-purple flames. The base of the left-hand brazier is ornamented with the five crosslets of the Pazzi arms, and from the inner handles of both braziers depends a band with the motto DARDANT DESIR. Round the green background runs a narrow bordure of manganese-purple (used throughout for gules) figured with a fillet raguly argent. The border has recessed within it a wide garland of fruit and leaves, each on a branch tied with a white band. The border was fired in fourteen sections, and the central area consists of seven or eight main pieces. There is some local damage and restoration. As shown by Durrieu (1908), the armorial bearings are those assumed by René of Anjou (1409–80) in the last months of 1466, when he was offered the crown of Aragon by the Catalans. The letters IR must therefore be interpreted as his own initial and that of his second wife, Jeanne de Laval. The close association of the Pazzi family, and especially of Jacopo de' Pazzi, with King René of Anjou is illustrated in documents published by Lecoy de la Marche (1873, passim), and is reflected on the stemma, where one of the two braziers carries the crosslets of the Pazzi arms. Maclagan/Longhurst (1932, i, pp. 30–31) observe that the design of the central part of the roundel is French not Italian, and may have been made from a drawing supplied by the herald of King René of Anjou. The stemma is universally accepted as a work of Luca della Robbia; the earliest dating proposed for it is about 1466 and the latest about 1475. When it was acquired by the museum in 1861, it was stated by Robinson (1862, pp. 54–57) to have been removed 'only a few years ago' from a villa which was 'in the immediate vicinity of Florence, and was latterly known as the Villa Panciatichi-Ximenes.' According to Robinson, this was 'even still known as the villa "Loggia dei Pazzi".' The Loggia dei Pazzi at Montughi is now known as the Villa Costantini (for which see Carocci, i, pp. 187–8, and Lensi Orlandi Cardini, 1954, pp. 111–12, pl. 113–14). This villa was owned by Jacopo de' Pazzi. After the Pazzi conspiracy of 1478, the architect Giuliano da Majano put forward a claim with the Uffiziali dei Ribelli for work 'nella chasa di Firenze e a luogo di villa a Montughi e al capitolo di Santa Croce," and it may be that the commissioning of the stemma was bound up with the extension of the Montughi villa. According to Robinson, the relief was originally let into the face of an external wall at a considerable height from the ground. V. Herzner (1976 (i)) notes that the Pazzi palace and villa were both acquired by Franceschetto Cybo at the end of the fifteenth century, and suggests that the stemma may have been removed from one to the other. This is improbable.

22 Madonna and Child with two Angels. Ashmolean Museum, Oxford.   Plate 90A

Pigmented stucco: diameter 40 cm.
Provenance: James Jackson Jarves; C. Drury Fortnum.

At one time covered with bronze paint, the relief was cleaned in 1956, revealing a crude polychrome surface dating substantially from the fifteenth century. On the back is incised a circle with irregular decoration in the border and the cursive inscription: 'formato adj 17 di gennaio 1428'. Within the circle is a crown, above which are incised the words:

> formosi nel
> chasotto di Nich
> olo i chossa.

The substance of the first inscription is not in doubt. In the second the word 'chasotto' has also been transcribed as 'gabinetto,' and the word 'chossa' as 'gesso'. A number of other reproductions of the composition are known. Among these are (i) a version formerly in the Von Bülow collection, Berlin, in an original frame painted with the *Risen Christ and four Franciscan Saints* and datable, on account of the presence of San Bernardino, after 1450; (ii) a version in terracotta in the Louvre (No. 424), somewhat smaller (diameter 34 cm.) and blunter than at Oxford, with traces of surface pigmentation; (iii) a rectangular variant in pressed leather formerly in the Kaiser Friedrich Museum, Berlin (No. 89). These versions are discussed by Marquand (1914, Nos. 105–110). The attribution of the Oxford relief to Luca della Robbia, proposed by Bode (1885, p. 184; 1905, p. 73; and elsewhere), is accepted by Schubring (1905, pp. 8, 84, pl. 89) and A. Venturi (vi, p. 555) and initially by Marquand (1894, pp. 2, 4–5), and is rejected by Marquand (1914, pp. 257–9), Reymond (1897 (ii), pp. 111–120), and Cruttwell (1902,

pp. 130–2, 349). The relief is ignored by Planiscig. The surface of the Fortnum relief suggests strongly that it was moulded from a low relief in bronze, of which the handling resembled that of the later circular *Madonna and Child with six Angels* (Cat. No. 45). While the two angels and the drapery forms of the Virgin's cloak are Ghibertesque, the types throughout are closely related to those of Luca della Robbia, and there can be little doubt that the lost bronze original was produced by Luca prior to the date inscribed on the reverse of the stucco squeeze, 1428.

23 Madonna and Child. Musée Jacquemart-André, Paris (Inv. 2453).   Plate 90B

Stucco: 30 × 22 cm. (right arm of Virgin restored).

Another version of the composition is recorded in Berlin (Kaiser Friedrich Museum, No. 1721 (Sch. 77), formerly. Dimensions: 37 × 28 cm.), and is accepted as a work by or after Luca della Robbia by Wulff (1917, pp. 229–30) and Schottmüller (1933, p. 28). A third version exists in the Museo Bardini, Florence (Alinari 17220). The Berlin example was bought in Florence in 1890. Gavoty (1975, No. 29) mistakenly relates the scheme to an 'exemplaire original en terre cuite émaillée' at Nynehead. The two compositions are not closely related, and the Nynehead *Madonna* (Cat. No. 64) is an independent work by Andrea della Robbia. For Marquand (1914, p. 243, No. 95) the design 'reflects Luca's mature style and doubtless represents one of his compositions.' The wide flat head of the Virgin recalls that in the *Madonna and Child with two Angels* at Oxford (Cat. No. 22), and the date inscribed on the Oxford relief (1428) offers an indication of the probable date of the present composition. The type of the Child, with chin drawn in and head turned down, recalls that of the angels in the Ashmolean relief.

24 Madonna and Child. Bode Museum, Berlin (D.D.R.), No. 1794 (Sch. 78).   Plate 92

Pigmented terracotta: 61 × 38 cm.
Provenance: Purchased in Florence 1891.

The group is modelled in one with a shallow base receding at the corners. The dress of the Virgin is of red and gold brocade, her blue cloak is lined with green, and her veil mauve. Her hair is gilt. In the border of her mantle, to the left of the Child's left foot, is the word DOMINVS. There are no traces of enamelling. The relief is accepted by Bode (1905, p. 77, pl. 226) as a work of Luca della Robbia of the fourteen-forties, and is exhibited as a work by Luca della Robbia in the Bode Museum (Berlin, 1964, fig. 2). It is catalogued by Schottmüller (1933, p. 29) as a work in the style of Luca della Robbia. There can be no reasonable doubt that Bode's attribution to Luca is correct, since the type of the Child is inseparable from that of the seated child on the right of the *Players on the Cithara* on the Cantoria. Points of resemblance include the pinched features, the large ears, the stiffly modelled limbs and the rendering of the torso. A small pigmented terracotta *Madonna* in the Kunsthistorisches Museum, Vienna (Benda bequest) is closely related to this relief, and is perhaps by Luca della Robbia. It may have been modelled ca. 1430–4.

25 Madonna and Child. Duveen Bros. Inc., New York (formerly). Plate 91A
Pigmented stucco: 62·5 × 54 cm.

Versions of the relief in stucco exist in the Bode Museum, Berlin (D.D.R.) (I. 64), the Museo Bardini (Lensi, 1923–4, p. 503), the Musée Jacquemart-André, Paris (Gavoty, 1975, No. 19), the Detroit Art Institute and the Albertinum, Dresden. All of them seem to have been made from a single mould; the best preserved example is that illustrated here. The composition is ascribed by Bode (1902, p. 168) and Wulff (1917, pp. 232–3) to Luca della Robbia, by Schottmüller (1933, p. 34) to an unidentified sculptor active about 1450, and by Schlegel (1962, pp. 4–12) and Gavoty (*loc. cit.*) to Buggiano. It is associated by Schlegel with three other pigmented stucco *Madonnas* of which examples exist in the Staatliche Museen, Berlin-Dahlem: (i) I. 1724, in which the Child is shown leaning back over the left arm of the Virgin (other versions in San Donnino at Villamagna (Fig. 26) and in the Musée Jacquemart-André), (ii) I. 146, in which the Child is shown standing beneath the Virgin's extended cloak (Fig. 27; other versions in the Carmine, Florence, and in a Florentine private collection), and (iii) I. 142, where the Virgin is shown in full face and the Child is represented with legs apart as though alarmed (another version in the De Ridder collection, Paris). Of these reliefs, I. 142 is accepted as a work of Luca della Robbia by Planiscig (1948, p. 48, fig. 100–1). All four reliefs are ignored by Marquand. The ungainly, inflated Child in I. 1724 is related to that in the *Madonna* by Buggiano at the back of the altar in the Sagrestia Vecchia, and the Child in I. 142 is related to the heads of cherubs in the spandrels of the Cappella Cardini in San Francesco at Pescia, which are also by Buggiano. The case for regarding these two compositions as Buggiano's is therefore, as argued by Schlegel, very strong, and it is likely that I. 146 is a work by the same artist. The present relief, on the other hand, is more coherent and sophisticated in design; the Child recalls that in Luca della Robbia's *Friedrichstein Madonna* (Cat. No. 28) and the geometrical structure of the figures also recalls the work of Luca. It seems reasonable to separate this composition from the other three, as a putative work by Luca della Robbia of 1435–40. Like that of the three stuccos by Buggiano, its style is Brunelleschan, and does not, as claimed by Bode, reveal the influence of Donatello.

26 Madonna and Child. Kaiser Friedrich Museum, Berlin (formerly), No. 62. Plate 91B
Terracotta covered with pigmentation over traces of enamelling: 41 × 32 cm.

For this relief, which was destroyed in 1945, see Cat. No. 27.

27 Madonna and Child. Statens Museum for Kunst, Copenhagen (Inv. 5482). Plate 93
Enamelled terracotta: 39·5 × 29 cm.
Provenance: C. F. von Rumohr, Dresden, 1847 (No. 4375).

The figures are enamelled in white on a blue-enamelled ground. The haloes are gilt. The eyes have blue irises and dark pupils. The relief is accepted by Bode (1906, p. 28n.), but is relegated by Marquand to an appendix (1914, pp. 226–7, No. 64) dealing with works in the manner of Luca della Robbia. Though not otherwise discussed in the literature of the artist, it is of importance as the only Madonna relief in enamelled terracotta which is directly associable with the style of the Cantoria reliefs. The relation of the Virgin's head to the ground recalls that of heads in the *Players on the Cithara* and the free modelling of the hair, bound by a fillet, resembles that of the figure on the extreme left of the *Choral Dancers*. The drapery forms have an analogy in the *Lamentation over the Dead Christ* on the Peretola tabernacle, and it is probable that the relief likewise dates from after 1435. A slightly larger variant of the composition (41 × 32 cm.), formerly in the Kaiser Friedrich Museum, Berlin (M. 62. For this see Schottmüller, 1933, p. 27), shows the Child fully clothed, His right foot resting on the wrist of the Virgin with His right knee raised, and the two haloes modelled in relief rather than painted. According to Schottmüller (*loc. cit.*), and Marquand (1914, pp. 227–8, No. 65), the Berlin relief was pigmented naturalistically over traces of white glaze. It is argued by Schottmüller that the enamelling was applied as a basis for pigmentation, and by Marquand and Bode that it represents an abortive attempt at glazing, which was then concealed with paint. The Berlin version is variously regarded as contemporary with the Copenhagen relief (Bode, Schottmüller) and as 'a free copy made probably towards the end of the fifteenth century' (Marquand). In the absence of the Berlin version, it is tempting to infer, from its faulty enamelling and its compositional connections with Buggiano, that it may have been made prior to the fully enamelled Copenhagen relief, and thus may represent the first stage in the development of reliefs in enamelled terracotta.

28 The Friedrichstein Madonna. Albright-Knox Art Gallery, Buffalo (N.Y.) (Inv. No. 29.4). Col. Plate XXV
Polychrome enamelled terracotta: 46·5 × 38 cm.
Provenance: Stated to have come from a Capuchin church at Santa Fiora (unconfirmed); Léon Somzée, Brussels (Somzée, 1904, iii, p. 58, No. 1142, as atelier of Luca della Robbia); sold by Madame Somzée 1913; purchased from the Bottenwieser Galleries, New York, by Seymour H. Knox 1929 and presented to the Albright-Knox Art Gallery.

The relief was first published by Camille de Roddaz (1882, pp. 388–9, repr.) with a tentative attribution to one of the nephews of Luca della Robbia. In 1888 a second version was purchased in Florence by Graf Dönhoff-Friedrichstein and was presented by him to the Kaiser Friedrich Museum (No. 143); for this reason the relief is commonly known as the *Friedrichstein Madonna*. The example in Berlin was destroyed in 1945, and the Buffalo relief is the only surviving example of the composition. The height of the Berlin relief is given by Schottmüller (1933, p. 24) as 47·5 cm.; it is likely that the two reliefs, which appear to be identical, were of precisely the same size. According to Schottmüller (*loc. cit.*), the glaze of the *Friedrichstein Madonna* was 'ergänzt'. From reproductions it seems that a small area above the Virgin's girdle and a second area in the Child's robe above the thigh were filled in with paint. The glaze in the Buffalo relief is also imperfect, and has flaked at a number of points (e.g. on the Child's robe across the thigh, on the upper surface of the Virgin's left hand, and in the surrounding white frame). Part of the extensive damage to the Buffalo *Madonna* may be due to faulty firing, but in addition the relief seems to have been dropped and extensively broken and repaired. The most serious damage is in the front of the head of the Child, where fragments of white enamelled terracotta have been arbitrarily replaced and the original form is lost. The two figures are glazed in white, with violet eyes; there are traces of pinkish glaze in the eyelids of the Child. The decoration of the corners seems to have been intended as illusionistic inlay. Three of the blue circles are plain, while one, in the upper left corner, is broken by small white spots. Photographs suggest that the decoration of the circular motif in the upper left corner of the *Friedrichstein Madonna* was treated in the same way. There is a presumption that the *Madonna* dates from about 1440 rather than from any later time. The imperfect glazing of both versions of the composition would also seem to argue a relatively early date. It is likely that the Buffalo and Berlin reliefs were made from a single mould.

29 Corsini Madonna. Musée Jacquemart-André, Paris (Inv. 1772, No. 30).   Plate 94A
Pigmented stucco: 44 × 22·5 cm.

The relief, which is known as the *Corsini Madonna*, seems to have enjoyed great popularity. A circular version in enamelled terracotta in the Palazzo Corsini, Florence, published by Reymond (1904) as an autograph Luca della Robbia of ca. 1470, is strongly polychromatic. Against a blue background decorated with gilt rays the Virgin wears a blue cloak with a turquoise blue lining, over a violet dress heightened with gilding, while the Child, Who has a cruciform halo, is dressed in green and pale blue. It was inferred by Reymond, from comparison with the *stemma* of the Arte dei Medici e Speziali on Or San Michele, that this colouring was characteristic of the late work of Luca. The attribution is rejected by Marquand (1914, pp. 239-40, No. 85: 'possibly this is an original by Luca himself, but probably a replica by another hand'). While the Corsini relief itself almost certainly dates from the late fifteenth or early sixteenth century, there can be little doubt that the composition depends from a lost original by Luca della Robbia, which may have been evolved about 1440. As noted by Marquand (*op. cit.*, p. 241, No. 87) the composition recurs in a wreath supported by two putti in the lintel of a stone doorway in the Ospedale di Santa Maria Nuova. No autograph version of the composition by Luca della Robbia survives. A blue and white enamelled version from the Percy

Strauss collection is at Houston (Marquand, No. 89. Ex-Beckerath, Berlin), and another is in the Philbrook Art Center at Tulsa (Middeldorf, 1976, pp. 34-5). The composition is otherwise known through examples in stucco (Marquand, No. 88, Hainauer collection, Berlin, later Duveen, New York; *ibid.*, No. 86, Bardini, Florence, Schubring, 1905, p. 81, fig. 85, as the example in the Palazzo Corsini; Marquand, *op. cit.*, No. 93, Santa Maria in Castello, Genoa), in unglazed terracotta (Marquand, No. 92, Berlin, Kaiser Friedrich Museum; *ibid.*, No. 90, Beckerath collection, Berlin), and in cartapesta (*ibid.*, No. 91, Berlin, Kaiser Friedrich Museum, No. 93, I. 1722, not circular). A rectangular example is in the Musée Jacquemart-André (Gavoty, 1975, no. 30). The diameters of the circular examples vary between 28 and 36 cm. Despite the lack of an autograph original, the composition is of some importance in the sequence of Luca della Robbia's *Madonnas*, and is most closely related to, though perhaps a little later than, the *Friedrichstein Madonna* at Buffalo. An early dating for the lost original is maintained by Middeldorf.

30 Madonna and Child with Saints Dominic, Thomas Aquinas, Albertus Magnus and Peter Martyr.
Galleria Nazionale delle Marche, Urbino.

Figs. 23, 24, Plate 95

Enamelled terracotta: 93 × 234 cm.

The Urbino lunette is of particular importance as the only representation of the Virgin and Child by Luca della Robbia in enamelled terracotta that is exactly datable. The door over which it was set was designed by Maso di Bartolomeo, and was paid for in the summer of 1449 (Yriarte, 1894, pp. 55-56). The commission for the lunette seems to have been placed with Luca della Robbia through Maso di Bartolomeo, and is the subject of the following entry in the *Libro di Conti di Maso di Bartolommeo di Firenze dell' anno 1449* (c. 1, 25t.): '1450, 19 di Giugno. Lucha di Simone della robbia de dare adì 19 di giugno f. quattro doro valsono L. 18 b. 8 et p. me da Frate bartolomeo daurbino. E questi furo p. parte di pagame[n]to dicerte Figure che detto lucha mi debba fare p. mettere nella porta durbino cioè una nostra dona sā piero martire e sandomenicho. E di sopra in uno frōtone uno idio padre in uno tondo p. prezo di f. quarante cioe f. XL...L. 18 b. 8.' (Ms. cart. del sec. XV nella Biblioteca Nazionale Centrale di Firenze, Palazzo Baldovinetti, No. 70, published by Marquand, 1914, p. 115, and Yriarte, 1894, p. 64).

The lunette was restored prior to 1914, and it was recognised by Marquand (*op. cit.*, p. 114) that 'the Madonna's face has been injured so much that we have no certainty concerning the form of her eyes, nose or mouth. The Child's face is also much damaged.' The made-up sections were removed from the relief in 1973 when it was transferred to the Palazzo Ducale at Urbino (see Urbino, 1973, pp. 222-7, No. 53). The present condition may be described as follows:

ST. DOMINIC. Head, neck and upper part almost perfectly preserved. Break through habit to right forearm.

ST. THOMAS AQUINAS. Fairly well preserved. Fractures across face below eyes and on cowl. He holds a book inscribed DE FRVCTV OPERVM TVORVM SATIABITVR TERRA.

VIRGIN AND CHILD. Nose and upper lip of Virgin missing, and veil to left of head broken. Fractures across face. Glaze largely removed on right side and on veil across shoulder and on right arm. Glaze removed from shoulder and head of Child, where the terracotta is otherwise intact. Extensive glaze loss on right thigh. The extremities of the scroll are original (EGO S ⟨VM LVX MVN⟩ NDI).

ST. ALBERTUS MAGNUS. Glaze loss on raised right hand and glaze loss on cowl.

ST. PETER MARTYR. Section missing from the centre of the forehead through the left eye. Extensive fracture and loss of glaze through the neck, the cowl of the habit and the left elbow.

In the circumstances in which it is shown in the Palazzo Ducale at Urbino, the relief can be studied more closely than any other work by Luca in enamelled terracotta. The figurated area was glazed and baked not in three parts as Marquand supposed, but in eleven sections: (i) body of St. Dominic up to line of cowl, (ii) head and cowl of St. Dominic, (iii) head of St. Thomas Aquinas to line below cowl, (iv) body of St. Thomas Aquinas from top of book to base, (v) body of Virgin and lower part of Child to lower edge of scroll, (vi) upper part of Child and scroll, (vii) head and shoulders of Virgin, (viii) upper part of Albertus Magnus to join below wrist and under cowl, including top of adjacent palm, (ix) bottom of figure of Albertus Magnus to edge of book held by St. Peter Martyr, (x) head of St. Peter Martyr to bottom edge of cowl, (xi) lower part and hands of St. Peter Martyr. The background is filled in with irregular sections of blue enamelled terracotta with a depth of 3·3 cm.

31 **Madonna and Child with two Angels.** Bode Museum, Berlin (D.D.R.), (Kaiser Friedrich Museum, Sch. 74, Inv. 2967). Plates 96, 98–100
Enamelled terracotta: 83 × 154 cm.

The relief was purchased for the Kaiser Friedrich Museum in 1905 from a London dealer, with a statement that it was originally over the door of a private chapel in the Mugello (Schottmüller, 1933, p. 26). No further information about its origin is available in the archive of the Staatliche Museen, Berlin-Dahlem, or of the Bode Museum. Marquand (1914, pp. 69–70, No. 16) questions the autograph character of the angels. His account of the relief is vitiated by comparison with the Via dell'Agnolo lunette in the Bargello, which was executed at a considerably later date by Andrea della Robbia. The closest analogies for the drapery forms of the robes of the Virgin and of the angels occur in the *Resurrection* lunette in the Cathedral (completed 1445) and in the Apostle roundels in the Pazzi Chapel, in certain of which (e.g. SS. Simon and Thaddeus) the torsion of the figure is related to that of the central Virgin in the lunette, while in others (e.g. SS. John the Evangelist and Matthew) the rich drapery forms are closely comparable. For Marquand, the type of the Child Christ suggests an earlier dating than the Christ in the Urbino lunette (1449–50). The probable date of the lunette is, how-

ever, the first half of the fourteen-fifties. The style of all three figures is strongly influenced by that of Michelozzo.

The width of the relief (154 cm.) is considerably less than that of the lunette from San Pier Buonconsiglio (240 cm.) or the Via dell' Agnolo lunette (222 cm.), and the presumption is that it was set over the entrance to a small chapel by or in the style of Michelozzo. Having regard to its probable date, it is likely to have had a stone frame, like the lunette at Urbino, not a moulded or floreated terracotta surround. No similar relief is mentioned in the account of Della Robbia reliefs in the Mugello prepared by Chini (1876, pp. 97–101), or by Brocchi (1748). It probably, therefore, originates from a chapel in a villa not described in either book. This may have been the Michelozzo chapel adjacent to Il Trebbio, the doorway of which measures 150 cm. across the open aperture and 161 cm. with the lintel supports, and is now surmounted by a stone lunette dating from the present century. There is some doubt as to the date of Michelozzo's activity at Il Trebbio, which is mentioned in 1427 in the Catasto return of Giovanni di Bicci de' Medici as 'uno luogho adatto a fortezza per mia abitazione.' Michelozzo's work on the structure has been variously dated after 1451 (Fabriczy, 1904), when under the division of the property of Giovanni di Bicci de' Medici Caffaggiolo passed to Cosimo il Vecchio and Trebbio to Pierfrancesco di Lorenzo, to 1427–36, when Michelozzo was employed by Cosimo il Vecchio on the reconstruction of the nearby convent of Bosco ai Frati, prior to 1427 (Gori Sassoli, 1975, p. 13 ff.), ca. 1422–3 (Caplow, ii, pp. 595–7), and ca. 1420 (Patzak, ii, p. 71). All and any of these datings would be consistent with the hypothesis that the Mugello lunette was made in or after 1451 for the chapel at Il Trebbio.

Il Trebbio (for which see also G. Baccini, 1897) was sold by the Grand-Duke Ferdinand II to Giuliano Serragli (transaction completed 1645), and was bequeathed by Serragli (d. 1648) to the Filippini of the oratory of San Firenze in Florence. In 1799 after the entry of the French troops the properties of the Congregation of San Firenze at Trebbio and Sassuolo were expropriated, and though the property was later restored to the Filippini, they were evicted in 1864 from the greater part of their premises in Florence, and in 1868–9, in the course of a legal action brought by the Bigallo, were finally deprived of Il Trebbio (for this see A. Cistellini, 1967). The property was acquired after this date by Principe Marcantonio Borghese. A great part of the contents of the house were dispersed under Borghese ownership.

32 **Madonna and Child with two Angels.** Palazzo di Parte Guelfa, Florence. Plates 97, 101
Enamelled terracotta: 120 × 240 cm.

The relief stood over an external doorway of San Pier Buonconsiglio, where it is described by Vasari (Vasari-Milanesi, ii, p. 175: 'la Nostra Donna, con alcuni angeli intorno molto vivaci'). It was still in place in 1677, when it is mentioned by Bocchi-Cinelli (pp. 215–6: 'S. Pier Buonconsiglio vicino alla pescheria, sopra la cui porta in un arco sono alcune figure di Luca della Robbia, le quali non meno dell'altre opere sue spirano grazia, e divozione insieme'). According to Richa (vii,

p. 303) the church was subjected to a 'rinnovazione totale' in 1736 by the then rector, Cosimo Trotti, 'non essendovi rimaso del vecchio, se non se [sic] poche armi di Famiglie, ed una Immagine di Maria col Figlio in collo, che si vede fattura in mezzo rilievo di Luca della Robbia, collocata sopra la porta al di fuori, e delle armi in alto della facciata.' The parish served by the church (for which see Paatz, iv, pp. 614–15) was abolished in 1785, and after a period of use as an oratory for a Confraternity, the building was secularised in the middle of the nineteenth century and was pulled down in 1890. The enamelled terracotta relief was removed from the lunette in 1884 (see *Arte e Storia*, 10 March, 1890, p. 48), and after a period of storage was exhibited from 1890 in the Museo Nazionale (Supino, 1898, p. 443, No. 29). It was removed in 1932 and installed over a doorway in the Palazzo di Parte Guelfa (for this see *Firenze*, i, 1932, No. 5, p. 24), from which it was removed during the 1939–45 war as a precautionary measure and in which it was subsequently reinstalled. Its present condition is explained, first by the fact that it was removed from its setting and wrongly reinstalled in 1736 (an old Alinari photograph 9767 shows it in position in the late nineteenth century), second that it was reassembled (with some modifications) in 1890 in the Bargello and third that the installation was again revised after 1945. The frame originally consisted of a double leaf-and-dart and egg-and-dart white moulding outside a floreated frieze, inside which was an inner white frame with leaf-and-cord mouldings immediately adjacent to the relief. In the form in which it was replaced on San Pierino in the eighteenth century, the white frames were transferred to the interior of the floreated frieze, which was therefore longer than it had been originally and included areas of make-up. The outer white frame was reduced at this time. When the relief was installed in the Bargello, this faulty articulation was preserved, and though it has now been rectified, this has been done at the cost of inserting substantial areas of make-up in the outer white frame and some make-up at the base of the floreated strip. The pieces of the frieze were themselves wrongly assembled in 1736 when a number of the sections were inverted. This was corrected in the 1890 Bargello installation. The head of the Child has been repaired and there is some make-up over His right eye. From a technical standpoint the lunette is badly integrated, and the wide repaints over joins impair its aesthetic effect.

In the fifteenth century the *Patronato* of San Piero Buonconsiglio was vested in the Signoria, and in 1444 a letter was dispatched by the Signoria to the Archbishop of Florence (for which see Richa, vii, pp. 300–1) protesting the Archbishop's refusal to appoint a rector elected by the parishioners and approved by the Signoria. By 1446 the rector was Messer Lionardo de' Falladanzi da Orta, who held the post jointly with the incumbency of San Miniato fra le Torri. A relief of the Virgin and Child by Luca della Robbia is recorded by Richa (iv, p. 71) over the entrance to San Miniato fra le Torri. According to Paatz (iv, p. 298), this was removed in 1785, and in 1792 it is referred to by Follini-Rastrelli (iv, p. 206) in the past tense ('Vi era pure una bellissima Madonna di Luca della Robbia'). This work cannot be traced.

The San Pierino lunette is adversely criticised by Marquand (1914, pp. 45–48, No. 8), who observes that 'in the

Virgin and Child Luca was probably dependent on some other master' and considers that in its construction Luca 'falls short of his usual perfection.' There is no reason to suppose that the four figures are not original and wholly autograph works. The relief has been variously dated before 1440 (Marquand, *loc. cit.*), before 1443 (Bode, 1902, pp. 119–20, and elsewhere), before 1450 (A. Venturi, vi, p. 566), between 1450 and 1460 (Reymond, 1897 (ii), p. 101; and Schubring, 1905, pp. 73–76) and about 1465 (De Foville, 1910, pp. 75, 127). The drapery of the flying figures is more advanced than that of the Christ in the *Ascension* lunette in the Cathedral (1446–51), and it is likely that the relief dates from about 1460.

33 Madonna and Child. Galleria dello Spedale degli Innocenti, Florence.　Col. Plate XXVI
Enamelled terracotta: 76 × 58 cm.

The earlier literature of this beautiful relief is superseded by L. Bellosi (1977, p. 226, No. 4), who establishes that it stood on a side altar in the Chiesa delle Donne of the Hospital in 1863, when it was ascribed to Agostino della Robbia. The relief was exhibited in the gallery from 1890. On the cartellino are the words: EGO SVM LVX MVNDI, and on the base is an inscription in white lettering from the *Magnificat*: QVIA RESPEXIT DOMINVS HVMILITATEM ANCILLE SVE. The Virgin points with the first finger of her right hand to the inscription on the base, and it is inferred from this by Bellosi that the relief was from the first intended for the edification of the congregation in the Chiesa delle Donne. By general consent the relief is dated by reference to the Urbino lunette of 1450. It may well be a somewhat earlier work. Cherici (1926, pp. 65–66, No. 93) proposes a date of 1446–9. Old photographs show that the edges of the Virgin's mantle, the cartellino and other parts of the relief were fortified with later paint. This was removed in 1925.

34 Madonna and Child. Metropolitan Museum of Art, New York (Altman Collection), 14.40.685.
Col. Plate XXVII
Enamelled terracotta: 80 × 56 cm.
Provenance: Conte Leonello di Nobili, Florence.

The relief is modelled without a background, the Virgin's head being modelled and fired separately. It is covered with white enamel, and the irises are pigmented grey-green (for this pigmentation see Marquand, 1912(i)). According to Marquand (1914, pp. 57–58, No. 13), it was 'on sale for several years in London and Paris before it found a home in the Altman Collection.' Bode (1910) states that it had been on the market for two years before it was acquired by Altman in or before 1910. There is no information as to the immediate source from which he obtained it (F. Haskell, 1970, p. 275). It is inferred by Bode from the absence of a background that the relief was originally the central section of a lunette. Marquand likewise notes that 'it resembles the André Madonna in having no background, and was probably designed to be set in a lunette over a door.' There is no confirmation that this was so.

Planiscig (1948, pp. 49, 71) rightly comments that 'segna con la sua maestà serena, con la calma sovrana che da essa si sprigiona, un'apice nell'arte di Luca.' The substitution of the head of the Virgin is a unique feature of this relief, and was presumably due either to a glazing failure in the original head or to a search after greater expressiveness. The relief is evidently later than the Urbino and Mugello lunettes, and seems to date from about 1455.

35 Madonna and Child. San Michele, Lucca.   Plate 102
Enamelled terracotta. A break in the background on the right extends though the neck of the Virgin and the left edge of the relief.

Now in a tabernacle over the first altar on the right of the church of San Michele, the relief was previously over an altar in the adjacent oratory of Santa Lucia (from which it is said to have been removed about 1910) and before that time was exhibited in a lunette over the door. It is recorded by Campetti (1917, p. 81) as a work of Andrea della Robbia, and was first ascribed to Luca della Robbia by De Nicola (1919). The attribution is accepted by Mather in an addendum to Marquand (1928, p. 148). When the relief was published by De Nicola, the hair, haloes, hems of the robe and mantle, girdle and cloth were covered with modern gilding, and the irises of the eyes were painted black. The gilding and overpaint have since been removed, and the pigmentation of the eyes is now characteristic of Luca della Robbia. The principal analogies cited by De Nicola are with the two *Madonnas* at Impruneta (which are of later date) and with the Demidoff and Nynehead *Madonnas* (which are early works by Andrea della Robbia). There can, however, be no doubt of Luca della Robbia's authorship of the present relief, in which the Virgin's retracted left shoulder recalls the Mugello lunette in Berlin (D.D.R.) and the pose of the Child shows affinities with that of the *Altman Madonna* in New York. The Lucca *Madonna* appears to be contemporary with the second of these works, and may have been produced about 1455. The form of the protruding porphyry base, which is cast in one with the relief, recalls that of the *Madonna* in the Spedale degli Innocenti.

There is no reference in any early source to a *Madonna* by Luca della Robbia made for Lucca. The relief appears, from its design, to have been intended to be shown externally, and was so exhibited on the oratory of Santa Lucia. It is possible that it is identical with a *Madonna* by Luca della Robbia which was removed from the entrance to San Miniato fra le Torri in Florence in the late eighteenth century (see Cat. No. 32 above).

36 Madonna of the Apple. Staatliche Museen,
      Berlin-Dahlem, M. 6 (Sch. 70).   Plate 103
Enamelled terracotta: 58 × 44 cm.
Provenance: Sir Francis Cook, Richmond; presented by Michaelis to the Kaiser Friedrich Museum Verein, 1896.

Modelled and glazed without a background. The irises are coloured pale blue with violet pupils, and the eyebrows are lightly indicated. Traces of gilding on the hair, the border of

the cloak, and the fillet, girdle and cuff. The group rests on a chamfered base, like that of the Innocenti *Madonna*, and on this account the two works are grouped together by Marquand (1914, pp. 116–17, No. 29) and dated about 1450. Bode (1900, pp. 25–26; 1905, p. 75, pl. 222; 1902, pp. 177–8) assigns the relief to Luca's middle years. Marquand's dating is rightly contested by Schottmüller (1933, p. 25), who regards the relief as 'noch qualitätvoller als das Exemplar im Florentiner Museum.' The relief is an even finer and more inventive work than the *Madonna with the Apple* in the Museo Nazionale, and seems to date from about 1455–60. Planiscig (1948, p. 71, No. 106) confuses the Berlin relief with that in the Bargello.

37 Madonna of the Apple. Museo Nazionale, Florence.
                                              Col. Plate XXVIII
Enamelled terracotta: 70 × 52 cm.

The relief was moved to the Galleria degli Uffizi from the Guardaroba of the Palazzo Vecchio on 29 July 1836, and from the Uffizi to the Museo Nazionale in 1869. It is thus, as established by U. Rossi (1893, p. 8, n. 3) and Supino (1898, pp. 442–3, No. 28), the single relief by Luca della Robbia with a certain provenance from the Medici collection. It is assumed that the relief entered the Medici collection before the end of the sixteenth century, and is perhaps identical with a relief listed in 1492 in the inventory of Lorenzo de' Medici (Müntz, 1888, p. 81): 'Una Nostra Donna di mezzo rilievo invetriata in su una ghocciola fitta nel muro', when it was in the *soffito* over the 'antichamera della chamera grande detta di Lorenzo.' Beneath the Virgin is a turquoise-blue base, chamfered like that of the Berlin *Madonna of the Apple* but with longer sides and a narrower front. The relief is made in one with its blue ground. The irises of the eyes are grey-blue, and the pupils violet. The eyebrows and eyelashes are not pigmented, and there is no evidence that the relief at any time had the gilded enrichment of the Berlin relief. The relief is accepted as autograph by all students of Luca della Robbia. Marquand (1914, pp. 118–19, No. 30) observes that 'the relation of mother and Son is not quite so intimate as that of the Madonna on the Impruneta frieze.' These two reliefs have it in common that the drapery beneath the Virgin's left hand is pulled in, so as to provide a narrow base for the silhouette. In the Berlin *Madonna of the Apple*, on the other hand, the base of the figure of the Virgin protrudes at right and left outside the support. For this reason the Bargello *Madonna of the Apple* is likely to be the later of the two reliefs, and may have been made about 1460.

38 Madonna and Child. Musée Jacquemart-André, Paris
      (Inv. 1799).   Plate 104
Enamelled terracotta: 74 × 48 cm.
Provenance: Pourtalès collection, Paris (sale Paris, 8 March 1865, No. 1865); Piot collection, Paris (sale Paris, 21–24 May 1890, No. 6, bt. André, Fr. 17,000).

The relief (for which see Gavoty, 1975, p. 7, No. 27) is modelled without a background. The irises are light-blue with dark-blue pupils and violet eyelashes. With the exception of Cruttwell (1902, pp. 135, 151), who did not know it in the original and regarded it as an imitation of Luca's work, the relief is universally accepted as a work of Luca della Robbia. The only divergence of view arises from its date. On account of its relationship to the San Pierino lunette, it was ascribed by Marquand (1914, pp. 49-50, No. 9) to the decade 1430-40. This dating is adopted by Janson (1942, p. 330), Planiscig (1948, pp. 16, 63) and Brunetti (1962, p. 267). Bode (1887, pp. 193-4; 1889, p. 74; 1900, p. 23) associated it with the *Innocenti Madonna* as a work of the middle of the century. A dating ca. 1450-5 is accepted by Gavoty (*loc. cit.*). Schubring (1905, p. 81; 1919, p. 86) assigned it to a considerably later date, ca. 1470. Its affinities are with the San Pierino lunette rather than with the *Innocenti Madonna*, and it is likely to have been modelled about 1460.

39 Madonna and Child in a Rose-Garden. Museo Nazionale, Florence (No. 31).   Col. Plate XXX
Enamelled terracotta: 83 × 63 cm.

The relief has no provenance. According to Marquand (1914, pp. 121-2, No. 32), it was at one time regarded as a forgery. It was first published by Bode (1889, p. 5; 1900, pp. 17, 24n.; 1902, p. 158: 'Nach dem Vergleich mit den datierten Arbeiten ist diese trotz des genreartigen Motivs ernste und vornehme Komposition wohl nicht vor 1450 entstanden'), and is accepted by Reymond (1897 (ii), p. 101: 'voisine de la Vierge d'Urbino'), Marquand (*loc. cit.*: 'may be assigned to the decade 1450-60'), and Planiscig (1940, p. 36). Points of reference for the composition are supplied by the *Altman Madonna* in New York, where the two figures both look outwards to the right, and by the Urbino lunette of 1449-50, which offers analogies for the type and the extended left arm of the Child. The *Madonna* is likely to date from the early fourteen-fifties. Cruttwell (1902, pp. 122-3) dates it 1420-30.

40 Madonna and Child in a Niche. Metropolitan Museum of Art, New York (67.55.98).   Col. Plate XXIX
Enamelled terracotta: 46·5 × 38 cm.
Provenance: Emile Gavet, Paris (till 1895); Henry G. Marquand, New York (till 1903); Mrs. George T. Bliss, New York; bequeathed to the Metropolitan Museum of Art by Susan Dwight Bliss.

The two figures are enamelled in white with blue-grey eyes. The hair of both figures and details of the dress were originally heightened with surface gilding, of which traces remain. The niche and frame are glazed in light blue (described by Marquand as turquoise blue). Within the niche the moulding and striations are gilt. The two *stemmi* in the upper corners and the surface decoration of the front face of the niche are in applied gilt. There is a diagonal break in the lower right corner running through the Child's left leg and right foot, and the glaze in these areas and on the index finger of the Virgin's right hand has been renewed. The relief is the most beautiful and complex example of applied decoration in Luca della Robbia's work. It is presumed by Marquand (1914, p. 157)

that the two *stemmi* 'possibly record a union of the Bartorelli and Baldi families.'

A second example of the composition, evidently made from the same mould, exists in the Boston Museum of Fine Arts (46·5 × 38·5 cm. Formerly in the collection of Mrs. Quincy A. Shaw). In this version (Fig. 28) the Child is represented nude, and the Virgin's cloak extends to the right of His left leg. As noted by Marquand (1914, pp. 156-60, Nos. 42, 43), the modelling is somewhat blunter than in the *Bliss Madonna*. The hair of the two figures and the edge of the Virgin's cloak appear to have been gilt. There are no traces of gilding in the interior of the niche, where the surface is blue and the ribs are light or turquoise blue. The front face of the niche is green, and appears originally to have been gilded, and the circular discs for *stemmi* in the spandrels are void. It is possible that coats-of-arms in the spandrels have been effaced. Though less carefully executed than the *Bliss Madonna*, the *Shaw Madonna* is also a work of notably high quality.

The reliefs are accepted as works of Luca della Robbia by Bode, Marquand, Schubring, and Planiscig. The *Bliss Madonna* was initially ascribed by Reymond (1897 (ii), p. 204) to Andrea della Robbia. This attribution was later (1904, p. 98n.) abandoned in favour of a direct ascription to Luca della Robbia ('L'admirable Madonne qui faisait partie de la collection Gavet, à Paris, peut-être considérée comme une variante du motif de la Madone de Gênes. C'est aussi une oeuvre de la propre main du maître').

The relief is finer and more expressive than the surviving versions of the Genoa and Impruneta *Madonnas*, to which it is superficially related. It is probable that the composition was evolved about 1460. A date ca. 1438-40 was initially advanced by Marquand (1894, p. 14), who later concurred in a dating ca. 1450 proposed by Bode (1905, p. 74, pl. 227).

41 Madonna and Child. Detroit Institute of Arts.
Plate 105
Enamelled terracotta: 51 × 37 cm.
Provenance: E. Simon, Berlin. Purchased by the Detroit Art Institute 1929.

The Virgin is shown frontally, with head inclined towards the Child. Her right hand rests on His waist and thigh and her left hand is placed on His head. The Child's left foot extends over a flat white base with receding sides. He wears a tunic which is decorated at the base with a gilt pattern. The edge of the Virgin's mantle and her cuffs are decorated with the same motif, and there are extensive traces of gilding on her girdle, on the hair of both figures and in the haloes. The composition is commonly described as the *Genoa Madonna*, and is also known from other versions. Three of these are:

(i) Vienna, Kunsthistorisches Museum. Enamelled terracotta: 51 × 37 cm. Coll. Gustav Benda, Vienna (Benda, 1932, p. 14, No. 60). Till 1904, when it was purchased for the Benda collection, it was in a Gothic tabernacle in the courtyard of the Casa Serra in Genoa (Vico delle Mele No. 20). An Alinari photograph made of the relief in Genoa (15001) shows a horizontal break through the waist of the Virgin and much local damage, including the protruding left foot of the Child. The Vienna relief differs from other versions of the composition in that a curl of hair appears on the Child's forehead and another lock or curl is caught up against the Virgin's left hand. The folds of the mantle to the left of the head are more elaborate than in the other examples and suggest a dating ca. 1500.

(ii) Berlin-Dahlem, Staatliche Museen (K.F.M., No. 2332). Enamelled terracotta: 52 × 37 cm. Coll.: Sir Charles Eastlake (sale London, 1894, bt. for Kaiser Friedrich Museum). The relief is broken horizontally and there are breaks in the veil over the Virgin's head and on her nose. Some traces of gilding.

(iii) Florence, Museo Nazionale. Enamelled terracotta: 51 × 37 cm. The relief was formerly in the convent of Santa Lucia in Florence and later (1884) in the Accademia. An old Brogi photograph (20863) shows it in a much damaged state, with wide breaks across the Virgin's face and on the level of her right wrist. The present, much restored condition is seen in a modern (1972) Alinari photograph (63033). Marquand (1914, pp. 155–6, No. 41) describes the relief as a 'duller reproduction' of the three other versions, to which it is in fact greatly inferior.

It is argued by Bode (1906) that all four versions of the relief were made from a single mould in Luca della Robbia's shop. This claim is repeated by Schottmüller (1933, pp. 25–26: 'wahrscheinlich aus derselben Form gepresst'), and seems to be correct. A letter addressed by Bode to the then owner of the Detroit relief, E. Simon (cited in Friedländer, 1929, I, p. 86), declares that 'die Ihrige die schönste ist,' and this view is repeated by him in print (1906, p. 29: 'Dazu ist kürzlich ein viertes Exemplar gekommen, das schönste von allen') and is also cited by Valentiner (1938, No. 33: 'Dr. Bode claimed to be the finest of the four'). J. Walther (1929, p. 35) wrongly describes it as 'the only one of the four to show gilding in the borders of the garments and the haloes.' The relief dates from 1450–5.

42 Madonna and Child with a Lily Plant. Hyde Collection, Glens Falls (N.Y.)   Plate 106
Enamelled terracotta: 45·5 × 38 cm.

The composition of this relief, which is known as the *Rovezzano Madonna*, seems to have enjoyed great popularity, and versions of it exist in Sant' Andrea at Rovezzano, in the Liechtenstein collection, Vaduz, the Hyde Collection, Glens Falls, and elsewhere. The reliefs are moulded not modelled, and there is therefore no original. Marquand (1914, p. 262, No. 111) concluded that the reliefs 'reflect only approximately Luca's style,' and considered the Rovezzano example 'in modelling and glaze ... perhaps the worst.' While the glaze on the Rovezzano relief is imperfect, it is one of the earliest and most authentic examples of the composition. Also conspicuously fine and certainly produced in Luca della Robbia's studio is the version from the Eduard Simon collection, Berlin, now at Glens Falls (*ibid.*, pp. 263–4, No. 113). In the variant in the Liechtenstein collection, the

Virgin's veil is replaced by a fillet. This change seems to have been made in the shop of Andrea della Robbia, to which a version with three flying angels, formerly in the Shaw collection, Boston (*ibid.*, pp. 264–5, No. 114), must be attributed.

43 Madonna and Child. Victoria & Albert Museum, London (4411–1858).   Plate 107
Enamelled terracotta: 44·5 × 38·1 cm.

The Virgin is shown seated on the ground in profile to the left. Accepted by Robinson (1862, pp. 57–58) as based on a model by Luca della Robbia, it is looked upon as a work of Luca by Bode (1905, pp. 75, 81, pl. 200B; 1902, pp. 172–3). A second version from the Von Beckerath collection was in the Kaiser Friedrich Museum in Berlin (No. 2939/Sch. 72), and was regarded by Marquand (1914, pp. 266–7) as superior to the present example. Other derivatives from the composition are known (*ibid.*, Nos. 117–20). Though rejected by Marquand, the composition certainly reflects a late work by Luca della Robbia of the same date and in the same style as the *Rovezzano Madonna* (Cat. No. 42). For a more detailed analysis see Pope-Hennessy (1964, i, pp. 120–1, No. 100).

44 Madonna and Child in a Niche. Victoria & Albert Museum, London (5788–1859).   Fig. 29
Unglazed terracotta: 63·5 × 30·5 cm.

Purchased in Florence. A second version of the relief, from Santa Verdiana, Florence, was formerly in the Von Beckerath collection and later at Schloss Nijenrode (sale Amsterdam, Mensing, 10 July 1923, No. 45). The frames of the two reliefs are closely related and appear to be original. The scalloped pattern in the niche is better preserved in the Beckerath relief. Initially ascribed by Robinson (1862, p. 20) to Donatello, the relief was attributed to Luca della Robbia by Marquand (1894, p. 7) on the basis of resemblances to the *Virgin and Child with six Angels*. In Marquand's monograph (1914, p. 219) the latter relief was wrongly dismissed as modern, and the present relief was omitted. The attribution to Luca is accepted by Bode (1905, p. 76, pl. 192a; 1902, pp. 180–1), with a dating about 1430, Schubring (1905, p. 85), Fabriczy (1909, p. 43, No. 151), Wulff (1917, p. 234), Maclagan/Longhurst (1932, i, pp. 28–29), Planiscig (1948, pp. 29–30) and Pope-Hennessy (1964, i, pp. 117–18, No. 97). The authorship of the relief is not contingent on that of the Fortnum medallion (Oxford) or the *Virgin and Child with six Angels*, and it is considerably later in date than Bode and Planiscig suggest. It can hardly have been produced before 1460 and may well have been made a decade later. The two known versions of the relief are moulded not modelled, with some surface working. They are not, like the *Virgin and Child with six Angels*, moulded from a bronze relief, but are closely analogous to the *Rovezzano Madonna* and other moulded reliefs from the last decade of Luca's life. They represent either an exceptional late work, which was intended for pigmentation not enamelling, or a relief designed for glazing of which no version in enamelled terracotta survives.

Fig. 24. Luca della Robbia: *Lunette* (Cat. No. 30). Galleria Nazionale delle Marche, Urbino

Fig. 25. Luca della Robbia: *Disassembled Elements of the Visitation Group* (Cat. No. 10). San Giovanni Fuorcivitas, Pistoia

Fig. 26. After Buggiano: *Madonna and Child*. San Donnino, Villamagna

Fig. 27. After Buggiano: *Madonna and Child*. Staatliche Museen, Berlin-Dahlem

Fig. 28. Luca della Robbia: *Madonna and Child in a Niche* (Cat. No. 40). Boston Museum of Fine Arts

Fig. 29. Luca della Robbia: *Madonna and Child in a Niche* (Cat. No. 44). Victoria & Albert Museum, London

Fig. 30. *The Chapel of the Cardinal of Portugal*. San Miniato al Monte, Florence

Fig. 31. *Damascened Ornament of Bronze Door* (cf. Plate 112). North Sacristy, Duomo, Florence

Fig. 32. After Luca della Robbia: *Drawing of the Federighi Monument*
(cf. Plate 72). Sepoltuario Baldovinetti, Biblioteca Riccardiana, Florence

Fig. 33. Michelozzo(?): *Head in the Frame of the Bronze Door* (cf. Plate 112). Duomo, Florence

Fig. 34. Maso di Bartolomeo(?): *Head in the Frame of the Bronze Door* (cf. Plate 112). Duomo, Florence

Fig. 35. Maso di Bartolomeo(?): *Head in the Frame of the Bronze Door* (cf. Plate 112). Duomo, Florence

Fig. 36. Maso di Bartolomeo(?): *David with the Head of Goliath* (Cat. No. 57). Metropolitan Museum of Art, New York

Fig. 37. Ghiberti: *Fruit*. Detail from jamb of First Bronze Door. Baptistry, Florence

Fig. 38. Ghiberti: *Fruit*. Detail from jamb of Second Bronze Door. Baptistry, Florence

Fig. 39. Unidentified Sculptor: *Madonna and Child* (Cat. No. 56). Santissima Annunziata, Florence

Fig. 40. Unidentified Sculptor: *Madonna and Child* (Cat. No. 61). Museo dell'Opera del Duomo, Florence

Fig. 41. Andrea della Robbia: *Madonna and Child* (Cat. No. 64). Parish church, Nynehead, Somerset

Fig. 42. Andrea della Robbia: *The Demidoff Madonna* (Cat. No. 65). Toledo Museum of Art, Toledo, Ohio

Fig. 43. Andrea della Robbia: *Madonna and Child with two Angels* (Cat. No. 66). Museo Nazionale, Florence

Fig. 44. Della Robbia Workshop: *The Santa Maria Nuova Madonna* (Cat. No. 67). Museo Nazionale, Florence

Fig. 45. Andrea della Robbia: *The Via dell' Agnolo Lunette* (Cat. No. 69). Museo Nazionale, Florence

Fig. 46. Andrea della Robbia: *The Frescobaldi Madonna* (Cat. No. 68). Formerly Kaiser Friedrich Museum, Berlin

Fig. 47. Unidentified Sculptor (Luca della Robbia ?): *Crucified Christ* (Cat. No. 55). Santa Maria in Campo, Florence

Fig. 48. Unidentified Sculptor: *Mirror Frame* (Cat. No. 59).
Bode Museum, Berlin (D.D.R.)

Fig. 49. Andrea della Robbia: *Stemma of the Arte della
Seta* (Cat. No. 70). Or San Michele, Florence

Fig. 50. Workshop of Andrea della Robbia: *Ceiling of the Martini Chapel* (Cat. No. 71). San Giobbe, Venice

Fig. 51. Andrea della Robbia: *Temperance* (Cat. No. 72). Musée de Cluny, Paris

Fig. 52. Andrea della Robbia: *Prudence* (Cat. No. 74). Metropolitan Museum of Art, New York

Fig. 53. Luca or Andrea della Robbia: *Justice* (Cat. No. 73). Musée de Cluny, Paris

Fig. 54. Unidentified Sculptor: *The Alessandri Madonna* (Cat. No. 85).
Bode Museum, Berlin (D.D.R.)

Fig. 55. Unidentified Sculptor: *God the Father with four Cherubim* (Cat. No. 84).
Art Institute of Chicago

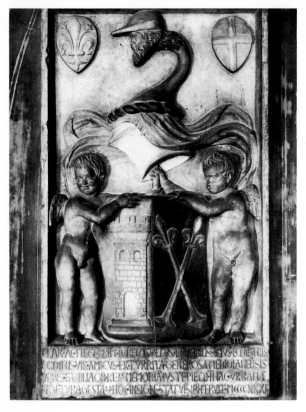

Fig. 56. Unidentified Sculptor: *Stemma of Amico della Torre* (Cat. No. 62). Museo Nazionale, Florence

Fig. 57. Della Robbia Workshop: *Stemma of Giovanni di Francesco Tornabuoni.* (Cat. No. 79). Palazzo Pretorio, San Giovanni Valdarno

Fig. 58. Della Robbia Workshop: *Stemma of Ruberto Leoni* (Cat. No. 81). Palazzo Pretorio, San Giovanni Valdarno

Fig. 59. Andrea della Robbia: *Stemma of the Della Stufa Family* (Cat. No. 82). Palazzo della Stufa, Florence

Fig. 60. Andrea della Robbia: *Bust of a Boy* (Cat. No. 76). Museo Nazionale, Florence

Fig. 61. Andrea della Robbia: *Relief Bust of a Youth* (Cat. No. 77). Bode Museum, Berlin (D.D.R.)

Fig. 62. Workshop of Bernardo Rossellino: *Bust of a Woman* (Cat. No. 78). Museo Nazionale, Florence

Fig. 63. Workshop of Luca della Robbia: *Angel* (Cat. No. 88). Musée Jacquemart-André, Paris

Fig. 64. After Luca della Robbia(?): *Madonna and Child with four Saints*
(Cat. No. 58). Louvre, Paris

Fig. 65. Unidentified Sculptor:
The Incredulity of Saint Thomas
(Cat. No. 86). Szepmüveszeti
Museum, Budapest

Fig. 66. Unidentified Sculptor:
Female Saint (Cat. No. 87).
Houston Museum of Fine Arts

45 Madonna and Child with six Angels.   Plate 94B

The composition is recorded in a number of examples in terracotta or stucco:

  (i) DETROIT, Institute of Arts. Coll.: Sir J. C. Robinson, London; Dreyfus, Paris. Repr. Valentiner, 1938, No. 35; Richardson.

  (ii) FULLERTON, Norton Simon Foundation. Coll.: Lady Eastlake (sale Christie's, 5 July 1894, No. 47, as Ghiberti, bt. Davis, £210); Charles Davis; Dr. Ludwig Mond; Violet Lady Melchett (sale Sotheby's, 18 June 1946, No. 122, bt. Lambert £160); Duveen, New York. The original state of the relief is shown in a plate in the Sotheby catalogue. After its acquisition by Duveen, some damaged areas were smoothed off in plaster, and the surface was covered with terracotta-coloured paint, giving the relief a wholly modern character.

  (iii) NEW YORK, Metropolitan Museum of Art. Coll.: Canessa; Pierpont Morgan, London and New York. Repr. Maclagan, 1913, pp. 38, 39, No. 18.

  (iv) PARIS, Louvre. Coll.: Campana. This example is rectangular, not circular, and measures 38 × 37 cm.

  (v) PARIS, Courajod Collection (formerly). Stated by Cavallucci and Molinier (1884, p. 281, under No. 473) to be superior to the version in the Louvre, and to be covered with bronze paint.

  (vi) ROME, Museo di Palazzo Venezia. From the Museo Industriale. Omitted by A. Santangelo, 1954.

  (vii) BERLIN, Kaiser Friedrich Museum (formerly). Coll.: Beckerath, Berlin. Gilded.

  (viii) LENINGRAD, Hermitage.

  (ix) AMSTERDAM, Lanz Collection (formerly).

The figurated areas of the reliefs are uniform in size (diameter approximately 33 cm.), and it is generally assumed, both by scholars who ascribe them to Luca della Robbia and by those who deny them to him, that they were moulded from a superior autograph original. There is no reason to follow Marquand in inferring from this fact that 'these plaques are modern,' though the surviving examples are unequal in quality and some of them may be of recent date. It has been argued that the lost original was in terracotta (Valentiner) and bronze (Bode; Schubring, 1905, p. 84). Luca's authorship is sustained by Bode (1885, pp. 184–5, and 1905, pp. 75, 76), Schubring, Venturi (vi, p. 555), and Valentiner, and denied by Reymond (1897 (ii), p. 127) and, after initial acceptance (1894, p. 6, Nos. 4–8), by Marquand (1914, pp. 229–31, Nos. 67–74). The analogies with authenticated works by Luca are too close to enable the lost original to be ascribed to any other hand. The figures of the Virgin and Child alone are reproduced, on a flat ground relieved by garlands, in the third quarter of the fifteenth century, in pigmented stucco reliefs in the Szepmüveszeti Museum, Budapest (Balogh, 1975, i, No. 56, pp. 63–64, ii, fig. 74) and in the Kunstgewerbe-museum at Leipzig. In a drawing after the design by a Pisanello follower in the Ambrosiana, Milan (F. 214 inf. 11) a number of details (e.g. the type of the Virgin and the angle of her head, the folds of her robe over and between the knees, and the heads of the outer angels to right and left) are modi-fied. If this drawing is accepted as a work of Pisanello, as it is by Degenhart/Schmitt (1960, pp. 84, 140 n. 37) but not by Fossi-Todorow (1966, p. 128, No. 183), it would be necessary to date the roundel before Pisanello's death in 1455. The composition is related by Bode to that of the Fortnum medallion (Cat. No. 22), and is assigned by him to the years 1428–30. The nearest point of reference for the drapery forms of the Virgin's cloak and for the clouds which support the feet and body of the Virgin occur in the Pazzi Chapel *Apostles* of the mid-fourteen-forties, and it is likely that the relief was made about this time.

46 Two Angels with Candlesticks. Musée Jacquemart-André, Paris (Inv. 1773).   Plates 108–111

(a) Angel with left leg extended and right knee drawn up, looking over the left shoulder and holding the base of a candlestick on the right thigh. Bronze (with traces of gilding): height 67·5 cm. (Gavoty, 1975, No. 21).

(b) Angel with right leg extended and left knee drawn up, looking over the right shoulder and holding the base of a candlestick on the left thigh. Bronze: height 57·5 cm. (*ibid.*, No. 22).

Provenance: Signol sale, Paris, 17–20 December 1866, No. 101; Piot sale, Paris, May 1890, No. 13 (bt. Madame Edouard André, 50,000 fr.).

The first reference to the presence of bronze *Angels* on the balustrade of Luca's Cantoria occurs in the second edition of the *Vite* of Vasari (Vasari-Milanesi, ii, p. 170): 'Sopra il cornicione, poi, di questo ornamento fece Luca due figure di metallo dorate; cioè due Angeli nudi, condotti molto pulita-mente, siccome è tutta l'opera, che fu tenuta cosa rara.' The *Angels* are again mentioned by Baldinucci (i, p. 453): '. . . e sono di sua mano sopra il cornicione di quest'ornamento due angeli di metallo dorati,' and are mentioned for the last time in 1677 by Bocchi-Cinelli (p. 59): 'I due Angeli di bronzo indorati furono condotti da Luca con tanta pulitezza, e con tanta leggiadria che con parole isprimere non si potrebbe.' They seem to have remained in position on the Cantoria until the upper section was dismantled in 1688. In the catalogue of the Piot sale the present *Angels* were identified by Bonnaffé (1890, No. 13) as those described by Baldinucci on the Cantoria of Luca della Robbia.

   In the Signol collection, however, the two *Angels* were ascribed to Donatello, and an attribution to Donatello is endorsed by all earlier students save Milanesi (1887, p. 29). It is supported *inter alios* by Bode (1879, p. 100), Schubring (1907, pp. xxxiii, 55), A. Venturi (vi, p. 282–3), Kauffmann (1936, p. 118), Lisner (1960, p. 20), and Gavoty (1968, pp. 353–9, and 1975, Nos. 21, 22). It is suggested by Schu-bring (*loc. cit.*) that the *Angels* were made for the Cantoria of Donatello, and Corwegh (1909) presents a reconstruction in which the present *Angels* are seated on the Donatello Cantoria. As noted by Hadeln (1909, pp. 382–5), this results from a misconception as to the original placing of the two Cantorias. It has also been argued (Bertaux, 1910, p. 210, and 1913, pp. 416–17; Kauffmann, 1936, p. 118) that the *Angels* were made by Donatello in Padua in connection with the altar in the Santo, and by Seymour (1968, p. 235 n. 24) that they are by a North Italian Donatellesque sculptor. It is claimed by Gavoty (1968) that the bronzes are by two different hands, one, that looking over the left shoulder, by Donatello, and the other an 'imitation tardive' by a member of Donatello's shop. A mistaken attempt is made by Gavoty to link the *Angels* to a document published by Poggi (1909, No. 1315) recording a payment to Donatello of 23 February 1446, of eight hundred and ninety-six florins '. . . computando omne magisterium materiam tam marmi quam bronzi et omne compensum in predictis spiritellis et duas testas. . . .' It was later (1975) suggested by the same student that a document (Poggi, 1909, No. 1412) recording a payment to Michelozzo in 1451 for two *spiritelli* referred to works in gilded terracotta made by Michelozzo for Luca's Cantoria, which might have disintegrated and would have been replaced by the present *Angels* removed from their original position on the Cantoria of Donatello. The view that these or any other *Angels* stood on the parapet of Donatello's Singing Gallery is wholly conjectural, and it is rightly observed by Janson (1957, ii, p. 118) that 'there is no testimony linking such figures with Donatello's Cantoria.'

The attribution of the *Angels* to Luca della Robbia was revived by Lanyi (1939), and is accepted by Planiscig (1940, pp. 14–15, 30–31, and 1948, p. 64), Janson (*loc. cit.*), and Pope-Hennessy (1958, pp. 292–3; 1971, pp. 272–4). If the two *Angels* are those which stood on Luca della Robbia's Cantoria, we should expect them to show some affinity to the latest of the Cantoria reliefs, the *Choral Dancers*, and it is indeed in this scene that compelling analogies for the two figures occur. Though it is argued by Gavoty that the bronzes are by two different hands, there is nothing in the *Angels* that would compel us to attribute the models to two different artists.

Corwegh (*op. cit.*, p. 2) in his fallacious reconstruction of the Donatello Cantoria shows the Angel looking over the left shoulder on the left of the parapet and the second Angel on the right. Since the candelabra, of which the bases only are preserved, were designed to provide light for and in the Cantoria, we are bound to assume that the Angel looking over the left shoulder stood to the right and the second Angel to the left, looking outwards. It is argued by Lanyi that 'der Beschreibung Vasaris folgend, muss man sich die beiden Putten über der Mitte der beiden seitlichen Reliefs am Gesims sitzend vorstellen.' It is conceivable that they stood in this position, but there is nothing in Vasari's description to make such a conclusion mandatory.

On 31 December 1451, a payment for two 'spiritelli' for one of the two organ lofts was made to Michelozzo (Poggi, 1909, No. 1412): 'Michelozio Bartholomei, intagliatori, l. CXXXX pro magisterio auri et pictura et aliis rebus pro duobus spiritellis qui de novo fiunt pro retinendo super uno ex pergamis organorum.' The reference to pigmentation precludes the possibility that this document refers to two figures in bronze. In the absence of further documents it is impossible to tell whether the *Angels* were modelled, cast and chased by Luca della Robbia (who in 1445 contracted with Michelozzo for the bronze door of the North Sacristy of the Cathedral), or whether they were modelled by Luca and cast

and chased by Michelozzo or Maso di Bartolomeo (who from 1446 was also involved in the commission for the bronze door).

47 Sacristy Door. Duomo, Florence.

Col. Plate XXXI, Plates 112–121

Bronze: 410 × 200 cm., figurated panels 53 × 53 cm.

The documentation of the bronze door of the North Sacristy is very full and of extreme complexity. The basic documentation by Poggi (Nos. 1484–90, 1514–1608) was destined for the second part of his *Duomo di Firenze*, and is unpublished. Dr. Margaret Haynes has generously made available the accurate transcriptions of the documents from her thesis on the North Sacristy of the Cathedral, and a number of the documents have been checked and retranscribed on my behalf by Dr. Gino Corti. These are supplemented by Mather (1918, pp. 197–202), whose transcriptions include a substantial quota of mistakes. An element of confusion has been introduced into discussion of the history of the door in a mistaken article by V. Herzner (1976 (ii)), which is referred to below.

On 28 February 1437 it was decided to commission bronze doors for the two Sacristies of the Cathedral from Donatello (Poggi, No. 1484). The contract for the doors dates from 27 March (Poggi, No. 1488) and stipulated that the first door was to be completed by April 1439, and the second by April 1441. The two doors were to be paid for at unequal rates, 1,100 florins for the first and 900 florins for the second. The projected doors must have been designed by Donatello in the course of 1436, since a model for them was available at the beginning of the following year. Preliminary work on the first door seems to have been undertaken prior to March 1437, when a sum of 250 florins (representing a substantial portion of the total cost of the first door) had already been paid to Donatello.

Herzner (*loc. cit.*) concludes that the iconography of the doors was determined by Donatello, but there is no evidence whatever to show that this was so. On 26 April 1437, a stonemason, Nanni di Miniato, who had, at an early stage, worked on the Cantoria of Luca della Robbia, was detached to undertake at Donatello's expense unspecified work in connection with the doors. On 30 June 1439, a payment records the purchase of bronze 'per fare le porte della sagrestia che dee fare Donatello' (Poggi, No. 1514). There is no further reference to Donatello's bronze doors. In the course of 1443 he left Florence for Padua, where he was engaged, in January 1444, on the bronze Crucifix for the Santo. Before his departure he seems to have worked primarily in the Old Sacristy of San Lorenzo, where he executed two bronze doors and a number of stucco reliefs. On 21 June 1445, the contract for one of the two doors was cancelled (Poggi, No. 1551). Donatello, however, retained the contract for the second door, that of the South Sacristy, beneath his own Cantoria, and as late as 1459 is referred to as 'intagliatore e chondottore de le porte de la sagrestia.'

On 1 July 1445, it was decided by the Operaii that a new contract should be placed for the door of the North Sacristy with Michelozzo, who was to execute it 'secundum designum factum' (Poggi, No. 1553). It is argued by Herzner that this model was that made by Donatello, and that the present door is therefore based on Donatello's design. This case rests on a misunderstanding of the procedure in the Opera del Duomo, and on the assumption that any new design must have been made in the nine-day period between these meetings. There can be little doubt (in terms of the procedure of the Opera) that the decision to annul one contract and embark upon another was taken long before it was formally ratified, and that the new model by Michelozzo was prepared in the first half of 1445. The decision of 1 July 1445 was accompanied by the proviso that if, by the end of the following August, Luca della Robbia accepted certain conditions laid down by the Operaii, the commission should be allocated jointly to both sculptors. If Luca did not accept within the stipulated term, the door would be contracted to Michelozzo alone. On 24 December 1445 (Poggi, No. 1555B), it was agreed in principle that the door should be executed by Michelozzo, Luca della Robbia and Maso di Bartolomeo, and on 28 February 1446 (Poggi, No. 1560A inaccurately transcribed by Marquand, 1914, p. 197), the door was formally commissioned. The text of the commission reads as follows:

Florence, Archivio dell'Opera del Duomo, I.1.4 (Allogagioni, 1438–1475)

[1445/(s.c. 1446) February 28]

fol. 51r–52r:

Locatio facta Michelozo et aliis
pro porta prime sacrestie

In Dei nomine amen. Anno Domini ab eius incarnatione MCCCCXLquinto, inditione ottava, die vigesima ottava mensis februarii. Actum in audientia Operariorum infrascriptorum, presentibus testibus ad infrascripta omnia vocatis habitis et rogatis [*canc.*: Michelozio Bartolomei] Bartolomeo Simonis Folchi, Ristoro Ugolini Ristori et Iohanne Francisci domini Iohannis Zati. Nobiles et prudentes viri Anfrione Laurentii Pieri Lenzi et Matheus Antonii de Albertis, Operarii Opere cathedralis ecclesie S. Marie del Fiore civitatis Florentie, simul in audientia et loco eorum solite congregationis pro ipsorum offitio exercendo, intellecto qualiter Consules Artis Lane proxime preteriti, intellecta locatione facta Donato Nicolai die XXVII Martii 1437 de duabus portis pro duabus sacrestiis maioris ecclesie florentine, et intellecto qualiter dictus Donatus dictas portas non fecit, et iustis de causis dicti domini Consules unam de dictis duabus portis removerunt a dicto Donato et concesserunt licentiam prefatis Operariis dictam portam prime sacrestie locandi cui et quibus et pro eo pretio et prout sibi videbitur. Qui quidem Operarii visa dicta licentia, omni modo etc. locaverunt et concesserunt ad faciendum unam portam bronzi pro prima sacrestia Michelozio Bartolomei, populi S. Marci, et

Luce Simonis Marci della Robbia et

Maso Bartolomei,

sociis intagliatoribus, dictam portam modo et forma inferius descripta, prout apparet per scriptam factam manu dicti Michelozi, cuius tenor de verbo ad verbum talis est videlicet.

Gli Operai aluoghano e danno a ffare a

Michelozo una porta di bronzo per la prima sagrestia di S.
Lucha et Maria del Fiore, di quella altezza e largheza che
Maso s'aspetta e richiede alla forma già data alla detta

sagrestia, e di quella forma, modo et ornamenti che mostra uno modello al presente è apresso al detto Michelozo et compagni di questa forma, el quale modello debba stare nella audientia di detti Operai.

La detta porta di due pezi, et in ciaschuno pezo cinque quadri ornati di cornici dappiè, infra le quali cornici debbano i detti maestri fare fregi piani, lavorati alla domaschina, d'oro et d'ariento o d'ariento solo, come parrà a detti Operai. Et in ciaschun chanto de' detti quadri uno compassino, entrovi una testa di profeta, delle quali teste ne va dodici in ciaschun lato. Et in ciaschuno de' detti quadri tre fighure, cioè nel mezo di ciaschuno quadro uno tabernacolo di mezzo rilievo, lavorato alla domaschina, come i detti fregi, entrovi una figura a ssedere, di mezo rilievo, nominata chosì: che ne'primi due quadri di sopra e nel primo da man ritta la figura di Nostra Donna col Figliuolo in braccio, nell'altro la fighura di Santo Giovanni Batista, et in ciaschuno degli altri quadri, che restano otto, la fighura de' Vangelisti e de' doctori della Chiesa, e ciaschuno con due angioletti ritti da llato, fatti di mezo rilievo. E ne' rovescio di detta porta, i medesimi quadri che da ritto, riciuti di cornici come di sopra e come mostra detto modello, sanza alchuna fighura o altri ornamenti.

Et promettono detti Michelozo, Lucha et Maso tutte le dette chose fare e perfettamente conducere a uso di buoni huomini, infra'l tempo et termine di tre anni.

E i detti Operai debbano prestare al detto Michelozo, Lucha et Maso per supplimento del detto lavorìo inanzi, fiorini dugentocinquanta. E dipoi per aumento d'essa, ciaschuno mese, fiorini venticinque, et prout apparet in dicta scritta.

Et dicti Operarii debeant predictis, pro eorum magisterio et labore, florenos auri millecentum.

Et quia in dicto modello sunt additi certa ornamenta alla domaschina, seminati circha campum et in tabernaculis dictarum figurarum, que res non sunt conprense superius, pro qua agiunta abere [*sic*] debent illud plus quod declarabitur per offitium Operariorum pro tempore existentium. Et tenentur dicti Operarii dare dictis Michelozo, Lucha et Maso, pro faciendo predicta, materiam opportunam, videlicet bronzum, argentum et aurum, pertinentem dicte porte.

Que omnia promiserunt dicti Michelozus, Luchas et Masus conductores predicti, actendere et observare, sub pena florenorum auri mille.

Accounts for the purchase of bronze for the door run from 24 December 1445 (Poggi, No. 1555A), through 1446. There are records for the transfer of 'lib. 2000 dj bronzo da botegha dj Lorenzo dj Bartolucio ci prestò l'Arte de' Merchatanti' (Poggi, No. 1556), and of visits paid by Maso di Bartolomeo to Lucca, Pisa, Pistoia and Arezzo for the procurement of bronze (Poggi, No. 1565A). The two frames of the door were cast at the end of 1446. This is deducible from (i) a payment of 27 February 1447, 'pro operibus missis in lavando spazaturam bronzi telariorum sacrestie noviter gettatorum' (Poggi, No. 1566A), (ii) a payment of the same date to 'Michelozzo Bartholomei et sociis, conductoribus della porta della sagrestia l. LXIIII fp. pro parte solutione et pro solvendo pluribus personis qui eos adiuverunt in faciendo gettum telariorum dicte porte et carbonibus' (Poggi, No. 1566C), (iii) the fact that on 28 February 1447, Michelozzo was empowered to use, for the grille surrounding the altar of the chapel of St. Stephen, 'libre cinquecento cinquantasej che avanzò del gietto delle porte della sagrestia' (Poggi, No. 1099), and (iv) a small payment on 12 December 1446 to 'Giovanni d'Andrea di Maso, per vino dette loro quandro gitorono le porte' (Corti, from Arch. dell'Opera del Duomo, VIII 1.9, Quaderno di Cassa 1446, c. 32).

After the casting no further action seems to have been taken till 9 April 1461, when a contract was entered into with Giovanni di Bartolomeo, the brother of Maso di Bartolomeo (who had died in 1457), for the cleaning of the frames of the two wings of the door. This contract reads as follows:

Florence, Archivio dell'Opera del Duomo, i.1.4 (Allogagioni, 1438–1475)

fol. 72r–v: Yhs

In Dei nomine amen. Anno Domini ab eius salutifera incarnatione millesimo quadringentesimo sexageximo primo, inditione nona, die nona mensis Aprilis. Actum in Opera et loco et audientia Operariorum, et presentibus testibus ad infrascripta omnia vocatis habitis et rogatis Laurentio Lapi Iohannis Nicholini, Iohanne Francisci domini Iohannis de Zatis, Bernardo Mathei del Borra et Maso Iacobi Suchielli.

Egli è vera chosa che

Michelozo di Bartolomeo et   intagliatori, avendo avertenza
Lucha di Simone di Marcho della Robbia
a una allogagione a lloro fatta pe'gli Operai di S. Maria del Fiore, insieme con Maso di Bartolomeo ancora intagliatore oggi morto, insino al'anno MCCCC quarantacinque et del mese di febraio, [di]

una porta della prima sagrestia, cioè da due lati, con più ornamenti e lavori, come nella allogagione rogata per mano di me notaio infrascritto chiaramente appariscie.

Onde oggi questo dì detto, Michelozo et Lucha sopradetti, con protestatione nel principio mezo et fine del presente contracto apposta, ch'eglino non intendono per questo atto [sic=altro] contracto essere più o meno oblighati che erano inanzi al presente contracto, sono contenti et de consentimento et volontà et in presentia de'nobili huomini

Giovanni di Domenicho Giugni et   Operai di detta Opera a
Bartolomeo d'Agnolo Ciai   tutte le infrascripte cose
consentienti, aluoghano a Giovanni di Bartolomeo intagliatore, presente et conducente per se e con quella compagnia a llui piacesse, a

nettare detti telai, cioè detti due lati già gittati, e commettere e battitoi di detta porta et ristorare se alchuno manchamento fusse a detti telai, et que'lavorare in tutte le loro parti dal lato ritto e dal lato rovescio e da tutte le sue parti bene e diligentemente a uso di buono maestro. E tutte le predette chose fare intorno a detti telai che di nicistà sarà intorno a quelli, sì et in tal modo che niuna chosa manchi se non rizarli alla detta sagrestia.

E sono d'acordo detto Giovanni abbia per sua faticha et maestero et intero pagamento d'ogni chosa delle sopradette, fiorini dugento correnti, e quali gli Operai ànno a paghare a detto Giovanni o a chi lui dicesse, tempo per tempo, chome lavor[e]rà, e ànnosi a porre al conto della condotta tolta delle dette porti [sic] per detto Michelozo, Lucha et Maso.

E più s'à a ddare per l'Opera a detto Giovanni, a spesa d'Opera, quella quantità del bronzo manchasse per avergli a ristorare in alchuna parte, e simile cera, se bisogno n'avesse.

E debbe avere detto Giovanni per potere mettersi in punto di masseritie a tale lavoro appartenenti et opportune, fiorini dieci.

E debbe detto Giovanni lavorare o fare lavorare dette porte nell'Opera, e l'Opera adattarlo di luogho ydoneo.

E detto Giovanni dar forniti detti telai come detto, per di qui a mesi sedici, e quali sedici mesi cominciano adì primo di maggio futuro MCCCC LXI.

E decti Operari parendo loro, possino detto tempo prolungare per insino a mesi quatro in una volta o ppiù.

Giovanni di Bartolomeo was assisted in this work (Poggi, No. 1578) by Silvestro di Guglielmo and Simone del Bianco. Interim payments to Giovanni di Bartolomeo run from 27 June 1461 to 30 June 1463 (Poggi, Nos. 1579–1586A). On 17 December 1463 (Poggi, No. 1588), it was formally accepted that this work was complete ('intexo quelle avere facte e nette in perfetione sechondo l'aloghazione allui fatta per raporto di Lucha di Simone della Robbia, detto Lucha in presentia di detta Opera quelle accettò per ben fatte et in perfetione'). According to a document of 16 May 1464 (Poggi, No. 1590), a further sum of 100 lire was reported by Luca to be due to Giovanni di Bartolomeo for ten bronze panels for the back of the door ('per manifattura et maestero di dieci quadri fatti et posti dallato a dette porte dove ànno a stare le storie dinanzi').

On 4 August 1464, a new contract was prepared for the completion of the doors. Two closely similar versions of this contract survive in the Archivio dell'Opera di S. Maria del Fiore: (i) I.1.4 (Allogagioni, 1438–1475, f. 73v., 74r.), (ii) II.4.19 (Bastardello di deliberazioni e stanziamenti, 1462–1463, c. 72r.–73r.). A key passage in these documents is the statement that Luca had received no earlier payment for work on the bronze door. In (i) this reads: 'e detto Lucha non ebbe alchuna chosa, come appare pe' libri del proveditore di detta Opera,' and in (ii) it appears in the form: 'e detto Lucha non avere avere [sic] auto danaio, come apare pe' libri di di [sic] detta Opera.' The text of (i) reads as follows:

Florence, Archivio dell'Opera del Duomo. I.1.4 (Allogagioni, 1438–1475)

fol. 73v–74r: MCCCCLXIIII die IIII mensis Aghusti
Nobiles viri

Iacopo d'Ugholino Mazzinghi et   citadini honorevoli fiorentini e Operai dell'Opera di
Andrea di Giovanni della Stufa
S. Maria del Fiore della città di Firenze, insieme raghunati nel luogho della loro usata residentia per loro uficio esercitare, observate etc., intexo che nel'anno 1444 per loro anticessori e Operai che a quel tempo furono, fu alloghato a

Michelozzo di Bartholomeo intagliatore e   una porta di due
Lucha di Bartholomeo [sic] della Robbia e   pezzi e con più
Maso di Bartholomeo detto Masaccio   hornamenti, patti
e modi come nella alloghagione si contiene, per pregio e nome di preg⟨i⟩o di fiorini 1100 d'oro, come apare al libro allogha-gioni segnato I, c. 51. E intexo dette porte essere state circha ad anni 20 che mai non vi s'è su lavorato né fatto alchuna cosa. E dipoi intexo che nel'anno 1461 adì 9 d'Aprile di detto anno, fu alloghato pe'gli Operai, con licentia di detto Lucha, a Giovanni di Bartholomeo intagliatore, fratello di detto Maso, a neptare e apezzare e acconc⟨i⟩are detti telai e porti [sic] per pregio e nome di pregio di fiorini 200 d'oro, come appare in questo, c. 72. E intexo detti telai e porti [sic] esser poste da

llato e per al presente non vi si fare alchuna chosa. Volendo che detti porti abbino compimento, e intexo detto Maso di Bartholomeo essere morto e defunto più anni sono, e intexo anchora detto Michelozzo non esser più in queste parti e non ci avere a essere a questi tenpi, e qui non essere se nnone detto Lucha. E intexo che detti telai e porti che in quel tenpo che furono alloghati a detto Lucha e Michelozzo e Maso, loro avere auti circha di fiorini 400, e quali gli ebbono detto Michelozzo e Maso, e detto Lucha nonn ebbe alchuna chosa, come appare pe'libri del proveditore di detta Opera, e fiorini 200 dati a detto Giovanni di Bartholomeo per detta nettatura, che fanno in tutto la somma di fiorini secento in circha. E volendo i detti Operai che detti telai e porti abbian qualche volta efetto e conducergli a perfetione, intexo la volontà di detto Lucha et vedendo detto Maso morto e detto Michelozzo ase[m]ptato. Non vedendo alchuno modo sia migliore né in beneficio di detta Opera, e volendo anchora che detti telai e porti abbino efetto, bisongna acrescere alla alloghagione prima, ché altrimenti non si potrebbe fare nulla e sarebbe sanza ingnuno efetto e in danno della detta Opera. E veduto e considerato quello che fu da vedere e considerare, messo, fatto e celebrato solepne e segreto scruptinio a fave nere e bianche e optenuto il partito secondo la forma degli ordini: delibero-rono e alloghorono a detto Lucha di Bartholomeo [sic], presente e conducente in suo nome prop⟨r⟩io, a fare compiere e storiare dette porti e ongni altra e qualunque cosa come nella prima alloghagione si contiene, che l'abbino piena perfetione, per pregio di fiorini septecento, de'quali gli si debbe fare e paghamenti secondo lavorerà e in quel modo e forma parrà agli Operai che ne'tenpi saranno, dandogli l'Opera el bronzo e ottone per gettatura, come apare a detta alloghagione. El qual Lucha ratifichò.

ibidem, fol. 79r–v:
Alloghagione a Lucha della Robbia
(Another redaction of the above convention, with very little variants in wording.)

On 18 May 1465 (Settesoldi, Quaderni di Cassa, No. 41, 1464/65, 1 sem., c. 61: Mather, 1919, No. 15), Luca della Robbia was supplied with 'due pezi d'asse d'abeto secho per fare 3 modegli delle storie delle portj.' A month later, on 27 June (Mather, *loc. cit.*), a payment is made to 'Pasquino di Mateo intagliatore ... per parte di storie net(t)e per deto lucha.' This is the only evidence for the involvement in the project of Pasquino da Montepulciano. A further payment of uncertain date (assigned by Mather, *op. cit.*, No. 16, to the year 1464, but probably of 1465) was made in respect of 'lib. mille di charbonj per gittare le prime due storie'. Payments to Luca continue through 1466 and 1467. In the latter year, on 6 October, there occurs a reference (*ibid.*, No. 25) to 'ottone chonperato per gittare due istorie della porta della prima sagrestia,' and on 29 October, bronze was purchased from the sculptor Verrocchio. The record of this transaction is as follows:

Florence, Archivio dell'Opera del Duomo, VIII.1.46 (Quaderno di cassa, 1467)
fol. 46 verso:
Ottone chonperato per gittare due istorie della porta della prima sagrestia de' dare ...

E adì detto [29 October 1467] lire venticinque e soldi cinque e danari nove, dati ad Andrea del Verochio per libre 72 oncie 3 di bronzo, a soldi sette la libra, istimato per Martino ottonaio, avemo da lui per gittare l'ultime due istorie della porta della sagrestia che fa Lucha della Robbia, chome apare al giornale rosso, segnato M, c. [*lacuna*]................f.-L.25 s.5 d.9
Other small interim payments were made to Luca della Robbia in the course of 1468, 1469, 1470, 1471 and 1472. Numerous as these are, they do not form a basis for calculating the overall sum paid to Luca in connection with work on the door. A final payment of 130 florins (Poggi, No. 1605) was made on 27 June 1475 ('Prefati operarii ... intexo una alloghagione facta a Lucha di Bartholomeo della Robbia ... di certe porte e veduto quelle compiute non secondo il modello allui dato, questo presente dì rimasono d'accordo con detto Lucha che per insino questo dì Lucha resti avere f. CXXX di sugello, non obstante che per detta alloghagione dimostra più quantita, e fatto detto paghamento sia finita detta opera da ongni maggiore somma e così rinuntiò detto Lucha a ongni magg(i)ore somma.') A payment (Poggi, No. 1603) made on 23 December 1474 to Domenico di Domenico Pagni da Prato for models for the hinges suggests that the doors were set in place in the first half of 1475. The reliefs on the door represent (*left wing, top to bottom*) the Virgin and Child, Saint John the Evangelist, Saint Luke, Saint Ambrose and Saint Gregory the Great, (*right wing, top to bottom*) Saint John the Baptist, Saint Matthew, Saint Mark, Saint Jerome, and Saint Augustine. The twenty-four heads in quadrilobe medallions cannot be individually identified.

48 Madonna and Child with two Angels between Saints James and Blaise. Pescia, Palazzo Vescovile.

Plates 124, 125

Enamelled terracotta: 127 × 163 cm.

The altarpiece is accompanied by an inscription indicating that it was erected in the Chapel of the Palazzo Vescovile in 1847 (Di preziosi frantumi che per incuria de' ciechi nell'arte/giacquero negletti molti anni/questo egregio lavoro/di Luca della Robbia/restituirono al debito onore/di largizione di Pietro Forti/Vescovo disignato di Pescia/e le cure di Domenico Martini/Economo alla sede vacante/3 Aprile 1847). At the base of the pilasters are the *stemmi* (*left*) of the Ospitalieri di San Jacopo at Altopascio, and (*right*) of the Capponi family. The altarpiece is mistakenly stated by Burlamacchi (p. 71) to have been formerly in the church of San Pietro at Pescia, and by Marquand (1909, p. 329), on the basis of information supplied by an official of the Duomo at Pescia, to have been formerly in the church of San Rocco. The earliest description of the altarpiece occurs in Ansaldi (1772, p. 37), when it was in the church of San Biagio: 'Verso, dissi, la metà della Piazza vi è la piccola Chiesa di S. Biagio, dove l'Altare è ornato d'un Bassorilievo di terra cotta vetriata di Lucca della Robbia, con la B[eata] V[ergine], il S. Bambino, e li Santi Biagio, e Jacopo Apostolo.' The church or oratory was destroyed in 1784, and the altarpiece was then transferred to the private chapel in the Episcopal Palace at Pescia (for this see Ansaldi, 1816, p. 24: 'che preservato nella distruzione di quest' Oratorio seguita nel 1784 stà di presente collocato in una Cappellina privata del Palazzo Vescovile'). Pietro Forti, Bishop of Pescia, by whom the altarpiece was re-erected, was elected Bishop on 12 April 1847, and made his solemn entry into the town on 29 April of that year (see Nucci, pp. 41–53). According to Lami (xvi, p. 1340), San Biagio at Pescia was a dependency of San Jacopo at Altopascio ('E da sapersi inoltre, che la Chiesa di S. Biagio di Pescia era ne' tempi antichi de' Frati dello Spedale di S. Jacopo dell'Altopascio, la di cui Tavola dell'Altare è di basso rilievo, opera di Luca della Robbia, come scrive Francesco Galeotti'), to which the friars from Altopascio were transferred during the winter months. Lami also supplies the information (*op. cit.*, p. 1360) that San Biagio bore the Capponi arms on its façade. Marquand (*op. cit.*, pp. 332–3; and 1914, pp. 211–13, No. 59) infers from the presence of the Capponi arms that the altarpiece may date from after 1472, when the *giuspatronato* of Altopascio and of San Pietro in Campo was granted by Sixtus IV to the Capponi family. There was, however, an earlier Capponi connection with the order of the Ospitalieri, and Repetti (i, pp. 76–77) notes that 'quattro individui di questa nobile famiglia tennero consecutivamente dal 1446 in poi il regime dell'ospizio suddetto.' The principal affinities of the altarpiece are with Luca's work at Impruneta (mid-fourteen-sixties), and though the palette is less varied and less strong than in such characteristic works of the decade as the ceiling of the Chapel of the Cardinal of Portugal and the cupola in the portico of the Pazzi Chapel, the linear treatment of the forms would be difficult to reconcile with a dating before 1465–70.

49 The Adoration of the Magi. Victoria & Albert Museum, London (651–1865). Plate 122
Enamelled terracotta: 40·8 × 61·6 cm.
Provenance: Soulages collection, Toulouse.

When in the Soulages collection, the relief was reproduced (in reverse), along with a companion scene of the *Nativity*, by Du Sommerard (v, p. 237; atlas, vi, ch. xvi, pl. II). It was catalogued by Robinson (1856, p. 132, No. 438) as 'either from the hand of Luca, or an early work of Andrea', and subsequently (1862, p. 57, No. 438) as ascribed to Luca della Robbia. An attribution to Luca della Robbia is preserved by Cavallucci/Molinier (1884, p. 264, No. 373) and by Pope-Hennessy (1964, i, pp. 115–16, No. 95). It is given to the Della Robbia studio by Cruttwell (1902, p. 345), by Marquand (1922, ii, p. 73, No. 191) and by Maclagan/Longhurst (1932, i, pp. 52–53). The composition recurs in predellas by Andrea della Robbia in the Museo Civico at Montepulciano (1484) and San Bernardino at L'Aquila and, with additional figures, in Santa Maria degli Angeli at Assisi. The present relief is manifestly superior to these three examples, in that the sense of interval throughout the frieze-like composition is more classical, and the spatial content of the scene is more firmly defined. These considerations suggest that the present relief is a late work of Luca della Robbia, from which the other panels depend. The types find a parallel in the Pescia altarpiece, and it cannot be precluded that the relief formed part of a disassembled predella for this work. The companion

relief of the *Nativity* from the Soulages collection is untraced, but is likewise more closely related to Luca than to Andrea della Robbia. It also was copied by Andrea della Robbia in the three predellas noted above and in a single panel in the Metropolitan Museum. The third panel of the predella was presumably an *Annunciation*.

50 The Virgin adoring the Child. Parish church, Nynehead, Somerset. Plate 123
Enamelled terracotta: 70 × 60 cm.

Presented to the church in 1833 by the Rev. John Sanford, who was acquiring paintings in Florence from 1815 (see Nicolson, 1955). The relief was published by Marquand (1912(i)), as a work of Luca della Robbia. As noted by Marquand, the pose of the Virgin is midway between pure profile and three-quarter face. Subsequently (1914, pp. 51–52, No. 10) Marquand dated the relief before 1440, and observed that it formed 'an interesting parallel to Fra Filippo Lippi's adorations of the decade 1430–1440.' The pictorial parallels for this beautiful relief are considerably later in date, and the first related composition by Lippi that is exactly datable occurs in a drawing of 1457 (Florence, Archivio di Stato; Berenson, 1938, No. 1385). Compositions of the type seem to have been popular among painters in Lippi's circle, especially in panels by the Master of the Castello Nativity, about the middle of the century. Though the two main figures are glazed in white, with some gold enrichment in the hair of the Virgin and elsewhere, and the background is blue, the yellow and bluish-green straw beneath the Child, the dark-green lily stalks and the blue-grey base are polychromatic. Marquand rightly notes that the pistils and the stamens of the two lily plants have parallels in the lilies in the border of the San Pierino lunette and in the *stemma* of the Arte dei Medici e Speziali on Or San Michele. The relief seems to date from soon after 1465.

51 The Adoration of the Shepherds. Victoria & Albert Museum, London (7752–1862). Plate 126
Enamelled terracotta: diameter 139·7 cm.

Purchased in Florence from the Palazzo de' Mozzi, where a number of reliefs made by Andrea della Robbia for the chapel of the Compagnia di San Frediano were also preserved (for these see Milanesi, in Vasari-Milanesi, iii, p. 181n.). The relief is given to Luca della Robbia by Marquand (1894, pp. 5–6), who subsequently (1922, ii, pp. 48–50, No. 146) reascribed it to the workshop of Andrea. It is regarded as a work of Luca by Bode (1905, p. 78, pl. 193b; 1902, pp. 183–6), Schubring (1905, pp. 82, 86–87), Ybl (1930, i, p. 281), Maclagan/Longhurst (1932, i, p. 29) and Pope-Hennessy (1964, i, pp. 116–17, No. 96). Cavallucci/Molinier (1884, p. 267, No. 386) give it to Andrea, and Reymond (1897 (ii), pp. 127–9) and Cruttwell (1902, pp. 200, 242) ascribe it to Giovanni della Robbia. Bode, noting the indebtedness of the relief to Ghiberti, dated it about 1430. The connection is, however, with the Porta del Paradiso, not with the first bronze door, and the relief must therefore date from after 1452. In practice it is, as noted by Schubring, probably a work of 1460–70, or of an even later time. This late dating is confirmed by the border, which is moulded not modelled, and is of a type frequently encountered in the fourteen-seventies in the work of Andrea della Robbia.

52 The Virgin adoring the Child. Philadelphia Museum
of Art.   Plate 127
Enamelled terracotta: diameter 169 cm.
Provenance: Palazzo Alberti, Florence (unconfirmed); Bardini, Florence; Edmond Foulc, Paris.

The relief, which is concave, shows the Virgin turned to the right. Behind her are four flying angels, one of whom carries a cartellino inscribed: *Gloria in excelsis Deo*. Gold enrichment appears on the Virgin's head and dress and gold rays on the background. The roundel is contained in a circular fruit frame from the shop of Andrea della Robbia, which was stated by Foulc to have been purchased from another source. The relief is accepted as a work of Luca della Robbia by Bode (1900, p. 23; 1902, pp. 170–1, and elsewhere), Marquand (1894, p. 24; 1914, pp. 170–1, No. 51), Schubring (1905, p. 87) and Venturi (vi, p. 575). It is rejected by Reymond (1897 (ii), pp. 159–60), and Cruttwell (1902, p. 351) ascribes it to the Della Robbia atelier. The composition seems to date from the last decade of Luca's life. While it reflects the influence of Andrea della Robbia, it was evidently made before the Brizi *Adoration of the Child* at La Verna, where a similar group appears in reverse, and is indeed one of the sources from which Andrea's altarpiece depends. The Brizi altarpiece has beneath it the inscription: VERBVM CARO FATTV. EST. DEVIRGINE.M, and the subject of Luca's relief is likewise the Incarnation.

53 Relief Bust of a Lady. Museo Nazionale, Florence
(No. 73).   Plate 128
Enamelled terracotta: diameter 45 cm.

The relief, which has no provenance, entered the Bargello before 1898, when it was assigned by Supino (1898, p. 451, No. 73) to the Fabbrica dei Della Robbia. It is listed by Cruttwell (1902, p. 339, No. 67) among works by the Della Robbia atelier. Ascribed initially by Marquand (1914, pp. 234–5, No. 77) to the manner of Luca della Robbia, it was later republished by him as Andrea della Robbia (1922, i, pp. 34–35, No. 22). The attribution to Luca della Robbia is due to Bode (1900, p. 32; 1902, p. 188; 1905, p. 79, pl. 228) and is sustained by Planiscig (1940, p. 25; 1948, pp. 56–57, 73). It is ascribed to Andrea della Robbia by Baldini (1965, pl. 31). A second relief with the head of a Lady in the Louvre (Collection Thiers, No. 38. Diameter with foliated border 56 cm.) is variously described by Marquand (1914, pp. 235–6, No. 78) as a school copy and (1922, i, pp. 34–35) an inferior variant of the Bargello relief. The angle of the head differs from that of the present relief, the hair is differently dressed, the necklace is omitted, and the dress is fastened below the

throat with a jewelled clasp. In the Bargello relief the female figure wears a white chemise, which is visible above the edge of her green dress, and a pale-blue over-dress. Round her throat is a white necklace with a pendant pearl. Her head is covered by a kerchief decorated above and at the sides with a double row of pearls, with a jewel on the crown, and her hair is spread out in two tresses at the sides. The head, hair and jewellery are white, and the eyebrows, eyelashes and pupils are violet. The background is deep-blue.

The relief is modelled with great sensibility. There is no equivalent in the work of Andrea della Robbia for the bold and confident modelling of the blue surcoat, with its padded shoulders, for the delicately rendered edge of the chemise above the dress, for the indentation on the throat beneath the pendant pearl, for the modelling of the lips, eyes and eyebrows, or for the treatment of the hair beneath the kerchief. The bust finds a natural point of reference in Luca's *Prudence* and *Temperance* in the Chapel of the Cardinal of Portugal (Col. Plates XV, XVII), and is likely to have been modelled and glazed by Luca about 1465. The type is reminiscent of portrait busts by Desiderio da Settignano, and the relief represents the nearest point of approximation between Desiderio and Luca. While it is generally assumed that the head was designed as a portrait, it is also possible that it represents an ideal type of female beauty, as in the mirror frame from the workshop of Neroccio in the Victoria & Albert Museum. If this were so, it would form the prototype of the related head in the Louvre, where the modelling of the features and the loose descriptive rendering of the dress are characteristic of Andrea della Robbia.

54 Bust of a Lady. Museo Nazionale, Florence.
Col. Plate XXXII
Enamelled terracotta: height 40·5 cm.

The bust was transferred to the Bargello in 1921 from the Museo di San Marco, and does not therefore figure in the Supino catalogue. It was published by Toesca (1921, pp. 149, 158) as a product of the workshop of Luca della Robbia or an early work of Andrea della Robbia made when his style was not yet fully formed. A direct ascription to Luca della Robbia was accepted by Marquand (1928, pp. 150–1), who noted, correctly, that the eyes were 'coloured in Luca's habitual manner.' The bust is ignored by Planiscig, and is given by Baldini (1965, pl. 30) to Andrea della Robbia. As noted by Toesca in his perceptive analysis, the polychromy differs from that of Andrea della Robbia, and the yellow hair and the treatment of the face have close parallels in the *stemma* of the Arte dei Medici e Speziali on Or San Michele. The blue cloak, with its green lining revealed on the shoulders, and the edge of the mauve dress beneath are modelled with great confidence, and admit only of an attribution to Luca della Robbia ca. 1465–70. There is a firing crack on the right side of the hair and some damage to the surface of the cloak on the right shoulder. The blue diadem seems to confirm Toesca's conclusion that we have here to do with a reliquary bust; this is corroborated by a hole in the head for the attachment of a halo.

Doubtful Works (Cat. Nos. 55-58)

55 Crucified Christ. Santa Maria in Campo, Florence.

Fig. 47

Pigmented wood.

The Crucifix, which is listed by Paatz (iii, p. 172) as Floren-tine school, fifteenth century, is ascribed by M. Lisner (1970, pp. 60–61, 70) to Luca della Robbia. As noted by Lisner, the figure is covered with overpaint, and the forward locks of hair framing the face are broken. The fingers of the left hand have been made-up, and the Cross is new. For these reasons no firm attribution can be arrived at. The musculature and the structure of the cheeks are reminiscent of the Crucifix by Brunelleschi in Santa Maria Novella, but the lips are parted and the eyes are depicted as half-open. The type of Christ is compared by Lisner to that of the Christ on the Peretola tabernacle, and the figure is tentatively dated in the late twenties or early thirties. Pope-Hennessy (1976, p. 79) comments that 'the attribution to Luca, albeit at a rather later date than is implied in Dr. Lisner's comparisons, is far from impossible.' There is no evidence that Luca della Robbia practised as a sculptor in wood. Since, however, Donatello and Desiderio da Settignano both produced wooden sculptures, the possibility cannot be ruled out. It is known, moreover, that on 24 January 1491, Andrea della Robbia received a commission from the Opera del Duomo for a wooden figure of Christ with movable limbs for adoration on Good Friday, which was completed by 29 April of the same year (for this see Fabriczy, 1906).

56 Madonna and Child. Chiostrino dei Voti, Santissima Annunziata, Florence.

Fig. 39

Marble.

The relief was discovered by Lensi (p. 361) 'murata nella nicchia di un andito buio a capo di scala del convento.' It is presumed, probably correctly, to be identical with a relief ascribed to Michelozzo in the first edition of Vasari (Vasari-Ricci, ii, p. 63: '... et la Nostra donna di mezzo rilievo sopra il desco delle candele') and ascribed in the second edition to Pagno di Lapo Portigiani (Vasari-Milanesi, ii, p. 447: 'Fece anco sopra il banco, dove i Frati vendono candele, una mezza Nostra Donna di marmo, di mezzo rilievo, col Figliuolo in braccio, a grande quanto il naturale, molto divota'). The relief is again described by Bocchi (1592, p. 33) and Richa (viii, p. 45). It was installed in its present position in 1922–3. The identification is accepted by Paatz (I, pp. 93, 123, 150n. 171), who regards the relief as a work of Michelozzo of ca. 1450. This dating, like the two attributions of Vasari to Michelozzo and Pagno di Lapo Portigiani, is based on the assumption that the relief was executed concurrently with the Chapel of the Santissima Annunziata, which was designed by Michelozzo and executed by Pagno di Lapo, is dated 1448 and was dedicated in 1452. The scapular, worn over the Virgin's veil and held in place by her left hand, is omitted in two stucco variants of the composition (for one of these see Schubring, 1907, p. 130). Casalini (1959; 1964; and 1978, pp. 58–60)

associates the relief with the cult of the Madonna of the Snow.

The relief is ascribed to Luca della Robbia by Brunetti (1962), apparently with a relatively early dating, on the strength of comparison with the Jacquemart-André and San Pierino Madonnas. The connection between the present relief and these two autograph enamelled terracotta reliefs is generic. A point of reference for the style of the marble relief is provided by a better preserved and somewhat earlier marble relief by Michelozzo of the Madonna and Child on an inlaid ground in the Museo Nazionale, and Caplow (I, pp. 480–2) accordingly attributes it to Michelozzo or the Michelozzo shop, noting that the surface had been smoothed down or recut, probably in the nineteenth century. Gavoty (1975, No. 27) accepts the attribution of the relief to Luca della Robbia, as does Avery (1976, pp. 14–19), who suggests that it 'may date from the 1430's or even before.' He comments that the relief 'might tempt a hasty observer to regard the piece as a forgery.' The relief in its present reworked state is not at-tributable either to Michelozzo or to Luca della Robbia.

57 David. Metropolitan Museum of Art, New York.

Fig. 36

Bronze: height 33 cm.
Provenance: Chigi-Saracini, Siena; Piccolomini della Triana, Siena; Godefroi Brauer, Nice; Jules S. Bache, New York.

Exhibited at the Albright Art Gallery, Buffalo (Washburn, 1937, No. 125) as a work of Luca della Robbia, it was pub-lished by Wehle (1943, p. 286) as a work of Luca, and is now ascribed to a follower of Bartolomeo Bellano. The fullest photographic coverage of the statuette is supplied in Duveen (1944, No. 26), where it is described by G. Swarzenski as 'the only bronze by Luca della Robbia, besides the doors in the Duomo, Florence, and, specifically, the only known example of the master's conception of statuary in bronze. This out-standing and in every sense important work is linked with Luca only by modern criticism, and I cannot but say that, from the beginning and again and again this attribution seems to me one of the most ingenious, inspiring and substantially convincing revelations deriving from artistic intuition and thorough study.' In the same volume the bronze is ascribed by Langton Douglas to Luca della Robbia 'at some date before 1445.' Weihrauch (1967, pp. 79, 81) considers it a copy by Luca after Donatello, and dates it to the mid-1430's.

The model, which exists in a second version in the Linsky collection, New York, is distinct from the two known bronze statuettes of *David* by Bellano, of which the first, in the Philadelphia Museum of Art, may have been produced in Florence about 1466, and the second, in gilt bronze, in the Metropolitan Museum of Art, dates from later in Bellano's career. It is also distinct from a number of bronze statuettes of *David* sometimes ascribed to Bellano, of which the prime examples, all from a single Paduan workshop, are in The Frick Collection, New York, the National Gallery of Art,

Washington (Widener Collection), the Museo Correr, Venice, the Metropolitan Museum of Art (Untermeyer Collection), and the Victoria & Albert Museum. The present bronze is Florentine, and was made under the influence of the bronze *David* of Donatello, probably about 1455–65. It is a work of considerable distinction, and the possibility cannot be ruled out that it was modelled by Luca della Robbia and cast in the shop of Maso or Giovanni di Bartolomeo. Analogies for it in the work of Luca or in the heads on the bronze door of the Cathedral executed by other hands are not, however, such as to make this attribution mandatory. The parallels in Luca della Robbia for the carefully rendered folds of tunic are not in works in bronze but in modelled terracotta sculptures on a larger scale.

58 Madonna and Child with Saints John the Baptist, Francis, Peter and Paul. Musée du Louvre, Paris. (No. 753).   Fig. 64
Terracotta: width 37 cm.

The relief comes from the Campana collection, and entered the Louvre in 1862. A second version is recorded in the Szepmüveszeti Museum, Budapest. It is accepted as a work by or after Luca della Robbia by Bode (1902, pp. 182–3) and Schubring (1905, pp. 79, 84) and is ignored by Marquand. The Child, with left leg extended across the Virgin's lap, is closely related to that in the *Madonna and Child with six Angels,* and the type of the Virgin recalls that in the reproductive *Madonna with the Standing Child* in the Musée Jacquemart-André (Cat. No. 23). It is possible that the relief is a record of a lost relief of Luca della Robbia of about 1440. The evenness of the background and the platform on which the figures stand constitute arguments against the view that the relief was moulded from a bronze original, and we are bound to assume that, if the relief is original and is not a pastiche of somewhat later date, it reproduces a low relief in marble like that beneath the tabernacle of Buggiano in Sant'Ambrogio (for this see U. Schlegel, 1962). The height cited in the Louvre catalogue (51 cm.) includes the more recent upper section.

Works not by Luca della Robbia (Cat. Nos. 59–89)

59 Mirror Frame. Bode Museum, Berlin (D.D.R.) Fig. 48
White enamelled terracotta: diameter 61 cm., diameter of central aperture 17 cm.
Provenance: Boy, Versailles; Figdor, Vienna; purchased for the Kaiser Friedrich Museum, Berlin, 1935 (Inv. 7261).

The frame comprises eighteen heads copied or adapted from heads in the Cantoria reliefs of Luca della Robbia. The sources, analysed by Lanyi in a lecture at the Warburg Institute in London in 1940 of which notes were made by the late Professor Otto Kurz, are as follows:

1. Head from the extreme right of *Tambourine Players.*
2. Head of child in centre foreground of *Cymbal Players.*
3. Second head from right of *Tambourine Players.*
4. Head from extreme right of *Choral Dancers.*
5. Free adaptation, not a copy.
6. Head from extreme right of *Cymbal Players.*
7. Adapted from head to right of centre of *Tambourine Players.*
8. Head from upper left corner of *Drummers.*
9. Head of dancing boy in foreground of *Drummers.*
10. Adapted from head in centre of *Tambourine Players.*
11. Head to left of centre in *Tambourine Players.*
12. Head of dancing boy to right of centre of *Drummers.*
13. Second head from left of *Tambourine Players.*
14. Head from centre of *Drummers.*
15. Head to right of centre of *Choral Dancers.*
16. Third head from left of *Players on the Cithara.*
17. Third head from left of *Players on the Organ and Harp.*
18. Fourth head from left of *Players on the Organ and Harp.*

The five hands supporting the central wreath have no precedent in the Cantoria, neither is there a parallel for the tight-fitting garlands round the necks of five of the children. The angle of some of the heads is changed (e.g. No. 1 appears in full-face on the Mirror, but in the marble is turned slightly to the left) and with others the hair style is modified.

From the time of its first publication, the Mirror Frame has been regarded as a preliminary model by Luca della Robbia for the Cantoria reliefs. It is so considered by Bode (1905, p. 177), Doering-Dachau (1913, p. 22), Marquand (1914, pp. 25–27, No. 3: 'There can be little doubt that it is not the work of a copyist, but a sketch dashed off by the artist himself at a time when the faces of the boys and girls of the Cantoria were still fresh in mind'), Schottmüller (1921, p. xxxix), Falke (1929, p. 331; 1930, iv, No. 129), Planiscig (1940, pp. 15, 31; 1948, pp. 23, 65), and Negri Arnoldi (1972, p. 646). The attribution is rejected by Foratti (1919, p. 24: 'antica imitazione, eseguita forse nella prima metà del Cinquecento') and Lanyi (lecture cited), who concluded that 'the idea of copying details from a popular work of art, and using them for the decoration of an *objet d'art*, is typical of only one period in the history of art, the nineteenth century.' A recent publication of the Staatliche Museen (Berlin, 1964, p. 9) restates the traditional view that 'die Engelsköpfe sind so nahe verwandt den singenden Knaben auf Luca della Robbias berühmter Sängertribüne im Dom zu Florenz, dass man die rein dekorative Arbeit wohl für das eigenhändige Werk dieses Meisters halten kann.'

The possibility that the Mirror Frame is a work of Luca della Robbia made prior to or concurrently with the Cantoria reliefs can be ruled out. After the Cantoria was installed in 1438, its reliefs were imperfectly visible and were in effect inaccessible. Foratti's suggestion that the present roundel dates from the sixteenth century is difficult to sustain on this account. The Cantoria was not dismantled until 1688, when the five supports and the four reliefs between them were left in position and the six reliefs from the upper register were removed. It is possible that the frame dates from the late seventeenth or early eighteenth century, and the coarse, porous glazing has something in common with that of the enamelled terracotta roundels of the *Stations of the Cross* designed by Ciro Ferri in 1685 for SS. Quirico e Lucia at Ambrogiana (Montelupo). Conti in his life of Massimiliano Soldani (printed by Lankheit, 1962, pp. 240–3) records that Soldani in his youth took refuge at Galatrona, where 'ammirasi in quella Pieve di S. Gio. Batista un singolare e pregiatissimo battistero tutto storiato di piccole figure, un Ciborio, ed altri bellissimi lavori di terracotta della Scuola del celebre Luca della Robbia. ... Quivi pertanto il nostro giovane Massimiliano trovava tutto il suo Pascolo e tutta l'occupazione in disegnar e ricavare i modelli di dette Figurine, e formarne ancora di propria invenzione, con ottimo Gusto.' The commissioning of a tabernacle and paliotto by Cosimo III for Impruneta (1698, 1714) may also have directed the attention of Florentine baroque sculptors to Luca della Robbia's work. The relation of the heads in the frame to the surrounding moulding has something in common with that of, e.g., the gilt bronze roundel of *The Presentation of the Veil to S. Maria Maddalena de' Pazzi* in Santa Maria Maddalena de' Pazzi, Florence (1685–6), and the relation of the heads to one another may be compared with those of the Angels in Foggini's relief of *The Glorification of S. Andrea Corsini* in the Carmine (1677–83). A firm dating for the relief could be arrived at only on the basis of a thermoluminescence test.

It cannot be assumed that the relief was necessarily a mirror frame. It has a generic relationship to a number of quattrocento mirror frames, of which examples are in the Bibliothèque Nationale, Paris (marble, ascribed to Mino da Fiesole), the former Lanz collection, Amsterdam (cartapesta), the Victoria & Albert Museum (cartapesta after Neroccio; majolica; wood), and the Musée de Cluny. In these, however, the imagery, generally in the form of a female head, is related to the purpose the mirror was designed to serve. No such relationship exists in the present relief, and the two hands supporting the wreath at the base suggest that it may have been designed as a form of reliquary or for some other religious purpose.

60 Trumpeters. Victoria & Albert Museum, London (7609–1861).
Stucco: 54·3 × 54·9 cm.

The relief was catalogued in the Galleria Rinuccini (1845, p. 9, No. 57) as a 'modello pel basso-rilievo dell'organo di S. M. del Fiore.' It was subsequently accepted by Migliarini (1858, p. 41, tav. xlviii), Robinson (1862, pp. 53–54), Cavallucci/Molinier (1884, p. 370, No. 264), Cruttwell (1902, p. 52) and Maclagan/Longhurst (1932, i, pp. 29–30) as a sketch model by Luca della Robbia for the related relief on the Cantoria. It was condemned by Venturi (vi, p. 578n.) as a forgery, and is listed by Marquand (1914, pp. 225–26, No. 63) as an early stucco reproduction, and by Pope-Hennessy (1964, i,

pp. 119–20, No. 99) as a cast moulded from a free reduction of the marble relief, probably made before the dismantling of the Cantoria in 1688. The surface is damaged and repaired, and those areas in which the figures differ from the marble are extensively made up.

61 Madonna and Child. Museo dell'Opera del Duomo, Florence.
Fig. 40
Marble: 70 × 62 cm.

The relief may be identical with a *Madonna* 'nell'opera di Santa Maria del Fiore dove stanno gli operai' given by Vasari (Vasari-Milanesi, ii, p. 447) to Pagno di Lapo Portigiani. It was generally ascribed to Pagno di Lapo (Bode, 1905, p. 45, pl. 163; Fabriczy, 1903, p. 119; and other scholars) until the 'comedy of errors brought about by Vasari's spurious reasoning' was analysed by Janson (1942), who ascribed it to the young Agostino di Duccio. The attributions to Pagno di Lapo and Agostino di Duccio are rejected in a sound account by Brunetti (in Becherucci/Brunetti, pp. 282–3, No. 144). The ascription to Agostino di Duccio is certainly and that to Pagno di Lapo Portigiani probably incorrect. A dating proposed by Janson ca. 1435–40 is, however, very plausible. Galassi (1949, pp. 138, 253) notes 'certi allacciamenti con Luca della Robbia' and Janson regards the relief as carved under Luca della Robbia's strong influence, noting that its somewhat hesitant technique 'has its closest parallels in certain parts of the Cantoria of Luca della Robbia.' The closest connection is with the *Choral Dancers*, where the tendency towards the flattening of forms evident in the Child in this relief recurs and where the handling of the drapery is generally similar. It is not impossible that the sculptor of this relief worked on the final panel of the Cantoria. Brunetti suggests that 'forse non sarebbe infondato di studiarlo anche in rapporto colla formazione di Antonio Rossellino.' It is suggested elsewhere (p. 229 above) that the sculptor who carved the *Choral Dancers* from Luca's model may later have been associated with the Rossellino shop.

62 Stemma of Amico della Torre. Museo Nazionale, Florence.
Fig. 56
Marble (with traces of pigmentation).

The relief shows the arms of Amico della Torre, Podesta of Florence, (on the shield left a tower, right two sceptres set diagonally and crowned with fleur-de-lys, supported by two putti, surmounted by a helmet with a crest in the form of a male head in profile) and is inscribed: CLARVS(VS).AC. INTEGERRIM(VS).IVRE. CONSVLTVS.ET.NOBILISSIMVS EQVESTRI ORDINIS.VIR.AMICVS EX TVRRITA GENE ROSA MEDIOLANENSSIS VRBIS FAMILIE.B. RE(RVM). MEMORIAM.IVSTI.PIEG(HE) S(V) HAC VRBANA PRAE TVRAGESTA(RVM).HOC.INSIGNE STATV.SIBI.MERVIT. MCCCCXXXI. Above (*left*) is the lily of Florence and (*right*) the Croce del Popolo. It is argued by C. Avery (1976, pp. 19–23) that the relief is a work of Luca della Robbia executed immediately prior to the Cantoria. This case rests on resemblances between (i) the supporting putti and the figure on the left of the *Players on the Organ, Harp, and Lute* on the Cantoria and (ii) between the profile on the crest and the head of the right figure in the relief of *Philosophy* on the Campanile. The most impressive feature of the *stemma* is the linear handling of the crest. The resemblances between the putti and the children on the Cantoria are unspecific, and the figures are too nerveless and too little tactile to admit of a direct ascription to Luca della Robbia.

63 Mourning Virgin; St. John the Evangelist.
Santissima Annunziata, Florence.
Terracotta: height 165 cm.

The two figures, which flank an earlier Crucifix and are not fully in the round, are in the Villani Chapel in Santissima Annunziata, where they are first documented in 1644. They are implausibly ascribed to Luca della Robbia by Casalini (1978, pp. 11-60), with a conjectural dating of ca. 1430-50.

64 Madonna and Child. Parish church, Nynehead, Somerset.   Fig. 41
Enamelled terracotta: 75 × 45 cm.

Presented to the church in 1833 by the Rev. John Sanford, who had acquired it in Italy. The relief was published by Marquand (1912) as a work by Luca della Robbia of about 1450: 'Here we have a fragment of a lunette composition, from which the lateral angels and the basal clouds have been omitted.' There is no evidence that the *Madonna*, which is modelled and glazed in one with its blue ground, at any time formed part of a lunette. Two years later Marquand (1914, pp. 53-54, No. 11) advanced the dating of the relief to before 1440, on account of its affinities to the *Madonna* in the Musée Jacquemart-André (Cat. No. 23) and to the San Pierino lunette (Cat. No. 32). He noted, correctly, traces of gilding in the hair, of greyish blue in the irises and violet in the eyebrows and lashes, and the presence of a grey-blue base. The contention that this is an early work of Luca della Robbia cannot be seriously entertained. The Verrocchiesque type of the Child and the flat modelling leave little doubt that we have here to do with a work of Andrea della Robbia of about 1465. The relief is exceptional in that the figures have no haloes. It has been cut at the top to conform to the Gothic niche in which it was placed.

65 The Demidoff Madonna. Toledo Museum of Art.
Fig. 42
Enamelled terracotta: 73 × 48 cm.
Provenance: Marchese Carlo Viviani della Robbia, Florence (till February 1879); Prince Demidoff, Florence (sale 15 March 1880, No. 376); Duveen, New York.

The relief is accepted as a work of Luca della Robbia by Reymond (1897 (ii), pp. 109-10), Marquand (1894, p. 21; 1914, pp. 55-56, No. 12: 'may be assigned to the late thirties or early forties'), Bode (1900, p. 19; 1902, p. 162: 'etwa in den Anfang der vierziger Jahre zu setzen'; 1905, p. 73, pl. 243),

Schubring (1905, p. 81), Valentiner (No. 31: 'belongs . . . to the earliest glazed terracottas of Luca, of about 1440'), and Planiscig (1948, pp. 16, 63). Between its appearance in the San Donato sale and its re-emergence in the United States, the relief was not available for study, and it was not known to Reymond, Marquand and Cruttwell in the original. Cruttwell (1902, p. 134) none the less concludes that 'there is a Verrocchiesque feeling about the Child both in form and attitude, which suggests the idea that the relief is of comparatively late date, it may be by Giovanni himself when working most carefully, possibly assisted by Andrea.' The observation that the Child is Verrocchiesque is well founded, and the types of the Virgin and Child, the two arms posed flat across the relief plane, and the clouds beneath are characteristic of Andrea della Robbia. The relief is among Andrea's most impressive works, and dates from about 1465-70.

66 Madonna and Child with two Angels. Museo Nazionale, Florence (No. 27).   Fig. 43
Enamelled terracotta: diameter 100 cm.

The relief is wrongly stated by Marquand (1914, pp. 71-72, No. 17) to have come 'from the monastery of the Cappuccini,' and is described on this account as the Cappuccini Tondo. It is recorded by Paatz (iv, pp. 458-62), perhaps following Marquand, in the cloister of the Capuchin convent of Sant' Onofrio delle Cappuccine. The premises of Sant' Onofrio were modernised in 1720-4, and in 1726 were taken over by the Cappuccine, who save for a six year period between 1808 and 1814 remained there till the convent was suppressed. Supino (1898, p. 447, No. 48) describes a Della Robbia tondo transferred to the Museo Nazionale from the suppressed convent on 5 April 1867, but this is not identical with the present tondo, which Supino also catalogues but without a provenance (*op. cit.*, p. 442, No. 27). The relief shows the Virgin in half-length, above a base of clouds. The standing Child, naked and in full-length, is contained within her silhouette; He holds an apple in His extended left hand, and sucks the index finger of His right hand. To left and right are adoring angels with hands clasped in prayer, floating on clouds. The four haloes are yellow. The relief is glazed in five sections (main figures and cloud beneath, left angel and background, right angel and background, two sections of background beneath). The white frame, in six sections, is composed of alternating bunches of white roses, white field flowers and marigolds, tied with blue ribbon. Since the nineteenth century, the attribution of the tondo has been in dispute. Reymond (1897 (ii), p. 166 ff.) gives the relief and frame to Andrea della Robbia, as does Cruttwell (1902, p. 178), who appears to date it about 1489. The contrary case is stated by Bode (1889, p. 6; 1900, p. 18; 1902, pp. 159-60; 1905, p. 72, pl. 220), who regards the relief as a work of Luca della Robbia of the date of the San Pierino lunette, and the frame as a later product of the Della Robbia workshop. Hauptman (pp. 141-3) dates the relief ca. 1455. Marquand (*loc. cit.*) observes that 'the adoring angels are not so fine as those in Luca's lunettes, and the yellow haloes coloured by some assistant do not add to their beauty. However, in attitude, in type, in relative size, they are Luca's not Andrea's. . . . If we could eliminate these angels, with their yellow haloes and the crudely executed frame, critics would find little difficulty in admitting this charming Madonna to be the handiwork of Luca himself.' The relief is a characteristic early work by Andrea della Robbia. The cartoon of the Child, with the left arm extended across the Virgin's body and a finger of the right hand in His mouth, depends from Luca della Robbia's *Madonna of the Apple* in Berlin, but the flatter, less sophisticated posing of the figure has no parallel in Luca's work. The modelling of the Virgin's veil recalls that in the *Demidoff Madonna* at Toledo, but the type of the Child's head is close to Luca, and the relief is likely to date from shortly before the Via dell'Agnolo lunette of 1470/71. There is no reason to suppose that the frame is not integral with the relief.

67 The Santa Maria Nuova Madonna. Museo Nazionale, Florence (No. 88).   Fig. 44
Enamelled terracotta: 63 × 50 cm.

The relief is contained in its original gilt wood tabernacle. It shows the Virgin in full-face with head inclined slightly to her left, supporting the Child on her left hand and with her right hand pressed against the Child's right arm. The Child's left hand holds her little finger, and His right hand grasps her thumb. He wears a robe and a tunic with short sleeves terminating below the shoulder and an open neck, held in by a girdle. With the exception of the eyes, the figures are white. Both have white haloes, that of the Child depressed as though foreshortened. The blue background is covered with an applied design in gold, perhaps stencilled, composed of five-petalled flowers in circles separated by a cross-motif of four leaves. The background decoration has been removed by cleaning to the left of the Virgin's veil, to the right of her halo and above the shoulder of the Child. The figures now show no trace of surface gilding, but it is likely that gilded decoration was removed from the robes and haloes at the same time. The relief was transferred in 1900 from the Galleria di Santa Maria Nuova to the Uffizi, and was subsequently (1903) moved to the Museo Nazionale. The Galleria di Santa Maria Nuova (for which see Paatz, iv, pp. 31–64, and E. Ridolfi) resulted from edicts of the Grand-Duke Pietro Leopoldo of 1773 and of the Grand-Duke Leopold II of 1825 that works of art from suppressed convents in Florence should be put on public exhibition. After forty years of delay, the Gallery was opened in 1865. It contained two enamelled terracotta *Madonna* reliefs from the Della Robbia shop ('altri due di cosimil soggetto in terra invetriata della scuola dei Della Robbia'—Ridolfi, p. 22), of which the present relief was transferred to the Uffizi about 1900, and thence about 1903 to the Museo Nazionale. It does not appear in Supino's Bargello catalogue of 1898, but is presumably identical with a *Madonna* in a tabernacle from Santa Maria Nuova listed by Marrai (1907, p. 78) as 'depositato . . . nel Museo Nazionale.' There is no evidence of its original provenance. The relief is ignored by Reymond and Cruttwell, but is accepted as a work of Luca della Robbia by Bode (1900, p. 19; 1902, p. 161: 'ein

früheres Werk, um 1440'), Marquand (1914, pp. 119–20, No. 31: 'transitional between the Madonna of the Apple and the Genoese Madonna, now in the Benda collection, Vienna'), Planiscig (1948, pp. 48–49, 71) and Baldini (No. 21). Though the decoration of the ground recalls that of the frame of Luca's *Bliss Madonna* in the Metropolitan Museum of Art, New York, and the type of the Virgin depends from that of the *Madonna of the Apple* in the Bargello, an attribution to Luca is untenable on account first of the slack, flat modelling, and second of the type of the Child, which has no equivalent in authenticated works. The relief is distinct from the group of works which are ascribable to Andrea della Robbia, and is either by an unknown member of the studio or a very early work by Giovanni della Robbia, whose style is anticipated in the curly hair of the Child.

68 The Frescobaldi Madonna. Formerly Kaiser Friedrich Museum, Berlin (Inv. 2180/Sch. 71).   Fig. 46
Enamelled terracotta: 86 × 59 cm.
Provenance: Frescobaldi, Florence; Bardini, Florence; bt. for Kaiser Friedrich Museum, 1893.

The relief, which was destroyed in 1945, was fired in two pieces, and is described as showing traces of gilding on the hair, dress and clouds. It is accepted as a work of Luca della Robbia by Bode (1894, p. xliv; 1905, p. 224, p. 75), Wulff (1917, p. 238), Schottmüller (1933, p. 25), Cruttwell (1902, pp. 121–2) and Planiscig (1948, p. 72, No. 110). An element of controversy was introduced by Reymond (1897 (ii), pp. 120–3), who dismissed the relief as an 'oeuvre d'imitation.' Reymond's objections, e.g. to the fact that the Virgin is shown without shoes, were in part frivolous, but the relief is in a number of respects uncharacteristic of Luca della Robbia, and is likely to be an early work by Andrea della Robbia of about 1465. It finds its closest point of reference in the *St. Thomas* in the Pazzi Chapel. Both Marquand (1914, pp. 109–10, No. 26) and Schottmüller (*loc. cit.*) compare the relief with Luca della Robbia's *Madonna in a Rose-Garden* and with the panel of the Virgin and Child on the bronze door of the North Sacristy. Seated *Madonnas* in enamelled terracotta were undoubtedly made in the second half of the fifteenth century for private devotional purposes, and one is listed in 1492 in the Palazzo Medici in the apartments of Giuliano de' Medici (E. Müntz, 1888, p. 85): 'Uno colmo di tabernacolo de legname con piu ornamenti d'oro, alto br. 4½, largo br. 2⅔, dentrovi una Nostra Donna a sedere col bambino in collo, di mezzo rilievo et invetriato, f. 30.'

69 The Via dell'Agnolo Lunette. Museo Nazionale, Florence.   Fig. 45
Enamelled terracotta: 160 × 222 cm.

The relief shows the Virgin and Child with two Angels holding long-necked vases filled with lilies. The four figures are enamelled in white with coloured eyes. The Child is clothed, and stands on a ledge of cloud at the base of the relief holding a vertical scroll inscribed EGO SVM LVX MVNDI.

His right arm is raised in benediction, and He looks out in the same direction as the Virgin, to the left. The heads of the two angels are turned towards the spectator. There is some damage in the forward plane of the relief, notably to the right hand of the Child and the nose of the angel on the right, and local loss of glaze elsewhere. In the border, which shows alternating groups of white roses and white lilies with yellow stamens, some of the forward leaves are yellow and some of the rear leaves blue; this is due to technical miscalculation.

The lunette is described by Vasari (Vasari-Milanesi, ii, p. 175) as a work of Luca della Robbia: 'E sopra una porta d'una chiesina vicina a San Pier Maggiore, in un mezzo tondo, un' altra Madonna, ed alcuni Angeli che sono tenuti bellissimi.' Other references to the relief occur in Baldinucci (i, p. 454: 'Un'altra della Vergine con Gesù bambino, ed altre figure, è sopra la porta di una stanza che serve al presente per iscuola de' cherici di San Pier Maggiore, il qual luogo io trovo che fosse già il monastero delle monache, ovvero eremite, di San Giovanni Laterano') and Richa (i, p. 139: 'E facendomi dal luogo del Convento di esse, dirò, che questo era dove oggi si fa la scuola de' Cherici di S. Pier Maggiore, rimasa essendo sulla porta antica una bella Immagine di Maria di terra cotta, lavoro di Luca della Robbia'). The reference in all three cases is to the Convent of the Santucce, on the corner of Via dell'Agnolo and the present Via Verdi. After the convent was secularised, the lunette remained in place over the entrance to the house of Avvocato Tantini at 93 Via dell'Agnolo, till it was transferred in 1904 to the Bargello. The lunette of the Virgin and Child described by Vasari, Baldinucci and Richa is wrongly identified by Paatz (v, pp. 72–73) with a relief of the *Annunciation* in the style of Buglioni now in San Pierino.

On the strength of Vasari's account the Via dell'Agnolo lunette has been widely accepted as a work of Luca della Robbia. It was regarded by Cruttwell (1902, p. 126), when still in Via dell'Agnolo, as 'executed at the time of Luca's highest development' (with a note on damage to the glaze on the faces of the figures), and by Bode (1902, pp. 139–40) as an autograph work executed before 1443. Marquand (1914, pp. 66–69, No. 15) observes 'it is more reasonable with Dr. Bode to assign it to about 1440, rather than with Venturi to about 1450, or with Marcel Reymond and de Foville to about 1460'. A date of about 1450 is adopted by Planiscig (1948, pp. 39–40). It was, however, established by Horne (1915, p. 4) that the building history of the convent renders these dates untenable. Permission to found a convent in the vicinity of San Pier Maggiore 'col titolo di Eremite di S. Giovanni Laterano dell' Ordine Agostiniano' was granted by Pope Sixtus IV to Niccolosa degli Alfani in February 1470, and was confirmed in the following year when the convent was subordinated to the Roman hospital of Santo Spirito in Sassia. The foundress of the convent died before 1476 and the convent was suppressed in 1495. The premises were subsequently taken over by the nearby church of San Pier Maggiore. The relief cannot, therefore, have been commissioned before 1470 or 1471.

It is inferred from this by Del Bravo (pp. 25–26) that 'tutte le opere che fanno gruppo con la lunetta di San Pierino, il tondo dei Cappuccini, la lunetta mugellana di Berlino, la "Madonna del roseto", la "Madonna" tipo Rovezzano, la "Madonna" a mezza figura di Wellington ... sono da considerarsi dell'ultimo decennio di vita di Luca.' This theory presents some difficulty, in that the forms of the Virgin and Child and the two angels in the lunette do not conform to those in such late works of Luca as the reliefs in the Chapel of the Cardinal of Portugal and the Pescia altarpiece. The works named, moreover, do not constitute a group, since the Mugello lunette, the *Madonna in a Rose-Garden*, and the *Rovezzano Madonna* are characteristic works by Luca della Robbia, while the Cappuccini tondo and the Nynehead *Madonna* are putative early works by Andrea della Robbia. In the Via dell'Agnolo lunette the two solidly modelled angels are wholly lacking in the rhythmic subtlety of the paired angels on the bronze door in the Cathedral, and the flat postures of both the Virgin and the Child, with their free arms extended in a single plane, are characteristic of Andrea rather than Luca della Robbia. The border, with its alternating groups of single roses and lilies, finds a close point of reference in the frame of Andrea della Robbia's *Madonna of the Architects* of 1474 in the Museo Nazionale. There is thus no alternative but to regard the lunette as an independent work by Andrea della Robbia executed in or soon after 1470.

Marquand (*loc. cit.*) rightly observes that 'the construction of the frame does not exhibit the perfect joins seen in some of Luca's later works, as the separate blocks are not of equal size and the successive bands have neither alternating nor coincident joints, but are somewhat irregularly blocked out and put together.' Each of the two angels is modelled and glazed in one with the vase held in the hands, the lilies being modelled and glazed separately. The bodies of the Virgin and Child are modelled in one and the two heads are attached. The presence of a clothed Child is explained by Cruttwell (p. 125n) by the fact that the lunette was commissioned for a convent. The inscription EGO SVM LVX MVNDI recurs in the Innocenti and Altman *Madonnas* and in the Urbino lunette.

70 **Stemma of the Arte della Seta.** Or San Michele, Florence. Fig. 49
Enamelled terracotta.

The roundel shows two winged putti standing on clouds, supporting a shield with the arms of the Guild (a white doorway with violet bolt, rings and nails and a violet surround). The *residenza* of the Guild is decorated with a carving of a closed door supported by two putti. The leaves, however, are divided into six compartments instead of the four compartments shown at Or San Michele, and have a different surround. Staley (1906, pp. 204–35) observes that the doors were 'borrowed doubtless from the Porta Santa Maria' and associates the emblem with the protectionist provisions of the Guild. The roundel is framed in a band of fruit (quinces, grapes, pine-cones, oranges, pomegranates) made in nine pieces. The bunches of fruit are segregated from each other on a white ground, and as noted by Marquand (1914, pp. 134–6, No. 36) their dimensions are wrongly calculated. The attribution of the *stemma* to Luca della Robbia has frequently been doubted, but is defended by Bode (1900, p. 12; 1905, pl. 233) and Marquand (1893, pp. 159–60, and 1914, *loc. cit.*).

Marquand was, however, prepared to envisage the participation of Andrea della Robbia in the frame if the relief were executed ca. 1460. Paatz (iv, p. 493) ascribes the roundel to 'Luca und Andrea della Robbia, um 1450/60 (?).' The two winged putti are strikingly different in style from the Child in the *stemma* of the Arte dei Medici e degli Speziali, and their flat poses and featureless heads suggest that the whole work was commissioned from Andrea della Robbia about 1465.

71 Ceiling of the Martini Chapel. San Giobbe, Venice.

Fig. 50

Enamelled terracotta.

The vaulted ceiling of the Chapel is decorated with five roundels, each surrounded with a triple moulded frame in white-enamelled terracotta, a circle of fruit and foliage and an outer moulded frame. The five roundels show (*centre*) God the Father in half-length, with right hand raised in benediction and an open book inscribed with the Alpha and Omega in the left hand, surrounded by seven cherubim, (*right of altar*) St. Mark, facing to the left with an open volume of the Gospel and with the lion at shoulder height, (*left of altar*) St. John the Evangelist, also facing to the left with an open volume of the Gospel and behind, to the left, the eagle, (*right of entrance*) St. Matthew, facing to the right, in colloquy with the Angel, who supports a volume of the Gospel, (*left of entrance*) St. Luke, facing to the right, writing the Gospel in an open volume, behind which is the ox. The central roundel is set diagonally between the figures of SS. Mark and Luke and is not orientated on the altar or the entrance to the Chapel; this may result from inaccurate construction when the roundels were installed or from a later restoration. The roundels of the Evangelists are each cut on two sides through the foliated borders, which are composed of fourteen sections showing pine-cones, oranges, quinces and grapes, the light-coloured fruits alternating with the dark. The roundels are glazed in blue and white, and there is some white glaze in the blue clouds which cover the base of all five figures. Extensive gilding appears on all the roundels (e.g., in the *St. Matthew* on the hair, the edge of the halo, the girdle and edges of the dress, and in the halo, wings and hair of the Angel; in the *St. John* on the beak and feet of the eagle as well as on the main figure; and in the *St. Mark* on the mane and edges of the wings of the lion). The area between the roundels is filled with tiles containing a diaper pattern of projecting cubes, of which the faces are green, yellow and violet. The pattern of cubes is based on that of the ceiling of the Chapel of the Cardinal of Portugal in San Miniato al Monte. The ceiling was damaged by Austrian artillery in 1849, and is much made up, notably in the area to the right between the roundels of SS. Mark and Matthew.

As noted by Janson (1973, pp. 445–6), the four Evangelist roundels contain a number of elements derived from the upper parts of the Evangelist roundels in the Pazzi Chapel. The affinities are closest in the case of the *St. Luke* and the *St. John*. It is argued by Janson that 'the master of the San Giobbe Evangelists must have had a close look at the Pazzi Evangelists, probably while they were still in the Robbia workshop rather than after their installation.' While the roundels are loosely indebted to the Pazzi Chapel *Evangelists* (e.g., in the depiction of the open books), the connection is not close enough to admit of so precise an inference. If the Pazzi Chapel *Evangelists* were, as is likely, modelled about 1460 (for this see Pope-Hennessy, 1977, pp. 265–6) and the ceiling of the Chapel of the Cardinal of Portugal dates from 1461, the ceiling of the Martini Chapel must have been planned after this time. It is, moreover, established by Paoletti (pp. 74, 194) that Doge Cristoforo Moro, in his will of 29 October 1471, made provision for the completion of the Cappella Maggiore of San Giobbe and of two adjacent chapels, and that at this time the nave of the church did not extend beyond the present division between the Chapel of St. Margaret and the Martini Chapel. It follows that the construction of the Martini Chapel must have been begun at some time in the 1470s. Some light is thrown on the history of the chapel by Schmarsow (1891, pp. 230 ff.). The Martini, by whom the chapel was erected, had emigrated from Lucca to Venice, and the architecture of the chapel seems to have been due to a secondary Tuscan architect, not to the Lombardi. Its main feature is a marble altar, by an unidentified follower of Antonio Rossellino, which contains statuettes of SS. Francis, John the Baptist and Anthony of Padua, and originally included a relief of the Virgin and Child, now replaced by a modern mosaic. It is implied by Marquand (1914, pp. 213–19, No. 60) that a *terminus ante quem* for the construction of the chapel is established by the death of Antonio Rossellino in 1478, but this argument is nugatory in that the part played by Rossellino in the relatively undistinguished design of the altar is problematical. The attributions of the altar to Rossellino and of the ceiling to Luca della Robbia were questioned by Selvatico (p. 236), according to whom 'la sua volta è poi scompartita in circoli in cui stanno Evangelisti di terra cotta dipinti ed inverniciati alla guisa dei lavori della famiglia Dalla Robbia. Quelle mezze figure non sono gran cosa, ma rammentano senza dubbio il puro stile fiorentino d'allora.' Marquand (*loc. cit.*) ascribes the *God the Father* to 'the hand of an assistant' of Luca della Robbia, the *St. John the Evangelist* to Luca in a period of decline or to an assistant, and the *St. Luke* and *St. Matthew* substantially to Luca della Robbia.

The ceiling of the Martini Chapel manifestly was commissioned from the Della Robbia shop, since the framing of the roundels and the diaper pattern reproduce those at San Miniato al Monte and the garlands of fruit are of a type frequently encountered in later products of the Della Robbia studio. It is unlikely that Luca della Robbia was responsible for the figurative content of any of the roundels; in all five the handling is incompatible with Luca's autograph late works and particularly with the Pescia altarpiece. It is moreover difficult to reconcile the roundels with works executed by Andrea della Robbia after 1470. The *God the Father* is iconographically (but not stylistically) associable with a roundel of God the Father from the shop of Andrea della Robbia in the Galleria della Collegiata at Empoli, while the four *Evangelists* executed for Santa Maria delle Carceri at Prato by Andrea della Robbia in 1491, though themselves based on the Pazzi Chapel *Evangelists*, are different from and much superior to the roundels in the Martini Chapel.

72 **Temperance.** Musée de Cluny, Paris (No. 2793).
Fig. 51
Enamelled terracotta: diameter 170 cm.

There is some confusion as to the provenance of this and the related reliefs (Nos. 73, 74, 75 below). In the 1861 catalogue of the Musée de Cluny (Sommerard, 1861, p. 255, Nos. 2035, 2036, where *Justice* is wrongly described as *Faith*), it is stated that 'ces deux belles faiences (the present relief and the Cluny *Justice*) ont été executées pour l'Eglise San Miniato de Florence et sont décrites par Vasari.' According to a subsequent edition of the catalogue (Sommerard, 1883, p. 216), 'ces deux belles faiences, qui sont décrites par Vasari, proviennent de la décoration du palais des Pazzi, près de Florence.' This provenance is accepted by Marquand (1914, pp. 164–9, Nos. 47–50), who identifies the palace as 'possibly the Panciatichi-Ximenes Villa near Fiesole,' and notes that in a third relief from the series, the *Faith* now in the Villa Brauer, Nice, the cross held by Faith conforms to that in the *stemma* of the Pazzi family. It is suggested by Marquand (1912, pp. 169–74) that the roundels 'may have been originally intended for the Pazzi Chapel of Santa Croce, and that either the series was never completed or was never put in place. The medallions are apparently of the proper size for the spandrels, and would harmonize with Luca's Apostles on the walls of the chapel better than the four garish Evangelists which now complete its decoration.' The form of the cross is not unusual, and does not warrant this deduction. The attribution of the *Temperance* to Luca is accepted by Cruttwell (1902, p. 100). Bode (1900, p. 8.n 1) observes of the *Temperance* that 'in ihrer individuellen Bildung, namentlich des Kopfes, eher mit Anlehnung an einen Künstler in der Art des Antonio Pollajuolo entstanden ist,' and Planiscig (1905, p. 55) postulates collaboration with Andrea della Robbia. Marquand (*loc. cit.*) accepts the *Temperance*, the *Prudence* in the Metropolitan Museum and the Brauer *Faith* as constituents of a single decorative scheme, but infers that the Cluny *Justice* 'may have been in another series of medallions of greater diameter, of lighter backgrounds, filled with winged, not wingless, virtues.'

The discrepancies pointed out by Marquand are valid, and there can be little doubt that the fourth roundel was made for a different complex. The *Prudence* is loosely related to the corresponding Virtue on the ceiling of the Chapel of the Cardinal of Portugal; its composition is however the inverse of that in Luca's roundel. The commission for the San Miniato ceiling seems for this reason to constitute a *terminus post quem* for the four reliefs. Fine as its modelling is, the *Prudence* is less rhythmical than the corresponding figure at San Miniato al Monte, and the *Faith* and *Temperance* are posed with rigid verticality. The three figures seem to have been executed by Andrea della Robbia probably in the fourteen-eighties. The structure of the background conforms to that in the roundels of the Spedale degli Innocenti; also typical of Andrea della Robbia are the half-closed eyes. The frame is glazed in eight sections. The theory that the roundels were made for the Pazzi Chapel is almost certainly incorrect.

73 **Justice.** Musée de Cluny, Paris (No. 2794).   Fig. 53
Enamelled terracotta: diameter 170 cm.

See No. 72 above. The sky is differently modelled and pigmented from that in the three roundels with which the present roundel has been associated, in the Musée de Cluny, the Villa Brauer, Nice, and the Metropolitan Museum of Art. As noted by Marquand (1914, pp. 168–9, No. 50), there are also significant differences in the white outer moulding sufficient to rule out the possibility that the four roundels come from a single complex. There is some damage in the nose and sword hilt. The modelling of the feathers of the wings is of great accomplishment. While the pose of the figure recalls that of the *Justice* in the Chapel of the Cardinal of Portugal, the type is altogether distinct, and it is hardly possible that the relief was, as implied by Marquand, executed between 1450 and 1460, before the roundels in the Chapel. If by Luca, the *Justice* is a late work of about 1470–5.

74 **Prudence.** Metropolitan Museum of Art, New York (21.116).   Fig. 52
Enamelled terracotta: diameter 165 cm.

See No. 72 above. The roundel was acquired in Italy along with the roundel of *Faith* in the Villa Brauer, Nice, by Edward Cheney, of Badger Hall, Shropshire, probably in the third quarter of the nineteenth century. The two roundels later passed by inheritance to Alfred Capel-Cure, and were sold at auction by his heir, Francis Capel-Cure (London, Christie's, 4 May 1905, where they were bought by H. W. Harding for 500 gns). From Harding they passed to Godefroi Brauer, who sold one of them, the present relief, to the Galeries Heilbronner in Paris. The present roundel was purchased by the Metropolitan Museum of Art in 1921 at the Galerie Georges Petit, Paris (Heilbronner sale, No. 141).

75 **Faith.** Heilbronner collection, Paris, formerly.
Enamelled terracotta: diameter 165 cm.

See No. 72 above. For earlier pedigree see No. 74. The present relief was retained by Godefroi Brauer and installed in his villa at Nice (219 Boulevard du Mont Boron). According to Marquand (1928, p. 149), on Brauer's death the villa, and with it the roundel, became the property of the city of Nice. Information from the Musées de la Ville de Nice, however, leaves no doubt that the relief does not form part of the collection of the Musée de Nice. It was not included in the Brauer sale at Christie's (July 4/5, 1929). Enquiries made on my behalf suggest that it is still in Brauer's former house. The figure is shown frontally against a background of sky, holding in her left hand a chalice and in her right a cross. Like the companion roundels of *Prudence* and *Temperance*, the central roundel is framed in a border of fruit. Marquand (1912, pp. 169–74) notes that the present roundel has a cord-moulding in the interior of the frame, and infers that it may belong to a separate series of roundels of the three theological Virtues.

76 Bust of a Boy. Museo Nazionale, Florence, No. 75.

Fig. 60

Enamelled terracotta: height 33 cm.

The boy wears a blue cloak over a green dress, above which the edge of a white undergarment is visible. His head is turned slightly to the right, and his freely modelled hair is held in with a fillet. The white glaze on the hair is faulty. The eyebrows are painted in pale blue over violet, and there are traces of pale-blue pigment on the edges of the eyelids. The pupils of the eyes, turned to the right, are copper-brown. The bust is given by Supino (1898, p. 452, No. 75) to Andrea della Robbia (?). An attribution to Andrea della Robbia is advanced by Cruttwell (1902, p. 155), based on analogies with the putti supporting the *stemma* of the Arte della Seta on Or San Michele. Bode (1902, pp. 250–1) identifies it as a bust of Christ, and ascribes it to Luca della Robbia. It was at first regarded by Marquand (1914, pp. 231–2, No. 75) as a bust of Christ by Luca della Robbia (again on the strength of analogies with the Art della Seta *stemma*, which he accepted as a work of Luca), but with the rider that 'Andrea's cooperation or interference is indicated by the unusual colouring of the eyes.' Subsequently it was republished by Marquand (1922, I, pp. 32–33, No. 20) as an early work by Andrea della Robbia, which 'probably had no religious significance.' There is no hole in the head for a halo. An attribution to Luca della Robbia is precluded by the modelling of the face and hair, the pigmentation, and the nerveless folds of the blue cloak. These leave little doubt that we have here to do with a work executed by Andrea at about the same time as the conjectural date of the Arte della Seta *stemma*, that is about 1465–70. The face, framed by free-flowing hair, reveals the strong influence of Verrocchio. It is suggested by Schubring (1905, p. 123) that the bust must originally have been associated with a companion bust of the Young St. John. A bust of the Young St. John from the Beckerath collection, later at Krefeld, cited by Schubring, derives, however, from the Buglioni studio. A letter dispatched by Andrea della Robbia to Mantua on 28 June 1471 (A. Bertolotti, 1890, pp. 12–13; see above, p. 73 n.2) refers to the modelling of a bust for Federigo Gonzaga. This letter is interpreted by Bertolotti as a reference to a portrait bust of Federigo Gonzaga, but in view of the reference to the sale and remaking of the head it may refer to a bust of the type of that in the Bargello.

77 Relief Bust of a Youth. Bode Museum, Berlin (D.D.R.) (Inv. 2183).

Fig. 61

Enamelled terracotta: diameter 55·5 cm.
Provenance: Torrigiani, Florence; bt. for Kaiser Friedrich Museum, 1894.

The relief was ascribed by Bode first to Andrea and then to Luca della Robbia (1894, lxiv; 1902, p. 187), and is accepted as a work of Luca by Schottmüller (1933, pp. 26–27) and Cruttwell (1902, p. 89). For Planiscig (1948, p. 74) 'la collaborazione di Andrea non è esclusa'. The relief is twice discussed by Marquand, who initially (1914, pp. 205–6, No. 57) ascribed it to Luca della Robbia and regarded it as the original

of a number of roundels from the shop of Andrea della Robbia, with heads of youthful male figures, possibly Saints (in the Liechtenstein collection, from the Palazzo Antinori and elsewhere). Later (1922, pp. 26–27, No. 12), he ascribed it to Andrea della Robbia, with the rider that 'the guiding hand of Luca della Robbia is so evident in the execution of this bust that it might well be attributed to Luca himself.' Attractive as it is, the formal structure of the relief, and especially the treatment of the violet and green surcoat and the pale-blue dress, is too weak to admit of a direct ascription to Luca della Robbia.

78 Bust of a Woman. Museo Nazionale, Florence.

Fig. 62

Marble: height 45·5 cm.

From the collection of Cardinal Leopoldo de' Medici. The bust is given by Supino (1898, p. 416, No. 177) to an anonymous Florentine fifteenth-century sculptor, and by Steinmann (1903, p. 157.n 1) to Michele Marini. This attribution is rightly contested by W. Biehl (1915), who ascribes it to Luca della Robbia, with a dating ca. 1440–50. The closest point of reference for this distinguished work occurs in the two angels supporting the inscription at the base of Bernardo Rossellino's Bruni monument, and it is likely that the bust is by or from the workshop of Bernardo Rossellino and dates from ca. 1440–5.

79 Stemma of Giovanni di Francesco Tornabuoni. Palazzo Pretorio, San Giovanni Valdarno.

Fig. 57

Enamelled terracotta.

The shield shows the arms of Tornabuoni (Per saltire *or* and *vert*, a lion rampant counterchanged). On the lion's neck is an escutcheon with the red Croci di Popolo on a silver field. Beneath, on a fictive cartellino, is the inscription:

IOHAN.FRANCISCVS.TORN
ABONVS.VICARIVS.ET
COMISSARIVS.1478.1479.

The arms are those of Giovanni di Francesco Tornabuoni, uncle of Lorenzo de' Medici and patron of Ghirlandaio. The shield commemorates his appointment as Vicar and Commissary at San Giovanni Valdarno. The *stemma* was initially associated by Marquand (1914, p. 246, No. 99) with that of Ruberto Leoni as a product of Luca della Robbia's workshop, and was later (1919, p. 39, No. 37) given by him to Andrea della Robbia.

80 Stemma of the Martelli Family. Rijksmuseum, Amsterdam.

Enamelled terracotta: 125 × 79 cm.

The shield shows the Martelli arms (Gules, a griffin segreant *or* beaked *azure* langued *gules*), with the customary substitution of yellow for *or* and purple for *gules*. Marquand (1914, pp. 247–8, No. 100) gave the relief initially to the shop of Luca della Robbia in the late fourteen-seventies. In the absence of a label, its date, purpose and provenance cannot be established, but it may, as suggested by Marquand (*loc. cit.*), relate to Braccio di Domenico Martelli, who was a Prior in Florence in 1479. In a later volume (1919, pp. 114–15, No. 137) Marquand reattributed the *stemma* to the atelier of Andrea della Robbia with the date 1497 on the strength of two documents which, however, make no reference to this work.

81 **Stemma of Ruberto Leoni.** Palazzo Pretorio, San Giovanni Valdarno.   Fig. 58
Enamelled terracotta.

The shield shows the Leoni arms (*or*, a bend *gules* accompanied by two lions passant of same). Beneath is a fictive cartellino with the inscription:

RVBERTO.LIONI.
.MCCCCLXIII.

The year is that in which Ruberto Leoni held the office of Vicar and Commissary at San Giovanni Valdarno. The relief is plausibly given by Marquand (1914, p. 246, No. 98; 1919, pp. 13–14, No. 10) to the workshop of Luca della Robbia.

82 **Stemma of the Della Stufa Family.** Palazzo della Stufa, Florence.   Fig. 59
Enamelled terracotta: diameter 180 cm.

On a blue fluted disc is a shield with the Della Stufa arms (*argent*, two lions combatant *or*, in chief a cross coupled *gules*). Above the shield is a white dove holding a scroll inscribed with the words: AB OVO RVIT. The frame with a border of fruit is fired in eight sections. There is no means by which the *stemma* can be dated. While its form derives from that of the *stemma* of Jacopo de' Pazzi, the less distinguished border and the timid modelling of the lions on the shield suggest that it was commissioned from Andrea della Robbia. A much inferior *stemma* of Francesco di Lorenzo della Stufa on the Palazzo dei Priori at Volterra dates from 1478, and though given by Marquand (1919, p. 37, No. 34; 1922, i, pp. 43–44, No. 29) to Andrea, seems to be a product of Andrea della Robbia's shop.

83 **Madonna and Child with two kneeling Angels.** Pierpont Morgan Library, New York.
Enamelled terracotta.

The relief was purchased from the Palazzo Antinori, and was previously over the door of the Oratory of Santa Maria della Quercia at Legnaia (for this see Carocci, ii, p. 392: 'da qualche tempo è stata remossa una lunetta robbiana'). Published by Bode (1910) as a work of Luca della Robbia, it was later correctly reascribed by Marquand (1912, pp. 20–22) to 'some unknown follower of Luca della Robbia.'

84 **God the Father with four Cherubim.** Art Institute of Chicago.   Fig. 55
Marble: 57·8 × 78·5 cm.

The relief, which is in the form of a Gothic lunette, represents God the Father in half-length with right hand raised in benediction and left hand resting on an open book with the letters Alpha and Omega. Exhibited at the Heim Gallery, London, as a work of Luca della Robbia of ca. 1450, the carving is stated to have come from the church of San Martino a Mensola. There is no confirmation of this provenance. The carving is published by Negri Arnoldi (1972, p. 646, fig. 62), who claims that the 'attribution to Luca della Robbia cannot be contested on any grounds,' and dates the work 'at the same time as, or even before, the Cantoria.' C. Avery (1976, p. 23 ff.) also accepts the relief as a work of Luca della Robbia 'midway between the Peretola tabernacle and the Federighi tomb,' and considers it 'probably the finest rendering of the theme of *God the Father in Benediction* in Italian Renaissance sculpture.' In support of this attribution Avery adduces analogies between the carving of the Alpha and Omega on the book held by God the Father and those on the Peretola tabernacle; the differences in detail in the carving of both letters are in fact so wide as to preclude the possibility that they are by a single hand. The posture of God the Father has no valid parallel in Luca della Robbia's work, and two of the four cherub heads seem to be loosely based on heads from the Cantoria. The relief is a weak work which depends from Andrea as well as Luca della Robbia, and must be regarded as a pastiche dating either from the sixteenth century or from a more recent time. The Gothic form of the lunette reappears in the *Alessandri Madonna* in Berlin (D.D.R., see No. 85). The cruciform halo of God the Father, while technically admissible in a fifteenth-century representation, is of a type which occurs frequently in the work of Dossena (1878–1937) (e.g. in a version by Dossena of the *Madonna* from Rossellino's tomb of the Cardinal of Portugal in the Isabella Stewart Gardner Museum) and the striations between the cross-pieces are also found in works by Dossena (e.g. in a *Madonna* in the Museum of Western Art, Tokyo).

85 **The Alessandri Madonna.** Bode Museum, Berlin (D.D.R.), Inv. 139/Sch. 79   Fig. 54
Terracotta: 83 × 92·5 cm.
Provenance: Conte Alessandri, Florence; purchased for Kaiser Friedrich Museum, 1883.

The attribution of the relief to Luca della Robbia is sustained by Bode (1885, pp. 179–80; 1889, p. 8; 1900, pp. 24–25; 1905, p. 75, pl. 218; 1902, pp. 147–9), and is reiterated in the catalogues of Bode/Tschudi (1888, No. 113) and Schottmüller (1913, p. 36). The ascription to Luca, though not the authenticity of the relief, was dismissed by Reymond (1897 (ii), pp. 124–5) and by Marquand (1914, p. 228, No. 66), who writes: 'When we recall that a Niccolò Alessandri was one of the deputies charged with the supervision of Luca's Cantoria from 1432–1435, we are tempted to classify this relief with the early works of Luca della Robbia, but its execution betrays the work of a more nervous and less sedate artist, who nevertheless was strongly inspired by Luca della Robbia, especially by the medallions of the Pazzi Chapel.' It is omitted from the 1933 catalogue of Schottmüller, but is accepted as a work of Luca in the Bode Museum Berlin, 1964, p. 21). The relief seems to have been regarded by Bode initially as an early work of Luca, on account of the resemblance of the two angels to those in the Fortnum tondo of 1428 in the Ashmolean Museum, and later as a work of the period of the bronze door. The relief is exceptional not only in its Gothic form and in the fact that it was left unglazed, but also in its tentative handling, its stylistic inconsistencies and its rather trivial sentiment. On all these grounds it is likely to date from the second half of the nineteenth century. Its true date could be established by a thermoluminescence test.

86 The Incredulity of St. Thomas. Szepmüveszeti Museum, Budapest. Inv. No. 4974. Fig. 65
Terracotta: height 45 cm.
Provenance: Bardini, Florence; Adolph von Beckerath, Berlin; Beckerath sale (Lepke, Berlin, Kat. 1755, No. 66)

The two figures are unglazed. Traces of blue pigment are visible on the cloak of Christ. The head and right hand of Christ are missing. The group was first published by Cruttwell (1902, pp. 88–89) as 'closely connected with the work of the Bronze Doors in sentiment and in treatment.' Schubring (1905, p. 69; 1919, p. 86) suggests that it was made as a model for the group in the Mercanzia tabernacle on Or San Michele, which was later commissioned from Verrocchio. According to this theory, it would have been executed between 1463 and 1465, immediately after the enamelled terracotta *stemma* of the Mercanzia, as a competition piece. Marquand (1914, pp. 201–2, No. 55) states that 'the Mercanzia might naturally have first thought of entrusting the group to Luca della Robbia,' and accepts the attribution to Luca. Schubring's thesis is endorsed by, among others, Bombe (1916, p. 171) and Balogh (1975, i, pp. 61–62, No. 54, with full bibliography). There is no documentary or other evidence to indicate that a competition was held in connection with the Mercanzia group or that a commission to Luca della Robbia was contemplated. Marquand (*loc. cit.*) makes the pertinent observation that 'the only hesitation one might feel in attributing this group to Luca himself is whether, after having created so individual a type for S. Tommaso as that in the Pazzi Chapel, Luca could have so far retrograded as to represent that saint here as an ordinary angel.' Both figures depend from angels on the bronze door in the Cathedral, the upper half of the St. Thomas from the angel to the left of the *Virgin and Child* and the lower half from the angel to the left of *St. Luke*, and the Christ from the angel to the right of *St. John the Baptist* and the angel to the right of *St. Augustine*. It is possible either

that the Budapest model is a fifteenth-century pastiche derived from the bronze door or that it is a nineteenth-century forgery.

87 Female Saint. Museum of Fine Arts, Houston.
Fig. 66
Unglazed terracotta: 86·7 × 37·5 cm.
Provenance: Edith A. and Percy S. Straus Collection.

The relief, which has an arched top, shows a female saint posed frontally holding a palm leaf in her right hand and a book in her left. It is published by Planiscig (1948, pp. 29, 66, fig. 37) as 'opera certa di Luca' on the strength of supposed analogies to the angels on the Peretola tabernacle. There is no substance in this comparison. The relief has a superficial resemblance to work from the shop of Andrea della Robbia such as the enamelled terracotta figure of San Pantaleo at Stagliano (Marquand, 1922, ii, pp. 12–13, No. 115), but a thermoluminescence test would be required before it could be affirmed confidently that it dated from earlier than the nineteenth century.

88 Adoring Angel. Musée Jacquemart-André, Paris (Inv. 2014). Fig. 63
Enamelled terracotta: diameter 50 cm.

The figure is enamelled in white on an irregular concave blue ground; the glazing is defective, notably on the left hand and wrist, the front of the cloak and the nose and chin. Previously ascribed to the atelier of Andrea della Robbia, the relief is given by Gavoty (1975, No. 28) to the shop of Luca della Robbia, on the strength of analogies with the angels on the Peretola tabernacle.

89 Processional Cross. Museo dell'Opera del Duomo, Florence.
Silver: 75·8 × 57·5 cm.

The cross, which is double-sided, is identified by Wackernagel (p. 96) with a cross executed for the Duomo in Florence in 1514 by Antonio di Salvi. Steingräber (p. 105) ascribes the cross tentatively to Antonio di Salvi and relates the figures to the late work of Luca della Robbia, and specifically to the reliefs on the bronze door. A connection with Luca della Robbia and a dating ca. 1470–80 is accepted by Rossi (1964, p. 72). Brunetti (in Becherucci/Brunetti, ii, pp. 246–7) advances a direct ascription to Luca della Robbia and an assistant. While the Christ on the *recto* of the cross shows some resemblance to the Christ in Luca della Robbia's relief at Impruneta, the attribution is highly speculative, and is likely to be incorrect.

BIBLIOGRAPHY

ALBERTI. Leon Battista Alberti, *Opere volgari*, ed. Cecil Grayson, 3 vols., Bari, 1960–73

ALBERTINI. Francesco Albertini, *Memoriale di molte statue et picture sono nella inclyta Cipta di Florentia*, Florence, 1510

ANDREUCCI. Ottavio Andreucci, *Della Biblioteca e Pinacoteca dell'Arcispedale di S. Maria Nuova*, Florence, 1871

ANSALDI, 1772. Innocenzo Ansaldi, *Descrizione delle sculture, pitetture et architetture della città, e sobborghi di Pescia nella Toscana*, Bologna, 1772

——, 1816. ——, *Descrizione delle sculture, pitture, ed architetture della città, e diogesi di Pescia*, 2nd ed., Pescia, 1816

ANSELMI. Anselmo Anselmi, 'Le maioliche dei della Robbia nella provincia di Pesaro-Urbino,' *Archivio storico dell'arte*, 2ᵉ s., I (1895), pp. 435–48

ASH/FORSTER/HEFFNER. Lucius Junius Moderatus Columella, *On Agriculture*, ed. and trans. Harrison Boyd Ash, E. S. Forster and Edward H. Heffner, 3 vols., London and Cambridge, Mass., 1960–8

AVERY. Charles Avery, 'Three Marble Reliefs by Luca della Robbia,' *Museum Studies*, VIII (1976), pp. 6–37

BACCI. Pèleo Bacci, *Il gruppo pistojese della Visitazione, già attribuito a Luca della Robbia*, Florence, 1906

BACCINI. Giuseppe Baccini, *Le Ville Medicee di Cafaggiolo e di Trebbio in Mugello, oggi proprietà Borghese di Roma, cenni storici*, Florence, 1897

BALDINI. Umberto Baldini, *La bottega dei Della Robbia*, Florence, 1965

BALDINUCCI. Filippo Baldinucci, *Notizie dei Professori del Disegno*, ed. Ranalli, 7 vols. Florence, 1845

BALLARDINI. Gaetano Ballardini, *Le ceramiche del Campanile di S. Apollinare Nuovo in Ravenna*, Ravenna, n.d.

——, 1929 (i). ——, 'Sulla tomba Robbiana del Vescovo Federighi (1455–1459),' *Faenza*, XVII (1929), pp. 9–13

——, 1929 (ii). ——, 'An Unknown della Robbia Tilework Floor at Bologna,' *The Burlington Magazine*, LV (1929), pp. 121–8

——, 1964. ——, *L'Eredità ceramistica dell'antico mondo romano*, Rome, 1964

BALOGH, 1939. Jolán Balogh, 'Studien in der alten Skulpturensammlung des Museums der bildenden Künste, II,' *Az Országos magyar Szépmüvészeti Múzeum, Evkönyvei*, IX (1937–9), pp. 45–136

——, 1975. ——, *Katalog der ausländischen Bildwerke des Museums der bildenden Künste in Budapest*, 2 vols., Budapest, 1975

BARBET DE JOUY. Henry Barbet de Jouy, *Les Della Robbia, sculpteurs en terre emaillée*, Paris, 1855

BARGELLINI. Piero Bargellini, *I Della Robbia*, Milan, 1965

BARGILLI. Federigo Bargilli, *La Cattedrale di Fiesole*, Florence, 1883

BARTOLUCCI. 'Il Tabernacolo scolpito da Luca della Robbia per la Cappella di San Luca,' *Il Nuovo Osservatore Fiorentino*, Francesco Bartolucci, ed., 26 April 1885, pp. 65–7

BAXANDALL. Michael Baxandall, *Giotto and the Orators*, Oxford, 1971

BECHERUCCI/BRUNETTI. Luisa Becherucci and Giulia Brunetti, *Il Museo dell'Opera del Duomo a Firenze*, 2 vols., Milan, 1969–70

BELLOSI. Luciano Bellosi, *Il Museo dello Spedale degli Innocenti a Firenze*, Florence, 1977

BENDA. *Führer durch die Sammlung Gustav Benda*, Vienna, 1932

BERENSON, 1896. Bernard Berenson, 'Les peintures italiennes de New York et de Boston,' *Gazette des Beaux-Arts*, XV (1896), pp. 192–214

——, 1938. ——, *The Drawings of the Florentine Painters*, 2 ed., 3 vols., Chicago, 1938

BERLIN. Staatliche Museen zu Berlin, *Majolika-Plastik der italienischen Renaissance*, Berlin, 1964

BERTAUX, 1910. Emile Bertaux, *Donatello*, Paris, 1910

——, 1913. ——, 'Musée Jacquemart-André. L'art italien,' *Revue de l'Art ancien et moderne*, 1913, ii, pp. 413–38

BERTI. Giovanni Felice Berti, *Cenni storico-artistici per servire di guida ed illustrazione alla insigne Basilica di S. Miniato al Monte e di alcuni dintorni presso Firenze*, Florence, 1850

BERTOLOTTI. Antonio Bertolotti, *Figuli, Fonditori e Scultori in relazione con la corte di Mantova nei secoli XV, XVI, XVII*, Milan, 1890

BETTONI. Nicolò Bettoni, *Le tombe ed i monumenti illustri d'Italia*, 2 vols., Milan, 1822–3

BIAŁOSTOCKI, 1972. Jan Bialostocki, *Spätmittelalter und beginnende Neuzeit (Propyläen Kunstgeschichte 7)*, Berlin, 1972

——, 1973. ——, 'The Door of Death,' *Jahrbuch der Hamburger Kunstsammlungen*, 18 (1973), pp. 7–32

BIANCHINI. Raffaello Bianchini, *L'Impruneta, paese e santuario*, Florence, 1932

BIEHL. W. Biehl, 'Eine Marmorbüste des Luca della Robbia,' *Monatshefte für Kunstwissenschaft*, VIII (1915), pp. 147–9

BIGAZZI. Francesco Bigazzi, *Iscrizioni e memorie della città di Firenze*, Florence, 1887

BLANC. Charles Blanc, *Collection d'objets d'art de M. Thiers leguée au Musée du Louvre*, Paris, 1884

BLANKENBURG. Walter Blankenburg, 'Chor,' *Die Musik in Geschichte und Gegenwart*, F. Blume, ed., ii, Kassel, 1952

BOCCHI, 1592. Francesco Bocchi, *Sopra l'immagine miracolosa della Santissima Nunziata di Fiorenza*, Florence, 1592

BOCCHI-CINELLI, 1677. Francesco Bocchi, *Le bellezze della città di Firenze. . . . Scritte già da M. Francesco Bocchi, ed ora da M. Giovanni Cinelli ampliate ed accresciute*, Florence, 1677

BODE. Wilhelm Bode, 'Luca della Robbia als Porträtbildner,' *Das Museum*, II, 1897, pp. 69–72

——, 1878. ——, *Die Künstlerfamilie della Robbia*, Leipzig, 1878

——, 1879. ——, 'L'Exposition rétrospective au Trocadéro,' *Revue archéologique*, 1879, pp. 94–103

——, 1885. ——, 'Luca della Robbia,' *Jahrbuch der königlich preussischen Kunstsammlungen*, VI (1885), pp. 170–85

——, 1887. ——, *Italienische Bildhauer der Renaissance*, Berlin, 1887

——, 1889. ——, 'Luca della Robbia e i suoi precursori in Firenze,' *Archivio storico dell'arte*, II (1889), pp. 1–9

——, 1894. ——, 'Amtliche Berichte aus den königlichen Kunstsammlungen,' *Jahrbuch der königlich preussischen Kunstsammlungen*, XV (1894), p. xliii

——, 1897. ——, *Die Sammlung Oscar Hainauer*, Berlin, 1897

——, 1900. ——, 'Luca della Robbia,' *Jahrbuch der königlich preussischen Kunstsammlungen*, XXI (1900), pp. 1–33

——, 1902. ——, *Florentiner Bildhauer der Renaissance*, Berlin, 1902

——, 1905. ——, *Denkmäler der Renaissance-Sculptur Toscanas*, Munich, 1892–1905

——, 1905 (ii). ——, 'La Madonna di Luca della Robbia del 1428,' *Rivista d'arte*, III (1905), pp. 1–3

——, 1906. ——, 'Originalwiederholungen glasierter Madonnenreliefs von Luca della Robbia,' *Münchner Jahrbuch der bildenden Kunst*, I (1906), pp. 28–32

——, 1907. ——, 'Die Gruppe der Begegnung Mariä mit der Hl. Elisabeth in S. Giovanni fuorcivitas zu Pistoja,' *Kunstchronik*, XVIII (1907), pp. 513–16

——, 1910. ——, 'Neuentdeckte Bildwerke in glasiertem Ton von Luca della Robbia,' *Zeitschrift für bildende Kunst*, n.f. XXI (1910), pp. 305–7.

——, 1914. ——, *Die Werke der Familie della Robbia*, Berlin, 1914

——, 1916. ——, 'Luca della Robbia und sein neuester Biograph,' *Mitteilungen des kunsthistorischen Institutes in Florenz*, II (1912–17), pp. 71–80

——, 1921. ——, 'Ghibertis Versuche, seine Tonbildwerke zu glasieren,' *Jahrbuch der preussischen Kunstsammlungen*, XLII (1921), pp. 51–54

BODE/TSCHUDI, 1888. Wilhelm Bode and Hugo von Tschudi, *Beschreibung der Bildwerke der Christlichen Epoche*, Berlin, 1888

BOFFITO/MORI. Giuseppe Boffito and Attilio Mori, *Piante e vedute di Firenze*, Florence, 1926

BOMBE. Walter Bombe, 'Die Sammlung Adolph v. Beckerath,' *Der Cicerone*, VIII (1916), pp. 167–86

BONAFFÉ. Émile Bonaffé, *Catalogue de la vente E. Piot*, Paris, mai 1890

BOSTON. 'The Quincy Adams Shaw Bequest,' *Boston Museum of Fine Arts Bulletin*, XVI (1918), pp. 11–29

BROCCHI. Giuseppe Maria Brocchi, *Descrizione della provincia del Mugello*, Florence, 1748

BROCKHAUS. Heinrich Brockhaus, 'Die Sängerkanzeln des florentiner Doms in ihrer kirchlichen Bedeutung,' *Zeitschrift für bildende Kunst*, XIX (1908), pp. 160–1

BRUCKER. Gener Brucker, *The Civic World of Early Renaissance Florence*, Princeton, 1977

BRUNETTI, 1954. Giulia Brunetti, *Luca della Robbia*, Paris, 1954

——, 1958. ——, 'Luca Della Robbia,' *Enciclopedia universale dell'arte*, IV, 1958, pp. 252–8

——, 1962. ——, 'Note su Luca della Robbia,' *Scritti di storia dell'arte in onore di Mario Salmi*, II, Rome, 1962, pp. 263–72

BULST. Wolfger A. Bulst, 'Die ursprüngliche innere Aufteilung des Palazzo Medici in Florenz,' *Mitteilungen des kunsthistorischen Institutes in Florenz*, XIV (1970), pp. 369–92

BURCKHARDT/BODE. Jacob Burckhardt, *Der Cicerone*, ed. Wilhelm Bode, 5th ed., 2 vols., Leipzig, 1884

BURGER. Fritz Burger, *Geschichte des florentinischen Grabmals von ältesten Zeiten bis Michelangelo*, Strassburg, 1904

BURLAMACCHI. Marchesa L. Burlamacchi, *Luca della Robbia*, London, 1900

BURNS. Howard Burns, 'Quattrocento Architecture and the Antique: Some Problems,' *Classical Influences on European Culture, A.D. 500–1500*, R. R. Bolgar, ed., Cambridge, 1971, pp. 269–87

BÜTTNER. Frank Büttner, 'Der Umbau des Palazzo Medici-Riccardi zu Florenz,' *Mitteilungen des kunsthistorischen Institutes in Florenz*, XIV (1970), pp. 393–414

CAGNACCI. Marcello Cagnacci, *Impruneta e la sua Basilica*, Florence, 1969

CAIGER-SMITH. Alan Caiger-Smith, *Tin-glaze Pottery in Europe and the Islamic World*, London, 1973

CALAMARI. Giuseppe Calamari, *Il confidente di Pio II, Card. Jacopo Ammannati-Piccolomini (1422–1479)*, 2 vols., Rome, 1932–40

CAMPETTI. P. Campetti, *Guida di Lucca*, Lucca, 1912

CAPLOW. Harriet McNeal Caplow, *Michelozzo*, 2 vols., New York, 1977

CAPUTO. G. Caputo, *Lo scultore del grande bassorilievo con la danza delle Menadi in Tolemaide di Cirenaica*, Rome, 1948

CAROCCI, 1884. Guido Carocci, 'Il monumento di Benozzo Federighi,' *Arte e storia*, XIII (1894), pp. 169–71

——, 1896 (i). ——, 'I tondi robbiani in Toscana,' *Arte italiana decorativa ed industriale*, V (1896), pp. 29–31

——, 1896 (ii). ——, 'Le porte del Battistero di Firenze e l'ornamento imitato dalla natura,' *Arte italiana decorativa ed industriale*, V (1896), p. 69 ff.

——, 1897. ——, 'Le cantorie nella Pieve di S. Maria Impruneta ed un fregio robbiano,' *Arte italiana decorativa ed industriale*, VI (1897) pp. 65–6

——, 1904. ——, 'Il monumento del vescovo Benozzo Federighi e l'ornamentazione floriale robbiana,' *Arte italiana decorativa ed industriale*, XIII (1904), pp. 85–8

——, 1906–7. ——, *I dintorni di Firenze*, 2nd ed., 2 vols., Florence, 1906–7.

CARTARI. Vincenzo Cartari, *Imagini delli dei de gl'Antichi*, Venice, ed. 1647

CASALINI, 1959. Eugenio Casalini, O. S. M., 'La Madonna della Neve di Pagno di Lapo Portigiani (note storiche),' *Studi storici dell'Ordine dei Servi di Maria*, IX (1959), pp. 59–63

——, 1964. ——, 'Note di storia e d'arte: Luca della Robbia alla SS. Annunziata,' *La SS. Annunziata: Bolletino del santuario di Firenze*, LXVII (September 1964), pp. 12–14

——, 1978. Eugenio Casalini, *et al.*, *La SS. Annunziata di Firenze, Studi e documenti sulla chiesa e il convento*, II, Florence, 1978

CASOTTI, 1713. Giovambatista Casotti, *Relazione della venuta in Firenze della miraculosa immagine di Maria Vergine dell'Impruneta l'anno MDCCXI*, Florence, 1713

——, 1714. ——, *Memorie istoriche della miracolosa immagine di Maria Vergine dell'Impruneta*, Florence, 1714

CASPARY. Hans Caspary, *Das Sakramentstabernakel in Italien bis zum Konzil von Trient*, Trier, 1964

CAVALLUCCI, 1881. Camillo Jacopo Cavallucci, *S. Maria del Fiore, storia documentata dall'origine fino ai nostri giorni*, Florence, 1881

CAVALLUCCI/MOLINIER, 1884. Jacopo Cavallucci and Emile Molinier, *Les Della Robbia, leur vie et oeuvre*, Paris, 1884

CECCHERINI. N. Ugo Ceccherini, *Santa Maria all'Impruneta, notizie storiche*, Florence, 1890

CHASTEL. André Chastel, *Art et Humanisme à Florence au temps de Laurent le Magnifique*, Paris, 1959

CHERICI. U. Cherici, *Guida storico-artistica del R. Spedale di S. Maria degli Innocenti di Firenze*, Florence, 1926

CHEVALLIER/MANNHEIM. Paul Chevallier and Charles Mannheim, *Catalogue des objets d'art ... composant l'importante et précieuse Collection Spitzer*, Paris, 1893

CHIAPELLI. Alessandro Chiapelli, *Arte del Rinascimento*, Rome, 1925

CHINI. P. Lino Chini, *Storia antica e moderna del Mugello*, 4 vols., Florence, 1875–6

CHOMENTOVSKAJA. O. Chomentovskaja, 'Le comput digital, Histoire d'un geste dans l'art de la Renaissance italienne,' *Gazette des Beaux-Arts*, 6e per., XX (1938), ii, pp. 157–72

CICOGNARA. Conte Leopoldo Cicognara, *Storia della scultura dal suo risorgimento in Italia fino al secolo di Canova*, 7 vols., Prato, 1823–4

CISTELLINI. Antonio Cistellini, *Momenti gaudiosi e dolorosi della storia di San Firenze*, Florence, 1967

COCCHI. Arnaldo Cocchi, *Le chiese di Firenze dal secolo IV al secolo XX*, Florence, 1903

CORA. Galeazzo Cora, *Storia della maiolica di Firenze e del contado, Secoli XIV–XV*, Florence, 1973

CORRERA. L. Correra, 'Il tempio dei Dioscuri a Napoli,' *Atti dell'Accademia di Archeologia, Lettere e Belle Arti*, Naples, XXIII (1904)

CORTI, 1970. Gino Corti, 'New Andrea della Robbia Documents,' *The Burlington Magazine*, CXII (1970), pp. 749–52

——, 1973. ——, 'Addenda Robbiana,' *The Burlington Magazine*, CXV (1973), pp. 468–9

CORTI/HARTT, 1962. Gino Corti and Frederick Hartt, 'New Documents Concerning Donatello, Luca and Andrea della Robbia, Desiderio, Mino, Uccello, Pollaiuolo, Filippo Lippi, Baldovinetti and Others,' *The Art Bulletin*, XLIV (1962), pp. 155–67

CORWEGH. Robert Corwegh, *Donatellos Sängerkanzel im Dom zu Florenz*, Berlin, 1909

COVI. Dario A. Covi, 'Lettering in Fifteenth Century Florentine Painting,' *The Art Bulletin*, XLV (1963), pp. 1–17

CRISPOLTI. Virgilio Crispolti, *Santa Maria del Fiore alla luce dei documenti*, Florence, 1937

CROLL. Gerhard Croll, 'Dufays Festmusik zur florentiner Domweihe,' *Österreichische Musikzeitschrift*, XXIII (1968), pp. 538–47

CRUTTWELL. Maud Cruttwell, *Luca and Andrea della Robbia and their Successors*, London and New York, 1902

D'ACCONE, 1961. Frank A. D'Accone, 'The Singers of San Giovanni in Florence during the 15th Century,' *Journal of the American Musicological Society*, XIV (1961), pp. 307–58

——, 1971. ——, 'Music and Musicians at S. Maria del Fiore in the Early Quattrocento,' *Journal of the American Musicological Society*, XXIV (1971), pp. 1–50.

D'ADDARIO. Arnaldo d'Addario, 'Antonio Agli,' *Dizionario biografico degli Italiani*, vol. I, Rome, 1960, pp. 400–1

D'ANCONA, 1902. Paolo d'Ancona, 'Le rappresentazioni allegoriche delle Arti Liberali nel Medio Evo e nel Rinascimento,' *L'Arte*, V (1902), pp. 137–55, 211–28, 269–89, 370–85

——, 1914. ——, *La miniatura fiorentina (secoli XI–XVI)*, 2 vols., Florence, 1914

DANIEL. A. M. Daniel, 'Italian Sculpture at the Burlington Fine Arts Club,' *The Burlington Magazine*, XXI (1912), pp. 278–84

DARCEL, 1866. Alfred Darcel, *Catalogue de la vente Signol*, Paris, 17–20 décembre, 1866

——, 1869. ——, *Recueil de faïences italiennes des XV, XVI et XVII siécles*, Paris, 1869

DE FOVILLE. Jean de Foville, *Les della Robbia*, Paris, 1910

DEGENHART/SCHMITT, 1960. Bernhard Degenhart and Annegrit Schmitt, 'Gentile da Fabriano in Rom und die Anfänge des Antikenstudiums,' *Münchner Jahrbuch der bildenden Kunst*, XI (1960), pp. 59–151

——, 1968. ——, *Corpus der italienischen Zeichnungen, 1300–1450*, 4 vols., Berlin, 1968–

DEL BRAVO. Carlo Del Bravo, 'L'Umanesimo di Luca della Robbia,' *Paragone*, 285 (1973), pp. 3–34

DELLA TORRE. Arnaldo della Torre, *Storia dell'Accademia Platonica di Firenze*, Florence, 1902

DEL MIGLIORE. Ferdinando Leopoldo del Migliore, *Firenze città noblissima illustrata*, Florence, 1684

DE MÉLY. F. de Mély, 'La dorure sur céramique et l'émail de Jehan Fouquet au Louvre,' *Gazette des Beaux-Arts*, XXXIV (1905), pp. 281–7

DENEKEN. F. Deneken, *Zweiter Bericht des städtischen Kaiser-Wilhelm-Museums in Krefeld*, Krefeld, 1904

DE NICOLA. Giacomo De Nicola, 'A Recently Discovered Madonna by Luca della Robbia,' *The Burlington Magazine*, XXXV (1919), pp. 49–55

DENIS. Valentin Denis, 'La représentation des instruments,

de musique dans les arts figurés du XV siècle en Flandre et en Italie,' *Bulletin de l'Institut Historique Belge de Rome*, XXI (1940–1), pp. 327–45

——, 1944. ——, *De Muziekinstrumenten in de Nederlanden en in Italië naar hun Afbeelding in de 15ᵉ-eeuwsche Kunst*, Antwerp and Utrecht, 1944

DOERING-DACHAU. Oscar Doering-Dachau, *Die Künstlerfamilie della Robbia*, Munich, 1913

DOREN. Alfred Jakob Doren, *Studien aus der florentiner Wirtschaftsgeschichte*, 2 vols., Stuttgart, 1901–8

DOUGLAS, 1904. R. Langton Douglas, *Cantor Lectures on the Majolica and Glazed Earthenware of Tuscany*, London, 1904

——, 1946. ——, 'Recent Additions to the Kress Collection,' *The Burlington Magazine*, LXXXVIII (1946), pp. 81–5

DURRIEU. Paul Durrieu, 'Les armoiries du bon roi René,' Académie des Inscriptions & Belles-Lettres, *Comptes rendus*, 4 sér., 1908, pp. 102–14

DU TEIL. B. J. du Teil, 'Notice sur des oeuvres d'Andrea della Robbia en Flandre,' *Miscellanea di studi storici in onore di Antonio Manno*, II, Turin, 1912, pp. 391–402

DUVEEN. *Duveen Sculpture in Public Collections of America*, New York, 1944

FABRICZY, 1888. Cornelius von Fabriczy, 'Un alto-rilievo di Luca della Robbia,' *Arte e storia*, VII (1888), pp. 173–4

——, 1892. ——, *Filippo Brunelleschi, sein Leben und seine Werke*, Stuttgart, 1892

——, 1900. ——, 'Donatellos Hl. Ludwig und sein Tabernakel an Or San Michele,' *Jahrbuch der königlich preussischen Kunstsammlungen*, XXI (1900), pp. 242–61

——, 1903. ——, 'Pagno di Lapo Portigiani,' *Jahrbuch der königlich preussischen Kunstsammlungen*, Beiheft, XXIV (1903), pp. 119–36

——, 1904. ——, 'Michelozzo di Bartolomeo,' *Jahrbuch der königlich preussischen Kunstsammlungen*, Beiheft, XXV (1904), pp. 34–110

——, 1906 (i). ——, 'Nanni di Miniato, detto Fora,' *Jahrbuch der königlich preussischen Kunstsammlungen*, Beiheft, XXVII (1906), pp. 70–86

——, 1906 (ii). ——, 'Urkundliches über Andreas della Robbia Arbeiten für S. Maria del fiore,' *Repertorium für Kunstwissenschaft*, XXIX (1906), pp. 284–5

——, 1907. ——, 'Die Heimsuchungsgruppe in S. Giovanni fuorcivitas zu Pistoja,' *Repertorium für Kunstwissenschaft*, XXX (1907), pp. 285–6

——, 1909. ——, 'Kritisches Verzeichnis toskanischer Holzund Tonstatuen bis zum Beginn des Cinquecento,' *Jahrbuch der königlich preussischen Kunstsammlungen*, Beiheft, XXX (1909), pp. 1–88

FALKE, 1929. Otto von Falke, 'Aus der Sammlung Figdor. I. Kunstgewerbe,' *Pantheon*, IV (1929), pp. 325–34

——, 1930. ——, *Die Sammlung Dr. Albert Figdor*, 2 vols., Vienna, 1930

FOLLINI/RASTRELLI. Vincenzo Follini and Modesto Rastrelli, *Firenze antica e moderna, illustrata*, 8 vols., Florence, 1789–1802

FORATTI. Aldo Foratti, 'Note robbiane,' *Rassegna d'arte*, XIX (1919), pp. 22–32

FORTNUM. Charles Drury Edward Fortnum, *Descriptive Catalogue of the Maiolica . . . in the S. Kensington Museum*, London, 1873

FORTUNA. Alberto M. Fortuna, *Andrea del Castagno*, Florence, 1957

FOSSI TODOROW. Maria Fossi Todorow, *I disegni del Pisanello e della sua cerchia*, Florence, 1966

FRANCESCHINI, 1885. Pietro Franceschini, 'Il Tabernacolo scolpito da Luca della Robbia per la Cappella di San Luca,' *Il Nuovo Osservatore Fiorentino*, I (1885), pp. 65–7

——, 1892. ——, *L'Oratorio di San Michele in Orto in Firenze*, Florence, 1892

FREY, 1892 (i). Carl Frey, ed., *Il codice Magliabechiano*, Berlin, 1892

——, 1892 (ii). ——, ed., *Il libro di Antonio Billi*, Berlin 1892

FRIEDLÄNDER. M. J. Friedländer, *et al.*, *Die Sammlung Dr. Eduard Simon, Berlin*, 2 vols., Berlin, 1929

GAETA BERTELÁ. Giovanna Gaeta Bertelá, *Luca, Andrea, Giovanni della Robbia*, Florence, 1977

GALASSI. Giuseppe Galassi, *La scultura fiorentina del Quattrocento*, Milan, 1949

GALLERIA RINUCCINI. *Catalogo dei quadri ed altri oggetti della Galleria Rinuccini*, Florence, 1845

GAVOTY, 1968. Françoise de la Moureyre-Gavoty, 'Gli angeli reggicandelabro del Museo Jacquemart-André,' *Donatello e il suo tempo*, Florence, 1968, pp. 353–9

——, 1975. ——, *Musée Jacquemart-André, Sculpture Italienne*, Paris, 1975

GAYE. Giovanni Gaye, *Carteggio inedito d'artisti dei secoli XIV, XV, XVI*, 3 vols., Florence, 1839–40

GENNARI. Gualberto Gennari, 'Il pavimento robbiano della cappella Bentivoglio a S. Giacomo di Bologna,' *Faenza*, XLIII (1957), pp. 127–30

GERSPACH, 1896. Edouard Gerspach, 'Le tombeau de l'évêque Benozzo Federighi,' *Chronique des arts*, 1896, pp. 156–7

——, 1904. ——, 'Nouvelles acquisitions des musées de Florence,' *Revue de l'art Chrétien*, XV (1904), pp. 405–7

GIGLIOLI, 1904. Odoardo H. Giglioli, *Pistoia nelle sue opere d'arte*, Florence, 1904

——, 1905. ——, 'Le pitture del Andrea del Castagno e di Alesso Baldovinetti per la chiesa di S. Egidio,' *Rivista d'arte*, III (1905), pp. 206–8

——, 1906. ——, 'La cappella del Cardinale di Portogallo nella chiesa di S. Miniato al Monte,' *Rivista d'arte*, IV (1906), pp. 89–99

GINORI-CONTI. Piero Ginori-Conti, 'Un libro di ricordi e di spese di Lorenzo e Vittorio Ghiberti,' *Rivista d'arte*, XX (1938), pp. 290–303

GINORI LISCI, 1953. Leonardo Ginori Lisci, *Gualfonda, un antico palazzo ed un giardino scomparso*, Florence, 1953

——, 1972. ——, *I palazzi di Firenze nella storia e nell'arte*, 2 vols., Florence, 1972

GLASSER. Hannelore Glasser, 'The Litigation Concerning Luca della Robbia's Federighi Tomb,' *Mitteilungen des kunsthistorischen Institutes in Florenz*, XIV (1969), pp. 1–32

GNECCHI. Francesco Gnecchi, *I medaglioni romani*, 3 vols., Milan, 1912

GOMBRICH. Ernst Hans Gombrich, 'The Early Medici as Patrons of Art,' *Norm and Form*, London, 1966, pp. 35–57

GORI SASSOLI, 1975. Mario Gori Sassoli, 'Michelozzo e

l'architettura di Villa nel primo Rinascimento,' *Storia dell'arte*, XXIII (1975), pp. 5–51

GOTTI. Aurelio Gotti, *Le Gallerie di Firenze*, Florence, 1872

GRISEBACH. August Grisebach, *Der Garten: eine Geschichte seiner künstlerischen Gestaltung*, Leipzig, 1910

GRONAU, 1904. Georg Gronau, 'Zur Genesis der Robbia-Arbeiten, eine kunstgeschichtliche Konjektur,' *Kunstchronik*, XV (1903–4), pp. 193–6

——, 1907. ——, 'Pèleo Bacci, Il gruppo pistoiese della Visitazione, già attribuito a Luca della Robbia,' *Monatshefte der Kunstwissenschaftlichen Literatur*, III (1907), pp. 2–3

GRONAU, 1945. H. D. Gronau, 'The San Pier Maggiore Altarpiece: a Reconstruction,' *The Burlington Magazine*, LXXXVI (1945), pp. 139–44

GROTE, 1964. Andreas Grote, 'A Hitherto Unpublished Letter on Benozzo Gozzoli's Frescoes in the Palazzo Medici-Riccardi,' *Journal of the Warburg and Courtauld Institutes*, XXVII (1964), pp. 321–2

GUASTI, 1857. Cesare Guasti. *La Cupola di Santa Maria del Fiore*, Florence, 1857

——, 1865. ——, 'Di un maestro d'organi del secolo XV,' *Archivio storico italiano*, II (1865), ii, pp. 48–79

——, 1866. ——, *Capitoli della Compagnia della Madonna dell' Impruneta*, Florence, 1866

GURRIERI. Francesco Gurrieri, *Donatello e Michelozzo nel Pulpito di Prato*, Florence, 1970

GUSMAN. Pierre Gusman, *L'Art décoratif de Rome, de la fin de la République au IVe siècle*, 3 vols., n.d.

HADELN. Detlev, Baron von Hadeln, 'Robert Corwegh, Donatellos Sängerkanzel im Dom zu Florenz,' review, *Repertorium für Kunstwissenschaft*, XXXII (1909), pp. 382–5

HARTT, 1949. Frederick Hartt, *Florentine Art under Fire*, Princeton, 1949

——, 1970. ——, *A History of Italian Renaissance Art*, London, 1970

HARTT/CORTI/KENNEDY, 1964. Frederick Hartt, Gino Corti and Clarence Kennedy, *The Chapel of the Cardinal of Portugal, 1434–1459, at San Miniato in Florence*, Philadelphia, 1964

HASKELL. Francis Haskell, 'The Benjamin Altman Bequest,' *Metropolitan Museum Journal*, III (1970), pp. 259–80

HATFIELD. Rab Hatfield, 'Some Unknown Descriptions of the Medici Palace in 1459,' *The Art Bulletin*, LII (1970), pp. 232–49

HAUPTMANN. Moritz Hauptmann, *Der Tondo*, Frankfurt am Main, 1936

HEIKAMP/GROTE. Detler Heikamp and Andreas Grote, *Il Tesoro di Lorenzo il Magnifico*, ii, Florence, 1974, pp. 47–51

HERLIHY. David Herlihy, 'Santa Maria Impruneta: a Rural Commune in the Late Middle Ages,' *Florentine Studies—Politics and Society in Renaissance Florence*, Nicolai Rubinstein, ed., London, 1968, pp. 242–76

HERZEN. E. Herzen, 'Über den Maler Pietro degli Franceschi und seinen vermeintlichen Plagiarius, den Franziskanermönch Luca Pacioli,' *Archiv für zeichende Künste*, II (1856), pp. 231–44

HERZNER, 1973. Volker Herzner, 'Bemerkungen zu Nanni di Banco und Donatello,' *Wiener Jahrbuch für Kunstgeschichte*, XXVI (1973), pp. 74–95

——, 1976 (i). ——, 'Die Segel-Imprese der Familie Pazzi,' *Mitteilungen des kunsthistorischen Institutes in Florenz*, XX (1976), pp. 13–32

——, 1976 (ii). ——, 'Donatello und die Sakristei-Türen des florentiner Domes,' *Wiener Jahrbuch für Kunstgeschichte*, XXIX (1976), pp. 53–63

HILL. G. F. Hill, 'On the Early Use of Arabic Numerals in Europe,' *Archaeologia*, LXI (1910), pp. 137–90

HONEY. William Bowyer Honey, *European Ceramic Art from the end of the Middle Ages to about 1815*, London, n.d.

HOPF/STRUCK. Wilhelm Hopf and Gustav Struck, *Die Landesbibliothek Kassel, 1580–1930*, 2 vols., Marburg, 1930

HORNE. Herbert P. Horne, 'Notes on Luca della Robbia,' *The Burlington Magazine*, XXVIII (1915), pp. 3–7

HYMAN, 1972. Isabella Hyman, 'Filippo Brunelleschi', *Dizionario biografico degli Italiani*, XIV, Rome, 1972, pp. 534–45

——, 1977. ——, *Fifteenth Century Florentine Studies: the Palazzo Medici and a Ledger for the Church of San Lorenzo*, New York, 1977

JANITSCHEK. Hubert Janitschek, *Die Gesellschaft der Renaissance in Italien und die Kunst*, Stuttgart, 1879

JANSON, 1942. Horst W. Janson, 'Two Problems in Florentine Renaissance Sculpture,' *The Art Bulletin*, XXIV (1942), pp. 326–34

——, 1957. ——, *The Sculpture of Donatello*, 2 vols., Princeton, 1957

——, 1963. ——, 'Nanni di Banco's Assumption of the Virgin on the Porta della Mandorla,' *The Renaissance and Mannerism* (Acts of the Twentieth International Congress on the History of Art, vol. 2), Princeton, 1963, pp. 98–107

——, 1973. ——, 'The Pazzi Evangelists,' *Intuition und Kunstwissenschaft: Festschrift für Hans Swarzenski zum 70. Geburtstag am 30. August 1973*, Berlin, 1973, pp. 439–48

KAUFFMANN, 1960. Georg Kauffmann, 'Zu Donatellos Sängerkanzel,' *Mitteilungen des kunsthistorischen Institutes in Florenz*, IX (1960), pp. 55–9

KAUFFMANN, 1936. Hans Kauffmann, *Donatello, eine Einführung in sein Bilden und Denken*, Berlin, 1936

KENNEDY. Ruth Wedgwood Kennedy, *Alesso Baldovinetti*, New Haven, 1938

KENT, 1977. Francis William Kent, *Household and Lineage in Renaissance Florence*, Princeton, 1977

KRAUTHEIMER. Richard Krautheimer, *Lorenzo Ghiberti*, Princeton, 1956

KRISTELLER. Paul Oskar Kristeller, *Supplementum Ficinianum*, Florence, 1937–45

LABARTE. Jules Labarte, *Histoire des arts industriels au Moyen Age et à l'époque de la Renaissance*, 6 vols., Paris, 1864–6

LAMI. Giovanni Lami, *Deliciae eruditorum*, 17 vols., Florence, 1736–55

LANKHEIT, 1962. Klaus Lankheit, *Florentinische Barockplastik, die Kunst am Hofe der letzten Medici, 1670–1743*, Munich, 1962

LÁNYI, 1939 (i). Jenö Lányi, 'Kleine Beiträge zur Donatello-Forschung,' *Mitteilungen des kunsthistorischen Institutes in Florenz*, V (1939), p. 213.

——, 1939 (ii). ——, 'Problemi della critica donatelliana,' *Critica d'arte*, IV (1939), ii, pp. 9–23

LASCHI/ROSELLI/ROSSI. Giuliano Laschi, Piero Roselli, and Paolo Alberto Rossi, 'Indagini sulla Cappella dei Pazzi,' *Commentari*, XIII (1962), pp. 24–41

LAVIN. Irving Lavin, 'Bozzetti and Modelli. Notes on Sculptural Procedure from the Early Renaissance through Bernini,' *Stil und Ueberlieferung in der Kunst des Abendlandes* (Acts of the Twenty-first International Congress on the History of Art), Berlin, 1967, III, pp. 93–103

LAZZERI. P. Zeffirino Lazzeri, 'La Verna, il Commune di Firenze e l'Arte della Lana,' *La Verna, contribuiti alla storia del santuario*, Arezzo, 1913, pp. 275–94

LECOY DE LA MARCHE. Albert Lecoy de la Marche, *Extraits des comptes et mémoriaux du roi René pour servir à l'histoire des arts au XVᵉ siècle*, Paris, 1873

LEMAN. Henry Leman, *Collection Sigismond Bardac; faïences italiennes du XV siècle*, Paris, 1913

LENSI, 1922. Alfredo Lensi, 'Una scultura sconosciuta di Michelozzo nell' Annunziata di Firenze,' *Dedalo*, II (1921–2), pp. 358–62

——, 1924. ——, 'Il Museo Bardini: stucchi e terrecotte,' *Dedalo*, IV (1923–4), pp. 486–511

——, 1934. ——, *La Verna*, Florence, 1934

LENSI ORLANDI CARDINI, 1954. Giulio Cesare Lensi Orlandi Cardini, *Le ville di Firenze di qua d'Arno*, Florence, 1954

LERNER-LEHMKUHL. Hanna Lerner-Lehmkuhl, *Zur Struktur und Geschichte des florentinischen Kunstmarktes im 15. Jahrhundert*, Wattensheid, 1936

LETHABY. W. R. Lethaby, 'Majolica Roundels of the Months of the Year at the Victoria and Albert Museum,' *The Burlington Magazine*, IX (1906), pp. 404–7

LEVALLET. Geneviève Levallet, 'Les della Robbia et Palissy,' *Faenza*, XVIII (1930), pp. 101–14

LEVI D'ANCONA, 1962. Mirella Levi d'Ancona, *Miniatura e miniatori a Firenze dal XIV al XVI secolo*, Florence, 1962

——, 1977, ——, *The Garden of the Renaissance*, Florence, 1977

LISNER, 1955. Margrit Lisner, *Die Sängerkanzel des Luca della Robbia*, Dissertation zur Erlangung der Doktorwürde der Philosophischen Fakultät der Albert-Ludwigs-Universität zu Freiburg im Breisgau, 1955

——, 1960. ——, *Luca della Robbia: Die Sängerkanzel*, Stuttgart, 1960

——, 1970. ——, *Holzkruzifixe in Florenz und in der Toskana, von der Zeit um 1300 bis zum frühen Cinquecento*, Munich, 1970

LITTA. Conte Pompeo Litta, *Famiglie celebri d'Italia*, 13 vols., Milan, 1819–1902

LONGHI. Roberto Longhi, *Piero della Francesca*, Rome, 1927

MACLAGAN, 1913. Eric Maclagan, *Catalogue of a Collection of Italian Sculpture and other Plastic Art of the Renaissance*, Burlington Fine Arts Club, London, 1913

MACLAGAN/LONGHURST, 1932. Eric Maclagan and Margaret H. Longhurst, *Catalogue of Italian Sculpture*, Victoria and Albert Museum, 2 vols., London, 1932

MAÏER, 1965. Ida Maïer, *Les manuscrits d'Ange Politien*, Geneva, 1965

——, 1966. ——, *Ange Politien: la formation d'un poète humaniste (1469–1480)*, Geneva, 1966

MALTESE. Corrado Maltese, ed., *Le tecniche artistiche*, Milan, 1973

MANCINI. Girolamo Mancini, 'Il bel s. Giovanni e le feste patronali di Firenze descritte nel 1475 da Piero Cennini,' *Rivista d'arte*, VI (1909), pp. 185–227

MANNI. Domenico Maria Manni, *Osservazioni istoriche ... sopra i sigilli antichi de' secoli bassi*, 30 vols., Florence, 1739–86

MANSUELLI. Guido Achille Mansuelli, *Galleria degli Uffizi, le Sculture*, 2 vols., Rome, 1958–61

MARCHINI. Giuseppe Marchini, 'Maso di Bartolomeo,' *Donatello e il suo tempo*, Florence, 1966, pp. 235–43

MARCUCCI. Emilio Marcucci, 'Sul monumento funebre di Benozzo Federighi vescoco di Fiesole,' *Arte e Storia*, II (1883), p. 315

MARDERSTEIG. Giovanni Mardersteig, 'Leon Battista Alberti e la rinascita del carattere lapidario romano nel quattrocento,' *Italia medioevale e umanistica*, II (1959), pp. 285–307

MARKHAM SCHULZ. Anne Markham Schulz, *The Sculpture of Bernardo Rossellino and his Workshop*, Princeton, 1977

MARQUAND, 1893 (i). Allan Marquand, 'Some Unpublished Monuments by Luca della Robbia,' *American Journal of Archaeology*, VIII (1893), pp. 153–70

——, 1893 (ii). ——, 'A Search for Della Robbia Monuments in Italy,' *Scribner's Magazine*, XIV (1893), pp. 681–98

——, 1894. ——, 'The Madonnas of Luca della Robbia,' *American Journal of Archaeology*, IX (1894), pp. 1–25

——, 1895. ——, 'Luca della Robbia and his use of Glazed Terracotta,' *Brickbuilder*, 1895, pp. 249–51

——, 1902. ——, 'Robbia Pavements,' *Brickbuilder*, 1902, pp. 55–7, 98–101

——, 1907. ——, 'The Visitation of Luca della Robbia at Pistoja,' *American Journal of Archaeology*, XI (1907), pp. 36–41

——, 1909. ——, 'An Altarpiece by Luca della Robbia,' *American Journal of Archaeology*, XIII (1909), pp. 328–33

——, 1912 (i). ——, 'On Some Recently Discovered Works by Luca della Robbia,' *American Journal of Archaeology*, XVI (1912), pp. 163–74

——, 1912 (ii). ——, *Della Robbias in America*, Princeton, 1912

——, 1914. ——, *Luca della Robbia*, Princeton, 1914

——, 1914 (ii). ——, 'Luca della Robbia,' *Art and Progress*, V (1914), pp. 79–85

——, 1919. ——, *Robbia Heraldry*, Princeton, 1919

——, 1920. ——, *Giovanni della Robbia*, Princeton, 1920

——, 1922. ——, *Andrea della Robbia and his Atelier*, 2 vols., Princeton, 1922

——, 1928. ——, *The Brothers of Giovanni della Robbia*, Princeton, 1928

MARRAI, 1900 (i). Bernardo Marrai, *Le Cantorie di Luca della Robbia e di Donatello*, Florence, 1900

——, 1900 (ii). ——, 'La ricomposizione della Cantoria di Luca della Robbia,' *Arte italiana decorativa ed industriale*, IX (1900), pp. 82–4

——, 1907. ——, *La Primavera di Botticelli, le Cantorie di Luca della Robbia e di Donatello, la Sepoltura di Lemmo*

Balducci, *Opere d'arte dell'Arcispedale di Santa Maria Nuova*, Florence, 1907

MASSON. Georgina Masson, *Italian Gardens*, London, 1961

MATHER. Rufus G. Mather, 'Nuovi documenti Robbiani,' *L'Arte*, XXI (1918), pp. 190–209

MATTEUCCI, 1964 (i). P. Gualberto Matteucci, *La Verna di Frate Francesco e della sua prima gente poverella, 1213–1263*, Verna, 1964

——, 1964 (ii). ——, *Da Messer Orlando di Chiusi il dono del monte Verna e due edifici sacri sulla scogliera delle Stimate*, Verna, 1964

MATTHIAE. Guglielmo Matthiae, 'Un Luca della Robbia nella Cattedrale di Atri,' *Bolletino d'arte*, XLIV (1959), pp. 321–3

MATZ. Friedrich Matz, *Die Antiken Sarkophag-reliefs—IV. Die Dionysischen Sarkophage*, 4 vols., Berlin, 1968–75

MAZZUCHELLI. Giammaria Mazzuchelli, *Gli scrittori d'Italia*, 2 vols., Brescia, 1753–63

MEISS. Millard Meiss, 'Toward a more Comprehensive Renaissance Paleography,' *The Art Bulletin*, XLII (1960), pp. 97–112

MENCHERINI. P. Saturnino Mencherini, *Bibliografia alvernina*, Città di Castello, 1914

MICHEL. André Michel, 'La sculpture au Musée Jacquemart-André,' *Gazette des Beaux-Arts*, X (1913), pp. 465–78

MIDDELDORF, 1940. Ulrich Middeldorf, 'Two Florentine Sculptures at Toledo,' *Art in America*, XXVIII (1940), pp. 13–30

——, 1973. ——, 'Filarete?', *Mitteilungen des kunsthistorischen Institutes in Florenz*, XVII (1973), pp. 75–86

——, 1976 (i). ——, 'A Forgotten Florentine Tomb of the Quattrocento,' *Antichità Viva*, XV (1976), iii, pp. 11–13

——, 1976 (ii). ——, *Sculptures from the Samuel H. Kress Collection*, London, 1976

MIGEON. Gaston Migeon, 'La Collection de M. Edmond Foulc,' *Les Arts*, 4 (1902), pp. 1–8

MIGLIARINI. A. Michele Migliarini, *Museo di sculture del risorgimento raccolto e posseduto da Ottavio Gigli*, Florence, 1858

MILANESI, 1862. Gaetano Milanesi, 'Le *Vite* di Andrea del Castagno e di Domenico Veneziano,' *Giornale storico degli archivi toscani*, VI (1862), pp. 1–10

——, 1864. ——, ed., *Dell'arte del vetro per musaico, tre trattatelli dei secoli XIV e XV*, Bologna, 1864

——, 1869. ——, 'Lettere d'artisti italiani dei secoli XIV e XV,' *Il Buonarroti*, IV (1869), pp. 77–87

——, 1887 (i). ——, *Operette istoriche edite ed inedite di Antonio Manetti*, Florence, 1887

——, 1887 (ii). ——, *Catalogo delle opere di Donatello e bibliografia degli autori che ne hanno scritto*, Florence, 1887

MOISÈ. F. Moisè, *Santa Croce di Firenze*, Florence, 1845

MOLINIER. Émile Molinier, 'Une oeuvre inédite de Luca della Robbia. Le Tabernacle en marbre de l'église de Peretola, près de Florence,' *Gazette Archéologique*, IX (1884), pp. 364–70

MONTORIOLA. Karl Markgraf von Montoriola, *Briefe des Mediceerkreises aus Marsilio Ficino's Epistolarium*, Berlin, 1926

MORENI. Domenico Moreni, *Continuazione delle memorie istoriche dell' Ambrosiana Imperial Basilica di S. Lorenzo di Firenze*, 2 vols., Florence, 1816–17

MORISON. Stanley Morison, 'Early Humanistic Script and the First Roman Type,' *The Library*, XXIV (1943), pp. 1–29

MOROZZI, 1964. Guido Morozzi, 'Ricerche sull'aspetto originale dello Spedale degli Innocenti di Firenze,' *Commentari*, XV (1964), pp. 186–201

MOROZZI/PICCINI. 1971. G. Morozzi and A. Piccini, *Il restauro dello Spedale di Santa Maria degli Innocenti, 1966–1970*, Florence, 1971

MOSCATO. Arnoldo Moscato, *Il Palazzo Pazzi a Firenze*, Rome, 1963

MÜNTZ. Eugène Müntz, *Les collections des Médicis au XVe siècle*, Paris and London, 1888

MURRAY. Peter Murray, 'Art Historians and Art Critics—IV,' *The Burlington Magazine*, XCIX (1957), pp. 330–6

NEGRI ARNOLDI. Francesco Negri Arnoldi, 'An Exhibition of Italian Sculpture in London,' *The Burlington Magazine*, CXIV (1972), pp. 646–53

NERI DI BICCI. Neri di Bicci, *Le ricordanze (10 marzo 1453–24 aprile 1475)*, Bruno Santi, ed., Pisa, 1976

NICOLSON. Benedict Nicolson, 'The Sanford Collection,' *The Burlington Magazine*, XCVII (1955), pp. 207–14

NUCCI. Ermenegildo Nucci, *I Vescovi di Pescia dall'anno 1726 al 1908*, Pescia, 1937

OETTINGEN. Wolfgang von Oettingen, ed., *Antonio Averlino Filarete's Tractat über die Baukunst, nebst seinen Büchern von der Zeichenkunst und den Bauten der Medici*, Vienna, 1890

PAATZ. Walter and Elisabeth Paatz, *Die Kirchen von Florenz*, 6 vols., Frankfurt am Main, 1940–54

PÄCHT. Otto Pächt, 'René d'Anjou Studien,' *Jahrbuch der kunsthistorischen Sammlungen in Wien*, XXXIII (1973), pp. 85–126; XXXVIII (1977), pp. 7–106

PAOLETTI. Pietro Paoletti di Osvaldo, *L'Architettura e la scultura del Rinascimento in Venezia*, Venice, 1893

PAPINI. Roberto Papini, *Catalogo delle cose d'arte e di antichità d'Italia: Pisa*, 2 vols., Rome, 1912

PARRONCHI. Alessandro Parronchi, 'L'aspetto primitivo del Sepolcro Federighi,' *Paragone*, 179 (1964), pp. 49–52

PATZAK. Bernhard Patzak, *Die Renaissance- und Barockvilla in Italien, I. Palast und Villa in Toscana*, 2 vols., Leipzig, 1912–13

PERKINS. Charles Perkins, *Tuscan Sculptors*, 2 vols., London, 1864

PETRIOLI. A. M. Petrioli, *Luca della Robbia*, Milan, 1966

PHILLIPS. Claude Phillips, 'Esposizione della R. Accademia di Londra. Marmi e bronzi del Rinascimento italiano,' *Archivio storico dell'arte*, I (1888), pp. 97–101

PICCOLPASSO. Cipriano Piccolpasso, *Li tre libri dell'arte del vasaio*, Giovanni Conti, ed., Florence, 1976

PIEROTTI. Fra Adamo Pierotti, 'Un libro d'amministrazione del convento della Verna degli anni 1481–1518,' *La Verna, contribuiti alla storia del santuario*, Arezzo, 1913, pp. 156–74

PILLET/LEROY/MANNHEIM. Charles Pillet, Victor Leroy and Charles Mannheim, *Catalogue des objets d'art etc., vente à Florence au Palais de San Donato le 15 Mars 1880*, Paris, 1880

POTINR. Fortunato Pintor, 'Per la storia della Libreria Medicea nel Rinascimento,' *Italia Medioevale e Umanistica*, III (1960), pp. 189–210

PLANISCIG, 1940. Leo Planiscig, *Luca della Robbia*, Vienna, 1940

——, 1948. ——, *Luca della Robbia*, 2nd ed., Florence, 1948

POGGI, 1903. Giovanni Poggi, 'Mino da Fiesole e la Badia Fiorentina,' *Miscellanea d'Arte*, I (1903), pp. 98–103

——, 1904. ——, *Catalogo del Museo dell'Opera del Duomo*, Florence, 1904

——, 1906 (i). ——, 'Documenti sulla tomba Federighi di Luca della Robbia,' *Rivista d'arte*, IV (1906), pp. 156–7

——, 1906 (ii). ——, 'Per la storia della tomba di S. Giovanni Gualberto,' *Rivista d'arte*, IV (1906), pp. 158–9

——, 1909. ——, *Il Duomo di Firenze*, Italienische Forschungen herausgegeben vom Kunsthistorischen Institut in Florenz, II, Berlin, 1909

——, 1949. ——, Leo Planiscig, Bruno Bearzi, *Donatello: San Ludovico*, New York, n.d. [1949]

POINTNER. Andy Pointner, *Die Werke des florentinischen Bildhauers Agostino d'Antonio di Duccio*, Strassburg, 1909

POPE-HENNESSY, 1958. John Pope-Hennessy, *Italian Renaissance Sculpture*, London, 1958

——, 1964. ——, *Catalogue of Italian Sculpture in the Victoria and Albert Museum*, 3 vols., London, 1964

——, 1971. ——, *Italian Renaissance Sculpture*, 2nd ed., London and New York, 1971

——, 1976. ——, 'Margrit Lisner, Holzkruzifixe in Florenz und in der Toskana von der Zeit um 1300 bis zum frühen Cinquecento,' review, *Pantheon*, XXXIV (1976), pp. 78–80

——, 1977. ——, 'The Evangelist Roundels in the Pazzi Chapel,' *Apollo*, CVI (1977), pp. 262–9

——, 1979. ——, 'Thoughts on Andrea della Robbia,' *Apollo*, CIX (1979), pp. 176–97

PROCACCI. *Mostra di opere d'arte trasportate a Firenze durante la guerra e di opere d'arte restaurate*, Florence, 1947

PUCCINELLI. Don Placido Puccinelli, *Istoria dell'erioche azzioni di Ugo il Grande*, 1664

RABIZZANI. G. Rabizzani, 'Un gruppo pistoiese della Visitazione in S. Giovanni fuorcivitas,' *Bolletino storico pistoiese*, X (1908), No. 1

RAGGIO. Olga Raggio, 'Andrea della Robbia's Saint Michael Lunette,' *The Metropolitan Museum of Art Bulletin*, n.s. XX (1961), pp. 135–44

REPETTI. Emanuele Repetti, *Dizionario geografico fisico storico della Toscana*, 6 vols., Florence, 1833–46

REYMOND, 1987 (i). Marcel Reymond, *La sculpture florentine*, Florence, 1897

——, 1897 (ii). ——, *Les Della Robbia*, Florence, 1897 (ii).

——, 1904. ——, 'La Madone Corsini de Luca della Robbia,' *Rivista d'arte*, II (1904), pp. 93–100

RIC. Harold Mattingley, *et al.*, *The Roman Imperial Coinage*, 7 vols., London, 1923–66

RICHA. Giuseppe Richa, *Notizie istoriche delle chiese fiorentine*, 10 vols., Florence, 1754–62

RICHARDSON. E. P. Richardson, 'The Virgin and Child with Six Angels by Luca della Robbia,' *Bulletin of the Detroit Institute of Arts*, XXIX (1949–50), pp. 78–80

RIDOLFI. Enrico Ridolfi, *La Galleria dell'Arcispedale di Santa Maria Nuova in Firenze*, Rome, 1898

RITCHIE. Andrew C. Ritchie, ed., *Catalogue of the Paintings and Sculpture in the Permanent Collection*, Albright Art Gallery, Buffalo, N.Y., 1949

ROBERT. Carl Robert, *Die Antiken Sarkophag-reliefs—III. Einzelmythen*, 3 vols., Berlin, 1897–1904, and Rome, 1969

ROBINSON, 1856. John Charles Robinson, *Catalogue of the Soulages Collection*, London, 1856

——, 1862. ——, *Italian sculpture of the Middle Ages and period of the revival of art*, South Kensington Museum, London, 1862

RODDAZ. Camille de Roddaz, *L'Art ancien à l'exposition nationale belge*, Brussels and Paris, 1882

ROOVER. Raymond de Roover, *The Rise and Decline of the Medici Bank, 1397–1494*, Cambridge, Mass., 1963

ROSSI, 1964. Filippo Rossi, *Il bel San Giovanni, Santa Maria del Fiore, l'Opera del Duomo*, Florence, 1964

ROSSI. Umberto Rossi, 'Il Museo Nzaionale di Firenze nel triennio 1889–1891,' *Archivio storico dell'arte*, VI (1893), pp. 1–24

RUMOHR. C. F. von Rumohr, *Italienische Forschungen*, 3 vols., Berlin and Stettin, 1827–31

SAALMAN, 1958. Howard Saalman, 'Filippo Brunelleschi: Capital Studies,' *The Art Bulletin*, XL (1958), pp. 113–37

——, 1964 (i). ——, 'The Authorship of the Pazzi Palace,' *The Art Bulletin*, XLVI (1964), pp. 388–94

——, 1964 (ii). ——, 'Santa Maria del Fiore: 1294–1418,' *Art Bulletin*, XLVI (1964), pp. 471–500

——, 1966. ——, 'Michelozzo Studies,' *The Burlington Magazine*, CVIII (1966), pp. 242–50

SALMI, 1929. Mario Salmi, 'Francesco d'Antonio fiorentino,' *Rivista d'arte*, XI (1929), pp. 1–24

——, 1936. ——, *Paolo Uccello, Andrea del Castagno, Domenico Veneziano*, Rome, 1936

——, 1947. ——, 'Contributi fiorentini alla storia dell'arte: Ricerche intorno a un perduto ciclo pittorico del rinascimento,' *Atti e memorie dell'accademia fiorentina di scienze morali (La Colombaria)*, n.s. I, Florence, 1947, pp. 415–32

SALVINI, 1942. Roberto Salvini, *Luca della Robbia*, Novara, 1942

SALVINI, 1782. Salvino Salvini, *Catalogo cronologico de' canonici della chiesa metropolitana fiorentina*, Florence, 1782

SANPAOLESI. Piero Sanpaolesi, 'Aggiunte al Brunelleschi,' *Bolletino d'arte*, XXXVIII (1953), pp. 225–32

SANTANGELO. Antonino Santangelo, *Museo di Palazzo Venezia, Catalogo delle sculture*, Rome, 1954

SCHLEGEL, 1960. Ursula Schlegel, 'Ein Sakramentstabernakel der Frührenaissance in S. Ambrogio in Florenz,' *Zeitschrift für Kunstgeschichte*, XXIII (1960), pp. 167–73

——, 1962. ——, 'Vier Madonnenreliefs des Andrea di Lazzaro Cavalcanti genannt Buggiano,' *Berliner Museen*, XII (1962), pp. 4–9

SCHLOSSER. Julius von Schlosser, 'Giusto's Fresken in Padua und die Vorläufer der Stanza della Segnatura,' *Jahrbuch der kunsthistorischen Sammlungen des allerhöchsten Kaiserhauses*, XVII (1896), pp. 13–89

SCHMARSOW. August Schmarsow, 'Un capolavoro di scultura

fiorentina del Quattrocento a Venezia,' *Archivio storico dell'arte*, IV (1891), pp. 225–35

SCHOTTMÜLLER, 1906. Frida Schottmüller, 'Zwei neuerworbene Reliefs des Luca della Robbia im Kaiser-Friedrich-Museum,' *Jahrbuch der königlich preussischen Kunstsammlungen*, XXVII (1906), pp. 224–7

——, 1913. ——, *Die italienischen und spanischen Bildwerke der Renaissance und des Barocks in Marmor, Ton, Holz und Stuck* (*Königliche Museen zu Berlin, Beschreibung der Bildwerke der christlichen Epochen*, vol. 5), Berlin, 1913

——, 1921. ——, *Wohnungskultur und Möbel der italienischen Renaissance*, Stuttgart, 1921

——, 1933. ——, *Bildwerke des Kaiser-Friedrich-Museums: die italienischen und spanischen Bildwerke der Renaissance und des Barock, I. die Bildwerke in Stein, Holz, Ton und Wachs*, Berlin and Leipzig, 1933

SCHRADE. Hubert Schrade, *Ikonographie der christlichen Kunst, I. Die Auferstehung Christi*, Berlin and Leipzig, 1932

SCHUBRING, 1905. Paul Schubring, *Luca della Robbia und seine Familie*, Bielefeld and Leipzig, 1905

——, 1906. ——, 'Notizie di Berlino,' *L'Arte*, IX (1906), p. 387

——, 1907. ——, *Donatello, des Meisters Werke*, Stuttgart and Leipzig, 1907

——, 1919. ——, *Die italienische Plastik des Quattrocento*, Berlin, 1919

SECONDO PUGLIARO. Luigi Secondo Pugliaro, *Il convento della Verna e il commune di Firenze*, Florence, 1931

SELVATICO. Pietro Selvatico, *Sulla architettura e sulla scultura in Venezia dal Medio Evo sino ai nostri giorni*, Venice, 1847

SENNEVILLE. P. Senneville, 'Les musiciens de Luca della Robbia,' *Gazette des Beaux-Arts*, IX (1874), pp. 134–7

SEYMOUR, 1963. Charles H. Seymour, Jr., 'The Young Luca della Robbia,' *Allen Memorial Art Museum Bulletin*, Oberlin, Ohio, XX (1962–3), pp. 92–119

——, 1966. ——, *Sculpture in Italy, 1400–1500*, Harmondsworth, Middlesex, 1966

SHELL. Curtis Shell, *Giovanni dal Ponte and the Problem of other lesser Contemporaries of Masaccio*, unpubl. Ph.D. diss., Harvard University, 1958

SOMMERARD. A. and E. du Sommerard, *Les Arts du Moyen Age*, 5 vols., Paris, 1838–46

SOMMERARD, 1861. E. du Sommerard, *Musée des Thermes et de l'Hôtel de Cluny. Catalogue et description des objets d'art de l'Antiquité, du Moyen Age et de la Renaissance*, Paris, 1861

——, 1883. ——, *Musée des Thermes et de l'Hôtel de Cluny. Catalogue et description des objets d'art de l'Antiquité, du Moyen Age et de la Renaissance*, Paris, 1883

SOMZÉE. *Catalogue des monuments d'art antique, etc., composant les Collections de Somzée*, 3 vols., Brussels, 1904

STALEY. Edgcumbe Staley, *The Guilds of Florence*, London, 1906

STEGMANN/GEYMÜLLER. Carl von Stegmann and Heinrich von Geymüller, *Die Architektur der Renaissance in Toscana*, 11 vols., Munich, 1885–1907

STEINGRÄBER. E. Steingräber, *Der Goldschmied*, Munich, 1966

STEINMANN. Ernst Steinmann, 'Michele Marini, ein Beitrag zur Geschichte der Renaissanceskulptur in Rom,' *Zeitschrift für bildende Kunst*, XIV (1903), pp. 147–57

STEINWEG. Klara Steinweg, 'Die Kreuzigung Petri des Jacopo di Cione in der Pinacoteca Vaticana,' *Rendiconti della Pontificia Accademia Romana di Archaeologia*, XXX–XXXI (1957–9), pp. 231–44

SUPINO, 1898. Igino Benvenuto Supino, *Catalogo del R. Museo Nazionale di Firenze*, Rome, 1898

——, 1934. ——, 'Robbia,' *Thieme-Becker* (*Allgemeines Lexicon der bildenden Künstler*), XXVIII, Leipzig, 1934, pp. 413–17

THOMAS. David Thomas, 'What is the Origin of the Scrittura umanistica?' *La Bibliofilia*, LIII (1951), pp. 1–10

TOESCA, 1904. Pietro Toesca, 'Umili pittori fiorentini del principio del quattrocento,' *L'Arte*, VII (1904), pp. 49–58

——, 1921. ——, 'Sculture fiorentine del Quattrocento,' *Bolletino d'arte*, I (1921), pp. 149–58

TOLEDO. 'The San Donato Madonna Acquired,' *Toledo Museum News*, 87 (1939)

TOYNBEE. J. M. C. Toynbee, *The Adrianic School, a Chapter in the History of Greek Art*, Cambridge, 1934

TRACHTENBERG. Marvin L. Trachtenberg, *The Campanile of Florence Cathedral, 'Giotto's Tower'*, New York, 1971

ULLMAN/STADTER. Berthold L. Ullman and Philip A. Stadter, *The Public Library of Renaissance Florence*, Padua, 1972

URBINO. *Restauri nelle Marche, testimonianze acquisiti e recuperi*, exh. cat., Urbino, Palazzo Ducale, 28 June–30 September 1973

VACCARINO. Paolo Vaccarino, *Nanni*, Florence, 1950

VALENTINER. W. R. Valentiner, *Catalogue of an Exhibition of Italian Gothic and Early Renaissance Sculptures*, Detroit Institute of Arts, 1938

VAN BUREN. A. W. van Buren, 'Il proprietario della "Casa dei Grifi" sul Palatino,' *Rendiconti della Pontificia Accademia Romana di Archaeologia*, XVI (1940), pp. 57–61

VASARI–RICCI. Giorgio Vasari, *Le Vite . . .* (1st ed., Florence, 1550), ed. Corrado Ricci, Milan-Rome, n.d.

VASARI–MILANESI. Giorgio Vasari. *Le Vite . . .* (2nd ed., Florence, 1568), ed. Gaetano Milanesi, Florence, 1878ff

VENTURI, 1900. Adolfo Venturi, *La Madonna*, Milan, 1900

——, 1901–40. ——, *Storia dell' Arte italiana*, 11 vols., Milan, 1901–40

VESPASIANO DA BISTICCI. Vespasiano da Bisticci, *Le Vite*, Aulo Greco ed., 2 vols., Florence, 1970–6

VICENZI. Carlo Vicenzi, 'Di tre fogli di disegni quattrocenteschi dall' antico,' *Rassegna d'arte*, X (1910), pp. 6–11

VITRY. Paul Vitry, 'La Collection de M. Gustave Dreyfus,' *Les arts*, 72 (1907), pp. 1–32

WACKERNAGEL. Martin Wackernagel, *Der Lebensraum des Künstlers in der florentinischen Renaissance*, Leipzig, 1938

WALKER. D. P. Walker, 'Orpheus the Theologian and Renaissance Platonists,' *Journal of the Warburg and Courtauld Institutes*, XVI (1953), pp. 100–20

WALLIS. Henry Wallis, *Oak-leaf Jars*, London, 1903

WALSER. Ernst Walser, *Poggius Florentinus, Leben und Werke*, Leipzig and Berlin, 1914

WALTHER. Josephine Walther, 'The Genoese Madonna

by Luca della Robbia,' *Bulletin of The Detroit Institute of Arts*, XI (1929), pp. 34–5

WARBURG. A. Warburg, 'Italienische Kunst und internationale Astrologie im Palazzo Schifanoja zu Ferrara (1912),' *Gesammelte Schriften*, Berlin, 1932, ii, pp. 459–81

WASHBURN. G. B. Washburn *et al.*, *Master Bronzes selected from museums and collections in America*, Albright Art Gallery, Buffalo, New York, February, 1937

WEGNER. Max Wegner, *Die Antiken Sarkophag-reliefs—V., iii. Die Musensarkophage*, Berlin, 1966

WEHLE. Harry B. Wehle, 'The Bache Collection on Loan,' *The Metropolitan Museum of Art Bulletin*, n.s. I (1943), pp. 285–90

WEIHRAUCH. Hans Robert Weihrauch, *Europäische Bronzestatuetten, 15.–18. Jahrhundert*, Braunschweig, 1967

WILLS. Howel Wills, *Florentine Heraldry*, London, 1900

WINTERNITZ, 1960. Emanuel Winternitz, 'The Lira da Braccio,' *Die Musik in Geschichte und Gegenwart*, F. Blume, ed., viii, Kassel, 1960

——, 1961 (i). ——, 'The Survival of the Kithara and the Evolution of the English Cittern: a Study in Morphology,' *Journal of the Warburg and Courtauld Institutes*, XXIV (1961), pp. 222–9

——, 1961 (ii). ——, 'The Visual Arts as a Source for the Historian of Music,' *International Musicological Society Congress Report*, Kassel, 1961

WOHL. Hellmut Wohl, *Domenico Veneziano Studies*, unpublished Ph.D. diss., New York University, 1958

WOLFF. Fritz Wolff, *Michelozzo di Bartolomeo*, Strassburg, 1900

WOODWARD. W. H. Woodward, *La pedagogia del Rinascimento, 1400–1600*, Florence, 1923

WULFF. Oskar Wulff, 'Ein verkanntes Frühwerk von Luca della Robbia und des Künstlers Werdegang,' *Jahrbuch der königlich preussischen Kunstsammlungen*, XXXVIII (1917), pp. 213–52

WUNDRUM. Manfred Wundrum, *Donatello und Nanni di Banco*, Berlin, 1969

YBL. E. Ybl, *Toscana szobrászata a quattrocentóban*, 2 vols., Budapest, 1930

YRIARTE. Charles Yriarte, *Livre de Souvenirs de Maso di Bartolommeo dit Masaccio*, Paris, 1894

INDEX